Teaching Music through Performance in Beginning Band Volume 2

Other books and recordings
available from GIA Publications, Inc.:

Teaching Music through Performance in Band, Volume 1

Teaching Music through Performance in Band, Volume 2

Teaching Music through Performance in Band, Volume 3

Teaching Music through Performance in Band, Volume 4

Teaching Music through Performance in Band, Volume 5

Teaching Music through Performance in Band, Volume 6

Teaching Music through Performance in Beginning Band, Volume 1

Teaching Music through Performing Marches

Teaching Music through Performance in Orchestra, Volume 1

Teaching Music through Performance in Orchestra, Volume 2

Teaching Music through Performance in Orchestra, Volume 3

Teaching Music through Performance in Choir, Volume 1

Teaching Music through Performance in Choir, Volume 2

Teaching Music through Performance in Jazz

A recording of the works discussed in this volume is available
separately from GIA Publications, Inc. (CD-750)

G-7264

Teaching
Music
through
Performance
in Beginning Band

Volume 2

Erin Cole
Dennis W. Fisher
Cheryl Floyd
Linda J. Gammon
John O'Reilly
Marguerite Wilder

Compiled and Edited by Richard Miles

GIA Publications, Inc.
Chicago

For a complete searchable index of works covered in the Teaching Music Series, as well as audio clips of more than 900 pieces, visit the Web site www.TeachingMusic.org.

Teaching Music through Performance in Beginning Band, Volume 2
Erin Cole, Dennis W. Fisher, Cheryl Floyd,
Linda J. Gammon, John O'Reilly, Marguerite Wilder
Compiled and edited by Richard Miles
www.TeachingMusic.org

GIA Publications, Inc.
7404 S. Mason Avenue, Chicago, Illinois 60638
www.giamusic.com
Copyright © 2008 GIA Publications, Inc.
All rights reserved.
Printed in the United States of America.

G-7264

ISBN: 978-1-57999-712-0

Table of Contents

PART II: The Band Conductor as Music Teacher
Teacher Resource Guides

Acknowledgments

The following research associates are gratefully acknowledged for outstanding scholarly contributions to the Teacher Resource Guides:

Robert J. Ambrose
Director of Wind Studies and Ensembles
Associate Director, School of Music
Georgia State University
Atlanta, Georgia

Carolyn Barber
Director of Bands
University of Nebraska-Lincoln
Lincoln, Nebraska

Gene Bechen
Associate Professor of Music
Director of Bands
St. Ambrose University
Davenport, Iowa

Daniel A. Belongia
Assistant Professor of Music
Assistant Director of Bands
Illinois State University
Normal, Illinois

Glen Scott Bersaglia
Assistant Director of Bands
University of Michigan
Ann Arbor, Michigan

William Berz
Professor of Music
Mason Gross School of the Arts
Rutgers, The State University of New Jersey
New Brunswick, New Jersey

John Cody Birdwell
Director of Bands
University of Kentucky
Lexington, Kentucky

David Martin Booth
Director of Bands
Wright State University
Dayton, Ohio

George R. Boulden
Associate Director of Bands
University of Kentucky
Lexington, Kentucky

C. Kevin Bowen
Director of Bands
Wake Forest University
Winston-Salem, North Carolina

Sheryl Bowhay
Conductor
Edmonton, Alberta, Canada

Gordon R. Brock
Chair/Director of Bands
University of North Florida
Jacksonville, Florida

Andrea E. Brown
Director of Athletic Bands
Assistant Director of Bands
Austin Peay State University
Clarksville, Tennessee

Matthew G. P. Brunner
Associate Instructor, Department of Bands
Indiana University Jacobs School of Music
Bloomington, Indiana

Pamela Bowen Bustos
University of Wisconsin-Superior
Superior, Wisconsin

James C. Chesebrough
Assistant Professor Band/Music Education
Keene State College
Keene, New Hampshire

Phillip L. Clements
Associate Director of Bands
Conductor, Symphonic Winds
University of Miami
Coral Gables, Florida

Jeff Cranmore
McKinney High School
McKinney, Texas

Susan Creasap
Associate Director of Bands
Morehead State University
Morehead, Kentucky

Katrina Lyn Davilis
Director of Bands
Music Department Chairperson
Thoreau Middle School
Vienna, Virginia

Patrick Dunnigan
Florida State University
Tallahassee, Florida

Catherine R. Fisher
Band Director
King George Middle School
King George, Virginia

Ricky L. Fleming
Director of Bands
Buffalo State College
Buffalo, New York

Richard A. Greenwood
Professor of Music
University of Central Florida
Orlando, Florida

Craig V. Hamilton
Director of Bands
Ouachita Baptist University
Arkadelphia, Arkansas

Eric L. Harris
Associate Director of Bands
Tennessee Technological University
Cookeville, Tennessee

Linda A. Hartley
Professor of Music, Coordinator of Music Education
University of Dayton
Dayton, Ohio

Glen J. Hemberger
Director of Bands
Southeastern Louisiana University
Hammond, Louisiana

Jennifer Kitelinger
Doctoral Conducting Associate
University of North Texas
Denton, Texas

Shannon Kitelinger
Doctoral Conducting Associate
University of North Texas
Denton, Texas

Kenneth Kohlenberg
Director of Bands, Professor of Music
Sinclair Community College
Dayton, Ohio

Christopher B. Knighten
East Carolina University
Greenville, North Carolina

Gina M. Lenox
Masters Conducting Associate
University of North Texas
Denton, Texas

Andrew Mast
Lawrence University
Appleton, Wisconsin

Wendy McCallum
Instrumental Music Education Specialist
Brandon University
Brandon, Manitoba, Canada

Linda R. Moorhouse
Associate Director of Bands
Louisiana State University
Baton Rouge, Louisiana

Donald Morris
Band Director, McClintock Middle School
Conductor, Charlotte Concert Band
Charlotte, North Carolina

Chad Nicholson
Associate Director of Bands
Colorado State University
Fort Collins, Colorado

James Popejoy
Director of Bands
University of North Dakota
Grand Forks, North Dakota

David Ratliff
Director of Bands
Madison Southern High School
Berea, Kentucky

John Stanley Ross
Director of Bands
Appalachian State University
Boone, North Carolina

Scott A. Stewart
Emory University
Atlanta, Georgia

Susan L. Taylor
Director of Bands
Anderson University
Anderson, Indiana

Andrew Trachsel
Doctoral Conducting Associate
University of North Texas
Denton, Texas

Kirsten Trachsel
Director of Bands
Boyd Independent School District
Boyd, Texas

John Wacker
Western State College of Colorado
Gunnison, Colorado

Lane Weaver
DMA Candidate/Teaching Assistant
University of Kentucky
Lexington, Kentucky

Mark Whitlock
Director of Bands
University of Minnesota–Duluth
Duluth, Minnesota

Jason Worzbyt
Associate Professor of Bassoon
Associate Director of Bands
Indiana University of Pennsylvania
Indiana, Pennsylvania

Michael Yonchak
DMA Candidate/Teaching Assistant
University of Kentucky
Lexington, Kentucky

Christian Zembower
Director of Bands
East Tennessee State University
Johnson City, Tennessee

Research assistance by:

Kevin Norton
Graduate Research Assistant
Morehead State University

Mark R. Webster
Graduate Research Assistant
Morehead State University

Music selection coordinator:

Dennis W. Fisher
Professor of Conducting and Ensembles
University of North Texas

Author submission coordinator:

Marguerite Wilder
Conductor and Clinician

PART I

THE TEACHING
OF MUSIC

CHAPTER 1

A Journey to Creativity through Musical Changes

Marguerite Wilder

In the first volume of *Teaching Music through Performance in Beginning Band*, Larry Blocher challenged us as music educators to think about early band experiences that may have been pivotal points in our own music education endeavors. In this volume, I challenge you to think about some of the pivotal points of *teaching* music education:

- How and when did you develop an organizational plan to ensure your students had the ability to transfer what they heard into musical performance? How do you develop and improve the critical listening skills of your students?

- How and when did you develop an organizational plan to track your students' progress?

Starting My First Year

Like so many first-year instrumental teachers, I was the only band teacher for five elementary schools. At times I envied the classroom teachers who could talk to and learn from other veteran teachers in their schools. I felt as though I needed feedback and help, so I asked one of my colleagues, John Mote, to come and observe me teaching my class of twelve beginning band students.

At the time, my big concern was that my class was held on the stage of the cafeteria during lunch. The curtain was closed, so it was considered a "real" classroom—unfortunately, a typical situation for many elementary band directors. But little did I know that *where* I taught was the least of my worries. I was soon to realize that it was not *where* I was teaching, but *how* I was teaching that mattered most.

1

My class began. I started with a warm-up of whole notes/whole rest, and then moved on to rhythm exercises. Next I asked the students to individually play their prepared songs. I often gave multiple opportunities for students to "pass off" the song; I thought that was one of the better parts of my teaching strategy. But after class, John Mote pointed out to me that the students who had practiced and worked on their music often played the song correctly on the first try. He also observed that as I moved from one student to the next, they would receive two, three, or maybe four chances to play the song. His question to me was, "How do you decide how many chances each child gets to play the assigned song for credit?" I did not have a hard-and-fast answer for him. I tried to explain my way around the question by saying, "Sometimes a student makes a small, simple mistake. The student knew it and I knew it, and they knew I knew it. I give them another chance." But I realized from John's question that some of the students who got the most of my attention had not practiced at all. They practiced taking their instruments home on the bus and bringing them back to school on the bus; the sad part is the instruments were not out of their cases while at home. Why was I giving so much attention to these students? I was basically ignoring the students who *had* worked on their music. Was the reason why some of the students did not practice at home my fault? Could it be that some of the students did not have the ability to tell if the rhythms and melodies they played were correct? Where my students motivated to practice? Did they have an understanding of the goals? Did they realize when they reached specific goals?

As a beginning music teacher, I wanted to give my students the best possible education. I wanted them all to be good. I wanted them all to exceed. These are wonderful goals for teachers and their students. I was giving and they were receiving. I thought, what could be better? I found that in my giving, I was also taking responsibility for my students and *from* my students. I was being responsible for everything and everyone. I was trying to make the students, the classes, and the band program be my vision of the best. It seemed that the ownership of the program, the music, and the students was mine alone; I don't think I was sharing anything. Did my students really understand what they had performed? Did the students have any ownership in their music experience?

Let me back up a little here...I considered myself very fortunate to get my first teaching job in the neighborhood where my family lived. I was very excited about teaching and wanted to get a head start before fall classes began. So over the summer, I asked neighborhood children if they were in band. When I found a current band student, I asked the normal questions: What do you like most about band? What do you play? How long have you played? What can you play? What band method book are you using, and how far did you get in the book? I soon found that my survey did not have to be so complicated. If students had been in band for one year, they were on page 15 of the first book. If students had completed two years of band, they had completed the first book. Now I do believe in being thorough; I consider myself a slow, methodical teacher, especially during the beginning years. But did students really need to spend an entire school year on ten pages and a second year to finish the book? Did the students actually understand the music, or did they just learn the songs by rote?

Going one step further: Is there any evidence of accountability of student learning, or did a student just happen to play the song correctly?" As a beginning band teacher, I felt I needed an organized and systematic approach to assessment. In *Assessing the Developing Child Musician* (GIA, 2000), Timothy Brophy gives these definitions for assessment and measurement: "*Assessment* is defined as the gathering of information about a student's status relevant to one's academic and musical expectations. *Measurement* refers to the use of a systematic methodology to observe musical behaviors in order to represent the magnitude of performance capability, task completion, or concept attainment."

The block teaching system involves more class playing than individual playing. For example, the entire class plays page 6, number 1 until it "sounds" like page 6, number 1; then the class moves on to page 6, number 2, and so on. I have visited schools to work with students during the latter part of the year. What I have often found is that the band class is on "page 20" (or so) of a method book, and most of the group is playing that page pretty well. Yet when I ask the class to go back to the beginning portion of the book to play a song for me, they have great difficulty playing a song they "learned" four months ago. So while the class may be on "page 20" of a method book, is every child actually there? Is student progress being tracked individually? Many teachers would say they assign certain songs in the method books to be heard individually; the reality, however, is that most of the tunes are being played in a group setting. So how do teachers assign an individual grade? As with all grading systems, there will be a bell curve on the performance scores. Some students receive a "C" and some an "A" on the individual song performance. Should teachers, then, keep progressing through the book with students who continually get Cs? We all know the answer is no. If your group played at a 70 percent accuracy level, you could not identify the tune. But how do we as teachers individualize with so many students in a classroom?

The reality is that beginning band students enter class with a wide range of musical abilities. It would be wonderful if all students entered beginning instrumental class meeting the National Standards for Music. Some students come from great general music programs, and they can listen, move, sing, play, and create. Other students come from programs that have experienced major cuts, and they have little or no musical experience.

So where do we start? I would be overjoyed if entering students could handle Content Standard #1 for grades 5 through 8: Singing, alone and with others, a varied repertoire of music. Consider that the first Content Standard is singing. This would seem to indicate that it must be important, yet in so many instrumental programs, we give up our biggest crutch in music—we quit singing! (More on this later.)

That Was Then

When I first started teaching, I spent a great deal of time on music theory and the naming and labeling of music notes and rhythms. I was such a diligent teacher that I made sure my students knew all of the lines and spaces before they even took out their instruments. I even had them learn the grand staff (even if the trombones would never play in treble clef and the flutes would never play in bass clef). I thought they might need to know this someday! I was teaching signs before experience and symbols before sound. (In mathematics, it would be like teaching the Pythagorean theorem before students understand fractions.)

Why did I expect my students to know all of the names of notes? I was requiring them to learn materials they would not need for a long time. For example: Why did I require my beginning trumpet player to know all of the notes on all of the lines and spaces? Just think about that: Would you intentionally introduce a beginning trumpet player to high F? Not likely. (The first time I skied a black diamond run on the ski slope was *not* on purpose— I was lost!) A beginning trumpet player on high F would also be lost! So now I teach on a need-to-know basis.

Back in the "dark ages" when I began teaching band, the methods books did not provide musical background for the songs; there wasn't really any grounding for any type of music making. We started off with whole notes: "Play–2–3–4, Rest–2–3–4, Play–2–3–4," etc. Can you think of a song that goes like that? Where is the pitch center, or lack thereof? Did we give our students any information that would help them make a musical decision? A mathematical decision, maybe, but not a musical one.

I would also use a tuner so I could "tell" students if the sound was flat or sharp. And some used Dr. Beat to give a steady pulse to the playing. But were either of these two approaches musical? Were students given an opportunity to listen and adjust before using outside aid?

This Is Now

Now back to this century…Many music educators today have "smart classrooms" with a great deal of technological support; others have great stereos. But at either end of the spectrum we are at least providing musical background, with CDs that are in tune and in time. Students have models for their instruments—even the tuba players! There is so much musical information available, even in the simplest of accompaniments. Recorded examples provide several benefits to beginning band students:

- Students have a great model for good tone quality.
- Students can hear how a song should sound.
- Students have an opportunity to play in tune with professionals who are in tune.
- Students have an opportunity to match articulation and play "inside" the sound of the model.

And now back to the first Content Standard—singing. The first exercise my band students do is sing. I really think our National Standards could be reduced to a saying by James Froseth:

"Listen, move, sing, play, and create."

Schleuter (1977) states: "Songs that students already know through singing are the most effective musical material for beginning instrumentalists. This allows an instrument to become an extension of the voice." Singing is the best tool for learning how to play in tune. Most instrumentalists play consistently in tune if they sing in tune. Harris's (1977) evidence supports this assumption; he found that vocalization improved instrumental intonation of junior and senior high school instrumentalists. The lyrics to a song give meaning and expressiveness to the music. It is so helpful to have recorded examples of songs to be performed. This is one of the cornerstones of the Suzuki approach to teaching music.

> Experiences with pictures attached, even when they involve looking at picture books and learning new words, are not as valuable (as learning through the ears) because the child needs to learn sooner rather than later to go beyond just naming things that can be seen.
>
> Language that always comes from pictures attached will produce different brain organization than that which must be processed only through the ears.

Whatever the cause, studies have shown that early experience with careful, analytic listening can dramatically improve auditory processing, listening comprehension and, in turn, reading ability—even in children with an inherited weakness.

—Jane Healy
Endangered Minds (1990)

Literacy is a symbolic system of what we understand in music. Singing is the primary basis for musical literacy. So I really believe we should incorporate singing as a vital part of every band class.

Call-and-Response Warm-Ups Using Solfege

I typically start my band classes with call and response. Students play by ear the first five notes of the B-flat concert scale. I then change the context from note names to solfege syllables. By using a movable *Do* solfege, I eliminate the need to use note names and concert pitches for "by ear" exercises. Don't worry...I still use note names and concert pitch after critical listening skills have been developed. At that point we can assign symbols and names to melodic and rhythmic patterns and songs.

The First Five Notes:

1. Associate B-flat concert with the syllable *Do*.

2. Associate C concert with the syllable *Re*.

3. Associate D concert with the syllable *Mi*.

4. Associate E-flat concert with the syllable *Fa*.

5. Associate F concert with the syllable *So*.

When singing or playing for the band class, always remember this very important principal: **Sing or play *for* the class—not *with* the class.** This concept was adapted from John Feierabend's *Conversational Solfege* series (GIA).

The following **by ear** call-and-response sequence is in B-flat concert. The patterns are examples of students playing **clarinet or trumpet**.

Teacher sings: *Do – Do – Do*
Students play: B-flat – B-flat – B-flat (concert pitch)
Trumpet and clarinet play: C – C – C (their pitch)

The following examples are exercises for B-flat instruments.

Teacher sings: *Do – Re – Do*
Students play: C – C – C

Teacher sings: *Do – Re – Mi*
Students play: C – D – C

Teacher sings: *Do – Re – Mi – Mi*
Students play: C – D – E – E

Teacher sings: *Do – Re – Mi – Fa*
Students play: C – D – E – F

Teacher sings: Do – Re – Mi – Mi – Fa
Students play: C – D – E – E – F

Teacher sings: Do – Re – Mi – Fa – So
Students play: C – D – E – F – G

Teacher sings: Do – Re – Mi – Fa – So – So
Students play: C – D – E – F – G– G

Teacher sings: So – So – So
Students play: G – G – G

Teacher sings: So – Fa – Mi – Re – Do – Do
Students play: G – F – E – D – C – C

Suggested Variations:

- Adjust patterns to the ability level of the class.
- Make up new patterns using the first five notes of the B-flat concert scale.
- Change the articulation.
- Change the dynamics.
- Change the rhythms.

Extending the Range Downward:

Later extend the range lower so it will encompass low F to F concert.

Teacher sings: Do – Ti – Do
Students play: C – B – C

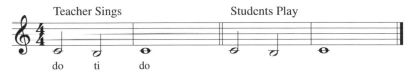

Teacher sings: Do – Ti – Do
Students play: C – B – C

Teacher sings: Do – Ti – Do – Do
Students play: C – B – C – C

Teacher sings: Do – Ti – La
Students play: C – B – A

Teacher sings: *Do – Ti – La – La*
Students play: C – B – A – A

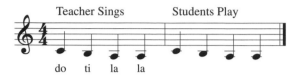

Teacher sings: *Do – Ti – La – So*
Students play: C – B – A – G

Teacher sings: *So – So – So*
Students play: G – G – G

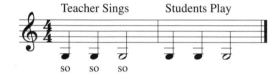

Teacher sings: *So – So – La – Ti – Do*
Students play: G – G – A – B – C

Suggested Variation:

When students have achieved success with this type of warm-up, reverse the exercises. You play the pattern, and have the students respond by singing the correlating solfege syllables. For example:

Teacher sings: C – C – C
Students sing: *Do – Do – Do*

Teaching Songs by Ear

During the first days of beginning band class, when you are teaching students how to take their instruments out of the case, hand and body positions, etc., introduce a song that you will teach the students later by ear. Sing the song alone and then with accompaniment. Some examples include:

- *Hot Cross Buns*
- *Mary Had a Little Lamb*
- *Down by the Station*
- *Oh, When the Saints Go Marching In*
- *Jingle Bells*
- *Twinkle, Twinkle, Little Star*

When you later return to these songs:

1. Sing the song.
2. Solfege the song.
3. Play the song "by ear."

Eventually the students will be able to write the song they learned "by ear." Following are examples of this process:

Hot Cross Buns

1. Sing the song.

Hot Cross Buns - Words

Hot cross buns,   Hot cross buns,   One cent, two cent, Hot cross buns.

2. Solfege the song.

Hot Cross Buns - Solfege

mi   re   do   mi   re   do   do   do   re   re   mi   re   do

3. Play the song "by ear."

Hot Cross Buns - "By Ear"

Mary Had a Little Lamb

4. Sing the song.

5. Solfege the song.

6. Play the song "by ear."

Most method books come with great background music for these songs. After the students can sing and play the songs alone, then add the accompaniments.

Rhythm

In my experience, I have found the best way to teach rhythm is through the use of rhythm flashcards with musical accompaniment. By using

flashcards, I am able to place a rhythm pattern into musical context. If I write a rhythm example and ask the students to "count" the rhythm, they can often give me the correct "numbers," but they are unable to play or sing that same rhythm with musical accompaniment. If students are not able to place rhythm patterns into a musical context, then I feel we are teaching "bad math."

Following is my recommended rhythm teaching sequence. Before I begin, I select the patterns found in the songs to be played in class.

1.   Teach a rhythm pattern through movement using musical accompaniment. An example of this is found in *Music for Movement* (book and CD), by James Froseth, Albert Blaser, and Phyllis Weikart (GIA Publications, 1981).

2.   Teach how the rhythm sounds by singing or playing the rhythm to a musical background.

3.   Teach how the rhythm looks by using rhythm flashcards with a harmonic background.

4.   Assess the students by having them sing and play the rhythm patterns found on the flashcards.

The following examples of rhythm flashcards were developed by James Froseth and Albert Blaser. They show the correlation between cut and common time.

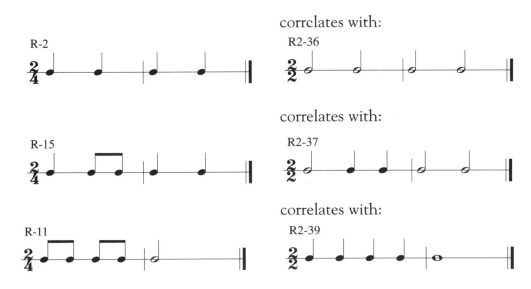

James O. Froseth. Rhythmic Flashcards, Set One (M421) and Set Two (M423).
Flashcards and compact disc. Chicago: GIA Publications, 1984, 2001.

Create

Even though I knew students should listen, move, sing, play, and create, I rarely focused on the "create" part of the Standards. The "create" part is, according to Jeffrey Agrell in *Improvisation for Classical Musicians* (GIA, 2007), "…something that has been missing from the students' music education from the beginning: a chance to experiment, explore, and use their imaginations to create their own music, and to understand music—at last—'from the inside out.'"

When I first began to teach, my students always had to play "Ms. Wilder's way" to get credit for the song. Through my experience, I have found that students gain so much more musical understanding when they create. So now my students still have to play the song correctly to receive credit for the song, but they also receive credit for playing their version after playing the original version correctly.

After students have mastered a song through singing, solfege, "by ear," and then by reading, have them play their version of the song. Beginning band students may be hesitant to "make up" their version of a song, so be sure to give them examples of an improvised song: they could take out the first note of every measure, change articulation, change dynamics, etc. At first, give students the example and have them play it. Later, they can begin to write their own examples. I have found that students derive great pleasure from sharing and teaching their version of a song with their classmates. This is a win-win experience since all versions are correct. The students are pleased to go home and tell their family how the entire band class played their song. This is the beginning of creating and improvisation.

Consider the words of Charles Young of the University of Wisconsin–Steven Point:

> Imagine a world where you could only use other people's pre-existing printed words when speaking to someone else. If you could only use the ideas of other people to communicate instead of your own thoughts, feelings, and attitudes, your personal and cultural language would be dead from a lack of creative expression. Unfortunately, too many musicians live only in this kind of world, taught to speak and read exclusively the ideas of others (composers). Very few musicians are encouraged to speak for themselves.
>
> —Charles Young
> Foreword, *Improvisation for Classical Musicians* (2008), Jeffrey Agrell

Playing Alone

Most learning takes place when a child sings or plays by himself or herself. Attempt to have every child sing and or play by him or herself at least once during every class. Studies have suggested that students perform better and learn more effectively when they are given the opportunity to make music independent of others. Individual assessment then becomes a simple extension of normal classroom activities.

—Dr. John M. Feierabend
The Hartt School of Music
at the University of Hartford

Repetition is the key to mastery. Instrumental students are learning a language. They are not able to pick up a melody and have ownership of it after only just a few days of contact. As music educators we must present the concepts and techniques to our students over and over again if they are to truly have an understanding of the language of music. So I searched for ways to motive my students to practice to the point of mastery. According to Dr. Tim Lautzenheiser, we all learn three to four times more in an environment of **joy!** Most people would say they enjoy playing games.

Over the years, I developed a classroom organizational and management technique that motivates students and monitors individual progress regardless of instrumentation, class size, or varying ability levels of students. While using many of the materials, method books, and music found in today's music classes, this sequential approach is directed toward the teaching of music fundamentals.

Sample Sequential Approach to Teaching Music Fundamentals

Teaching through Rain, Sleet, Snow and a 7th Grade Fire Drill

Pass-Off Round

I.   GROUP PARTICIPATION

     A.   Students sit in the pass-off-order of exercises completed.
        (Mixed instrumentation: This placement is not concert order.)

        Example:
        1.   Student A (clarinet) is on page 10, #2.
        2.   Student B (tuba) is on page 10, #3.
        3.   Student C (trombone) is on page 10, #3.
        4.   Student D (trumpet) is on page 11, #4.
        5.   Student E (flute is on page 12, #3.

     B.   Pass-off round begins. *(Group plays every 10 to 15 seconds.)*

        1.   Group plays exercise of Student A—page 10, #2.
        (This playing serves as a model for some students while acting as a review of music fundamentals for more advanced students.)

        2.   Group is involved in silent practice while an individual student (Student A) is actually playing his/her exercise (page 10, #2).

        3.   Group plays exercise of Students B and C—page 10, #3.

        4.   Group is involved in silent practice while an individual student (Student B) is actually playing his/her exercise (page 10, #3).

        5.   Group is involved in silent practice while an individual student (Student C) is actually playing his/her exercise (page 10, #3).

        6.   Group plays exercise of Student D—page 11, #4.

        (This pattern continues through the order until all students have had one turn during the pass-off round.)

II.   INDIVIDUAL PARTICIPATION

     A.   Student plays pass-off exercise with entire group.

     B.   Student plays pass-off exercise by himself/herself.

        1.   Student starts at the beginning of the exercise.

        2.   Student plays through the exercise to the end with no stops or replaying portions of the music.

(cont.) 3. Student observes all repeats as well as first and second endings.

    4. Student performs with correct posture (body, hands, instrument), embouchure, breathing, pitch, rhythms, articulations, dynamics, etc.

C. Performance possibilities:

    1. Student plays song correctly on the first attempt and receives a pass-off.

    2. Student makes a mistake, "buys" an extra turn with an "ET" coupon, and then plays song correctly.

    3. Student makes a mistake, "buys" an extra turn with an "ET" coupon, and then plays song incorrectly.

    4. Student makes a mistake and does not use a coupon.

    5. Student's turn is over and pass-off round moves to the next student.

(An "ET"—or extra turn—is earned for each 30 minutes of practice. Students turn in a practice note signed by the "consenting adult of his/her choice." The ET coupon can be used once per exercise. An ET can also be earned by writing a report on a composer, attending a pre-approved live concert, or viewing a video on music. With the use of the ET coupons, the responsibility for a second chance to perform an exercise is controlled by the students.)

III. TEACHER PARTICIPATION

A. Teacher starts round with Student A by asking the page and number of the song (exercise) being performed.

(By starting with the student closest to the beginning of the book, these songs can also serve as a warm-up or a review of material for more advanced students in the class.)

B. Teacher starts song with a count-off or a musical introduction.

C. Teacher monitors group performance:

    1. Active participation
    2. Correct posture, breathing, etc.
    3. Correct playing

D. Teacher monitors individual performance of the pass-off exercise.

    1. Student receives pass-off for correct performance.

    OR

    2. Student makes a mistake.

        a. Student "buys" an extra turn.
          (Teacher starts song again at the beginning.)

(cont.)   b.   Student does not "buy" an extra turn because he/she:
              (1) Does not have an ET coupon.
              (2) Decides more practice is needed on the exercise.

    3.   Teacher monitors group participation of silent practice.

    (Teacher may reward individual students for involved silent practice with an ET coupon, which usually increases group attention and participation.)

E.   Teacher continues round with Student B by asking the page and number of the song (exercise) being performed.

F.   Teacher starts song with a count-off or a musical introduction.

G.   Teacher monitors group performance:

    1.   Active participation
    2.   Correct posture, breathing, etc.
    3.   Correct playing

If Student A is successful in performing the pass-off exercise correctly, the teacher marks the song with a large "P", and then adds the date and his/her initials (e.g., P. 12/19/07 M.W.).

If Student A is unsuccessful in performing the pass-off exercise correctly, the teacher circles the mistake(s) and shows the exercise to the student.

(By dating the pass-off, the teacher, parents, and students can track performance progress. The initials indicate which teacher approved the pass-off.)

Regular Round

The pass-off method can be used in a variety of ways. If the class is of reasonable size, the regular round can be used daily. A student may stay in the round as long as he/she remains in the pass-off line. When the turn comes to a student, he/she will play with the group on his/her exercise and then continue to play the exercise from the beginning as if he/she observed a repeat. This keeps the class moving quickly and avoids a second count-off by the teacher.

    Example:
    1.   Student A (clarinet) is on page 10, #2.
    2.   Student B (tuba) is on page 10, #3.
    3.   Student C (trombone) is on page 10, #3.
    4.   Student D (trumpet) is on page 10, #5.

A.   Student A starts the round on page 10, #2.

B.   The group plays page 10, #2.

C.   Student A individually successfully performs Page 10, #2.

D.   The round is now on page 10, #3.

(cont.)

E.   The group plays page 10, #3.

F.   Students A, B, and C will each have a turn playing page 10, #3.

G.   Students A and C have passed off page 10, #3, and are now on page 10, #4.

H.   Student B did not pass off the song and is still on page 10, #3.

   The seating order is now:
   1.   Student B (tuba) is on page 10, #3.
   2.   Student A (clarinet) is on page 10, #4.
   3.   Student C (trombone) is on page 10, #4.
   4.   Student D (trumpet) is on page 10, #5.

I.   The group plays page 10, #4.

J.   Students A and C each have a turn playing page 10, #4. Both students pass off page 10, #4, and are now on page 10, #5, with Student D.

   The seating order is now:
   1.   Student B (tuba) is on page 10, #3.
   2.   Student A (clarinet) is on page 10, #5.
   3.   Student C (trombone) is on page 10, #5.
   4.   Student D (trumpet) is on page 10, #5.

K.   The group plays page 10, #5.

L.   Only Student A passes off page 10, #5, and is now on page 10, #6. Students C and D are still on page 10, #5.

   The seating order is now:
   1.   Student B (tuba) is on page 10, #3.
   2.   Student C (trombone) is on page 10, #5.
   3.   Student D (trumpet) is on page 10, #5.
   4.   Student A (clarinet) is on page 10, #6.

LIGHTNING ROUND

This type of round can be used with a limited amount of time for pass-off. The student is allowed only one chance to play the exercise he/she is on. A student may **not** "buy" an extra turn in this type of round. A **super lightning round** is played without the group performance of the exercise. Students must be ready for the count-off. No hesitation, ready, play! The teacher can use this round the last few minutes of class. If the class is small enough, everyone can have one last chance to play.

PARTNERSHIP PASS-OFF

Two or more students are involved in ensemble playing. The student playing the melody line will actually receive the pass-off. The student(s) playing the other lines will receive an ET coupon for their participation in the ensemble. This process is a good tool to stress ensemble balance and blend.

(cont.)   PARTNER PICK

When a student passes off his/her assigned exercise for the round, he/she may pick any other student to play an exercise. This round is a bonus turn for the chosen student. If the chosen student plays his/her exercise correctly, he/she receives a "free" pass-off, and the first student receives an ET coupon. This allows the better-prepared students to move faster through their exercises without the teacher giving them an extra pass-off turn. The prepared students will usually be picked because of the assumption that they will complete their pass-off and the first student will acquire a "free" ET coupon.

LAS VEGAS

A student may select any exercise from the book he/she has not passed off. The student may bet up to 5 extra turns that he/she can successfully pass off the exercise. The teacher will lay "odds" on the bet. (Example: A student bets 2 extra turns that he/she can pass off page 17, #2. The teacher, knowing the difficulty level of the exercise and the ability of the student, will place an odd of 4 on the bet. The student could earn 8 extra turns if he/she passes off the exercise, or the student could lose the 2 extra turns he/she bets.) This approach is a good change of pace for a student who is "stuck" on an exercise or has just arrived at a difficult exercise.

TEAM COMPETITION

Divide the class into two or more teams. Teams should have equal numbers of woodwind, brass, and percussion instruments, as well as male and female players. A point system may be set up by the teacher and the class. (Example: 2 points for most exercises in the book, 5 points for difficult exercises, 10 points for scales played by memory.) Students can earn points for their team by attending concerts; watching video programs; writing reports on instruments, composers, etc. The teacher can award "team" bonus points when all team members are involved in the silent practice while an individual is playing. Good posture, hand position, tone quality are often given bonus points. The team with the most practice notes turned in receives bonus points. Points can even be acquired by being the first team set up and ready to go, with all members in their place. (The team captain will raise his/her hand with great dignity and calmly notify the teacher of this achievement.)

ESSENTIAL IN THE BAND ROOM—an egg timer (or stopwatch with an alarm). The timer is set to ring every 1 to 5 minutes throughout the class. If the egg timer goes off while a line is in progress, then the song is now worth 3x to 5x the number of team points originally assigned. If the timer goes off between teams, the bonus points go to the next team, provided the student passes off his/her exercise.

BAND SQUARES

This game is set up like Tic-Tac-Toe and Hollywood Squares. Nine students set up the board. They sit in three rows of three. Draw a Tic-Tac-Toe grid on the chalkboard. Two students are chosen to be the players. Assign Player 1 the X and Player 2 the O. When the player chooses a student who can successfully play his/her pass-off exercise, the appropriate X or O will be placed on the corresponding Tic-Tac-Toe board. If the chosen student does not pass off his/her exercise, he/she will leave the band square set-up. A new class member will now occupy the vacated space on the Tic-Tac-Toe board. This will continue until the game is won or tied.

(cont.)   LET'S MAKE A DEAL!

If a student can play his/her pass-off exercise correctly, he/she may choose to play Let's Make a Deal! The student will choose Door #1, Door #2, or Door #3. Behind each door is a different prize: free ET coupons, loss of ET coupons, a melody line to a popular rock tune or commercial, or silly tunes (like nursery tunes). Another option could be a turn where a student could play as many songs as he/she can until he/she makes a mistake, or a student could be given a free 30-minute private lesson with the teacher.

BAND BASEBALL

Divide the class into two teams—The Braves! and someone else. Set up the room like a baseball diamond. Place a chair and a stand where 1st, 2nd, and 3rd bases should be. The teacher's podium serves as home plate. The team captain for each team sets the batting order. Students have the opportunity to play up to 4 exercises in this game.

Example: Student 1 plays his/her first exercise and moves to the 1st base chair and stand. At this point, he/she can choose to stay or play another exercise in an effort to move to second base. If the student plays the second exercise correctly, he/she moves to second base. Same for 3rd base and home plate. However, if the student makes a mistake and is not able to complete the song using an extra turn, the student's turn is over and the team has acquired its first out. Three outs and the other team comes to bat.

MAIN RULE: No arguing with the umpire or YOU'RE OUT!

GRAB BAG

Fill a bag with questions that, when answered correctly, can earn the student extra turns, actual pass-off, or extra points for his/her team.

Example: Key signatures, musical terms, a request to play a certain exercise of scale or passage from Concert Music. Who composed the piece *Three London Miniatures?* Who composed the piece *In the Shining of the Stars?* Who composer the piece *Under Three Flags?* Who composed the piece *Cobb County Festival?*

SUMMARY

With the pass-off method, everyone is involved during the entire class. The students will be playing the line with the group, or they will be involved with silent practice while another student is playing for a pass-off. On average, the group will be playing every 30 seconds. Students will play review material, current material, and new material during each pass-off round. In our quick fix, instant results from computers, TV remote control society of today, students have few opportunities to practice mastery by practicing a song (or concept) over and over until they achieve mastery. The pass-off system offers this opportunity to students.

REPETITION IS THE KEY TO MASTERY!

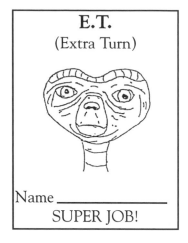

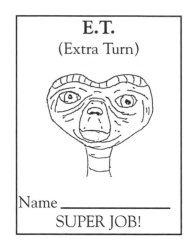

Plan B

In my teaching, I have found that students learn in a variety of ways, so I approach the same subject in as many ways as possible. I like to refer to my "additional" ways to teach the fundamentals as my **Plan B**. Following are examples of "additional" (Plan B) ways to teach the fundamentals.

Scales – Plan B:

Scales are as easy as (1) one, (2) two, (3) three!!
Administer two exams, with all questions on both exams being of equal difficulty. Make the questions available for study before the exam. One exam has two questions, and the other has five questions. All questions must be answered to pass—all or nothing. It does not matter which exam is chosen. Remember that all questions are of equal difficulty and will be available for study before the exam. Logic suggests the exam with two questions would be chosen.

Taking this concept into consideration, why then would teachers ask their beginning band students to memorize scales with more than three items to remember? Why try to remember five sharps? Wouldn't it be much easier for students to remember two natural notes, with all the remaining notes being sharp? Why read a key signature as five sharps? Why not read it as if every note is sharp except for the two natural notes of B and E?

When teaching scales to students, consider trying this approach. Most beginning band students have a working knowledge of several basic scales. The B-flat concert scale is the first scale introduced in most method books. Many students understand the concept of seven letter names in music, with the three arpeggio notes being the first, third, and fifth degrees of the scale. Students playing concert-pitched instruments know that the B-flat scale has two flats: B-flat and E-flat. If students understand that this scale has five natural notes and two flat notes, then they should understand that the B-natural scale is just as easy to play. When students play the B-natural scale, they tend to think the scale has two natural notes and five sharp notes. Instead, have them look at the B-natural scale as having two natural notes, and all the other notes are sharp.

Some teachers suggest that students should learn notes this way: In the first lesson, show the students the names and fingerings for seven natural notes. The students come back for the next lesson with the knowledge of seven natural notes. In the second lesson, show the students seven sharp notes, and in the third lesson show them seven flat notes. From this point, it is easy for students to understand the concept of one, two, or three types of notes, with the rest of the notes being all natural, all sharp, or all flat. Now that's as easy as 1–2–3!

You should never think more than three sharps, flats, or naturals per scale. There are seven letters in music. All scale note name combinations must add up to seven. (By the way, this approach drives theorists nuts!) Here are some examples:

THINK "1"
1 flat or 1 sharp or 1 natural

G – A – B – C – D – E – **F-sharp** – G
1 sharp + 6 naturals = 7

G-flat – A-flat – B-flat – C-flat – D-flat – E-flat – **F** – G-flat
1 natural + 6 flats = 7

F – G – A – **B-flat** – C – D – E – F
1 flat + 6 naturals = 7

THINK "2"
2 flats or 2 sharps or 2 naturals

The B scales think "2." They are the B and E scales.

B-flat – C – D – **E-flat** – F – G – A – **B-flat**
2 flats + 5 naturals = 7

B – C-sharp – D-sharp – **E** – F-sharp – G-sharp – A-sharp – **B**
2 naturals + 5 sharps = 7

The D scales also think "2." They are the F and C scales.

D-flat – E-flat – **F** – G-flat – A-flat – B-flat – **C** – D-flat
2 naturals + 5 flats = 7

D – E – **F-sharp** – G – A – B – **C-sharp** – D
2 sharps + 5 naturals = 7

THINK "3"
3 flats or 3 sharps or 3 naturals

The E scales think "3." They are the B, E, and A scales.

E-flat – F – G – **A-flat** – **B-flat** – C – D – **E-flat**
3 flats + 4 naturals = 7

E – F-sharp – G-sharp – **A** – **B** – C-sharp – D-sharp – **E**
3 naturals + 4 sharps = 7

The A scales think "3." They are the F, C, and G scales.

A-flat – B-flat – **C** – D-flat – E-flat – **F** – **G** – A-flat
3 naturals + 4 flats = 7

A – B – **C-sharp** – D – E – **F-sharp** – **G-sharp** – A
3 sharps + 4 naturals = 7

Many auditions use five chromatically adjacent scales, so I have my students use these scales played for their instrument (not a concert pitch scale). I suggest these five scales because they are the easiest!

B-flat scale
B scale
C scale
D scale
D-flat scale

The most you have to think is "2"!

- The B-flat and B scales have 2 — B and E.
- The D-flat and D scales have 2 — F and C.
- The C scale is 7 naturals — no flats and no sharps.

Remember:
The goal of the audition is
2 BE FIRST CHAIR! = 2 BE FC!

Sight-Reading – Plan B:
Are our students dependent or independent?

Advanced music students find themselves in auditions for chair placement, regional and all-state groups, and even auditions for music school. Part of most every audition is individual sight-reading. How well prepared are the students for the sight-reading exercises? Do they have the independent skills that confidently carry them through the exercise? Good fundamental playing techniques carry the students through most of the sight-reading. But what about the rest? Do they have a valid and sequential plan for the exercise? Do the students know their characteristic playing patterns when sight-reading, or is that the responsibility of the teacher?

When working on sight-reading with instrumental students, many teachers do not let the students learn from the sight-reading experience. Many one-on-one sight-reading sessions go like this: The teacher reviews the sight-reading guidelines with the student. The student is usually given a thirty-second block of time to study the exercise. The student performs the exercise. After the exercise is completed by the student, the teacher points out performance errors. Unless the exercise is recorded, it is very difficult for the student to be aware of how he/she actually performed the exercise. In this scenario, the teacher is the active participant in correcting mistakes. The teacher has taken the responsibility for knowing the student's sight-reading traits. The student may truly want to improve and learn, but he/she is still dependent on the teacher's observations and evaluations.

How quickly do students learn to recognize their deficiencies? Can they play an active part in the process of identifying and correcting sight-reading mistakes? **Yes, they can!** Active rather than passive learning is the best and quickest way to independence. It is a student's responsibility—not the teacher's—to improve his/her sight-reading techniques. It is the teacher's responsibility to teach the needed skills, but it is the student's responsibility to improve his/her own musicianship.

The following method is one that I have found seems to dramatically improve the sight-reading skills of conscientious students within a few short weeks:

MATERIALS NEEDED

- Skill-appropriate packet of sight-reading exercises
- Tape and tape recorder / CD and CD burner
- Timer or stopwatch
- Notebook or log for keeping a record of mistakes and how to correct them

PROCEDURE

By using the following procedure, students are ready to actively improve their sight-reading technique:

1. The student sets the timer for 30 seconds and studies the sight-reading exercise during that time period.

2. After turning on the recording device, the student records his/her performance of the exercise to the best of his/her ability.

3. The student turns off the recorder and practices the sight-reading exercise until he/she can perform it correctly. The student now knows how the sight-reading exercise sounds.

4. The student replays and assesses the recording of the sight-reading exercise.

5. The student writes down the mistakes and how to correct them in his/her notebook.
   (In the beginning, students may need to replay the originally recorded sight-reading performance several times.)

6. The student turns in the recorded exercises with the evaluation of his/her performance. The teacher checks the recorded exercises and the student evaluation to see how accurately the student assessed the performance. If the student missed a problem, the teacher and student can listen to the performance together and work on the problem.

Students will begin to recognize their own performance patterns, both good and bad. (For example, a student may see that he/she missed D-flat concert or certain rhythms in 6/8 time.) They will learn how to approach the sight-reading materials in a more efficient manner because they are not dependent on the teacher's feedback. They will be able to make decisions about which components of the music require careful attention and which are usually played correctly. The students will acquire the skills to sequentially and *independently* work through the sight-reading materials.

This same procedure can be used in a full band situation to allow the group to assess their performance. This critical listening exercise helps students to listen and to adjust individual and group performances. The students learn to listen to the individual sections and how they relate to the group performance as a whole.

Rhythmic Reinforcement – Plan B:

One of my goals for each band class I teach is that somewhere, somehow my students have an outstanding musical experience. Each class should have an esthetic experience for all to experience. Now I realize this is sometimes hard to achieve in the beginning months of instrumental instruction and performance. But I often think of the wonderful way in which John Feierabend reinforces rhythmic reading through the use of classical music in his *Conversational Solfege* series (GIA). The exercises in this series provide reinforcement of emerging literacy skills, and they also enable students to listen to wonderful classical examples with greater attention.

Can Can — Example #1

The musical track for the "Can Can" by Jacques Offenbach is intended for use as support music while students practice chanting rhythm patterns. I like to play this piece and have the students maintain some steady beat motion while they echo rhythm patterns and read rhythm patterns.

The main theme occurs four times in the music:

1. First time, students read and chant the rhythms as written.

2. Second time, students read and chant the rhythms, except when a square is placed under the note. (This is an example of rest (silence) within the concept of the whole of a piece.)

3. Third time, students read and chant the rhythms, except when a triangle is placed under the note. (This is an example of rest (silence) within the concept of the whole of a piece.)

Can Can by Jacques Offenbach from Conversational Solfege – Level 1

4. Fourth time, divide the class in half. Group 1 reads and chants the notes, except when a square is placed under the note. Group 2 reads and chants the notes, except when a triangle is placed under the note.

Not only are you reinforcing sound and silence within a rhythmic pattern—you are developing ensemble skills!

In the Hall of the Mountain King — Example #2

For beginning students, another good example is "Hall of the Mountain King" (also part of the *Conversational Solfege* series) to reinforce a steady beat, eighth note, quarter note, half note reading.

This activity is supported by the music of "Hall of the Mountain King."

1. Students perform the entire page with repeats three times.

2. Students perform the following motions while reading the rhythms:

    *   For all pairs of eighth notes, tap the right leg with the right hand, and then tap the left leg with the left hand.
    *   For all quarter notes, clap hands once.
    *   For all half notes, clap hands once and pull the top hand away in an arch.

In the Hall of the Mountain King from Conversational Solfege – Level 2

Peer Gynt Suite

Perform entire page with repeats three times.

CD #2, Track #8

John Feierabend

So I wish for you and all your students these skills…The primary skills for successful music teaching are:

Modeling skills
Aural and visual discrimination skills
Diagnostic skills

The primary skills for successful music learning are:

Imitation skills
Aural and visual discrimination skills
Skills to independently analyze, generalize, and synthesize

—Dr. James O. Froseth
Emeritus, University of Michigan

Materials and Sources

Agrell, Jeffrey. *Improvisation for Classical Musicians*. Chicago: GIA Publications, 2008.

Feierabend, John M. *Conversational Solfege, Level 1*. Chicago: GIA Publications, 2000.

Feierabend, John M. *Conversational Solfege, Level 2*. Chicago: GIA Publications, 2000.

Feierabend, John M. *Conversational Solfege, Level 1*. Classical music selections (CD-526). Chicago: GIA Publications, 2002.

Froseth, James O. *Rhythmic Flashcards, Set One* (M421). Flashcards and compact disc. Chicago: GIA Publications, 2001, 1984.

Froseth, James O. *Rhythmic Flashcards, Set Two* (M423). Flashcards and compact disc. Chicago: GIA Publications, 2002, 1984.

Froseth, James O. *Do It! Play in Band*. Book and compact discs. Chicago: GIA Publications, 1997.

Lautzenheiser, Tim. *Everyday Wisdom for Inspired Teaching*. Chicago: GIA Publications, 2005.

CHAPTER 2

Establishing an Effective Rehearsal Procedure for Middle School Students

Erin Cole

Setting middle school students up for success from the beginning is key! Besides teaching the needed fundamentals of instrumental music, students need routine and structure within the rehearsal procedure.

Starting your beginners off with a routine in the first year of playing will enable you to have very successful seventh/eighth grade rehearsals. The students will already be accustomed to a rehearsal routine, which will result in a very disciplined ensemble that will be able to rehearse very well.

Entering the Classroom

Students should enter the room quietly.
This may take time to develop consistently with middle school students, but stick with it. Depending on the atmosphere of your school, students often enter a classroom excited by what is going on in the hallways. You must establish the behavior and level of noise that is acceptable in your band room and be consistent with enforcement, even if the expectation is much different than that of the other teachers in the school.

Students should listen to recordings of the music they are working on as they enter the room.
Students will immediately focus on the rehearsal and get in the right frame of mind when they hear their music being played. As soon as students get settled, they should air play or "tizzle" along with the recording. This gives them something to do before rehearsal starts and gets them focused.

Students should read the rehearsal plan found on the board.
Come up with an exact time for each class to start rehearsal each day. Write that time on the board (e.g., "Time: 9:27"). Expect the students to be unpacked, quiet, and ready to start rehearsal at that time each day. It is also a good idea with beginners to put a few reminders, such as "Enter the room quietly!" or "Do not unpack yet." Written reminders will help the students adjust to the routine. Underneath the time that is written on the board, list the warm-ups and the pieces to be rehearsed. Next to each piece, you can even note the specific measure numbers you want to work on.

Having the plan for rehearsal written on the board lets students know what is expected of them and shows them you have put a lot of thought and preparation into the rehearsal.

The director should be in the band room, supervising students.
This could be at the front of the room, at the door to the classroom, in the instrument storage room, or anywhere supervision is needed. Be as visible and observant as possible. If there is more than one band director, have different places that each director stands to supervise the students coming into the room.

When the Director Gets on the Podium

Students immediately stop what they are doing and get quiet as soon as the director gets on the podium.
If students have unpacked and assembled their instruments, they should go to ready position. Make sure the music stands are at a height so the students can see both you and the music at the same time while maintaining perfect posture.

All students' eyes must be on the director on the podium.
The classroom should be completely silent. You should be able to address the ensemble in a normal speaking voice; you should not have to raise your voice at all. Inform the students of the plan for rehearsal that day.

Incorporate positions throughout the rehearsal.
Rest, ready, and play positions should be used throughout the rehearsal.

Rest Position:
Students sit with instrument on lap (uniform position for each section), with their back against the back of the chair.

Rest Position

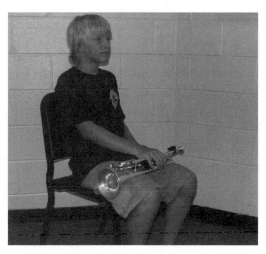

Ready position:
Students move up on the front three inches of the chair and sit with perfect posture: straight backs, feet flat on the floor, and instruments straight up and down on the right knee (or a position close to that depending on the instrument). Each section of the band has a uniform ready position. (For tuba and euphonium players, this is the same as their playing position.) Students should go to ready position every time you step on the podium or otherwise instruct them to go to this position during rehearsal.

Ready Position

Play position:
Students bring the instrument up to correct playing position (again by section). Posture should not change from ready to play position. Students should know to go to this position when you bring your hands up to conduct.

Play Position

For example: Once the band is finished playing, bring your hands down. Students immediately go to ready position and they do not speak or make any sounds on their instruments. Choose the positions to be used, provide detailed instructions, and continually reinforce this practice. Let the positions do the work for you! If a routine is established, the students will become accustomed to that routine, and you will not have to deal with talking and behavior issues. The students will be more actively engaged in the rehearsal, and you will do more teaching. Detailed instruction and a firm commitment to the procedure will result in better rehearsals.

During Rehearsal

Maintain a proper student rehearsal procedure.

- Throughout the rehearsal, students should maintain correct technique by incorporating the positions.

- Students should not talk during rehearsal. Remind them that there is no talking in rest, ready, or play position.

- Students should only play their instruments when instructed. Playing out of turn is not acceptable.

- All eyes should be on you when you are speaking.

Praise students often for exhibiting correct rehearsal procedure and proper behavior. Positive reinforcement motivates students!

Pace the rehearsal.

Pacing the rehearsal is very important to student motivation. It is your responsibility as director to pace the rehearsal appropriately so the educational objectives are met and at the same time the students are actively involved.

When rehearsing sections, be careful not to neglect other students for long periods of time (e.g., percussion). This only encourages misbehavior.

Employ "tizzling" (air playing) in rehearsal.

Tizzling is beneficial to the students as well as the director. Tizzling allows the students to actively finger the notes and push air through the instrument in rhythm. As the students go through the musical passage without playing out loud, you will hear what the students are tizzling and be able to make any corrections before the students play out loud.

A great time for tizzling is when students are coming into the room and getting ready for the rehearsal to start. I like to have a recording of the piece playing that the students will be rehearsing that day. As soon as the students are settled and ready, they immediately begin to tizzle with the recording that is playing. This gets the students mentally focused before rehearsal even starts.

Model for the students.

Modeling great tone quality is very helpful to the students. Play for your students as often as possible. You will see that their tone will mature at a much faster pace when they hear and emulate characteristic tone quality.

Take volunteers!

When students are playing lines in the book, warm-ups, or scales, take volunteers! Students love to show off and play in front of the class.

Taking volunteers promotes self-confidence and keeps students motivated. It also provides an opportunity for you to hear students individually and give feedback.

At the End of Rehearsal

- Always give students feedback on how the rehearsal went that day. Offer positive feedback or even suggestions to make the rehearsal better the next day.

- Give the students practice homework for the next day's rehearsal.

- Tell the students the plan for the next day's rehearsal.

Transitioning to *Daily Routine for Band*

The Tapp Middle School Band has been using *Daily Routine for Band* to establish the necessary foundations that have become inherent in our program. (See excerpts from *Daily Routine for Band* starting on page 40.)[1] It is very easy to transition from a disciplined approach with the rehearsal procedure to *Daily Routine for Band*, which we use every day as our warm-up. I am able to spend quite a bit of time on a beneficial warm-up. We have established a very routine approach, which consists of breathing exercises, buzzing exercises, scales, lip slurs, and chorales. The warm-up is an opportunity for learning through review or an introduction of new fundamental concepts. Because the classes are so disciplined, we are able to spend half of the class period on the fundamental warm-up routine, and the students are able to focus on that task.

As students progress from beginning band to seventh/eighth grade band, we transition from the elementary book to the intermediate book. At the intermediate level, the students are challenged much more on each warm-up exercise. The scales become more difficult, and many sections of the band now play two octaves. The chromatic scale exercise is also integrated into our daily warm-up.

The chorale in A-flat is a fantastic way to work on legato style, maturity of sound, balance, blend, tone, and intonation. This particular chorale is very useful because it begins with the woodwind family (mallets with woodwinds) and brass family (percussion and timpani with brass) playing at separate times, and then playing as a full band on the last phrase. This allows you to address balance, blend, and intonation within the woodwind and brass sections individually and as a complete ensemble.

Keys to Success

- Give clear instructions.

- Offer reminders about proper rehearsal procedure.

- Maintain balance between routine and variety.

- Establish high expectations.

- Acknowledge commitment from both you (the director) and the students to establish and maintain consistent proper rehearsal technique.

Photo by Jolesch Photography. Used with permission.

Midwest Clinic 2004
Tapp Middle School Symphonic Band (Powder Springs, GA)
Cobb County School District

Excerpt #1. The Breath and the Breathing Chorale.

Air is as vital to wind players as it is to life. The mastery of the air will not only enhance your fundamentals, but also raise your performance abilities. Success on any wind instrument is dictated by how well we manage our air.

The "Breathing Chorale" was developed to coordinate both the inhale and exhale breath within actual literature. A student can now see how the air relates to the music. By using this revolutionary approach, breathing becomes an easy part of your Daily Routine!

How it works
Use air and don't sound actual pitches! The notes on the page are for air durations only.

Brass
Move the air as fast as possible through the instrument without activating the lips. The proper playing embouchure must be used during this process even though <u>no pitches</u> are being created on the instrument. Changing notes provides varying resistance on each instrument. Trombones use 7th position on E naturals.

Woodwind
Create a "Hissing" sound on the syllable "sss" in coordination with the music. Teeth together with lips slightly apart will help facilitate this action. Move the air as fast and aggressively as possible. This will create resistance and develop breathing stamina.

Percussion
While the woodwinds and brass work on breathing the percussion part is designed to get the wrists and fingers moving while concentrating on fundamental strokes. Good stick control on every percussion instrument must be developed. This control should also be refined during full band rehearsal. Please note that the sticking for the eighth notes in the snare drum part is written for a Right Hand Lead.

Key Points to Establish

Students must breathe in time. Let the breathing become a part of the musical rhythm. If the entrance is on beat 1, breathe on the prior beat 4.

Students must not stop the breath. The air either moves into the respiratory system or out. Air never stops between each motion.

Every breath must be as large as possible. Students must fill up the entire respiratory system.

Students must keep excellent posture. Lifting from the waist up and gently rolling the shoulders back will allow the ribcage to open up. This will allow maximum air in the chest area. Any movement of the shoulders should be induced by the expansion of the chest.

Finale
A daily dose of the "Breathing Chorale" will not only elevate fundamentals, but also raise awareness on how the breath is coordinated with the music. Incorporating the "Breathing Chorale" on a day-to-day basis aids in the awareness of how the breath helps create musical ideas and concepts.

 Daily Routine for Band - Elementary

Excerpt #2. Tone Production & Embouchure Development.

Do not underestimate the power long tone exercises have in improving sound. The thought of doing long tone exercises can seem a bit unappetizing. Because of this we tend to stay away from them. Many long tone exercises are built around sustaining one isolated tone before switching to another. This new exercise offers a fun and exciting way to involve long tones as you travel through your Daily Routine.

How it works

Brass
- Play the exercise on the instrument. This improves tone production and develops pitch recognition. Encourage consistent air speed.
- Play the exercise on the mouthpiece only. This enhances tone production, pitch accuracy, range extension, endurance, and airflow. With so much at stake, it becomes imperative that you include mouthpiece buzzing in your daily routine.
- Interchange on the instrument or mouthpiece as needed.

Woodwind
- Play the exercise on the instrument working on tone production and embouchure strengthening. Encourage consistent air speed.
- Use this exercise to supply pitch reference for our mouthpiece playing colleagues.

Percussion
- Make sure the percussionist "overlaps" the multiple bounce strokes (no break in the sound from hand to hand).
- Make each multiple bounce stroke last as long as possible. Also keep constant and steady hand motion throughout the exercise.
- The mallet part is designed to focus on playing eighth notes while moving in a stepwise motion up and down the keyboard.

Benefits of Tone Production
Improves on tone sonority
Develops better air flow and air management
Improves on pitch accuracy
Develops stamina
Improves embouchure strength

Finale
Remember to encourage each student to focus on each individual note in pursuit of tonal perfection. Time well spent on this exercise will result in an astonishing amount of growth fundamentally. There is no denying that if this exercise is performed on a daily basis, students in your ensemble will hear drastic improvements in the creation of mature sounds and sonorities.

Daily Routine for Band - Elementary

Sample Exercises:
Breathing Chorale—Bassoon

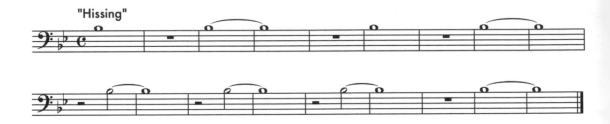

Breathing Chorale—Mallet Percussion

Tone Production—Flute

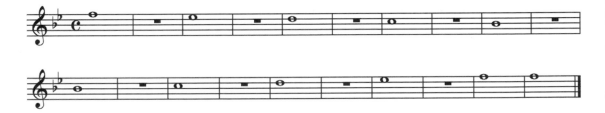

Tone Production—Trumpet

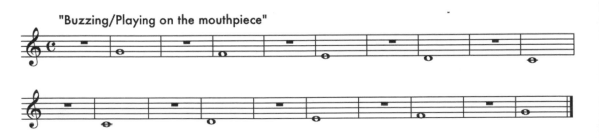

Excerpt 3. Flexibility & Embouchure Strengthening.

Without question, flexibility and embouchure strengthening exercises are one of the staples in building fundamentals. These exercises were developed not only to help one move fluidly and effortlessly throughout the entire range of the instrument, but also help build embouchure strength and endurance.

B
R
A
S
S

In slurring in the upward direction

Encourage your brass students to increase the air speed while raising the back of their tongue. This will help facilitate an effortless sound as you move through the partials.

In slurring in the downward direction

Encourage your brass students to lower the back of the tongue and increase the volume of air. During this process, the aperture becomes bigger as the lips inside the cup of the mouthpiece become more relaxed. This creates less tension within the cup allowing the lips to vibrate generously and produce an unforced sound throughout the entire register of the instrument.

W
O
O
D
W
I
N
D
S

Flutes
Goal: tone quality and aperture size awareness

Pay careful attention to the size of the aperture and stability of the embouchure during sustained pitches. While playing these mid-range exercises, be sure to reinforce the importance of clear tone quality. These exercises are also the perfect opportunity to introduce vibrato to the developing flute student.

Double Reeds
Goal: correct embouchure formation and breath support

The manner in which the double reed vibrates is controlled by the embouchure. In order to achieve the best possible sound it is imperative that the student uses good breath support.

Clarinets
Goal: enhance tone and embouchure consistency.

Encourage the student to achieve an unchanging embouchure throughout the range of the instrument. This exercise can also be used to reinforce correct right hand thumb position.

Saxophones
Goal: create a smooth, fluid tone quality over the range of the instrument.

A solid and steady stream of air must be used while changing from pitch to pitch. Encourage the student to achieve an unchanging embouchure throughout the range of the instrument.

P
E
R
C
U
S
S
I
O
N

Keyboards

Focus on developing single stroke rolls on one pitch at a time. Notice the slur markings when the pitch changes on every beat. The percussionist should strive to keep the hand motion constant to resemble the air of the woodwind and brass players...no break in sound! All of the notes should sound smooth and connected.

Snare Drum

Designed to develop three other basic rudiments, the paradiddle, flam, and flam taps. For the paradiddle, starting with quarter notes the percussionist can really focus on the sticking before progressing to eighth notes. The sticking patterns for the flams makes the percussionist concentrate on one hand at a time before alternating and developing the fluid sticking pattern for flam taps.

Daily Routine for Band - Elementary   9

Flexibility/Embouchure Strengthening—Horn

Exercise #2

Flexibility/Embouchure Strengthening—Snare Drum

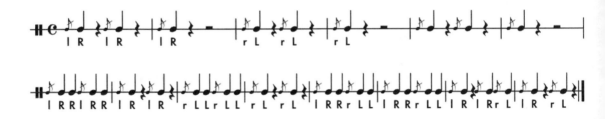

Excerpt 4. Scales, Finger Dexterity and Chorales.

The next three skills must be developed on a day-to-day basis. The ability to make precise, coordinated finger and hand movements is an important component of playing an instrument. How well the hand motion can be manipulated is just as important as all other aspects of playing. Sloppy or lazy movements will result in inaccurate and poor performances. Developing great technique will only enhance great fundamentals.

Why Practice Scales?
Scales are the "building blocks" of music.

Winds/Mallets
- In practicing scales and arpeggios the student must execute many of the physical movements required in playing music.
- Scale work can be used as a tool to improve physical dexterity, responsiveness, range extension, and sight-reading.
- Simply playing scales, backwards, forwards and in lots of other patterns establish hand patterns that can then be translated directly to music we play.

Snare Drum
- The snare drum part takes the "buzz" roll development to the next step, 16th notes.
- Each measure is designed to set up a "check" pattern for the hands without the roll.
- Once the percussionist has developed the rhythmic portion, then it is simply time to add the multiple bounce strokes. Make sure the hands are even in timing and the "buzz" strokes are long and smooth.

Finger Dexterity
Sloppy technique with fingers, slides or hands/wrist will cause:
Poorly executed notes
Articulation issues
Rhythmic discrepancies
Inaccurate slurs

Why play Chorales?
Chorale work is the perfect vehicle to get that mature sound out of your ensemble! Involving daily chorale use is a fun way to develop air management, balance, blend, phrasing, finger timing and tone.

All chorales should be played in a legato style and tempo that is moderately slow. These chorales can also be used for study of precise intonation within the wind section. This exercise builds physical stamina in the percussionist's hands. Other common percussion instruments are included here to work on the "delicate" touches needed in a chorale style.

Finale
Increasing student awareness of good finger/hand technique, balance and blend on an everyday basis will only help improve their fundamental development. Taking care of fundamentals can only inspire great performances.

 Daily Routine for Band - Elementary

Sample Scale Exercises:
B-flat Concert Scale—Alto Saxophone

B-flat Concert Scale—Trombone

B-flat Concert Scale—Snare Drum

Sample Chorales:
Chorale #2 in B-flat—Flute

Chorale #2 - in B♭

Chorale #2 in B-flat—Trumpet

Chorale #2 - in B♭

Chorale #2 in B-flat—Timpani

Chorale #2 - in B♭

(Bb,C & F)

Getting Ready for Beginning Band—Questions and Answers

Question: When are instrument demonstrations done?
At Tapp Middle School, we do instrument demonstrations at an open house in the band room for two nights in August each year. The students can hear and see the instruments, try them, and sign up for the instrument for which they seem best suited.

We also do another demonstration once school starts for the entire sixth grade student body in the theater, where the band directors and high school students demonstrate the different instruments. I feel it is important to have not only the band directors demonstrate the instruments but also students who play very well and are not much older than the sixth graders. This allows the beginners to see that it is possible to play an instrument extremely well within just a few years.

Question: How is instrument selection done?
During the band open house in August, the sixth grade students come to the band room to see all of the different instruments offered in our band, and they actually try them out. There are different stations for the different instruments, with a band director at every station. (This includes the Tapp band directors as well as other band directors in the local area who we pay to come and help at the stations.) The students go around to the different stations and try as many instruments as they want. They take the mouthpiece test at each station and, time permitting, try to play the actual instrument.

The students have a paper they take with them to the various stations. The director at each station marks the student's paper with a specific code that indicates how the student did.

When the students are finished trying all of the instruments, they take their paper to the checkout table, which is run by the head band director. The head director then looks at the paper and determines which instrument each student was most successful on. The director then guides the student and his/her parent(s) in the direction of that specific instrument, explaining the importance of playing and choosing the instrument the student was most successful on.

For the most part, the parent(s) and the student are happy with the same instrument, but occasionally you may need to ask the parent(s) and student to consider the second best instrument for the student to reach an agreement.

We do not sign up all of the students during the two open house nights. We sign up the rest of the students once school starts, usually during the first week and a half after the demonstration open house. This is done during connections time, when we take student out of class to test them on the instruments the same way we do at the open house.

Question: Do you have a set instrumentation for beginning classes?
I do keep track of how many of each instrument we sign up each night, and I do try to encourage students to consider the instruments we need the most while still making sure the students are best suited for those instruments.

Once it seems like we are at maximum numbers for a specific instrument (e.g., percussion, saxophone), then we explain to students that those instruments are no longer available. This can sometimes be a sensitive situation, as I want to give as many students as I can the opportunity to experience band. However, before I make an exception, I call the student's parent(s) to explain the need for the child to consider other instruments. If I am ultimately faced with losing a student who feels very strongly about playing a particular instrument, at that point I will make an exception.

Question: What about color instruments?
At Tapp, we do start beginners on bassoon, oboe, and horn. However, we do strongly recommend private lessons for these specific instruments because they are generally more difficult to learn. Most of our students take lessons on these instruments. But if you cannot get enough students to take lessons at your school, consider hiring professional bassoon, oboe, and horn players to come in a few times (during the first year of playing especially) to give the students masterclasses.

Question: How do you approach beginners?
I think it is very important to split up beginner brass, woodwind, and percussion students as much as possible in the first year of playing. While at the same time I feel it is important to have full band every now and then to teach concepts such as balance, blend, etc., within the full ensemble, the students benefit greatly from very frequent like instrumentation instruction in that first year!

Question: How do you incorporate your discipline approach into your first lesson?
I teach students my discipline routine starting with the first day: how to come into the room, where to sit, and how to properly behave and rehearse. I then gradually start incorporating the techniques presented in this chapter. I have found that the sooner you introduce these concepts, the easier it is to establish the routine so it becomes second-nature for the students. They will consistently rehearse properly and behave, so you can focus on teaching!

Question: How do you set up your classroom for each rehearsal?
I make sure all the chairs and stands are set up correctly in their rows, nice and neat. When there is order in the classroom, students are more likely to enter the room in an orderly manner.

Question: When do students start full band?

At Tapp, we do not start full band until November, when we begin to prepare for the first concert. Prior to that, we split up woodwind, brass, and percussion every day. But at that point, we only have full band rehearsal once or twice a week.

CHAPTER 3

Beginners or Musicians: The Risk/Reward of Musicianship

Dennis W. Fisher

Beginning a new instrument or developing skills on any instrument is a daunting and sometimes intimidating experience. Necessarily, much focus is placed on the mechanics and techniques of producing pleasing and acceptable sounds. After all, if students cannot produce a good sound, they cannot recreate the music.

The creation of organized sound is based on musical performance fundamentals that are only achieved through meticulous and methodical preparation and practice. However, placing the focus on the mechanics and techniques of producing good sound, without the pleasure of turning that sound into music, often creates a barrier to achieving musicality and musicianship. So as students mature and obtain increased technical facility required by the increasing demands of advanced repertoire, great care needs to be taken to ensure that they also achieve greater musicality and musicianship.

I have found that the reason many students want to begin playing in band is because they want to make the great music they heard on CD, TV, radio, or at a live performance. What they hear really appeals to them and they want to do it, too. They select an instrument and then come to beginning band with great excitement and expectation.

Then comes the reality: Playing any instrument is a very complex process that demands a highly elevated level of multi-tasking. It is our job as music educators to prepare our students and assist them in mastering the multi-tasking processes of playing an instrument. Following are some of the many tasks students must accomplish:

Preparation for playing:
1. Open the case.
2. Carefully remove and assemble the instrument.

Physical aspects of playing:
3. Use proper posture.
4. Use proper hand position.
5. Create the proper embouchure.
6. Breathe properly.
7. Create the sound.
8. Change pitches with finger dexterity (as well as embouchure and air adjustments for brass).

A new written language to learn:
9. Recognize and translate note names and rhythmic values.

Critical thinking, decision making, execution:
10. Correlate the knowledge of the musical language and apply manual dexterity and movement.
11. Use air appropriately to produce sound in the proper register.
12. Adjust sound with air/embouchure to refine intonation.
13. Use air to create different volume levels.
14. Use speed appropriately for accurate tempos.
15. Listen to others and adjust to match their pitch, volume, and speed.
16. Watch the director and interpret his/her instructions for pitch, volume, and speed.
17. Practice and play to the best of your ability so as to enhance the rehearsal and contribute to the improvement of the ensemble.

Beautiful and enjoyable music is created when all seventeen tasks above take place *simultaneously*. With beginning band students, however, these tasks often represent new or unfamiliar skills requiring much attention by a brain that's not accustomed to complex multi-tasking. Every effort must be made to help students execute each of the skills above successfully. Careful practice is required to improve and correct any errors.

The sheer volume of information concerning the technical and other objective aspects associated with playing an instrument can overwhelm beginning students. As a result, they often focus only on the technical goals of playing an instrument. The art of mastering an instrument requires a positive attitude that focuses on the joy and thrill of music making. But how is it possible to create a positive musical experience while negotiating so many technical tasks? It is easy and convenient as directors to get so immersed in mastering the technical skills that we rationalize not getting to the musical aspects of mastering an instrument. Or worse, we assume that if we master the technical skills with our students, then we are being musical.

As directors, we must remember that the purpose for playing an instrument is to *experience music*, not just produce sounds. We must teach

students how to do that and then give them permission to do it! Let's consider what we can and should do.

- Develop critical thinking in young musicians that will enable them to become independent decision makers.
- Develop critical listening skills.
- Create style and musical personality beyond the notes.
- Rehearse with techniques to achieve musicianship.
- Let the reward be worth the risk.

Developing Critical Thinking in Young Musicians

Critical thinking skills are absolutely essential for young musicians to become independent decision makers. Making independent decisions about music and putting the students in action is central to their flexibility and ability to create music from sound.

For example, students must make decisions concerning how to start sound. They must correlate the shape of the embouchure, amount and speed of air, style of articulation, and adjustment of intonation based on what they see on the page of music. They must interpret what the conductor is doing. And they must adjust and adapt to what they are hearing from other players around them. They must anticipate what the appropriate sound should be and how to create it. While all the last-minute reminders and admonitions directors give to students may seem to be an efficient way to teach skills, it often inhibits the students from making their own decisions—ultimately *decreasing* efficiency.

Decision making can be incorporated into the teaching process in this way: Start an excerpt without instruction, and then review the students' responses. Ask yourself:

- What did they remember to do?
- How did they do it?
- Did they make the right decisions?
- Were they able to adapt?

This same technique can be applied to virtually all aspects of playing an instrument, from articulation to dynamics to interpretation of symbols. It teaches how to use the mechanics of music both intelligently and wisely. After all, knowing what to do is the intelligent aspect of learning; putting that knowledge into practice is the wisdom.

Developing Critical Listening Skills in Young Musicians

Developing critical thinking easily dovetails with developing critical listening, and then *responding* to that listening. Too often students listen only to "their part" and not to the music that is being played around them, to which they are contributing. As directors, we provide reinforcement by constantly reminding them to watch the key signature, tap their foot, count the rhythm, and use correct hand position, embouchure, air, fingerings, etc. We remind them to listen to what they are playing—and even to listen to the person next to them.

How often are students asked to listen to other instruments and adapt to the ensemble? How often are they guided toward what to listen to? Students must understand the importance of listening and proportionalizing to the group and to the music. We must teach them how to move their listening around to hear what others are playing and to then proportionalize what they are playing to others. A little time spent doing this each day will enable students to adapt and react more quickly, effectively, and independently. Rather than wait for instruction from you, students will begin to make those decisions independently.

So how does all of this contribute to the concept of musicianship? The ability to respond and adapt to musicality relies on listening and flexibility. Independent decision making and critical thinking absolutely contribute to students' success in converting sound to music—and creating a positive musical experience.

Creating Style and Musical Personality Beyond the Notes

"There ain't nothin' wrong with that." This is a favorite quote used by a band director friend to describe a performance that is non-offensive in all aspects of the technical performance, but devoid of musical expression and meaning. This is the type of comment we would expect to hear for a band seeking to please a panel of adjudicators and achieve a First Division rating at a contest, especially where the primary determination of success hinges on the more easily judged objective aspect of making music.

While the objective creation of sound does allow us to access the music, it does not *create* the music. The music is created outside of the notes. I often tell students that "sound is created by the notes and rhythms, but style and music is created between the notes." This statement serves to continually remind students that making sound is only the beginning. We have not succeeded until we have created the music.

A parallel example I often use in clinics or rehearsals is to read the text of a great historical speech, such as The Gettysburg Address. I recite the text to the students in a monotone voice, with no attention to punctuation, phrasing, inflection, or meaning. After asking the students what they just heard, they always correctly respond with "The Gettysburg Address." I explain that what they heard was the text, but not the speech. I then do my best Abraham Lincoln impression and recite the speech with the appropriate passion and meaning. The looks on the students' faces and in their eyes always tell me that "they get it."

I immediately ask the students to play through a section we have just been rehearsing—without any instruction from me—and the results are astounding. They instantly recognize what to do; they already know how to do it, they just need to be reminded of how important it is…musicianship.

Rehearsing with Techniques to Achieve Musicianship

Elements for achieving musicianship in young students include such things as:

- Phrasing
- Ear mapping
- Dynamic contrast
- Articulation style
- Elastic tempo
- Interpretation

These elements function not only individually but also in combination with all other elements. You cannot do one without doing all.

Phrasing:

Phrasing is much more than playing from one rehearsal number to the next and knowing where to breathe. To establish phrases is to organize the musical sounds based on many other elements that provide meaning to the music. I explain it as the "sentence structure" we use with written and spoken language. In language, there are specific rules for organizing text into meaningful thoughts. That same concept exists in music, only there are different means of providing punctuation. Melody, rhythm, and harmonic cadences are but a few of the ways to punctuate music.

These rules also dictate how to stress certain words, add inflections of volume, and either speed up or slow down speech patterns for meaning and effect. We all know this and we do it naturally and effortlessly. When we want more meaning and emphasis, we increase these inflections without inhibition. Yet with student musicians, we are hesitant to do the same and, worse yet, to encourage and allow them to do it. This is one of the first steps of interpretation.

By using the elements of harmony, rhythm, and expressive contrast, students can find and express the *music* that exists beyond the notes. In

teacher preparation, we all studied harmony and how cadences are used to organize music and affect expression; different cadences elicit different responses and emotions. Virtually all of that exists in band music! All we have to do is transfer that knowledge and use it to help mold and expose the music to our students.

One way to do this is to isolate and rehearse phrases. Establish how cadences create a phrase and play only that phrase, just as you would isolate a written or spoken sentence. Speak a sentence with no inflection; then repeat the same sentence with the inflections that give it meaning. Don't be afraid to move the emphasis around to show different interpretations of meaning. Now do the same with the musical phrase. Give different emphasis to different parts of the phrase with stresses, *crescendos/decrescendos*, and possibly changes of tempo to show how different meanings can be created.

Next try going beyond the indications of the composer who explicitly marks *crescendo/decrescendo*, accelerando/poco ritardando. Experiment by varying proportions. Overdo one thing, then another, then in different combinations. This will force the students to look outside of the notes, and they will immediately become more flexible.

These exercises and techniques will serve to create options for interpretation and expression, but more importantly, they will begin to show students (and remind directors) that interpretation of expressiveness and meaning cannot be written down—it must be discovered.

Starting with slow and lyrical music is much easier and convenient, but it is always amazing how this practice transfers to all styles of music. We always have the encouragement of the composer to do this. Now we must follow through and do it.

Ear Mapping:

The simple concept of ear mapping is merely a different way of establishing the listening and adapting component of music making. Essentially, this is moving the listeners through the music, just as if each had the full score to refer to. By creating an aural map of the music, we can address issues of balance, blend, intonation, dynamic contrast, nuance, and inflection, as well as other issues that give us access to the music and not just the sound. Additionally, the music becomes multi-dimensional and not mono-dimensional. The listeners hear the music come to life and develop its personality—just as the composer intended.

There are three groups of listeners who experience this: (1) the **conductor-listener**, (2) the **performer-listener**, and (3) the **listener-listener**. If both the conductor-listener and performer-listener are engaged in ear mapping, then the listener-listener (the audience) will experience it as well. The listener-listener will never experience it *unless and until* the conductor-listener and performer-listener do.

It is always interesting that we seem to focus on preparing a performance primarily for the listener-listener (the audience or the adjudicator). Yet all of the time spent on preparation, score preparation, and rehearsal for the conductor-listener and performer-listener far exceeds the actual performance time. The conductor-listener and the performer-listener live with the music far longer than the listener-listener. It is often said that every rehearsal is a performance; we must instill that mindset in our students. The more they become listeners at every stage, the more effective and enjoyable their music making will be. A musical moment in a rehearsal is just as magical as in a performance.

Dynamic Contrast:

Too often the contrast and intensity between dynamics is compromised to the point where it is virtually imperceptible. It is easy to "imagine" the dynamics rather than actually create contrast. But when creating contrast, students must understand that they cannot compromise tone quality as they play louder or softer, so control is a key component. By establishing a scale of dynamic intensity and continually reviewing it, students will become more consistent with dynamics. Begin by setting the *mezzo* levels of dynamics, and work to louder and softer dynamics incrementally. This allows students to continue using good-quality tone production as they gradually expand their dynamic range.

Also continually remind students that "all dynamics are not created equal." This is especially true in ensemble playing, as melodic dynamics and accompanying dynamics must be treated differently. A *forte* is not always a *forte*. For example, a *forte* on clarinet and a *forte* on trombone cannot be the same if students are to achieve balance and tonal blend. By the same token, a melodic *forte* and an accompanying *forte* must be treated differently. This is where ear mapping, listening, and independent decision making take place. The students must be responsible for participating in the ensemble sound to create music. When they know what to listen for and how to adapt, they will no longer just be playing their parts. They will begin balancing themselves within the ensemble and playing in proportion to the other instruments.

Articulation Style:

Another key component of giving sound personality and life, and creating music, is pronunciation of the sound—articulation. It is, in essence, the *consonants* of *consonance*. Imagine if there were only five vowels of speech to use in expressing language. It would be the same to hear music with no articulation at all, only sound. To demonstrate this, create a sentence that uses only vowels. What you hear is humorous and sounds somewhat ridiculous. But it represents a dramatic and shocking reminder of how important consonants are in language. Lack of consonants in speech destroys clarity and meaning.

Lack of articulation in music also destroys clarity and meaning. No amount of volume, emphasis, or attempted nuance makes it better. Playing it louder doesn't help; playing it faster doesn't help. We can hear the outline of the music, but clarity, style, personality, and meaning are missing.

This also demonstrates how lazy we can become when using and pronouncing consonants when we speak. This same "laziness" or carelessness can transfer to how we start sound or articulate in music. It is also reflected in how we play each note (i.e., whether it has qualities like space, emphasis, resonated release). Articulation creates the personality, meaning, and style of the music. Without this, there is only sound. Again, the music is created *between* the notes.

Elastic Tempo:

A key element of musicianship is elastic tempo, or the "pushing/pulling" of time. It is virtually impossible for composers to notate every nuance they imagine or feel as they are putting their thoughts on the page. Thus, the concept that there is more music *not* written on the page comes into play as conductors and composers try to read each other's minds regarding musicianship.

With many pieces of music, adhering to printed or suggested tempos with metronomic regularity is essential. The style and intent of many pieces would be destroyed if the pulse did not remain consistent throughout. However, in many other instances, the style and intent could be greatly enhanced by the use of elastic tempo. The goal is to find the music beyond the notes; it frequently exists outside regulated pulse. Just as we vary the speed of our speech to highlight meaningful words or thoughts, so, too, could we apply those same principles to the expression of music.

Considering that music is rarely static and that it is either *going to* somewhere or *coming from* somewhere, we can begin to make decisions about the appropriateness of using elastic tempo and to what degree. Much of the thinking that goes into making these decisions is intuitive, as it is based on experiences and feelings. For example, how we have heard a similar passage before is often a guide to how we might approach it with our bands—and that is a great place to start. Obviously, the fact that we heard someone else do it a certain way that was meaningful to us opens the door. Imitation is not always a negative, especially when trying to recreate a mood, a feeling, or something that is particularly passionate. Such intuition is the result of exposure and experience, and we can often trust it.

There are other techniques for deciding when to push and pull tempo, and to what extent. Phrase shape, harmonic cadence and structure, suspensions, altered chords, transitions, and modulations are but a few of the elements to consider when determining the appropriateness of elastic tempo. Here are some opportunities when elastic tempo would be appropriate:

- As phrases rise and fall within a musical line, it is often appropriate to push forward or relax tempo.

- Within the context of a longer overall phrase that might end with an interesting harmonic structure, a more exaggerated pulling back on the tempo could create a special musical moment—one to linger on for emotional effect.

- The tension created by the composer when a suspension or any other creation of dissonance followed by resolution can and should be highlighted.

- Repetition of a musical phrase with new harmonic treatment or in a new key is another perfect time to utilize elastic tempo.

Movement is a wonderful way to manipulate emotion in whatever way is appropriate. Often composers will provide some guidance with written tempo changes: accelerando, ritardando, or other explicit changes. The use of poco and molto as descriptors highlight the intent even more. That works great for the obvious. However, nuance is almost impossible to notate, and it is that application of honest nuance that transforms a really fine performance into a truly memorable musical experience.

During an honor band clinic, a student came up to me following an extended rehearsal segment of a slow, expressive piece and said, "Do you realize you're not keeping the same tempo?" My response was, "Yes, and *thanks* for noticing!" His follow-up comment was the most meaningful, though, when he said, "Yeah, that's really cool; I like it."

Interpretation:
The artistry of including nuance, inflection, passion, and meaning in the music—beyond the sound of the notes—is the whole purpose behind this chapter. How we interpret the intent of a composer is first on the list. But using the guides the composer has put on paper is only a start. The risk/reward in making such musical decisions is enormous. Just as we try to recreate the intent of any important author or orator when we read and re-read their words, so must we attempt to recreate the intent of a composer in the rehearsal and performance of that composer's work.

Once composers complete a musical work, they must trust that conductors and their ensembles will do their best to faithfully recreate the work. The obvious inclusion of the right notes at the right time becomes enhanced by an interpretation of the composer's intent. As conductors, we are a composer's advocate as we try to "get inside their head" to communicate on their behalf. One of the wonderful aspects of the entire *Teaching Music through Performance*

in Band series is the opportunity to become "friends" with the composers. The teaching guides include information on the composers, which enables readers to become acquainted with them and with their intent.

Also key to recreating and interpreting style is accurate adherence to the musical elements of articulation. Decisions regarding the use of staccato, legato, marcato, accents, etc., directly affect whether an interpretation of style is correct. Style is the *character* of the music, which helps to give it personality—the music beyond the notes.

In essence, interpretation is the sum total of all of the elements of phrasing, ear mapping, dynamic contrast, articulation style, and elastic tempo.

Letting the Reward Be Worth the Risk

As mentioned earlier, students must be taught, encouraged, and given permission to engage and initiate concepts and practices on their own. Critical thinking and using the information they are taught is central to their success. Too often, students are told to "wait until you're told" to make changes in the music. As a result, fear of the negative or of making an error only inhibits or eliminates critical thinking.

When rehearsing, insist that students make decisions. No student is too young to be introduced to the independence of musicianship. This decision making and critical listening can be based on comparing one part to another, isolating individual parts so everyone can hear, or any other rehearsal technique you commonly use.

Here's an example: If you want to rehearse all the low brass for an accompaniment figure, point out to students that the accompaniment initiates the process of ear mapping. You can still rehearse rhythm, articulation, note accuracy, intonation, speed, etc., but at the same time you are creating a role for that voice in the total ensemble—one that the students are aware of, no matter what their part. In essence, you are beginning to create a full score in their ear. Equally, when you rehearse a melodic element with the same emphases, you create a proportional priority for the students. They can now easily realize that all parts are not created equal all the time. The element of ear mapping will begin to take on meaning, and the students can then start making independent decisions about how to apply their part in the music—in proportion to other voices.

Many would say that students do not have the maturity and experience to do this at the beginning, in beginning band. Exactly...that's where we as directors come in. The old adage, "You can pay me now or pay me later," is absolutely true. Time spent exposing the students to these concepts from the very beginning allows us to incorporate musicianship throughout the entire rehearsal process, not just at the end for the public performance. Time spent exposing students to this in beginning band will carry over into their approach to making music as they mature and encounter new music requiring even greater musicianship.

Again, **every rehearsal must be treated as a performance**, no matter the age or maturity level of the students. How many times does making beautiful music get ignored because we just ran out of time? By incorporating it from the very beginning, every time, you will be amazed at how quickly the notes begin to expose the music, not just the sound.

You must foster and allow independence in student expressiveness. Easily said, but as trained directors/teachers/conductors, don't we possess all the knowledge and shouldn't we make all the decisions? That seems practical enough. But when we place that responsibility on our students—even our beginning students—we will see the excitement level and musicianship explode from our ensemble. The students take ownership of the music—it's theirs!

Allow your students to play without you conducting or without a metronome or any other outside influence. You can conduct the entrance and the cutoff—better yet, allow the students to start themselves. After a few attempts, they will come to agreement on tempo, style, dynamic contrast, etc., because they are listening to each other. They begin "watching" with their ears; all of the elements of ear mapping, flexibility, expression, and response will take over. Everyone will benefit from doing this periodically in rehearsal, even for a short period of time. It is at this point that everything really comes together. Every student becomes a listener, every student is involved in the music, and every rehearsal becomes a performance.

So the responsibilities are many, and they are shared—by the director/teacher and the students. There is risk/reward in coloring outside the lines in music. Often we let the perceived consequences of the risk get in the way. We choose to play it safe: "There ain't nothin' wrong with that." As a result, we diminish (or eliminate) the reward, or the musical payoff.

Playing music and experiencing the emotion of music is why the students are there—and why you are there. Incorporate the musicianship element every day, and the reward will be indescribable.

CHAPTER 4

Confessions of a Music Junkie

Cheryl Floyd

I guess at one point or another, I tried to follow traditional advice about programming for my band: If the piece is for first-year players, there should only be one part per instrument; the second year, only two parts; etc. It is important to avoid D-flat or G major because it's really hard to play in tune in those keys. Consider selecting a piece to showcase your best section and hide your weakest one. It is important to avoid multi-movement pieces for contests because you have to start and stop so many times. Young players don't like Renaissance music because they just don't understand it!

Don't get me wrong: all of this is great advice for anyone who is just starting out. Even now, several of these thoughts do come into play as a second- or even third-level consideration as I select music for my bands. But after my first few years in the classroom, I realized that both my students and I were missing out on many musical gems.

By the way, I select pieces much like I buy clothes and shoes—with my heart and certainly not with my head. Does it sparkle? Are there beautiful, rich colors? Is this a single spectacular piece that could set off the rest of my outfit—I mean, our program?

I enjoy listening to a new piece. If it gives me goose bumps, then I think about how to teach it to my students. How can I sell it to them? How can I break it down so the music might touch them like it touched me? What kind of lesson plan would work for my band? I love recordings. If I am interested after a first listening, I buy the recording. If within the first minute or so I am not taken with a piece, I skip to the next track.

The music must make me feel good inside. The goose-bump test that I referred to above works for me. The goose-bump test also helps me know whether or not a piece is almost ready for performance. Every concert has a variety of pieces that are fun to teach, perform, and listen to. Remember that the parents in the audience have hopefully listened to their own children practice their individual parts at home over and over again!

Does each concert have at least one piece that any father could whistle as he walks out the door? My dad attended every concert that each of my three siblings and I performed. If we didn't play a standard march or at least one piece with a beautiful melody, he felt cheated. I love more contemporary selections such as Michael Colegrass's *Old Churches* or Thomas Duffy's *Crystals*, but a concert that showcases only one type of music could distance some of your very best patrons! Here are some of my thoughts:

- I know that I am on the right track when I can't wait to program the piece again!

- I know that I am in trouble when I get bored with a particular piece. By then, my students have been tired of it for much longer than I have.

- I do not learn the piece with my students. I study ahead of time and use a rehearsal lesson plan.

- As a rule, I do not perform pop music, even with my beginners.

- I always try to make it real! There are a number of ways I do this:
  –Read performance notes to the class.
  –Play recordings for the class.
  –Have students interview composers over the phone.
  –Have student announcers read performance notes at a concert.

- It's all about the music: If the music is good, it will almost teach itself!

Some people like to have a theme for each concert. Many schools have a Halloween concert that their community looks forward to every year. Our school community loves our Veterans' Day program, which showcases the talents of our entire music, drama, and art departments. Our high school music and drama departments combine with a local dance studio to perform *The Nutcracker Suite* each December. Several local high school programs enjoy an early spring "pops" concert.

So what do I consider as I program for my band?

- Is the piece unique?

- Is it unlike anything else in our middle school (or other level as appropriate) repertoire?

- Have my students been exposed to this genre?

- Is there a uniqueness of orchestration?

- Are there unusual combinations of instruments that create new and interesting timbre for the ensemble and the audience to enjoy? Our dear friend, Dr. Ron Nelson, liked to refer to instrument combinations, like the cloboe (clarinet plus oboe). Several former students of mine liked the flumpet (flute plus trumpet).

Also, I'm always interested in a young composer or a composer who has written a limited number of pieces for young band. I look at the selection of titles from the smaller, less well-known publishing companies to find some boutique-like pieces.

And, of course, I consider the percussion requirements: which instruments are called for and how many players are needed. Although if I do not have an instrument that is required in the selection, I figure out a way to beg, borrow, or buy one! If that is not an option, however, and you are sure combining parts is not an option, then consider having a percussionist from another ensemble cover one of the lesser percussion parts. Or if you can spare a player from a larger section (such as flute or clarinet), this could work even better!

You must also take a careful look at the solo requirements. Since I work with middle school players, I avoid E-flat clarinet solos at all costs...unless the composer has suggested an alternative! We usually do not have a piccolo player in our non-varsity seventh/eighth grade band, but I have been known to ask the best flute player to play the piccolo solos up an octave on the flute!

Initially, I never consider whether or not the key signature is a problem. Range is also not a first-level concern—unless the first trumpet part has high C above the staff! And I never worry about whether or not my students will like the music! They are 11 through 14 years of age, and they like what they know! If it's real music and I believe in the piece, I know I can teach my students to love the piece. And so can you!

I also don't worry too much about trying to hide weak sections or showcase the stars. A good friend of mine, Verda Herrington, once programmed *Incantation and Dance* with what she unabashedly admits was a very weak flute section. Guess what? The flute players worked hard and improved tremendously—and the performance was a big success!

I try to find opportunities for interdisciplinary units. Maybe we could share a unit with our seventh grade science teachers as we prepare Anne McGinty's *Clouds*. Or perhaps we could involve the eighth grade American history teachers as we prepare Robert Jager's *The World Turned Upside Down* for music festival in the spring. One year, our second band was working on Frank Ticheli's *Portrait of a Clown*, so the art classes created many different pieces of clown art that were displayed not only in our rehearsal hall, but all over our school!

Also, don't be afraid to ask for student feedback. I do a survey at the end of every year. (Note: Administer the survey only after all pieces listed have been performed in public.) I list all of the pieces we played during the school year (even the football pep tunes) and ask the students to rate each piece using a rating scale of 1–5 (1 being low and 5 being high). Just last January, I had my Symphonic Band students rank our nine Midwest pieces in order of preference. Their top three pieces were *Hill Country Flourishes*, *Dancing at Stonehenge*, and *Solid Men to the Front*—our three most challenging pieces!

Beginner Programming

Take a look at the beginning band repertoire page (see page 36). You will notice that, for the most part, our holiday concert program is the same from year to year. Think about it...these pieces are new to the beginners. Many beginners have attended their older siblings' concerts and listened to brothers and sisters practice their parts at home, and they often ask specifically if and when they will learn those pieces. This is a very Suzuki idea—that in order to make appropriate progress, students must learn/study/perform certain pieces in a certain order.

Using familiar pieces for holiday and spring concerts also helps me know exactly what my students must be able to do range-wise and rhythmically to have a successful concert—which is the goal! I do not spend money every year trying to find the perfect beginner selections. However, that doesn't mean I am against trying a new selection if one happens to pass my goose-bump test.

I always try to get more than one performance out of a piece. Notice that *Chant for Percussion* is performed on our Holiday Concert and again on our Fifth Grade Program in February. *Crown Point March* is programmed on our Fifth Grade Program and then again on the Spring Music Festival and the Spring Concert.

This allows us to focus on fundamentals (not on repertoire) during the beginner year. Once the students are in a performing ensemble, the time for extending technique and range is *very* limited.

Sample Beginning Band Repertoire Page

Hill Country Middle School Beginning Band 2005- 2006

Holiday Concert

1. Jing A Ling Bells, arr. Sandy Feldstein and John O'Reilly
2. The Hanukkah Song, arr. Michael Sweeney
3. Tannenbones, Timothy Loest
4. March of the Kings, arr. John Kinyon

Fifth Grade Program (recruiting concert)

1. Crown Point March, Bruce Pearson
2. Bandroom Boogie, arr. Andrew Balent
3. Chant for Percussion, arr. Andrew Balent

Schlitterbahn Music Festival

1. Crown Point March, Bruce Pearson
2. Serengeti Dreams, Robert W. Smith
3. Mystery of the Maya, John Edmondson

Spring Concert

1. Crown Point March, Bruce Pearson
2. Serengeti Dreams, Robert W. Smith
3. Mystery of the Maya, John Edmondson
4. Two Minute Symphony, Bob Margolis

Hill Country Middle School Beginning Band 2006- 2007

Holiday Concert

1. Jing A Ling Bells, arr. Sandy Feldstein and John O'Reilly
2. The Hanukkah Song, arr. Michael Sweeney
3. Chant for Percussion, arr. Andrew Balent
4. March of the Kings, arr. John Kinyon

Fifth Grade Program (recruiting concert)

1. Crown Point March, Bruce Pearson
2. Smoke on the Water, arr. Paul Murtha
3. Chant for Percussion, arr. Andrew Balent

Schlitterbahn Music Festival

1. Amberwood Overture. Ann McGinty
2. Crown Point March, Bruce Pearson
3. Mystery of the Maya, John Edmondson

Spring Concert

1. Amberwood Overture, Ann McGinty
2. Crown Point March, Bruce Pearson
3. Mystery of the Maya, John Edmondson
4. Two Minute Symphony, Bob Margolis

For second- and third-year students, I have a standard format that I follow every year:

Hill Country Middle School Symphonic Band 2006- 2007

Pep Rally/Football game tunes

1. Hill Country Middle School Song
2. Hill Country Middle School Fight Song
3. Crunchtime
4. El Fuego
5. Louie, Louie
6. Shout It Out

Fall Concert

1. Hill Country Flourishes, Steven Barton
2. Joy, Frank Ticheli
3. The Lowlands of Scotland, Larry Daehn
4. Solid Men to the Front, Sousa/Byrne

Veterans Day Program

1. God Bless America, John Moss, arranged for band, choir, and orchestra,
2. Marches of the Armed Forces, Michael Sweeney
3. Hill Country Flourishes, Steven Barton
4. Solid Men to the Front, Sousa/Byrne

HCMS/UT Symphony Band Joint Concert

1. Variations on a Sailing Song, Carl Strommen
2. Air and March, Purcell/Gordon
3. Journey Down Niagara, Chris Tucker
4. Dancing at Stonehenge, Anthony Suter
5. Solid Men to the Front, Sousa/Byrne

Midwest Preview Concert, December 12, 2006
Midwest Band and Orchestra Clinic Concert, December 21, 2006

1. Hill Country Flourishes, Steven Barton
2. Air and March, Henry Purcell/Phillip Gordon
3. Dancing at Stonehenge, Anthony Suter
4. Variations on a Sailing Song, Carl Strommen
5. Journey Down Niagara, Chris Tucker
6. The Lowlands of Scotland, Ralph Vaughn Williams/Larry Daehn
7. Joy, Frank Ticheli
8. Whirlwind, Jodie Blackshaw
9. Solid Men to the Front, John Philip Sousa/Frank Byrne

Most middle school bands are expected to perform at a couple of pep rallies or football games during the fall semester. Our pep rally/game tunes are the same every year! Our eighth graders are responsible for teaching our seventh graders both in and outside of class. Peer teaching empowers older players and makes it possible for you to work on *real* music during band class. Our pep rally/football game tunes are as follows:

- *Hill Country Middle School Song*
- *Hill Country Middle School Fight Song*
- *El Fuego*
- *Louie, Louie*
- *Crunchtime*
- *Shout It Out*

Our Fall Concert always includes a standard march. My students love King marches! Everyone gets to play all of the time, and just about everyone has a great part (except for the horns and the tubas). They love tinkering with the music: play first time only, lower the clarinet part an octave the first time through the trio, or even add additional percussion parts! Next we have a "mellow-yellow" piece, something in a slower tempo and perhaps a bit more reflective. Finally, we have an ABA overture (maybe something off of our approved contest list). I try to make sure this selection challenges all of my students in one way or another. Keep in mind that, for young players, a piece is only worth practicing if it has a lot of black notes! I have found that the following pieces work well with my students at this point in the year:

- *Dona Nobis Pacem*
- *Blue Ridge Saga*
- *Overture on a Minstrel Tune*

We usually conclude our Fall Concert with one of our pep rally tunes. Remember my dad? He always loved this part!

Our Veterans Day Program is next. This is the only thematic concert we do regularly. It is a much-anticipated event for our school community every year. We repeat several selections from our fall concert, including the march. We also perform a salute to our Armed Forces, and we always include *God Bless America* with our combined band, choir, and orchestra.

Our other concerts might look something like this:

Holiday Concert
- Festival of Hanukkah

along with either:
- A march I am considering for Spring Music Festival
- A movement or two from a multi-movement piece I am considering for Spring Music Festival
- Something secular, like *Dashing through the Snow*
- Something sacred, like Frank Ticheli's *Amazing Grace*

Spring Music Festival
- A standard Sousa march

  Although this year we are programming William Latham's *Brighton Beach*. We need a change!
- A multi-movement work, such as *Courtly Airs and Dances*, *Suite Provençal*, or *Rikudim*

  This is usually a project piece for us. We learn a movement or two for the holiday concert, add another movement for Spring Music Festival, and maybe finish it up for our May Music Festival.
- Something new—a commission or a treasure, such as Anthony Suter's *Dancing at Stonehenge*

May Music Festival
- A novelty march, such as *The Whistler and His Dog*, *The World Turned Upside Down*, or a paso doble
- A completed project piece, such as *Suite Proveçal*
- Something new
- Something completely different, such as *Star Wars*, a Beach Boys medley, an ethnic piece, an aleatoric selection (*Old Churches*, *Snakes*, *Crystals*, *Whirlwind*)

Build your wardrobe of pieces: your basic selections (such as your school song and fight song), standard pep tunes, patriotic pieces, and perhaps a classic holiday concert piece or two. Add to that pieces that add color and sparkle...your accessories, if you will! Also consider "something old, something new, something borrowed, and something blue":

something old . . . . This might be a piece you have done before, which you feel comfortable teaching again. It might be a perfect fit for your group!

something new ....This might be a brand new piece you have just discovered, or a new publication or a recommendation from a friend or colleague, or maybe even a commissioned work!

something borrowed ....This might be a piece that was written for a different medium that has been transcribed for band.

something blue ....This might be something jazzy, or something with rich and beautiful colors, or something in a minor key. It may even be a slow piece.

Use your imagination. If you can, plan ahead for the entire year. Store your winter pieces away for the next season. Invest in quality pieces that last a lifetime—following are some of my favorites!

Cheryl Floyd's Favorites for Middle School Band

TITLE	COMPOSER
1. *American Riversongs*	Pierre La Plante
2. *The Battle Pavane*	Susato/Margolis
3. *The Blue Orchid*	William Owens
4. *Cajun Folk Songs**	Frank Ticheli
5. *Cajun Folk Songs, Set II*	Frank Ticheli
6. *Caprice*	William Himes
7. *Clouds*	Anne McGinty
8. *Courtly Airs and Dances**	Ron Nelson
9. *Cradlesong*	Steven Barton
10. *Crystals*	Tom Duffy
11. *Dancing at Stonehenge*	Anthony Suter
12. *Danses de Fantasie*	Jan de Haan
13. *Domingo Ortega*	Charles Wiley / Ledesma/Oropesa, ed.
14. *Down a Country Lane*	Copland/Patterson
15. *Early English Suite*	Dunscombe/Finlayson
16. *Fa Una Canzona*	Larry Daehn
17. *Figaro*	Allier/Rhoads
18. *For the New Day Arisen*	Steven Barton
19. *Fortress*	Frank Ticheli

20. *Hill Country Flourishes**   Steven Barton
21. *Joy*   Frank Ticheli
22. *Korean Folk Rhapsody*   James Curnow
23. *March on a King's Highway*   Pierre La Plante
24. *Old Churches*   Michael Colgrass
25. *Portrait of a Clown*   Frank Ticheli
26. *Prairiesong*   Carl Strommen
27. *Puszta!*   Jan Van der Roost
28. *The Red Balloon*   Anne McGinty
29. *Renaissance Fair**   Bob Margolis
30. *Rikudim*   Jan Van der Roost
31. *Rhythm Machine*   Timothy Broege
32. *Sang!**   Dana Wilson
33. *Shenandoah**   Frank Ticheli
34. *Sinfonia Six*   Timothy Broege
35. *Snakes!*   Tom Duffy
36. *Soldiers Procession and Sword Dance* Bob Margolis
37. *Songs for America*   Berlin/Curnow
38. *Suite Provencal*   Jan Van der Roost
39. *Three Russian Cameos*   William Rhoads
40. *Twilight in the Wilderness**   Christopher Tucker
41. *When Johnny Comes Marching Home* Bruce Pearson
42. *The Walls of Zion*   Greg Danner
43. *Whirlwind*   Jodie Blackshaw
44. *The Whistler and His Dog*   Arthur Pryor/Balent
45. *The World Turned Upside Down*   Robert Jager

*commissioned work

CHAPTER 5

Great Beginnings: Warm-Up Strategies for Success

Linda J. Gammon

Setting the tone and focus of each rehearsal is essential to the success and development of young musicians. The warm-up process is without a doubt the most important period of time during each rehearsal and provides students the opportunity to prepare physically, mentally, and musically. Often we as directors settle into the same repetitious and mundane exercises that lack creativity and fail to contribute the developmental skills necessary for our students' musical growth. Varying and challenging warm-up activities are key to the success of any band program.

The following strategies will help in the development of a systematic warm-up procedure that gives consistency and focus to rehearsals, reinforces playing fundamentals, teaches listening skills, and develops technique. By always warming up musically, students will reinforce the skills necessary to transfer to the performance of their literature. Insist on the best posture, hand position, breathing techniques, tone quality, and focus at all times.

Performing a few warm-up exercises with quality is far better than numerous exercises with no attention to detail. Strive to create a variety of warm-up exercises to go well beyond just playing the concert B-flat scale known by some young students as "the" scale. Great beginnings in each rehearsal will ensure actively engaged young musicians and contribute to the students' successful musical growth.

Setting the Stage

A structured and well-defined routine contributes greatly to the success of the warm-up period. Students who enter a band room that is neat and orderly sense an environment where serious learning will take place. Follow a procedure for unpacking and storing cases; define the amount of time to complete this task and avoid as many distractions as possible so class may start in a timely fashion before students become restless or lose focus.

An important part of a young musician's development is listening to recordings of exemplar models of both individuals and ensembles. Some directors have found that playing recordings during the entrance and exit of the band period helps set the tone for the rehearsal as well as quiet the students as they go about their tasks. The listening experience may illustrate style, historical periods, culture, and characteristic tone of an individual instrument or ensemble, and should be considered as part of the beginning and/or ending of each rehearsal.

Place a daily agenda on the board so students are responsible for preparing the necessary equipment as soon as they enter the room. When the schedule allows, distribute materials and music on the students' seats to save time and avoid disruption during the rehearsal. Create a plan for collecting practice records, forms, and money. Some directors have found a lockbox to be helpful when collecting forms and money. Avoid repairing instruments at the beginning of rehearsal by establishing a before-school, after-rehearsal, or after-school rule for such repairs.

Establish a signal for silence before the rehearsal begins, and insist on immediate silence and focus. Students seem to learn better if they are required to stop all activity and focus quickly on the director at the beginning of each class period. Try to start the warm-up activities immediately by actively engaging the students. Minimize announcements at the beginning of the class period so students do not lose focus and become distracted.

Develop a routine for students to check the height of their music stands before each rehearsal begins. The stand should be high enough so each student has excellent posture with an eye-level line of sight above the stand to the director. This position allows the head to be upright and free of tension, and lets the air flow freely. Reinforce this often, and students will adjust their stands automatically each day.

Students today are visual learners: Present as much information as possible in visual form through the method book and with the use of overheads, recordings, chalkboards, and other media. Keep all explanations simple, and present new information in small segments. Consider utilizing games to reinforce and review concepts. Set high standards, and do not accept anything less. Keep your procedures consistent, but vary the method of delivery to keep the students' minds alert and focused.

At the end of rehearsal, follow a regular procedure for packing up and returning all equipment to the proper storage area. Ask students to return stands to their original position and clean the area around their seating area before dismissing them in an orderly manner. Students appreciate a well-organized environment in which to learn, and with the proper expectations, they can be a huge help in maintaining the neatness of the room.

Breathing

Daily breathing exercises help students understand the efficient use of air; they are an essential part of each rehearsal. These developmental exercises should be a priority; they not only serve to prepare the students physically and mentally, but they are an integral part of tonal development in young students. The sequential development of characteristic tone quality and intonation cannot be achieved without proper use of the air stream.

The use of breathing exercises at the beginning of rehearsal sets the tone for a silent, focused environment and develops the concept of an open air stream, greater air capacity, and control. Breathing improves ensemble awareness, attacks, and releases. All students, including percussionists, should perform all exercises on a daily basis. It is just as important for percussionists to understand the breathing process so they enter on time with the rest of the ensemble.

Breathing exercises should start slowly; instruct the students to properly inhale, exhale, and develop a proper air stream.

1. Review proper posture, whether sitting or standing. This is essential for students to experience proper breathing techniques and to reinforce proper focus.

2. Instruct the students to inhale through their mouth and then exhale, keeping the throat open and the tongue flat. Remind them to keep their shoulders and neck relaxed so as not to create tension.

3. Ask the students to think about breathing to the bottom of their chair while expanding the belt area.

4. Explain that breathing should be steady and supported at all times. The air must be turned around quickly without holding it in.

5. Ask the students to use their hand to visualize the length of the air stream as they inhale, exhale, and direct their air towards a target. Visualizing the air stream assists students in playing through notes, phrases, and over bar lines.

6. As an option, ask the students to hold the top of a small piece of paper in front of their face with their thumb and forefinger. Using the proper air stream, students should be able to blow the paper away from them as they use a steady exhale.

7. Use a variety of counts and tempos to create daily breathing exercises while constantly reinforcing a focused air stream.

8. Encourage students to take a full breath regardless of the number of counts and to turn the air around quickly on the exhale.

Some teachers have successfully utilized breathing tubes in the development of these exercises. A short piece of PVC pipe or other small tubing may be used, as this aids the students in keeping the throat open.

1. Instruct the students to place the breathing tube between their teeth while gently holding it with their lips.

2. Ask the students to use the tube to perform a variety of breathing exercises.

3. Once the students become comfortable, instruct them to breathe through their mouthpiece.

4. Then instruct the students to breathe with the mouthpiece on the instrument.

Inhale	Exhale
4	4
4	6
4	8
2	4
2	6
2	8
2	12
1	6
1	8
1	12
1	16
Quick	6
Quick	8
Quick	12

Singing

Singing should be a daily part of each band rehearsal because it is a very important step for developing a musician's ear. Daily singing will help to improve tone quality and pitch center, as well as foster mental and physical preparation. It will help to alleviate a "pinched" sound often produced by younger instrumentalists, and it will enhance ensemble skills such as timing, balance, blend, and intonation. Percussionists should also be directed to participate in all vocal activities, as they, too, must develop pitch discrimination to tune and play timpani.

Students, like many directors, may at first be reluctant to sing. Over time and with practice, though, everyone should be able to hear improvement in intonation, tone quality, and ensemble responsiveness.

1. Remind students that posture and breathing are the same for singing as for playing. Make sure the students think about opening the back of their throat.

2. Explain that vocalizing will improve tone quality, pitch, and ensemble responsiveness.

3. While demonstrating proper posture and breathing, sing a concert B-flat for the class. This note is in a very comfortable range for most young students.

4. You may wish to use a pitch source as a reference point. Direct the students to hum the pitch first before singing it on an "oh" sound.

5. Ask the students to sing the concert B-flat using proper breath control and an open throat. You may wish to use scale degree numbers or solfeggio. Scale degree numbers will assist students in learning scales and set the stage for improvisation.

6. Sing the first five notes of the concert B-flat scale, and direct the students to echo sing together.

7. Vary patterns using the five notes of the concert B-flat scale. Initially sing the pattern and have the students echo sing the pattern back before playing the pattern on their instruments.

8. Over time, ask the students to simply sing and play the patterns with scale degree numbers or solfeggio without you singing them first.

Singing Examples
(using scale degree numbers or solfeggio):

Singing Example #1

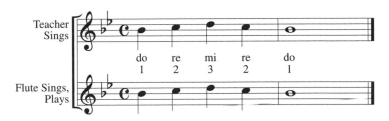

Singing Example #2

Singing Example #3

Singing Example #4

Singing Example #5

9. Next, demonstrate the concert B-flat arpeggio and ask students to sing and play back the arpeggio. As an option and as they become comfortable with this pattern, demonstrate and ask the students to sing a concert B-flat minor arpeggio.

Singing Example #6

10. Direct a student to play a simple pattern, and then ask the class to sing the pattern back. This activity encourages creativity and is one of the first steps for ear training.

11. Sing a variety of patterns using these notes to create "call and response" warm-ups. These activities develop listening skills necessary for ensemble performance.

Alternate the singing and playing activities for each rehearsal to build confidence in singing and improve intonation. As students become more confident, they should be able to sing concert B-flat without relying on a pitch source. Begin by asking the students to think about the pitch, hum it and then sing it aloud. Over time and with practice, everyone should be able to hear improvement in intonation and tone quality.

1. When the students have mastered the concert B-flat patterns, direct them to sing concert F using the same progression of steps.

2. As students become comfortable with concert F, add concert C, E-flat, and A-flat. Eventually the band will be able to sing and play around the circle using a variety of scale patterns.

3. Alternate the singing, playing, and buzzing activities in each rehearsal to build confidence and develop improved intonation.

4. As students become more comfortable, divide the class in half and have one group sing and hold concert B-flat while the other group sings up and down the five-note pattern. Then reverse the group assignments. Vary patterns using the five notes of the concert B-flat scale, and continue to divide the class into groups to create harmonies.

5. Once students become more comfortable in two-part singing, consider singing simple four-part chorales.

Transfer this newly acquired skill to sight-singing simple patterns from your method book.

Long Tones and Scales

Good tone production with a characteristic sound is the most important musical element for young students. Long tones will reinforce playing fundamentals, such as posture, breathing, and embouchure. After completing daily breathing exercises, perform a variety of long-tone patterns. As an option, ask the brass players to buzz on their mouthpieces. Instruct them to hold the mouthpiece with their thumb and first two fingers as they play the patterns. As the students' skills increase, the variety of patterns will expand and the possibilities will become endless.

1. Using any key, sustain scale tones for a variety of beats, with rest between. Change the duration on a daily basis to make students concentrate and think more.

a. Hold 7	Rest 3
b. Hold 5	Rest 1
c. Hold 9	Rest 5
d. Hold 11	Rest 3

2. As the students progress and are able to play more notes, sustain tones using the circle of fourths or fifths, and vary note lengths and rests.

3. Use scale patterns to perform only portions of scales in a variety of keys. When students can play any portion of a scale with any pattern, then they truly know the scale. Vary the activity by using the scales the students know and adding others as they learn them.

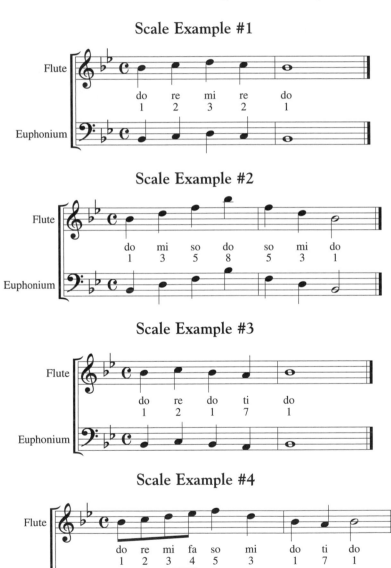

Lip slurs develop evenness of tone between notes; consistent tone and embouchure expand the range for young players, especially in the upper register. Lip slur exercises can be found in numerous method books or can be easily created using a music writing program. Remind students to keep the air stream steady while maintaining energy throughout each note as well as throughout the entire lip slur.

Scales are a fundamental part of a musician's education. Air speed and an open throat are necessary in the upper ranges to avoid pinched sounds. With beginners, accuracy of pitch and quality of tone are far more important than the speed at which the notes are played. Vary the activities and exercises so students truly know and understand a scale rather than just preparing them for a scale test.

As students learn their scales, encourage them to produce notes with good tone quality and pitch center on both the lower and upper notes of the scale. Also remind them to support the lower pitches and avoid spreading the tone quality on the upper notes by maintaining a firm embouchure and a focused air stream. Make sure the students:

1. Say the key signature.

2. Spell the notes, ascending and descending.

3. Say the notes as they finger or air stick the notes, ascending and descending.

4. Learn as many octaves as possible, even if the upper notes may seem a bit difficult.

5. Play the scale while looking at the notes and thinking the notes in their head.

6. Play the scale by memory.

Perform scale exercises slowly to reinforce playing fundamentals and to develop varying articulations. In the beginning, students should understand the following articulations:

*   **Staccato** is a light start to a note with good tone quality for a short duration.
*   **Legato** is a light start to a note with good tone quality and full duration.
*   **Tenuto** is a note with good tone quality and full duration.

The chromatic scale is another playing fundamental students must add to their repertoire. Consider teaching the chromatic scale in segments:

1. Teach half an octave, and then expand to one octave.

2. As students become comfortable, expand to one and one-half octaves, and then to two octaves.

3. Remind the students that this exercise will take time. Explain that they must achieve one level before moving to the next.

Regular testing can assist in motivating students and encouraging them to practice. Although large classes create some challenges in this area, some recommended testing options follow:

1. Test a few students or sections for part of the period over time.

2. Test the entire class in a class period while they complete a rhythmic, vocabulary, or creative worksheet.

3. Assign several scales to be tested, and place the name of each scale in a cup. When you call the student's name for testing, draw one of the scales out of the cup. This allows students to be prepared for numerous scales but only perform the assigned scale.

4. Listen to students perform in small groups and isolate the students who need further assistance.

5. Ask students to prepare audio tapes.

6. Videotape the students performing the assigned scales.

Chorales

The use of chorales is an important part of the rehearsal; they reinforce many of the basic playing fundamentals. Chorales develop breath control, pitch, balance and blend, shaping of phrases, contour, and control. They also allow students to concentrate on listening skills. They develop sight-reading, tone quality, note duration, intonation, dynamics, and ensemble precision. Singing chorales and asking students to visualize a focused air stream also helps to reinforce good tone and phrasing.

A good practice is to develop a repertoire of three or four chorales for the year. Use these throughout the year to reinforce and expand skills, which will enhance your ensemble's tonal maturity and ability to follow the conductor. Remind students to increase the air stream between notes to create a smooth slur. Encourage students to blow to the end of the notes or phrases to avoid allowing the air stream to deteriorate or go flat before the release. Keeping the embouchure set and simply allowing the air to stop will help to create a resonate sound.

Inform students that louder dynamic levels require a greater volume of air, and softer levels still require a consistent and focused air stream. Never allow students to play beyond their best sound, and make sure they always use control at all dynamic levels and all ranges to create quality tone production. Ask students to critically listen, correct ensemble problems by identifying the problem areas, and then offer and demonstrate solutions to the problems during the rehearsal.

Intonation

Intonation is a constant issue for bands. There are many different approaches to tuning an ensemble; the most successful approaches in the long term are those that train the students to hear and distinguish "in tune" from "out of tune" and place the responsibility on their shoulders. Singing, critical listening, and other activities to develop this skill are very important and should be regularly emphasized.

Good intonation is achieved by constantly listening and adjusting. Students must be able to identify problems and make the proper adjustments. To do this, listening skills must be taught and sequentially developed. From the start, use the word "listen" often in rehearsal. Allow students the opportunity to show you they are listening. Students need to realize that instruments are never perfectly in tune, and they need to make it their responsibility to play in tune each time they practice or perform.

Relying only on electronic tuners causes the ear to shut down or turn off. Tone quality and intonation or tuning should never be separated. The control of air is necessary for good tone, and tone is necessary for good intonation. Emphasize to students that they should always be in *tone* before trying to be in *tune*. Many times intonation problems are a result of poor tone quality. Control of the air is one of the most important factors in producing a characteristic tone.

Students must be able to hear intonation problems themselves. They must be reminded and taught to fit into the sound of others. Once they hear a problem, they need to come up with the solution to fix the problem and adjust the pitch. Always remind students to make tuning adjustments with their slides and tuning mechanisms before attempting to adjust their embouchures.

Tuning is never ending and must be stressed every day during the entire rehearsal.

Developing procedures for both individual and ensemble tuning is very important. Below are some suggested guidelines:

Individual Tuning:

1. After a sufficient period of warm-up, encourage students to play with a natural, relaxed tone at a *mezzo forte* volume.

2. Ask the students to listen to a pitch reference, sing the pitch, and hum the pitch. The students should play and match the pitch before making the necessary adjustments, and then listen to the pitch reference again, play, match, and adjust.

Students must be able to hear their part, hear the parts of others, and know how they fit into the sound. They must develop the concept of the ear, know correct set-up of the instrument, and know what the next pitch will sound like.

Ensemble Tuning:

A portion of each rehearsal should be devoted to aspects of ear training and tuning to properly sequence the development of these skills. The warm-up period, which should be concentrated and meaningful, is the time to warm the instrument, develop the embouchure, reed, and prepare the ears. Students must understand that they need to be concerned about tuning.

1. Allow time for individual students to critically judge their tuning. Simply instructing students to push in or pull out does not develop their ear. Poor tone production and lack of air support will have a negative effect on an individual's or a group's ability to play in tune. Good balance and tone production will go a long way in the development of a good ensemble tone center.

2. Always emphasize proper posture, breath support, and hand position; these are all important factors in tuning and being able to play in tune.

3. During a full band rehearsal, individual tuning should not be part of the daily routine. Once students know where to set their tuning slides and mechanisms, only minor adjustments should be necessary. Students must set their instrument slides (brass), head joints (flute),

barrel joints (clarinet), mouthpieces (saxophone), and reeds (oboe and bassoon) in the same place every day to gradually refine the individual and ensemble pitch center.

Rhythmic Development

The use of rhythm patterns improves sight-reading skills and helps to create clarity and precision within an ensemble. This fosters independence, accuracy, and confidence for individuals as well as the total ensemble. As students learn and perform new rhythms, their attacks and releases should be together, vertically aligned, and well defined.

When reading new rhythms, remind students to always use good posture, hand position, and air support; playing fundamentals must always be maintained, even when sight-reading. Vary tempos and styles as students become more confident with new rhythm patterns. Constantly emphasize a counting system, subdivision for notes and rests as well as internal pulse. Practicing with a metronome helps to internalize pulse and aids in the students' technical facility and dexterity.

Create or use rhythm cards as part of the warm-up process by using some of the following suggestions:[1]

1. Introduce or review a new rhythm in each rehearsal.

2. Use several cards during a block of time, but change the order in each rehearsal.

3. Divide the band into sections or small groups, and ask each group to play the rhythm as the others listen for accuracy. Award one point for each correctly performed rhythm.

4. Create a play down activity, and ask students to eliminate them-selves when they make a mistake.

5. Provide upbeat accompaniment and have students perform the rhythms with the background music.

---

1. Two sets of rhythm flashcards, developed by James Froseth and Albert Blaser, are available from GIA Publications; they come with an accompaniment CD containing multiple tracks of music in a variety of styles, tempos, and meters—lively backgrounds for building rhythm skills.

Rhythm card examples:

Rhythm Example #1 – 2/4

Rhythm Example #2 – 2/4

Rhythm Example #3 – 4/4

Rhythm Example #4 – 6/8

As students become comfortable with scales, you may wish to combine scale and rhythm development by playing any rhythm pattern on each scale degree. This will reinforce the scales and promote further rhythmic development.

The next step would be to add a variety of patterns, group them in eight measures, and perform each measure on a different scale degree. To incorporate yet another playing fundamental into the warm-up, vary the articulation. The key is to keep the students reading and building on their fundamentals as they build their literacy.

Sight-Reading

Sight-reading and sight-singing are integral components to a music program, and they may be incorporated into the warm-up. Establishing, practicing, and implementing procedures for sight-reading and sight-singing will result in a more successful band program. Students will develop individual and group reading skills with increased accuracy, which will lead to life-long enjoyment of music.

Sight-reading is an authentic assessment for measuring fundamental skills both individually and as a group. Short exercises of 4, 8, or 16 measures may easily be included as part of the warm-up period. Select passages or exercises that are not too difficult or beyond the performance abilities of the group to achieve success and not discourage the students.

Develop a sight-reading procedure to follow each time a new line, excerpt, or entire music selection is read for the first time. Prior to playing, instruct the students to silently scan the music and look for:

- Title and composer
- Time signature
- Key signature
- Tempo
- Accidentals
- Rhythm patterns
- Technically challenging passages
- Melodic range and intervals
- Dynamics, expressive markings
- Articulations
- Roadmap signs and symbols
- Fermatas

Then lead the students through a guided practice, which may include the following exercises:

1. Say the note names.
2. Clap the rhythm.
3. Count/Speak the rhythm.
4. Sing.
5. Tizzle (*sst* sound) and finger/air stick.
6. Play silently as the director conducts.

The length and timing of the warm-up period will vary greatly depending on the length of the class period, the time of the year, and the developmental level of the group. At the beginning of the school year, a large portion of each rehearsal should be devoted to the warm-up process, with the greatest emphasis on breathing, singing, tone production, and chorales. As the year progresses, the warm-up period should include a greater emphasis on intonation, scales, and rhythmic development.

Individual musical responsibilities taught and reinforced throughout the warm-up period are integral to the success of any band. Always make tone your highest priority, along with a great understanding of the effect of air stream, embouchure, hand position, and posture. Together, these are crucial in the enhancement of characteristic tone quality. These good fundamental habits will ensure continued growth and development.

If you are organized, you have time to teach. Always remember to be fair and consistent, and maintain a sense of humor. Be flexible, professional, and organized, and provide positive feedback while showing your enthusiasm and passion for teaching. Always maintain high standards and strive for excellence, as it is worth the reward.

CHAPTER 6

Nurturing Creativity: From Making Up Accompaniments to Composing for Beginning Band

John O'Reilly

In the spring of 1960, I embarked on my first real teaching experience by way of the required practice teaching that was part of my music education degree from the Crane School of Music in Potsdam (NY). As a percussion major, I had been grouped with other band students for instrumental methods courses and was pretty well prepared to go out and demonstrate my brass and woodwind teaching skills. Unfortunately, my first assignment in the Colonie School District near Albany, New York, was with a very fine violinist who had developed one of the top orchestra programs in New York State. I'll never forget that first day when we were headed to one of the three elementary schools in the district. My supervising teacher, Ed, asked about my background, and I don't think he was very happy about getting a "drummer" who had an interest in composition as his new practice teacher.

We arrived at the first school, and I watched the fourth grade students take out their violins along with their teacher. I had only played a little cello during my one semester of string methods and was really not prepared to help much in this class. Trying to keep out of trouble, I gravitated toward a piano that was in the corner of the room. At one point during that first class, Ed asked me to play a melody on the piano to help the young violinists. I was glad to be able to help out a little; I certainly wasn't going to pick up a violin and make a fool of myself. As the class progressed, I became a little more confident

and began making up accompaniments for the exercises and songs being played. The students really liked having the musical support while they struggled with their lessons, and Ed at least found a way to utilize his new practice teacher.

As we were driving to the high school, where I was to get my first shot at conducting the band, Ed suggested that I take home a violin and start working through the book the students were using. I, of course, took his advice and learned a great deal about string teaching from this master teacher.

I continued to provide accompaniments for the string students as well as the like-instrument wind classes I was assigned to. In those days, method books didn't come with an accompaniment book or CD recording. I was fortunate to have had good training in keyboard harmony, so making up accompaniments on the spot was easy for me (although the wind classes were more challenging than the strings because everything had to be played in concert pitch while looking at a B-flat Clarinet or E-flat Alto Sax book). Nonetheless, providing a harmonic background made the beginning classes a lot more musical. I subsequently included written piano accompaniments in the band and string methods I developed for publication.

After graduation, my first teaching job was in East Meadow, a suburb of New York City on Long Island. I taught in that district for ten years and had the pleasure of working at all levels with both band and orchestra students. At my last concert, I conducted the high school wind ensemble and symphony orchestra, playing some significant standard repertoire. A good percentage of the performers were students I had worked with in the fourth grade ten years earlier.

My first four years of teaching were devoted exclusively to elementary school, where I taught like-instrument classes. Students were "pulled out" of their classrooms for thirty minutes once a week to go down to the basement, where I had a small area set aside for lessons. In addition to the weekly lesson, the students played in either the beginner or the fifth/sixth grade band, which met for forty-five minutes once a week after school. Although a large segment of the United States starts beginners in fairly large, mixed-instrument classes, the experience I had is still pretty much the "norm" for New York and several other eastern states.

Due to the like-instrument structure of my program, I used the *Breeze Easy Method*, co-authored by John Kinyon. (It is interesting to note that several years later, I became John's editor at Alfred and was proud to co-author several books with him.) The *Breeze Easy Method* was a pretty straightforward book that didn't offer anything in the way of "creative activities." I found that I needed to come up with some of my own ideas. Fortunately, there was an old upright piano in my teaching area, so I used it in my teaching. I also remember spending my "free time" on my own writing. In addition to my teaching, I was working on my master's in composition/theory at Columbia University.

After teaching the students how to put their instruments together and make their first sound, I would do a variety of rote activities before getting into the method book. Following are some examples:

1. Have a class of clarinets play an open G and sustain it while you provide an interesting accompaniment.

2. Play the following arpeggiated accompaniment at a slow tempo.

Next play the same progression with simple rhythmic patterns in a variety of Latin, rock, and jazz styles.

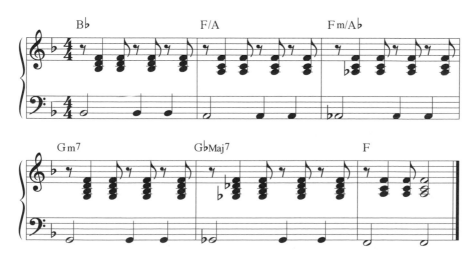

3. Another simple idea is to have the clarinets sustain their G for four beats and then rest for four beats. You can then play a simple "oompah" style accompaniment, with a single note in the left hand and chords in the right. (If you don't play the piano or have a piano available, use a guitar or autoharp.)

Another beginning activity that worked well for me is simple call and response or audiation exercises. I liked to teach my students their first five notes by rote before getting into the method book. If using a band method, those first five notes would be concert B-flat, C, D, E-flat, and F. All band methods teach these notes in the first few pages. Some start with D and go down, while others start with D and go up. Still others start with F and go down to B-flat. It doesn't really matter because the first five notes are introduced in the first few pages of all books. The best part about these starting pitches is that they are in a good singing range for young children, and singing is a critical activity for all instrumentalists.

1. Starting with just one note, play or sing simple rhythm patterns to the students, and have them sing the patterns back. Have them finger the notes on their instruments while they are singing.

2. Have the students play the patterns back to you.

3. Gradually expand the range of notes used, continuing to have the students sing first.

Don't be afraid to use some interesting rhythms for this activity; don't limit yourself to the rhythms presented in the method book. As your students get comfortable with this activity, have them make up patterns and become the leader. You can also have students write down their patterns before playing them. String teachers influenced by the Suzuki method have been using these rote techniques for many years. They are especially effective with beginners before they start reading music, but they are also fun, creative activities that can be used at any level.

Once we started using the method book, I occasionally played the piano to accompany the students. I found this particularly helpful when they were playing the exercises beginning with a whole note followed by a whole rest. I would play simple chord patterns, and sometimes I would write down the chord symbols if I came up with a particularly interesting progression. I never dreamed I would write a method myself, but when I did, I made sure all of the exercises and melodies had simple accompaniments with chord symbols in the teacher's score. My first method, *Alfred's Basic Band Method* (1977), co-authored with Sandy Feldstein, also had a cassette recording of the piano parts available. Unfortunately, the pitch was so unreliable with cassette players that few people found the recordings helpful. When Sandy and I wrote *Yamaha Band Student* in 1987, we also developed CD recordings with rhythm section recordings, which made practicing more interesting for students. (The pitch on a CD is always correct if properly recorded.) Every band method written after Yamaha has included optional CD accompaniments. Some books now include the CD with the book. Mark Williams and I co-authored *Accent on Achievement* in 1997. That series includes a CD that is also an interactive computer program, which allows students to change the tempo and record themselves. *SmartMusic* technology supports several band methods and includes assessment software in addition to accompaniments. In my opinion, beginning band students have a more interesting, creative experience if they use these types of materials during part of their practice time.

The national standards for music encourage instrumental teachers to include music history and theory in their classes. In addition, Standards 3 and 4 specifically talk about improvising, composing, and arranging. Incorporating these standards into beginning band can be a real challenge. Some methods have music history and theory built into the book, while others provide supplementary materials.

In many teachers' minds, improvisation is something that only happens in high school jazz band with a select few students. In actuality, performers at all levels benefit greatly by learning how to do simple improvisation. The examples below, which are excerpts from *Accent on Achievement,* are designed to foster creative thinking at a beginning level.

Sample Exercise #1

ACCENT ON LISTENING

1. Play "Mary Had a Little Lamb" by ear.
2. Write in the missing notes to complete the song.

20

This exercise gives students a chance to figure out a song "by ear," yet some notes are provided to help them in the beginning. Another part of this exercise is to ask students to think of a song they like and figure out how to play it. However, they most often think of songs that contain notes they don't yet know. So another way to approach this exercise is to suggest five-note standards, such as *Lightly Row* and *Jingle Bells*. Some students will be able to do this with ease, while others will find it very frustrating. For the most part, though, students are able to figure out the missing notes in *Mary Had a Little Lamb*.

Sample Exercise #2

ACCENT ON CREATIVITY: Variation on Lightly Row

Create your own variation by changing some of the quarter notes into pairs of eighth notes.

German Folk Song

36

Another activity that students will generally be able to do with relative ease is to create a variation of an existing melody. In this exercise, they change quarter notes into pairs of eighth notes. I suggest that students try to do this first by improvising. Obviously, you should demonstrate some examples before they try.

After the students have created several variations, instruct them to write down their favorite. As you might suspect, some students will be able to play interesting variations but will have a difficult time figuring out how to write them down. This is a great way to reinforce the teaching of this critical rhythmic concept.

Sample Exercise #3

ACCENT ON CREATIVITY: This Old Man
Choose your own orchestration for this melody.

American Folk Song

69

In this example, students have an opportunity to provide their own orchestration for a short piece of music. This forces students to focus on the variety of instruments in the band and to think about how they can be used to make a simple musical statement more interesting. This is a fairly simple exercise for beginning band students to do, and it is a fun activity for the ensemble to play.

Sample Exercise #4

ACCENT ON CREATIVITY: Rhythmic Improvisation
Improvise your own rhythms in each measure using only the pitches shown.

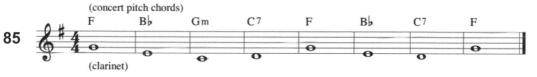

85

This fun improvisation exercise uses just one note per measure and works well for all students. Some students will be very conservative in what kind of rhythms they play, while others will try all sorts of variations. Encourage students to play a variety of rhythms. Some students will find a rhythm they like and play it over and over again.

A logical extension of this activity is to add passing and neighboring tones to turn the rhythm into a real melody. This activity works best with accompaniment. The chords indicated are in concert pitch. Piano, guitar, or autoharp work well. If you are using the AOA method book, there is a rhythm section recording that repeats the chord progression four times.

Sample Exercise #5

ACCENT ON CREATIVITY: Free Improvisation
Concert Pitch Chords E♭, Cm, A♭, E♭, E♭, Cm, A♭, E♭

102

Using the five pitches shown, improvise your own melody using any rhythms you know. You may play these notes in any order, repeat notes, or use rests.

This exercise gives students five notes to work with. Explain that the notes make up a pentatonic scale. My experience with this exercise has shown that a slow tempo and a lot of slurring work best. If you are using the AOA method book, there is a pop-style accompaniment on the CD for further enhancement.

Sample Exercise #6

ACCENT ON CREATIVITY
Create your own composition containing a balance of unity and variety.

119

1. Copy the first two measures into measures 5 and 6 to create unity.
2. Compose new music for the remaining measures to add variety.
3. Play your composition.

This exercise gives students an opportunity to compose and notate a short composition. This very structured activity can be a rewarding experience for all children. As part of this exercise, it is important that the students get to play their pieces for the whole class.

    While I was teaching beginning band I was also very active as a composer, writing many compositions as part of my study for my master's in composition and theory. I was fortunate enough to have some of my more difficult, contemporary-style original works published by G. Schirmer, Bourne, Shawnee Press, and Kendor.

    At the same time, I continually wrote for my own students. When I began teaching in 1962, there wasn't near the volume of music available for young band that we have today. There was an abundance of simple marches and arrangements of folk songs and classical themes, but very little in the way of more serious concert music. I found that my students enjoyed playing pieces in modes other than major and minor. They also responded well to simple changes of meter. Being a percussionist, I had experienced playing in band without having much to do. As a result, my first pieces for young band always had interesting percussion parts, and I have continued that practice through the years.

Like all beginning bands, I had some strong sections and some very weak ones. I was able to customize pieces that worked just right for a particular ensemble. My students really appreciated my creative efforts; I would try to keep them involved by playing new music on the piano and asking them for title suggestions. Some of the pieces I wrote during those early years were subsequently published by Alfred.

After a brief stint as a college theory teacher, I left teaching altogether to become editor-in-chief for Alfred, where I spent thirty-five years developing a wide range of performance series and methods for band, orchestra, and choir. My own writing and the editorial direction Alfred took were directly affected by my own teaching experiences.

I don't have to tell you how rewarding it is to teach beginners. Having worked at all levels, I can honestly say those first years of teaching beginning band gave me the most satisfaction. I had no one to blame but myself if the band didn't sound the way it should. When I was a high school band director, I could blame all the weaknesses on "the feeder system." Likewise, my beginners responded well to all the creative activities I tried to interject into their classes. But at the high school level, the pressure to perform at a higher level often superseded experimenting with creative activities.

All of us are creative in our own way, and I encourage you to try some of the ideas presented in this chapter—and, of course, develop additional activities that add a whole different dimension to your own program.

PART II

THE BAND CONDUCTOR AS MUSIC TEACHER

Teacher Resource Guides

PART II: The Band Conductor as Music Teacher

Teacher Resource Guide

Andante Con Moto

Symphony No. 5, Movement II

Franz Schubert
(1797–1828)

arranged by Stephen Bulla
(b. 1953)

Unit 1: Composer/Arranger

Franz Schubert was born in the musically charged city of Vienna on January 31, 1797. He is considered by many to have been the musical heir to the city's most celebrated musicians, Mozart, Haydn, and Beethoven. His father, a schoolteacher, was an avid amateur musician and arranged for his seven-year-old son to audition for Antonio Salieri. Considered in retrospect as a less-than-stellar composer, Salieri held the tremendously prestigious position of music director at the Austrian court. Salieri deemed young Schubert acceptable and listed him as an approved singer of services for one of the imperial chapels. By age eight, Schubert was studying piano, violin, counter-point, voice, and organ.

In 1808, Schubert's membership in the chapel choir allowed him to enroll at the Imperial and Royal City College, an outstanding boarding school for non-nobility. During his five-year stay, the teenager received a first-rate education and, as a member of the school's violin section, became enamored with the works of Haydn, Mozart, and the early symphonies of Beethoven. He studied composition with Salieri, but discontinued lessons after two years because the instructor's emphasis on Italian opera did not complement the student's admiration of the Viennese composers.

In 1813, Schubert followed the same career path as his father. Teaching still allowed time for composition, and these early years proved incredibly productive. A creative burst between 1814 and 1816 expanded his compositional output to over 300 solo songs, four masses, numerous chamber works, two acts of his first opera, and five symphonies. While most of these works received private performances, the twenty-year-old Schubert had yet to receive public performances or recognition for this body of work.

Schubert continued to compose, and although some of his music was published and performed, most of the music published during his short life was for voice or piano; he did not live to see any of his orchestral works in print. This fact and ill health made the composer's short life terribly frustrating. When Franz Schubert died in Vienna on November 19, 1828, less than a quarter of his music had appeared in print.

Stephen Bulla received his degree in arranging and composition from Boston's Berklee College of Music. For three decades he has been staff arranger to "The President's Own" U.S. Marine Band and White House Orchestra. His musical arrangements have been featured on the PBS television series "In Performance at the White House" and performed by many artists including Sarah Vaughan, The Manhattan Transfer, Mel Torme, Doc Severinsen, Nell Carter, and Larry Gatlin. Mr. Bulla is a member of ASCAP (American Society of Composers, Authors, and Publishers) and has received that organization's Performance Award annually since 1984. His commissioned concert works include instrumental compositions that are performed and recorded internationally. His wind band compositions are published by DeHaske Music and Curnow Music Press. For more information on Mr. Bulla, visit his Web site, Bulla Music, at http://www.bullamusic.com.

Unit 2: Composition

This work is a skillful transcription of the opening themes from the second movement of Franz Schubert's Symphony No. 5 in B-flat Major, D.485. Originally composed for flute, two oboes, two bassoons, two horns, and strings, this now popular symphony was written in 1816 when Schubert was just nineteen years old. The movement highlights Schubert's skill as a melodist and his mastery of balanced structure. The influence of Haydn and Mozart is very strong, and many hear direct quotes from melodies written by the latter.

Stephen Bulla has maintained the movement's original key of E-flat major and presents the original melodies from the A section of the ABABA movement with only slight rhythmic simplification. The structure of the three-minute work is significantly shorter than the original, eliminating the B section's melodic material and harmonies in C-flat major for obvious reasons. The final bars of the original work return as a coda. This piece offers a terrific opportunity for the development of melodic style and expression. While playable by young bands, the work maintains a high level of musical integrity.

Unit 3: Historical Perspective

Franz Schubert was known during his lifetime as a composer of lieder. Most of his other compositional efforts were not published, and in some cases not even performed, until after his death. The Fifth Symphony is recognized as one of his earliest quality instrumental pieces, and has become a popular piece in today's orchestral repertoire. Schubert's early symphonies were written for and performed by a private orchestra, which was a slightly augmented version of the Schubert family string ensemble. The works owe much to the symphonies of Haydn, Mozart, and the early works of Beethoven. These first six symphonies continue the Viennese tradition of inspired melodies within slightly relaxed phrase structures. The enjoyable, good-natured themes continue to attract audiences to this music more than two hundred years after its creation.

Schubert's search for a more independent style of symphonic writing proved a significant challenge. Between 1818 and 1822, despite numerous attempts, only one symphony was completed, and it was in draft form. Schubert abandoned this seventh symphony in E major (D.729) before it was completely scored. Even Schubert's most famous symphonic work, his Symphony No. 8, was also known as the "Unfinished Symphony" (D.759). It was not until 1825, after seven years of attempts, that Schubert was successful in completing his cumulative symphonic work, Symphony No. 9 the "Great" C Major (D.444).

Unit 4: Technical Considerations

Andante Con Moto is scored for flutes, oboe, clarinets 1–2, bass clarinet, alto, tenor, and baritone saxophones, trumpet 1–2, horn, euphonium T.C., trombone/euphonium B.C./bassoon, tuba, timpani(2), mallet percussion, snare drum, bass drum, suspended cymbal, triangle, and a piano accompaniment. The work is complemented by the interesting timbres of the oboe and horn parts, which are not mere doublings of any single part. These instruments should be included whenever possible; their pitch and harmonic content are covered in other parts, however, which allows for performances when these instruments are not available.

The piece is in 3/4 meter and is marked "Slowly" with a tempo of a quarter note = 80. The arranger's "Program Note" more correctly translates the title as "at a medium tempo with motion."

The movement is in the key of E-flat major, but because of the harmonic excursions and secondary functions common to the period, players should be familiar with the chromatic scale. For most instruments the range requirements are no more than an octave. First trumpets and horns will need to play up to written C5, and the first clarinets cross the break playing from written E-flat4 up an octave and a third to written G5. The low woodwinds and low brass perform the same material in convenient octaves to ensure adequate coverage of the bass line. The mallet player must be able to play two- to four-bar melodic passages, but the remaining percussion parts are technically very simple. These players must be aware that the function of these parts is strictly supportive.

In his "Notes to the Conductor" the arranger mentions the importance of sustained, legato playing in this work. Mr. Bulla suggests rehearsing the areas in which the melodic material is combined in the upper woodwinds and trumpets for both "blend and rhythmic match." Players need to recognize the difference between slurred and non-slurred articulations, and there is a section of slurred melody against staccato notes in the bass line. A successful performance of this piece will obviously require the ability to play sustained passages with good tone quality at a controlled dynamic level.

Unit 5: Stylistic Considerations

Andante Con Moto demonstrates the profound influence that Mozart had on Schubert. The players must be able to perform the simple and lyric melodies, a style common in most second movements of both composers' symphonies. Light and precise articulations are required. The symmetrical phrases befit music from the Classical era.

Mr. Bulla includes extensive dynamic markings in his score, but they should be observed with the following in mind. Originally written for what would today be considered a chamber orchestra, this symphony was given the appellation "The Symphony without Trumpets and Drums." Players of this arrangement must perform elegantly at controlled and reduced dynamic levels, and the percussion and brass players must add to, not dominate, the overall sound of the piece.

Unit 6: Musical Elements

MELODY:

All of the melodic material in this arrangement is drawn from Schubert's original work. The opening theme shown in Example 1 is heard first in the upper woodwinds in measures 4–11. It is repeated a second time with added first trumpet in measures 12–19. The four-bar phrase structure is apparent, and all players must strive to carefully match rhythm, tone, and articulation.

EXAMPLE 1. Opening Theme (mm. 4–11)

The second theme, found in measures 20–37 (Example 2), is more involved than the first. It is presented in the first clarinet, with supporting material in the horn. The players should note that the opening phrases are again four bars in length, but the section contains an extended six-bar phrase (mm. 28–33), and there is a great deal more dynamic shaping indicated in the score.

EXAMPLE 2. Second Theme (mm. 20–37)

The theme in the coda (mm. 48–56) is a duet pairing the first clarinet and trumpet against the alto saxophone and horn as shown in Example 3.

EXAMPLE 3. Coda Theme (mm. 48–56)

The two lines of the duet should complement each other and players should know that the upper part covers the separation between the two four-bar phrases in the lower part. The accent mark and *mf* marking in the fourth measure of both parts adds a bit of weight and volume before the *decrescendo* to *mp.* Players should lean into the note with increased air rather than use a distinct articulation.

HARMONY:
The harmonic progression in the first nineteen measures functions cleanly in E-flat major, with secondary dominants occurring only at cadence points. At measure twenty the harmony becomes a bit more complex. A brief flirtation with F minor (mm. 20–23) combined with the dynamic shaping of the melody and cadences containing a 4–3 suspension (m. 23) and an augmented dominant (m. 27) create added tension. In measures 28–37, secondary functions, 4–3 suspensions, and diminished triads support first a six-bar and then a four-bar slide to the dominant, which sets up the return of the more relaxed and less harmonically active opening theme. The coda (m. 48–56) reemphasizes E-flat major using the progression I–V7/IV–I–V–I.

RHYTHM:
The rhythmic content in this piece is not challenging. Listed as a Grade 1.5, it contains dotted half notes, half notes, dotted quarter notes, quarter notes, eighth notes, and quarter notes tied to eighth notes. As always, it is important that players feel an internal pulse to maintain rhythmic accuracy; however, they must never allow the rhythmic feel to override the overall legato style of the piece.

TIMBRE:

The scoring of *Andante Con Moto* emphasizes the blending of timbres rather than the contrast of individual colors. Good tone, intonation, and balanced dynamics are essential to the creation of this blended sound. Along with learning the correct techniques of tone production (posture, air, and embouchure) the players must have a concept of what constitutes a good tone. Directors should be sure to demonstrate the desired sound through live and recorded performances.

Accurate intonation requires an internalization of the pitch. The best way to improve melodic and harmonic intonation is to have young players sing the music.

Dr. W. Francis McBeth has defined the principles of balanced dynamics. Simply put, lower-sounding instruments need to play louder than higher-sounding instruments. In this piece, the low woodwinds and low brass need to have more presence than the upper woodwinds and brass. The same is true within the sections of the ensemble. Second-part players need to project more than players on the first part.

All of these concepts may be practiced at each rehearsal during the tuning process. Players should internalize (sing) the tuning pitch, then play the tuning note with their best tone possible, placing their sound within the ensemble sound. Rather than sustain their tuning note indefinitely, students should enter and exit the group tone several times. If they can hear themselves outside of the ensemble sound, they may be out of tune, requiring adjustment of the instrument. They also may have poor tone quality or are just playing too loud. Insist on a homogenous sound during the tuning process and the players will more easily be able to attain it in a performance.

Unit 7: Form and Structure

SECTION	MEASURE	EVENT AND SCORING
Introduction	1–3	Added by arranger and taken from the last three bars of the opening theme
Opening Theme	4–11	Melody is scored for the upper woodwinds with harmonic support from the horn, alto saxophone, and low brass and woodwinds
	12–19	Fuller scoring of opening theme with trumpet 1 added to the melody and percussion providing rhythmic support

Section	Measure	Event and Scoring
Second Theme	20–37	The second theme played by the first clarinet with supporting material in the horn; the opening phrases are four bars in length, but the section contains an extended six-bar phrase (mm. 28–33); a great deal more dynamic shaping is indicated in the score
Opening Theme	38–45	Opening theme returns in a slightly varied form, scored for full ensemble including percussion
Repeat	20–47	Repeat of measures 20–47
Coda	48–58	New melody in the coda; a duet pairs the first clarinet and trumpet against the alto saxophone and horn

Unit 8: Suggested Listening

Wolfgang Amadeus Mozart:
    Minuet finale from Sonata for Violin in F Major, K.377
    Serenade in E-flat Major, K.375
    Serenade in C minor, K.388(384a)
Franz Schubert:
    Symphony No. 5 in B-flat Major, D.485
    Octet in F-major, D. 72
    Ave Maria, arr. Frank Ticheli (for band)

Unit 9: Additional References and Resources

Downes, Edward. *The New York Philharmonic Guide to the Symphony*. New York: Walker and Co., 1976.

Garofalo, Robert J. *Improving Intonation in Band and Orchestra Performance*. Ft. Lauderdale, FL: Meredith Music Pub., 2000.

McBeth, W. Francis. *Effective Performance of Band Music*. San Antonio, TX: Southern Music Company, 1972.

Stedman, Preston. *The Symphony*. Englewood Cliffs, NJ: Prentice Hall, Inc., 1992.

Winter, Robert (text), Maurice J.E. Brown with Eric Sams
    (work-list): "Schubert, Franz (Peter)," Grove Music Online,
    ed. L. Macy (Accessed 3 June 2007), http://www.grovemusic.com

Contributed by:

James C. Chesebrough
Assistant Professor Band/Music Education
Keene State College
Keene, New Hampshire

Teacher Resource Guide

A New World Adventure

Douglas Court
(b. 1963)

Unit 1: Composer

Douglas Court was born in 1963 in Toronto, Ontario, Canada. He holds a bachelor degree in music education from the University of Toronto with further study in composition completed at the University of South Florida.

Court worked as a freelance trumpeter while in Toronto and performed with a variety of groups including the Canadian Opera Company orchestra. He also spent five years performing and touring with the Canadian Staff Band.

Court has a long history of musical involvement with The Salvation Army. His early musical training came through this organization, and he spent extensive time working with young musicians as Florida's Divisional Music Director for The Salvation Army from 1986 through 1995. His responsibilities included organizing summer music conservatories, teaching private lessons, and conducting both youth and adult ensembles.

In addition to his many instrumental and vocal pieces published by The Salvation Army, Court's catalog of work includes numerous band pieces including several works for beginning bands. Recent compositions include a solo written for Philip Smith, principal trumpet of the New York Philharmonic, and a suite for euphonium written for Steven Kellner of the United States Marine Band.

Since 1994 Court has pursued composition full time, writing for Curnow Music Press, and now lives in Atlanta, Georgia.

Unit 2: Composition

A *New World Adventure* is a single-movement work that is sixty-five measures in length. Marked *Allegro marcato*, it is written with a time signature of 4/4 and a tempo marking of quarter note = 120. Performance time is approximately two minutes and fifteen seconds. Tonality is centered primarily around the D-natural minor scale (D Aeolian mode) with a shift to F major near the end. The texture varies from short trumpet soli passages to moderately voiced scoring to full tutti sections. Monophonic, homophonic, and polyphonic techniques are all used. The scoring includes one part each for flute, oboe, alto saxophone, and F horn, while clarinets and trumpets are both divided into two separate parts. All low woodwinds and low brass play in unison or octaves and parts are condensed to one line in concert pitch on the score. Percussion parts include mallet percussion (bells), timpani (also doubles on crash cymbals), percussion one (snare drum and bass drum) and percussion two (triangle, shaker, tambourine, and suspended cymbal). A minimum of five percussionists is required, but six is preferable. A piano accompaniment part is also included.

The work draws inspiration from the story of French explorer Etienne Brule. Although no specific song is referenced, the melodies and character of the piece are folk-like in nature. The composer provides the following program note:

> In 1608, Etienne Brule, a young boy of 15 and protégé of explorer Samuel de Champlain, arrived in Canada. Brule impressed Champlain with his courage after surviving a harsh winter. Champlain, in an attempt to cement relations with the Algonquin and Huron Indians, sent Brule to live the life of an Indian with the family of an Algonquin chief. At the same time, a young Algonquin brave was brought to Champlain to learn the ways of the white man. This exchange led to greater understanding of the two races and led to new discoveries and adventures in the new world of North America.

Unit 3: Historical Perspective

Published in 2002 as part of Curnow Music's *Focus on Fundamentals* series, *A New World Adventure* provides conductors an opportunity to introduce beginning bands to program music depicting stories and characters of the North American frontier. Researching and listening to similarly inspired pieces will help students understand ways to better portray the spirit of the music during performance. The conductor might lead a brief discussion on common qualities of music inspired by old west or pioneer times. Attention should be given to musical aspects such as articulation, phrasing, melodic and harmonic intervals, tonality, and tempo. Students might experiment with alternative ways of playing the melodies and countermelodies of *A New World Adventure* to determine how they might be made to sound more or less programmatic. Because the melodies have folk song characteristics, conductors might also wish to provide a number of listening or playing examples of Canadian folk songs, which should lead to a more meaningful performance.

On a larger scale, time might also be spent contrasting the characteristics of program music and absolute music.

Unit 4: Technical Considerations

A New World Adventure is written using instrument ranges within the capabilities of very young players. All parts are written within the span of an octave except for the oboe and higher low brass and low woodwinds which cover a ninth. Both clarinet parts stay under the break with the second part extending to G3. The timpani plays two notes: D3 and A2. Wind and mallet players should be familiar with the D natural minor and F major scales.

Most melodies and countermelodies are scored in two or more parts and are usually doubled in other instruments, either in unison or at the octave. Although some independence exists between the separate clarinet and trumpet parts, in most instances the two parts play in unison or harmonize together. The alto saxophone and horn lines are identical with the exception of six measures. Accidentals are used sparingly, and courtesy accidentals are provided when the altered notes return to their original pitches. Percussion parts support the winds yet retain a sense of function and independence. Due to the extensive doubling and inclusion of a piano reduction, this piece is suitable for a young band lacking complete instrumentation.

Articulation markings include staccato, accents, slurs, and tenuto, with quick dampening required of the timpanist. The crash cymbals must also be choked. Dynamic markings are essentially uniform for the entire ensemble and range from *mezzo piano* to *forte*. Most dynamic changes are accomplished through *crescendos* or *decrescendos*.

Unit 5: Stylistic Considerations

In his notes to the conductor the composer offers that, "solid, well-marked tonguing will create the desired style though much of the piece." Indeed, *A New World Adventure* should focus on a spirited and articulate style. Most melodies and countermelodies are declamatory in nature and use minimal legato or slur markings. Even so, musicians must avoid allowing their articulation to cause too much separation between notes, thus destroying the musical flow. Melodic and countermelodic lines rely primarily on stepwise motion and leaps of a third or a fourth. Wider leaps are more common in the bass line, but no part has any leaps greater than a fifth. Breath marks are placed throughout the piece to aid in phrasing.

Slurs generally happen between moving eighth notes, although the alto saxophone and horn do have slurred quarter notes. The flute and clarinet parts enter with a group of four slurred eighth notes in measure 2. Additionally, the trumpets and upper woodwinds have a handful of "slur two, tongue two" eighth notes. An extended series of slurred ostinato eighth notes occurs in the flute and oboe in measures 30–33. The conductor and players should lend a careful ear to this ostinato figure to ensure consistent tone quality and length, particularly toward the end of the passage. To help build uniformity, spend a few moments practicing with a metronome, starting slowly and working toward the performance tempo. Also, the ostinato should be carefully balanced under the melody and countermelody.

The composer adds several accents beginning at measure 46. The *forte* dynamic should help younger players execute these notes. In some parts the accents occur on the first of two slurred eighth notes. To build an appropriate and uniform concept of accents, the conductor might demonstrate a measure or two of quarter notes or eighth notes with various accent patterns. Different sections of the band could take turns repeating the accent patterns back to the conductor until a greater sense of consistency is reached. Individual students might also enjoy leading the ensemble in their own accent patterns. Other articulations to note include repeating staccato eighth notes in the trumpet part in measures 17–24 and the tenuto quarter notes of the low brass and low woodwind pedal point from measures 38–41.

Because this piece uses melodies and countermelodies rather extensively, the conductor is presented with several opportunities to explore the concept of balance. For each section of the piece the conductor should help students determine which players have melody, countermelody, and supporting material. The conductor can then lead the band through a series of balance experiments varying dynamic levels of the melody, countermelody, or support, preferably while recording the results. By playing back the recording and discussing the results, students can better understand the effects of proper or improper balance. They should also be able to take individual responsibility for good balance during performance.

Unit 6: Musical Elements

MELODY:
All winds and mallet percussion players play either melody or countermelody at some point during the piece. Because most melodies are written with antecedent and consequent phrases, the conductor might distribute the melodies of *A New World Adventure* to each musician, transposed appropriately. The conductor can help young musicians discover the

"question-and-answer" role of these phrases by having a section or individual play one of the antecedents followed by a different section or individual playing the corresponding consequent. Time could also be spent on allowing students to improvise their own antecedent and consequent lines.

Several other compositional techniques can be found throughout *A New World Adventure*. The first nine measures may be seen as call and response between the trumpets and the entire ensemble. The alto saxophone and horn enter at measure 18 with a fragment of the subsequent melody beginning at measure 21. The melodies occurring in measures 30–37 and 38–45 are variations of the theme from measures 21–30. Imitation occurs in measures 38 and 39 as the trumpet statement is repeated at the unison by the upper woodwinds and mallet percussion. A short sequence is found in measures 51 and 52 in the mallet percussion. The previously mentioned ostinato (flute and oboe in mm. 30–33) and pedal point (bass voices in mm. 38–41 and mm. 50–54) could also be isolated for teaching purposes.

HARMONY:

A New World Adventure could be used to introduce a minor tonality to a young band as soon as their first or second concert. Because the piece modulates to F major the conductor can also demonstrate how relative major and minor scales employ the same key signature. The use of the natural minor (or D Aeolian) scale—particularly its lack of accidentals—should help make this concept especially clear to young musicians. The conductor might further wish to address the concept of suspension which appears prominently in measures 17–24. A few altered chords appear throughout the piece, and several ii–V–I progressions are used after the change to F major. Chord symbols are provided in the piano accompaniment. Overall, the harmonic structure should be very "hearable" to a beginning band.

RHYTHM:

All rhythms in this piece are appropriate for young players. Half notes, quarter notes, and eighth notes provide most of the rhythmic vocabulary with occasional appearances of dotted half and dotted quarter notes. As the piece climaxes the snare drum provides greater rhythmic activity with the appearance of sixteenth notes in measure 54.

Rhythmic patterns are often repeated in melodic, countermelodic and supporting lines, yet they are varied enough to remain engaging. The former characteristic should help build ensemble confidence, while the latter retains the interest of young players.

TIMBRE:

All musicians should strive for a solid, well-supported sound that is never timid. Encourage students to play with a spirit and boldness that reflect the courage and resolve of those who lived in the North American frontier. The minor setting helps beginning level musicians portray these ideas. Similar character should also extend through quieter moments. Give special attention to passages with softer dynamics (measures 10–16, 21–29, and 50–54) to avoid smears and imprecisions. The conductor might choose to rehearse these sections at a full dynamic, repeating them at softer and softer volumes while striving for consistency of attack, tone and release. Players should also endeavor to keep a uniform sound quality through each *crescendo* and *decrescendo*.

Unit 7: Form and Structure

SECTION	MEASURE	EVENT AND SCORING
Theme 1	1–9	Two-measure trumpet calls followed by tutti responses
Theme 2	10–17	Clarinet 1 antecedent followed by a consequent phrase from all upper woodwinds and mallet percussion
Interlude	17–20	Trumpets with repeated rhythmic figure followed by theme 3 fragment in alto saxophone and horn
Theme 3	21–30	Upper woodwinds and mallet percussion play theme 3 through measure 24 with countermelody in alto saxophone and horn; trumpets continue rhythmic figures from the interlude; the melody is traded between the alto saxophone and horn and flute, oboe, trumpets, and mallet percussion in measures 27–30
Variation	30–37	Theme 3 varied in clarinets and trumpets; countermelody in low brass and low woodwinds; rhythmic figures are in the alto saxophone and horn; flute and oboe have the eighth-note ostinato; texture thins and briefly becomes monophonic during the second part of the phrase before building to next section

Section	Measure	Event and Scoring
Variation	38–45	Trumpets with theme 3 variation at *forte*, imitated by upper woodwinds and mallet percussion; alto saxophone and horn have counter material; bass voices provide a tonic pedal point in measures 38–41; the tonality shifts to F major in measures 42–45
Transition	46–54	Accented downbeat confirms F major followed by trumpet accents and eighth-note motion in woodwinds, horns, and bass voices; tutti *decrescendo* into *mezzo piano* at measure 54; dominant pedal point, sequential material and *crescendo* build to coda
Coda	55–65	Rhythmic and melodic fragments recalled from previous sections and established in F major; antecedent/consequent phrasing leads to final accented tonic triad

Unit 8: Suggested Listening

Aaron Copland:
> *Appalachian Spring*
> *Billy the Kid*

Douglas Court:
> *Champions in the Quest*
> *Rise Before the Sun*
> *True North*

James Curnow, *Canadian Folk Song Rhapsody*

Antonin Dvorak, Symphony No. 9 in E Minor, "From the New World"

Percy Grainger, *Lincolnshire Posy*, Movement I, "Lisbon"

Clare Grundman, *Kentucky 1800*

Ralph Vaughan Williams, *Folk Song Suite*, Movement I, "March – Seventeen Come Sunday"

Dan Welcher, *Zion*

Unit 9: Additional References and Resources

Battisti, Frank, and Robert Garofalo. *Guide to Score Study for the Wind Band Conductor*. Fort Lauderdale, FL: Meredith Music Publications, 1990.

Court, Douglas. *A New World Adventure*. Wilmore, KY: Curnow Music Press, Inc., 2002.

"Douglas Court." http://www.curnowmusicpress.com/douglascourt.htm (accessed April 18, 2007).

"Etienne Brule." http://www.britannica.com/eb/article-9016763/Etienne-Brule (accessed May 15, 2007).

Harris, Fred E., Jr. *Conducting with Feeling*. Galesville, MD: Meredith Music Publications, 2001.

Contributed by:

Lane Weaver
DMA Candidate/Teaching Assistant
University of Kentucky
Lexington, Kentucky

Teacher Resource Guide

A Sailor's Odyssey
David Bobrowitz
(b. 1945)

Unit 1: Composer

David Bobrowitz was born in Brooklyn, New York, on February 21, 1945. Bobrowitz is a freelance bass trombonist, pianist, composer, and arranger. He taught in the Great Neck Public Schools in New York for thirty years, serving as band and orchestra director and as a music department chairman before he retired in June 2000. He received a bachelor of science degree from the Mannes College of Music, majoring in trombone performance and studying with Simon Karasick. Bobrowitz went to Teachers College, Columbia University, where he earned a master's degree in music education. He studied composition with Robert Russell Bennett. Bobrowitz has composed works for orchestra, concert band, jazz band, chorus, and piano with grade levels ranging from 2 through 5.

Unit 2: Composition

A Sailor's Odyssey was composed in 2004 and is based on the song "The Drunken Sailor." After a brief introduction the melody is stated and then repeated with variation-like treatment. Known as a "sea shanty" or "work song," this song was known to be sung as sailors turned the capstan to raise the sails or the ship's anchor. Many verses can be found in different publications and recordings. In each four-line verse, the first line is sung three times and followed with "Early (sung "ear-lye") in the morning." "What shall we do with a drunken sailor," "Put him in the brig until he's sober," "Put him in a boat and row him over," are three common verses. The chorus, "Way, hay (or Heave ho) and up she rises" refers to the hoisted sails or anchor. The work is 144 measures and two minutes, thirty seconds long.

Unit 3: Historical Perspective

Folk songs, especially those related to the sea and sailing, have been a source of inspiration for composers throughout the history of band music. The works of Gustav Holst (his Suites for Band), Ralph Vaughan Williams (*English Folk Song Suite* and *Sea Songs*) and Percy Grainger (*Lincolnshire Posy*) are perhaps the most significant twentieth-century band compositions that are based on folk songs. Several composers used "The Drunken Sailor" melody in their band works including Clare Grundman in his *Fantasy on American Sailing Songs* (1952), Anne McGinty in her *Sea Song Fantasy* (1994), and Elliot Del Borgo in his *Sea Trilogy* (2004).

Unit 4: Technical Considerations

The melody is in the Dorian mode and this work is written with a key signature of D minor, using accidentals to indicate B-naturals. Rhythms used include the eighth-and-two sixteenths pattern and the dotted eighth-and-sixteenth pattern. Prevailing throughout the work is an eighth rest on the beat followed with and eighth note entrance on the off-beat. This is first introduced as an accompanying motive but becomes the main motive in the tutti statement at measure 63. The percussion parts can be covered by six players, with parts available for up to three additional players.

Unit 5: Stylistic Considerations

Proper and effective articulation will result in a successful performance of this work. The composer has indicated many staccato markings on eighth notes. Care must be taken to play these lightly and in a bouncing style; they should not sound choppy. The middle section at measure 63 has the fullest scoring and the loudest dynamic, marcato accents on the eighth notes. This provides an excellent opportunity to teach an ensemble to play these heavy articulations with a balanced sound without over blowing or tonguing too hard.

Unit 6: Musical Elements

MELODY:
The folk song's verses and the chorus are all eight measures in length. The melodic shape of the chorus is very similar to that of the verse. The variations in the work are provided by changes in scoring and rhythm.

HARMONY:

With the melody stated in the D Dorian mode the harmony is taken from the key of D minor. This presents a fine opportunity to teach students the relationships between D minor in the natural and melodic forms and the Dorian mode on D.

RHYTHM:

The work is in a duple meter throughout. Continuous eighth notes are being played in most measures. Some players may be challenged by a recurring rhythm throughout the work in which there is an eighth rest on the beat (either on beat one or beat two) with an eighth note entrance on the off-beat. Another challenge may be for players to cleanly articulate the eighth-and-two sixteenths rhythm. Some players will undoubtedly be fooled by the two sixteenths-and-eighth rhythm in the penultimate measure.

TIMBRE:

In most of this work the woodwinds and the brasses are scored in opposition to each other. The composer accomplished this by alternating which section plays the chorus and verse and by scoring the melody in one section with an accompanying rhythm in the other section. At measure 109 the melody is played in a *hocket* or *Durchbrochene Arbeit* style with the flutes, oboes and alto saxophones playing one measure and the clarinets and trumpets playing the next.

Unit 7: Form and Structure

MEASURE	EVENT AND SCORING
1	Introduction
7	Verse stated in trumpets with original rhythm of eighth-and-two sixteenths
15	Chorus stated in flutes and 1st clarinets with original rhythm of dotted eighth-and-sixteenth
23	Verse variant in trombone, baritone, and tuba
31	Extension of measures 29–30
33	Verse variant in rhythmic augmentation stated in bass clarinet, bassoon, baritone saxophone, trombone, baritone, and tuba
43	Trumpets and horn added to melody line
45	Fourth stanza of verse (incomplete) stated in flutes, oboe, and clarinets in quarter notes
47	Fourth stanza (incomplete) repeated in alto saxophones and trumpets in eighth notes

MEASURE	EVENT AND SCORING
48	Fourth stanza (incomplete) repeated in bassoon, tenor saxophone, trombone, baritone, and tuba in eighth notes
49	Interlude with eighth notes on D and eighth rest-eighth note-quarter note motive
63	Verse variant in fullest scoring using eighth rest-eighth note-quarter note motive
71	Chorus variant added in alto saxophones, horn, and bells to the repeat of verse variant
79	Fourth stanza variant repeated at softer dynamic
81	Fourth stanza variant repeated at softer dynamic
83	Verse variant is begun and simplified in bass clarinet, baritone saxophone, and timpani
85	Verse variant is continued in flutes
87	Verse variant is continued in flutes, clarinets, bass clarinet, and baritone saxophone
101	Extension of measures 99–100
105	Interlude with rhythm from measure 63
109	Verse variant broken between flutes, oboe, and alto saxophones and the clarinets and trumpets
117	Verse variant repeat of measures 109–114
123	Fourth stanza in full scoring in half notes
127	Fourth stanza repeated in quarter notes
131	Flutes, oboe, clarinets trill on D and final cadence begins
141	Rhythmic motive from measure 63 stated final time
143	Rhythm of two sixteenths-and-eighth stated on D
144	Final eighth on D

Unit 8: Suggested Listening

Elliot Del Borgo, *Sea Trilogy*
Clare Grundman, *Fantasy on American Sailing Songs*
Anne McGinty, *Sea Song Fantasy*
Ralph Vaughan Williams, *Sea Songs*

Unit 9: Additional References and Resources

Rehrig, William H. *The Heritage Encyclopedia of Band Music.* Westerville, OH: Integrity Press, 1991.

Web sites:
www.grandmesamusic.com
www.shawneepress.com

Contributed by:

Kenneth Kohlenberg
Director of Bands, Professor of Music
Sinclair Community College
Dayton, Ohio

Teacher Resource Guide

A Summer Waltz

Murray Houllif
(b. 1948)

Unit 1: Composer

Murray Houllif received his bachelor of music education degree from the State University of New York at Potsdam and attained a master of music degree in percussion performance from the University of New York at Stony Brook. He studied with Raymond Des Roches, Richard Fitz, James Petercsak, Sandy Feldstein, and Bey Perry. During his career as a music educator, Murray served as the co-coordinator of percussion at North Texas State University in Denton, and as a band director and percussion specialist for the public schools of Smithtown, New York. He has recently retired from this position after thirty-two years of teaching.

Murray is a freelance percussionist in the New York-Metro area, and currently performs with the Atlantic Wind Symphony and Theatre Three. While a member of the Long Island Symphony under Seymour Lipkin and the Nassau Symphony directed by Andrew Schenk, he performed with notable musicians Dave Brubeck, Itzak Perlman, Stanley Drucker, Julius Baker, and Phil Smith. He is cofounder of the Ambira Mallet Quartet, which has performed many of his compositions. He endorses Pro-mark sticks and Grover Pro-Percussion products.

As a composer, Murray has more than 175 concert and pedagogic publications to his credit. His music is used and performed in universities, conservatories, and public schools around the world. He has been a recipient of the Percussive Arts Society Composition Award twice, and has contributed to the following professional journals: *Percussive Notes*, *The Instrumentalist*, *School Band and Orchestra Magazine*, and the *Music Educator's Journal*.

Unit 2: Composition

A *Summer Waltz* is a lyrical piece in 3/4 time. Unison rhythms, graceful melodies, and comfortable ranges make this an excellent repertoire choice for young bands. It is scored for standard concert band instrumentation, with two clarinet parts and two trumpet parts, and interesting percussion parts for six players on snare drum, bass drum, crash cymbals, triangle, tambourine, and bells. *A Summer Waltz* was published in 2005 by C. Alan Publications and is approximately two minutes in duration.

The piece is dedicated to his mother, Esther Houllif, and his kid sister, as a testament to supportive family. Murray notes that his mother would "cheerily tolerate my drum set practicing when I was a teenager. I had to stop when my Dad got home!" His sister Sandy, who played flute in her high school band, is now a high school band director herself.

Unit 3: Historical Perspective

A waltz is a dance in moderate triple time. The dance form originated in the late eighteenth century and became very popular in the early nineteenth century. The *Landler,* an Austrian country dance also in triple meter, as well as the German *deutsche Tanz* predate the waltz. Mozart, Beethoven, Schubert, and Weber are among the first composers to cultivate this form. Weber's *Invitation to the Dance* (1819) is one of the first pieces to exploit the characteristic rhythm and accompaniment associated with the waltz. Johann Strauss and Johann Strauss, Jr. developed the waltz into the ballroom dance phenomenon that was popular in Vienna in the early nineteenth century.

Unit 4: Technical Considerations

The concert B-flat key signature is consistent throughout the piece with accidentals providing the shift in tonality. To prepare students, practice the concert B-flat and concert F scales in daily warm-ups and exercises. The concept of 3/4 meter should also be addressed during an ensemble warm-up. Introduce movement to help students feel the lilting nature of the waltz. Establish a sense of pulse by having students sway back and forth while stepping on beat one. Once this becomes comfortable, have students incorporate tapping on the two weaker beats. This kind of movement exercise may be used independently or incorporated into daily exercises and scales. Rhythms are simple with the occasional dotted quarter eighth note syncopation occurring in the melodic line. Ranges are comfortable for students near the end of their first year of playing. A more advanced student should be assigned to the first clarinet and the first trumpet parts. The highest note for clarinet I is B5 (with an optional C6), and the highest note for trumpet I is fourth line D5. Special attention should be given to the bell part in measures 25 through 32 as it is written in thirds. This provides an ideal opportunity to introduce the double mallet grip to young percussionists.

Unit 5: Stylistic Considerations

A *Summer Waltz* can be used to teach students what roles their part plays within the context of the score. Careful attention must be given to the melodic line at all times. Take time during the rehearsal to isolate the melody, and have students document in their music the instruments have the melody in each statement of the theme. Another rehearsal strategy to help increase awareness of the melodic line is to have musicians stand up when they are performing the melody. This may help create a quantitative or visual reference to the number of musicians and the voices that perform the melodic line. Dynamics must also be approached with this same sensitivity. The tempo is marked *Gracefully*, and the quarter note = 80–88. Freedom of movement in the lyrical line is aided by various tempo markings: *Poco ritardando et crescendo, a tempo,* and *ritardando*. This flexibility teaches students to respond to the conductor. The greatest challenge of successfully performing A *Summer Waltz* will be encouraging students to play in a light, lyrical style. The waltz is a dance form that young people seldom experience today. Introduce students to the well-known waltzes of Johann Strauss; listening is a valuable tool in creating awareness of musical style.

Unit 6: Musical Elements

MELODY:
The melody in A *Summer Waltz* is mostly conjunct with the melodies at the B theme and the harmonized accompaniment lines providing contrast. The scales of concert B-flat major and the dominant, concert F major are the key centers. Diatonic structure is prominent; there is no use of chromaticism. The phrase structure is antecedent and consequent in that each phrase is constructed so as to require resolution by a second phrase of similar duration. All phrases are four measures in length with only the final phrase being extended and used as a coda. The graceful and lilting melody in the A and B sections is contrasted at the C section with a rhythmic tutti that is light and detached. This contrast in style, texture, and tonality provides an excellent opportunity to teach the rondo form of this piece.

HARMONY:
A *Summer Waltz* is based in the tonality of B-flat major and the relative dominant F major. Basic harmonic progressions allow students to identify with tonic-dominant chordal relationships. The tuba or lowest-sounding brass instrument plays the root of each chord throughout the work. Have students

listen to and hum or sing the tuba (low brass/woodwinds) part in the first eight measures to learn the simple chord progressions. Using a blackboard with a staff, have students identify the note names of the root of each chord, and place them on the staff. Next, take time to build a major chord above each root and explain that the building blocks of a major chord are scale degrees one, three, and five. Then, introduce the melodic line performed by the flute and clarinet I on top of the chord progression played by the low brass and woodwinds. With guidance, students should be able to pick out pitches in the melody that perform a harmonic function as well as a melodic function. The next step is to add the countermelody and go through the same process. Use the C section at measure 25 to discuss the tonic-dominant relationship as it relates to the harmonic structure of the composition. Explaining the role and function of the harmonic line teaches students to listen to and for other parts. This is also a valuable tool in creating balance and blend. The texture of *A Summer Waltz* is homophonic. The above exercise can also generate discussion about texture in music: When the melodic line is isolated it is considered monophonic, whereas when the harmonic foundation is added it becomes homophonic.

RHYTHM:

Triple meter and simple rhythmic structure create a lilting feel in *A Summer Waltz*. Rhythmic demands are minimal in this work. The smallest division is the eighth note with occasional syncopation in the dotted-quarter and eighth note figure. The challenge for young players will be performing the 3/4 meter in a fluid and connected manner. Using 3/4 meter in warm-ups and creating simple technical exercises that reinforce this will be valuable to achieving mastery.

TIMBRE:

Scoring each repetition of the melody with different combinations of instruments and instrumental families creates timbral contrast. This could generate a conversation about timbre and how it affects the character of a composition. Use Unit 7: Form and Structure as a resource to help isolate the instrumental voices and families. In this discussion, ask students to think about how using different instrumentation would affect the piece. For example, how would this piece be different if the melodic line was introduced by trombone or baritone? Draw attention also to the various ways the composer uses the percussion section as they are a significant timbral resource in this composition and in the wind band medium as a whole.

A *Summer Waltz* also presents an ideal vehicle for teaching blend and balance. For example, the first statement of the theme is played by flute and oboe. clarinet I and bells join on the repeat and clarinet II, alto saxophone and trumpets introduce a countermelody. When clarinet I and bells enter, the new color must blend and complement the existing flute/oboe line. As clarinet II, alto saxophone, and trumpets enter with the countermelody they must strive to maintain a balance with the melody in the upper woodwinds and bells. These conversations help students begin to understand the degree of sophistication that is required of them each time they perform in an ensemble setting.

Unit 7: Form and Structure

SECTION	MEASURE	EVENT AND SCORING
A	1–8	B-flat major; melody performed by flute/oboe with woodwind and French horn accompaniment; repeat of melody adds clarinet I and a countermelody with contrary motion in clarinet II, alto saxophone, and trumpet with the addition of low brass accompaniment; percussion: bells and triangle
B	9–16	Melody performed by alto saxophone and trumpet with woodwind/brass accompaniment excluding clarinet II, baritone saxophone and tuba; percussion: snare/bass drum
A	17–24	Melody performed by flute/oboe, clarinet I and II, alto saxophone and trumpet with woodwind/ brass accompaniment; percussion: snare/bass drum
C	25–33	F major; rhythmically cohesive tutti ensemble with melody performed by flute/oboe, divisi clarinet, alto saxophone and trumpet; low wood-wind/brass accompaniment; full percussion

SECTION	MEASURE	EVENT AND SCORING
A	34–45	B-flat major; melody performed by flute/oboe, clarinet I and alto saxophone with countermelody in clarinet II and trumpet; low woodwind/brass accompaniment; full percussion

Unit 8: Suggested Listening

Warren Barker, *An Irish Interlude*
John Corigliano, *Gazebo Dances*
Anne McGinty, *Red Balloon*
Johann Strauss, Jr.:
    By the Beautiful Blue Danube
    Tales from Vienna Woods

Unit 9: Additional References and Resources

Blom, Eric. *Everyman's Dictionary of Music*. Revised by Sir Jack Westrup. London, Great Britain: JM Dent & Sons Limited, 1975.

Dvorak, Thomas L. *Best Music for Young Band*, revised edition. Edited by Bob Margolis. Brooklyn, NY: Manhattan Music, 2005.

Longyear, Rey M. *Nineteenth-Century Romanticism in Music*, second edition. Englewood Cliffs, NJ: Prentice-Hall, Inc., 1973.

Miles, Richard, and Thomas Dvorak, eds. *Teaching Music through Performance in Beginning Band*. Chicago: GIA Publications, 2001.

Miles, Richard, ed. *Teaching Music through Performance in Band*, Volume 3. Chicago: GIA Publications, 2000.

Randall, Don., ed. *Harvard Concise Dictionary of Music*. Cambridge, MA: Belknap Press of Harvard University Press, 1978.

Web sites:
    http://www.c-alanpublications.com
    http://www.murrayhoullif.homestead.com

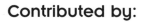

Contributed by:

Sheryl Bowhay
Conductor
Edmonton, Alberta, Canada

Teacher Resource Guide

An Irish Air

Robert Sheldon
(b. 1954)

Unit 1: Composer

Robert Sheldon was born in Chester, Pennsylvania, on February 3, 1954. He is an experienced music educator and composer with a bachelor of music in music education from the University of Miami and a master of fine arts in instrumental conducting from the University of Florida. Mr. Sheldon's teaching experience includes public school music in Florida and Illinois and conducting/music education/university bands at Florida State University. He is the conductor of the Prairie Wind Ensemble and is the Concert Band Editor for Alfred Music Publishing Company.

Sheldon's successful career is mirrored in his numerous honors and awards. He is the recipient of the American School Band Directors Association's (ASBDA) *Volkwein Award* for composition and the *Stansbury Award* for teaching. The American Society of Composers, Authors, and Publishers (ASCAP) recognized his outstanding works for concert band with eighteen separate *Standard Awards*. The International Assembly of Phi Beta Mu honored Sheldon by naming him *International Outstanding Bandmaster* of the year in 1990. Robert Sheldon and his music are represented in articles in *The Instrumentalist, Teaching Music*, and *School Band* and *Orchestra Magazine*.

Sheldon's compositions span a wide range of performance levels. He has composed commissioned works for school districts, state music associations, individual school band programs, all-state bands, various honor bands, and community bands. The title of the work often reflects the location or event that elicited the commission as in *Charleston Harbor Celebration*, Op. 119

composed for the Charleston Community Band of Charleston, South Carolina (Gr. 4, 2007). Tara Winds of Atlanta, GA, director David Gregory, commissioned *Chiaroscuro: Symphonic Dances in the Shades of Darkness and Light*, Op. 79 (Gr. 5, 2002). Other representative commissioned works include *An American Hymntune* (Gr. 1.5, 2005); *Appalachian Legacy*, Op. 46 (Gr. 4, 1995); *As a Wind from the North*, Op. 104 (Gr. 5, 2006); *Barrier Reef*, Op. 81 (Gr. 2, 2002); *Lost in Mammoth Cave* (Gr. 2.5, 2006); *Metroplex: Three Postcards from Manhattan*, Op. 110 (Gr. 4.5, 2006); and *Three Miniatures for Winds and Percussion*, Op. 99 (Gr. 3, 2005). Sheldon's works are found on virtually all selective music lists. Some popular titles for younger bands are *Pevensey Castle*, Op. 44 (Gr. 2.5, 1993); *An Irish Ballade* (Gr. 1, 2003); *Fall River Overture* (Gr. 3, 1981); and *Visions of Flight*, Op. 30 (Gr. 4, 1990).

Robert Sheldon maintains a busy schedule as a guest conductor, clinician, and composer.

Unit 2: Composition

An Irish Air is an arrangement of the Irish song "Molly Malone," also known as *Cockles and Mussels*. This new addition to the young band repertoire was published in 2006 by Alfred Publishing and is listed in the *Challenger Band Series*. The ballad is beautifully scored for bands with less-experienced players and is an excellent choice for teaching musical expression, phrasing, legato playing, and tone quality. Sheldon's simple and lovely setting employs only the verse of the song. The composer writes:

> Folk songs often have the very best melodic material, and I think interpretation of melody is one of the most important elements in teaching how to play music expressively, so I am often drawn to folk material. Because most folk tunes are necessarily very singable, they also often have limited ranges and easily accessible intervals, so they are terrific for young band settings. This is a tune I have known and enjoyed for many years.[1]

An Irish Air is listed as a grade 1.5 (easy) and is approximately two and one-half minutes in duration.

Unit 3: Historical Perspective

Molly Malone is considered the unofficial anthem of Dublin City, Ireland where a lovely statue of the fair lass stands on Grafton Street. Although legends abound, there is no substantial evidence to support the common misconception that Molly Malone was a real person. Indeed the reputed folk song was actually composed in the 1880's by James Yorkston as "a 'comic song' replete with mock pathos."[2] No known versions of the melody or lyrics exist prior to 1883, when the song was published in Cambridge, Massachusetts, with no listed composer. However, Francis Brothers and Day published the work in London a year later and listed Yorkston as the composer and Edmund Forman as the arranger. This 1884 edition also indicates that *Molly Malone* "was reprinted by permission of Messrs Kohler and Son of Edinburgh"[3] from which one may deduce that an earlier edition of the song had been published in Scotland. As the song gained popularity, Yorkston's name failed to appear on printed editions and therefore many people erroneously assumed that it was a traditional folk song. (For a fascinating look into the history and legend of Molly Malone, see *Irish Historical Mysteries: Molly Malone* by Sean Murphy at the Web site listed in Unit 9: Additional References and Resources.)

As is often the case with ballads, the story is a sad one: beautiful Molly Malone sells her wares on the streets of Dublin but alas, she falls ill of a fever dies at a young age. As with other folk songs (and folk-like songs) the lyrics may vary depending on the source. *Molly Malone* is no different with some modifications such as "wheeled" vs. "wheel'd," "but" vs. "and," and other minor differences. The lyrics below may be found on Sean Murphy's Web site. (See Unit 9.)

In Dublin's Fair City
Where the girls are so pretty
I first set my eyes on sweet Molly Malone
As she wheel'd her wheelbarrow
Through streets broad and narrow
Crying cockles and mussels alive, alive o!

Chorus
Alive, alive o! alive, alive o!
Crying cockles and mussels alive, alive o!

She was a fishmonger
But sure 'twas no wonder
For so were her father and mother before
And they both wheel'd their barrow
Through streets broad and narrow
Crying cockles and mussels alive, alive o!

Chorus

She died of a fever
And no one could save her
And that was the end of sweet Molly Malone
But her ghost wheels her barrow
Through streets broad and narrow
Crying cockles and mussels alive, alive o!

Chorus

Molly Malone has been recorded by numerous artists: including Burl Ives, Cisco Houston, the Limeliters, Sinead O'Connor, and the Wayside Trio. One of the best-known settings of the song for concert band is found in Clare Grundman's *An Irish Rhapsody.*

Unit 4: Technical Considerations

An Irish Air is scored in concert E-flat with a key change to concert F at measure 35. Students should be proficient in both keys. Accidentals are limited, however, concert D-flat appears in the second clarinet, trumpet, baritone, and tuba parts. The meter is 3/4 with a tempo of quarter note = 84. Students will need to be able to phrase a minimum of four measures in one breath while maintaining good tone quality. This may be challenging for developing players and additional work on breathing and tonal control may be necessary. Use long tones and play unison sustained melodies to improve breath support.

One challenging breath support development "game" is "Hold the Sheet of Toilet Paper Against the Wall." Every student takes a sheet of toilet paper (the lightness of it makes it a good choice for this exercise) and stands facing the classroom wall. Place the paper against the wall and hold it with one finger. Begin to blow air at the paper and remove the finger hold. The paper will stay in place if the student is blowing a supported air stream. In the initial phases of the game ask students to stand fairly close to the wall. As they develop better air support have them step further back. Time students to see who can hold the paper against the wall for the longest number of seconds. Hint: Some students may seek to improve their time by wetting a small section of the paper so that it sticks to the wall.

A critical, and often neglected, aspect of developing good tone quality is the art of listening. Students need a positive and appropriate "sound" model. A listening assignment could encourage students to listen to a recording of their instrument as performed by a favorite artist. Post a list of your favorite performers to give students a starting point. Make frequent listening assignments so that students will continue to have an aural picture of good tone quality. This will help them on a conscious and subconscious level and subtle adjustments in their sound will be evident as they begin to internalize the proper tone. Daily reminders about correct embouchure along with a visual check will ensure the development of proper playing techniques. Some band directors glue small mirrors on the corners of the music stands so that students may self-check. Use short verbal reminders such as "click" to help clarinet players remember to place the top teeth on the mouthpiece or "r.h." to remind horn players to properly place the right hand in the bell.

No breath marks are included in the score and parts of *An Irish Air* but the lyrics indicate where the breaths should be taken. Students should learn to sing the song before they play the piece. Stress proper use of air, diction, and tone as they sing. Use the same rhythms as those used in *An Irish Air* to avoid confusion when playing the band arrangement. All rhythms are basic variations of half notes, quarter notes, and eighth notes and are consistent with the grade 1.5 classification.

The instrument ranges employed in *An Irish Air* are within the capabilities of young players. The distinction between the first and second parts allows for a wide range of competency levels, challenging the more advanced player while providing an interesting part for the developing beginner. For example, the first clarinet part crosses the break while the second part does not. The first trumpet part extends to written E-flat5 but the second part only reaches written C5. The flute part ranges from B-flat4 to D-flat6. The horn players all play the same part and the range is written C4 to D5. Although this may be challenging for the young horn player, the part is cross-scored in the alto saxophones. Horn players who have already switched to the double horn will have an easier time negotiating the part because of the written D5. Players who are still on the single horn may try fingering written D5 with either 0 or 1. The open fingering is generally more in-tune but due to its proximity to open C5, may be difficult for some players to locate. Simple C5 to D5 exercises and arpeggios (C4-E-G-C5 and D-F-sharp-A-D) will develop control of these pitches. The range of the unison trombone part is C3 to E-flat4. Players need good tone and legato tonguing to successfully perform this part. While the concert E-flat4 is in unison with trumpets, the trombone part in general is independent of cross scoring and/or cues.

The percussion scoring is very simple: bells, suspended cymbal, triangle, and timpani. The suspended cymbal and timpani players need to know how to perform a basic roll; use softer mallets for the timpani and cymbal parts. The bell and triangle parts provide an excellent opportunity for teaching timbre. The entire band will benefit from listening as the bell player discovers which mallets best reflect the style and color of the piece. If your inventory allows, experiment with different size and weight triangles and beaters. Have the triangle player try various combinations and then guide the student to the best selection. This early exploration into the world

of percussion colors encourages players to consider choices beyond the ordinary. It allows students to develop an ear for color while engaging them in the music-making process. Consider a new kind of ear training test—"Name that mallet."

Dynamic contrast is essential for a musical performance. The dynamics range from *piano* to *forte* with interspersed *crescendos* and *decrescendos*. Try using a visual representation to explain the amount of contrast required by the ensemble. Select four students of varying heights to come to the front of the room, choosing the shortest and tallest members of the band as the *piano* and *forte* representatives, respectively. Arrange the students from tallest to shortest and explain that this is how much contrast is needed among the various dynamics. Where this example goes from here is a matter of imagination. Students can say their names at their designated dynamic level or use "1(*p*)-2(*mp*)-3(*mf*)-4(*f*)." Arrange the four students in different orders so the dynamics vary, such as *f-mp-mf-p*. Ask the students to create other ways of explaining dynamic contrast.

One of the most difficult concepts for young players is the production of the *piano* dynamic. Young players tend to use less air and less air speed, while the proper technique requires a small but steady, controlled air stream. Proper breath support is essential in the production of a clear, beautiful *piano* tone. The player will not be able to sustain or project the tone with a small air stream that lacks focus. Again refer to the "paper against the wall" exercise to demonstrate the feeling of focused air. Brass players need to avoid increasing mouthpiece pressure as this inhibits the lip vibration. Philip Farkas in *The Art of French Horn Playing* writes "when playing loud, let the embouchure 'take it easy' and depend on the air to do the work; when playing softly, make the embouchure tension do the heavy share of the work."[4] Once again, practicing long tones helps students develop this critical balance.

Unit 5: Stylistic Considerations

An Irish Air is a ballad and therefore its interpretation should be consistent with the lyrical, gentle nature of this genre. The moderate tempo, coupled with simple rhythmic material allows students to explore and develop their legato playing and musical expression. All ensemble members will benefit from preparing *An Irish Air* for performance. As students develop the techniques required for a successful musical rendering of *Molly Malone*, they strengthen the fundamentals necessary to perform lyrical, legato passages and compositions. Young players need a healthy diet of such works to help them develop breath support, tone quality, legato style, and musicality. The composer indicates: "Expression is the key to a good performance of this piece. It is scored to bring out warmth and blend, but the most important elements are the phrasing of the lines, and the emphasis on the accompanimental textures along with the tension and release created by the counter-point."[5]

Flute players will need to use plenty of air to extend their phrases to four measures. Trumpet players should be monitored for the "wah-wah" effect, which occurs when players push the air through the instrument note-by-note instead of through the phrase. All students need a strip of paper eight inches long and one inch wide to practice proper use of the air. Hold the paper so that the end of the strip dangles about eight inches in front of the mouth. Blow a stream of air against the paper. It will move away. Now do the same thing but add a series of quarter notes by articulating "too-too-too-too." If the student is supporting throughout the phrase the paper will remain extended. A paper that drops back toward the face between notes indicates that the student is stopping the air. Have all students practice this exercise on a regular basis. Trombone players will need to develop legato tonguing using a "dah" or "doo" articulation. Remind them to quickly move the slide while using fast air. Low woodwind, baritone and tuba players typically do not phrase with the rest of the band and they may try to breathe after every measure or two instead. However, isolating the low brass and woodwind parts and defining where the breath marks should occur will help these players understand that phrasing applies to all members of the ensemble.

Unit 6: Musical Elements

MELODY:
This beautiful folk-like melody lends itself quite naturally to expressive playing, however, young players have little experience with shaping phrases. *An Irish Air* is a setting of a song with a text, so the lyrics provide an ideal starting point for identifying phrases.

The process of teaching musical expression takes time and patience, but even very young players can be musical. Begin by recording the band as it plays mm. 11–27 and save this for later. Now have students listen to Irish tenor Michael Daly as he sings *Molly Malone* at www.michaeldalytenor.com and sing along with a MIDI file of the songs at www.ireland-information.com/irishmusic/cocklesandmussels.shtml.

Guide students into a musical and expressive rendition of the song by using these models or by personally performing it on an instrument. Explain that musicians make subtle adjustments to all musical lines by using small *crescendos/decrescendos* and by adding weight to notes through breath accents. One example that students may relate to is to make a simple statement such as "like pizza" using a monotone voice. Now say the statement again "I **LIKE** pizza" emphasizing "like." Repeat the statement but say "I like PIZZA." Encourage students to identify what makes this version different and

Example 1. An Irish Air

determine how this technique can be applied to music. Use "Three Blind Mice" and seek volunteers to perform a happy version, a sad version, a silly version, etc., and begin to define how musicians elicit an emotional response from listeners. This is pretty heavy information for young players but their imaginations will guide them when experience is lacking. Movie soundtracks provide an excellent example of how music can help us feel the action. Use a clip from a familiar (and appropriate) movie. Show it first without the sound and repeat with the volume turned on. This works best with clips that have no dialogue.

Expressive playing may come naturally to some students but most will need to be taught how to shape a musical line. Use the first phrase of *Molly Malone* to establish a tangible foundation for expressive playing: "In **Dub**lin's fair city, where **girls** are so **pret**ty." Ask students to slightly increase the volume on the boldfaced syllables. Now go back and add a gentle *crescendo* to the underlined syllables. Continue this process throughout the song; once the band members understand and can demonstrate this simple melodic enhancement it would be appropriate to discuss predictability. Listen again to the Michael Daly example and analyze his interpretation through the following guidelines:

1. Hand out the lyrics.
2. Ask students to circle the notes that have more weight as they listen.
3. Listen again and ask students to underline the syllables or phrases that *crescendo*.
4. Analyze the results and identify patterns and unexpected changes.

Play the section from mm. 11–27 again and apply the subtle changes. Ask students for their input and allow more advanced players to demonstrate their interpretation. Once the band is playing with expression, make a second recording of this section. Play back the earlier recording and compare it to the second version. Discuss the differences. Remember that it may take a day or two of work before the band is ready to record the second interpretation.

HARMONY:

An Irish Air is arranged in concert E-flat major and modulates to concert F major. The harmony reflects a combination of homophonic and polyphonic textures. The initial melodic statement (mm. 11–27) is accompanied by the low brass and alto saxophones playing simple chords. At m. 35 the texture becomes polyphonic with contrapuntal lines in the clarinets, bells, and flutes. Rehearse the individual parts separately. Have the students who are not playing tap their feet while counting and/or fingering their parts. The key to a beautiful performance rests on the tone quality and musicality of the supporting harmonic parts. Tune the chords from root to fifth to third and then add color tones. The composer uses the minor supertonic (ii) and submediant (vi) chords to enrich the basic tonality. Carefully scored seventh chords also enhance the supporting harmonic progressions. The final chord is F major (F-A-C) with an added ninth (G) to create interest and color. Similar color tones are found throughout the work, giving the piece a more mature sound than is typical of this grade level.

RHYTHM:

An Irish Air is arranged in simple 3/4 meter and requires an understanding of the dotted-quarter/eighth-note rhythm. Because slower works are more challenging for young players, use a metronome to establish the pulse and clap/say the rhythms prior to the first read-through. Begin at m. 19 and say the rhythm via the band's counting system. The example on the next page reflects all rhythms used in mm. 19–24 and includes arrows to indicate foot direction as established in the "Down-up" system:

Example 2. An Irish Air

An established counting system coupled with a metronome helps the band develop an internal pulse and a solid foundation in interpreting rhythms. A metronome can be linked to an amplifier to ensure that all students hear the set tempo, which is critical during the initial stages of rhythmic development. Use the metronome during every warm-up and refer to it often in rehearsals. As students demonstrate that the tempo has been internalized, use the metronome less for that piece. The foot tap will gradually give way to an internalized pulse but this, too, is a gradual process.

Timbre:

It is critical that students play with a characteristic tone before attempting to perform band music. All students need a frequent reminder to sit properly, hold the instrument at the correct angle, blow faster air, have several working reeds, and to form the correct embouchure. Students should listen to recordings of respected artists that model the desired tone quality. Just as one would not attempt to drive to South Dakota without a map, a young musician needs a musical "map" to direct him toward the right sound. If the school library has a collection of sound recordings, work with the librarian to select listening examples for each instrument. Encourage students to listen to these recordings by making listening assignments. Students may use programs like *SmartMusic* to records themselves and listen to their sound. Consider making a "taped" assignment and give students feedback on their performance.

Unit 7: Form and Structure

SECTION	MEASURE	EVENT AND SCORING
Introduction	1–11	Melodic motive passes from unaccompanied horn/alto saxophone for two measures to harmonically supported flute/trumpet 1/bells
Verse in E-flat:		
Phrase 1	11–19	Trumpet melody
Phrase 2	19–27	Flute/clarinet/trumpet melody
Transition	27–35	Trumpet melody based on the theme and transitional material that modulates to F concert; uses color tones, passing tones, accidentals, and moving eighth notes in the clarinet/oboe/flute parts to progress to new key; suspended cymbal roll begins in m. 31 and is joined by a timpani roll in m. 33; chord progression of D-flat/C7/F
Verse in F:		
Phrase 1	35–43	Trombone and baritone melody (cued in horn and alto saxophone); clarinets have moving eighth notes; simple quarter note bell part; descending dotted half notes in flutes and oboes
Phrase 2	43–51	Trumpet and alto saxophone melody; flute countermelody
Coda	51–59	The melody is broken into fragments and passes from the flute/oboe/bells (m. 51) to the clarinet/baritone (m. 52) and continues in the clarinet/alto saxophone/horn/trombone (mm. 53–54); the concluding five measures are a lovely progression F/D-flat/G dim7/F/F major with the ninth, G, for color

Unit 8: Suggested Listening

Stanley Applebaum, *Irish Suite*
John Edmondson, *Amazing Grace*
Percy Grainger, *Irish Tune from County Derry*
Clare Grundman, *An Irish Rhapsody*
David Holsinger, *A Childhood Hymn*
Sinead O'Connor, *Sean-Nos Nua* (Vanguard CD, B00006J420, 2002)
Images: The Music of Robert Sheldon, recorded by Washington Winds,
    WFR–104
Infinite Horizons: The Music of Robert Sheldon, recorded by Washington
    Winds, WW–1641

Unit 9: Additional References and Resources

Farkas, Philip. *The Art of French Horn Playing*. Evanston, IL: Summy-Birchard
    Co., 1956.

Murphy, Sean, "Irish Historical Mysteries: Molly Malone,"
    http://homepage.eircom.net/~seanjmurphy/irhismys/molly.htm/

Sheldon, Robert. www.robertsheldonmusic.com/.

Contributed by:

Susan Creasap
Associate Director of Bands
Morehead State University
Morehead, Kentucky

1 Robert Sheldon, email correspondence with author, May 28, 2007.
2 http://homepage.eircom.net/~seanjmurphy/irhismys/molly.htm.
3 Ibid.
4 Philip Farkas, *The Art of French Horn Playing*, Evanston, IL: Summy-Birchard Co., 1956, 28.
5 Robert Sheldon, email correspondence with author, May 28, 2007.

Teacher Resource Guide

Ariodante Suite

George Frideric Handel
(1685–1759)

arranged by Chuck Elledge
(b. 1961)

Unit 1: Composer

George Frideric Handel was a composer of the Baroque period best remembered today for his oratorio *The Messiah* (1741). He was born in Germany, studied extensively in Italy, and lived most of his adult life in London, where he became a British subject in 1727. His compositions span a wide variety of genres and include vocal music, opera, chamber music, organ, orchestral suites, and works for wind ensemble. He was perhaps best known in his day as a master of Italian opera seria. Two instrumental compositions, *Water Music* (1717) and *Music for the Royal Fireworks* (1749), are still widely performed by orchestras and wind bands. Handel's music had great influence on a generation of composers including Haydn, Mozart, and Beethoven. His contemporaries included Johann Sebastian Bach and Domenico Scarlatti.

Unit 2: Composition

Handel composed the opera *Ariodante* in 1734, which premiered in London the following year. The opera is in three acts and runs nearly three hours when performed in its entirety. The author of the libretto is unknown, but the text is based on writings by Antonio Salvi. The plot is typical eighteenth-century nonsense involving forbidden love, mistaken identity, infidelity, diabolical

144

schemes, murder, improbable plot twists, and the ultimate triumph of love. Forgotten for centuries, *Ariodante* was rediscovered in the twentieth century and is considered one of Handel's best examples of *opera seria*.

Ariodante Suite is a three-movement set arranged by Chuck Elledge using two dances (*gavotte* and *musette)* and a chorus extracted from various acts of the full work.

The published set includes parts for two flutes (no piccolo), oboe (no divisi), two clarinets, alto clarinet, bass clarinet, two alto saxophones, tenor saxophone, baritone saxophone, bassoon (no divisi), two trumpets (with straight mutes required for the second movement), French horn (one single divisi note at the end of the second movement), trombone (one single divisi note at the end of the first movement), baritone, and tuba (minimal divisi in octaves). The arrangement makes extensive use of doubling to ensure that important melodic and harmonic parts are covered by small bands or bands with weaker players. As such, the alto clarinet part is functionally optional. The bass line is coverable by various combinations of bass clarinet, bassoon, and/or baritone saxophone.

Elledge includes parts for numerous percussion players. These include timpani (one player, two drums required, tuned to B-flat and F for each movement), orchestra bells (one player), marimba/xylophone (one player), snare/bass drums (two players), and an additional part covering crash cymbals, triangle, finger cymbals, wood block, and tambourine (two players for some sections, but can be covered by one player). The numerous percussion parts provide many options for the conductor. It is advisable to carefully select and control all of the percussion parts for a stylistic performance.

The set includes an electric bass part that is designed to reinforce the bass part in ensembles with minimal instrumentation. Apply caution if using this part, as the electric-bass sonority is inconsistent with the desired Baroque-ensemble effect. (The part would fit better if performed on a traditional string bass.) Conductors should weigh the advantages of bass reinforcement against the disadvantage of inconsistent sonority.

The full set also includes a part for "rehearsal piano." This part is not a reduction of the complete arrangement, but rather a supporting part to be used in the absence of complete instrumentation. In other words, not all melodic and harmonic material is included. Using this part in performance (to support and encourage weaker players) requires careful examination to determine whether missing material (due to the absence of certain instruments) is covered.

Unit 3: Historical Perspective

A composer of wide-reaching significance, the importance of Handel's contribution to the world of music is without question. His total compositional output includes some 50 operas, 23 oratorios and 16 organ concerti, among many others. In a somewhat ironic historical twist, Handel, a German-born composer, is recognized today as an eighteenth-century master of English compositional style. This is attributable to his early interest in English composers (especially Henry Purcell), two important visits to London around 1710, and the ultimate decision to permanently relocate to England in 1712.

The Baroque *gavotte* (used in the first movement) is a French folk dance that was often incorporated into instrumental suites of the eighteenth century, most notably by Johann Sebastian Bach. It is based on the following rhythmic pattern:

The term *musette* (second movement) refers to a Baroque musical instrument similar to the bagpipes. It was popular as both a professional and amateur instrument. Handel's use of the term *musette* refers not to the actual instrument, but rather to the drone notes that occur within the harmonization (much like the drone created by bagpipes).

The *chorus* (third movement) is an arrangement of the instrumental introduction to the final chorus in Act III, not the actual chorus itself. Instrumental introductions were common in operas of the Baroque period.

Unit 4: Technical Considerations

The publisher lists *Ariodante Suite* as Grade 1.5 and the ranges and tessitura are consistent with these technical limitations. Notes are restricted to the concert B-flat scale, with accidentals appearing for brief modulations to the dominant key and for modality changes to the relative minor. (The first movement contains E-natural, B-natural, and F-sharp; the third movement contains only E-natural. There are no accidentals in the second movement.)

The wind parts move in mostly stepwise direction, but include some wider intervals as a result of melodic construction. While some of the wider intervals (sixths, sevenths, and octaves) will challenge young players, all are within reach of performers at this level.

The percussion parts call for flams in the snare drum, and open rolls in the timpani as well as the marimba/xylophone part. In all cases, a wide variety of percussion mallets are required.

Unit 5: Stylistic Considerations

The most challenging aspect of *Ariodante Suite* is producing a stylistic sonority consistent with music of the eighteenth century. The range limitations and extensive doubling inherently produce a sonority that is uncharacteristically heavy for music of the Baroque period. Conductors should encourage young players to reduce overall volume and articulate as lightly as possible. Conductors might also consider reducing the number of parts in some sections. This is possible thanks to the extensive doubling throughout the arrangement. From a purely stylistic perspective, this arrangement might be considered a Grade 2.

To further emphasize lightness, some of the percussion parts could also be reduced or eliminated. Mallet/stick selection for percussion will contribute to this goal.

Unit 6: Musical Elements

Numerous musical elements introduce (or reinforce) important concepts to the young student, including: time signatures (4/4; 3/4), key signature (B-flat major), written dynamics (*piano, mezzopiano, mezzoforte,* and *forte*), phrase markings (breath mark), terminology (allegro, moderato, allegro moderato, ritardando, divisi), and the graphic representation for *crescendo* (expanding lines) and *decrescendo* (contracting lines). Articulation markings are restricted to the use of staccato (second movement only), a few two-note slurs (all movements), and the occasional use of accented (>) notes in the percussion parts.

Elledge notes in the score that, during the Baroque period, the practice of terraced dynamics would apply in performance. In a seemingly contradictory scoring practice, Elledge liberally applies graphic notation (expanding and contracting lines) to indicate changes in volume. These markings are not part of Handel's original score and therefore are left to the interpretation of the conductor.

As noted above (See Unit 3: Historical Perspective) the *gavotte* is defined by a six quarter-note and one half-note rhythm. In *Ariodante*, the music used as source material for the first movement is derived from the *ballo* that occurs near the end of Act I. Elledge has rebarred Handel's music so that the previously illustrated rhythm is notated as follows:

Whether or not this editorial change is of consequence depends on how the conductor "hears" the effect of this rhythm on the melodic and harmonic lines. In the traditional Baroque *gavotte*, a natural emphasis occurs on the third quarter note and the half note (by virtue of falling on the first beat of the measure, all things being equal). In Elledge's adaptation, the natural emphasis falls on the first and fifth quarter notes. It could be argued that as a Grade 1.5 arrangement, this distinction has little meaning to the intended performers, but conductors may wish to keep this editorialized rhythm in mind if preparing the suite for contest or festival performance.

Elledge has made numerous additional changes to Handel's original material. Handel scored the *gavotte* material in F major, the *musette* material in D major, and the *chorus* material in G major. Elledge has transposed all sections of the suite to B-flat major. It is also noteworthy that, in addition to the rebarred *gavotte* rhythm (explained above), Elledge also transformed the *musette* music from 6/8 time to 3/4 time. The third movement receives a similar metric adjustment and all of Handel's original rhythms have been doubled (eighth notes become quarter notes, etc.), presumably to facilitate easier reading among young band students. These rhythmic transformations are less critical to correct performance, as they do not inherently change the natural metric emphasis.

Unit 7: Form and Structure

The first movement, "Gavotte," is in ABCA form with an added repeat of the first A section.

SECTION	MEASURE	EVENT AND SCORING
A	1–8	Theme I, key of B-flat major; measures 7 and 8 cadence to dominant chord (F triad); the section repeats
B	9–16	Theme II, key of G minor
C	17–22	Theme III, transition back to B-flat major
A'	23–32	Return of Theme I with slight variation, key of B-flat major

The second movement, "Musette," is in AABA form with a repeat of the last two sections to produce an overall AABABA form.

SECTION	MEASURE	EVENT AND SCORING
A	1–8	Theme I, key of B-flat major; melody in flutes and oboe
A	9–16	Theme I, key of B-flat major; melody in clarinet, alto clarinet, bass clarinet, bassoon, baritone sax, trombone and baritone
B	17–24	Theme II, key of B-flat major; melody in flutes and clarinets adding trumpets at measure 21
A	25–32	Return of Theme I, key of B-flat major
	33–34	Second ending to facilitate repeat of final B/A sections

The third movement, "Chorus," is in AABB form with an introduction and coda added by the arranger.

SECTION	MEASURE	EVENT AND SCORING
	1–4	Introduction, key of B-flat major.
A	5–12	Theme I, key of B-flat major; melody in low woodwinds and low brass
A	13–20	Theme I, key of B-flat major; melody in flutes, oboe, clarinets and trumpets with slight rhythmic variation from the first statement
B	21–28	Theme II, first phrase, key of B-flat major; melody in flutes and alto saxophones
B	29–36	Theme II, second phrase, key of B-flat major, melody in clarinets and trumpets with flutes added in measure 33; repeats back to measure 21
	37	Second ending measure to facilitate coda
	38–41	Coda

Unit 8: Suggested Listening

Ariodante, G. F. Handel (audio recording)
> Freiburger Baroqueorchester (McGegan); Harmonia Mundi, ASIN: B0000007ET

Ariodante, G. F. Handel (audio recording)
> Les Musiciens du Louvre (Minkowski); Archiv Produktion, ASIN: B0000060AK

Ariodante, G. F. Handel (audio recording)
> Munich Bavarian State Orchestra (Bolton); Farao Records, ASIN: B0006B2AEC

Unit 9: Additional References and Resources

Ariodante, G. F. Handel (DVD)
> English National Opera (Bolton), Image Entertainment, 1996. ASIN: B000055XSK

Dean, W. *The New Grove Handel*. New York: W.W. Norton & Company, 1997.

Hogwood, C. *Handel*. New York: Thames & Hudson, 1997.

Lang, P. H. *George Frideric Handel*. Mineola, NY: Dover Publications, 1996.

Contributed by:

Patrick Dunnigan
Florida State University
Tallahassee, Florida

Teacher Resource Guide

Ave Verum Corpus, K. 618
Wolfgang Amadeus Mozart
(1756–1791)

arranged by Mark Williams
(b. 1955)

Unit 1: Composer

Born into an artistic family, Wolfgang Amadeus Mozart was trained by his father, Leopold. As children, Wolfgang and his sister Maria traveled with their father throughout Europe, where the siblings astounded audiences with their virtuosic abilities. Mozart began writing music at a very young age and left an exhaustive compositional catalogue including opera, concerti, string quartets, and symphonies, as well as *harmonie* and choral music.

Unit 2: Composition

Ave Verum Corpus was written for Mozart's friend Anton Stoll, a school teacher and choir director in the small town of Baden, near Vienna. The work was originally scored for SATB choir, string orchestra, and organ. Mr. Williams's modern-day setting is for winds and percussion—glockenspiel, suspended cymbal, and timpani—and includes an optional piano accompaniment. The arrangement is written in E-flat major, one-half step higher than Mozart's original score.

Unit 3: Historical Perspective

Composed during the Turkish War (1787–1792), *Ave Verum Corpus*, K. 618, was written in June 1791. *Così fan tutte*, K. 588, had just received its premiere in Vienna one year earlier. Drawing from the Latin text, *Ave Verum Corpus* translates:

> Praise the true body
> Formed from the Virgin Mary
> Having suffered, sacrificed on the cross for man
> Whose side was pierced
> Water flowed with blood
> Before the body broken in the agony of death

Unit 4: Technical Considerations

The work requires sustained, broad phrases at a slow tempo (adagio, quarter note = 66). Intervalic leaps must be equally balanced to provide clarity through the tessitura and the contour of each line should be treated with special attention.

Unit 5: Stylistic Considerations

Use a rehearsal plan to implement pedagogical strategies and exercises in the areas of tone development, breath support, and ear training while preparing the work. The conductor may use several singing exercises, including but not limited to: harmonic and melodic arpeggios, chord progressions, and individual parts. To further encourage active listening, incorporate descriptive rehearsal phrases such as "fit inside the sound," "join the [horns]," and/or "color the texture with your sound." Couple discussions on period performance practices, with appropriate listening examples, into rehearsals as well.

Worthy of note, on beat three of measure 20, Mr. Williams rhythmically notates the would-be ornamentation (eighth-note grace followed by a quarter note) to represent the correct performance practice of Mozart's day in which the grace notes were performed on the beat.

Unit 6: Musical Elements

MELODY:
The melody incorporates broad leaps requiring the musicians to thoroughly support the line. The conductor must ensure that the lower notes speak at the same volume as the upper notes.

RHYTHM:
Because much of the composition is homorhythmic, it is crucial to give full attention to the direction of every line. All lines must possess forward motion, while creating a sense of contemplation and reflection (see Unit 3).

HARMONY:

With few minor alterations, Mr. Williams's arrangement retains Mozart's harmonic language and structure including: dominant and diminished-seventh chords, tonal modulations to flat keys, as well as ascending and descending chromatic pitches. These elements may require younger musicians to play in unfamiliar tonal areas; therefore, a thorough knowledge of pitch adjustment techniques and concepts—alternate fingerings, finger shadings, just intonation, and intonation tendencies—are beneficial.

TIMBRE:

Musicians should listen to vocal and string recordings of eighteenth-century music to better understand appropriate timbre and sound concepts. Due to the arrangement's orchestrational doublings, the conductor may also consider experimenting with the scoring.

Unit 7: Form and Structure

Ave Verum Corpus is through-composed and grouped into three larger sections.

SECTION	MEASURE	EVENT AND SCORING
Introduction	1–2	E-flat; reeds, horns, & low brass; *piano*
A	3–17	Tutti
Transition/ Cadential extension	18–21	B-flat; flutes, reeds, & low brass; *mezzo piano*
B	22–29	B-flat; tutti; *pianissimo*; moves to flat keys: D-flat & G-flat; returns to E-flat
C	30–46	E-flat; tutti, sans flute & oboe (m. 34: flute & oboe enter); *piano*

Unit 8: Suggested Listening

Mozart, Wolfgang Amadeus. "Adagio, Clarinet Concerto in A, K. 622." *Mozart: Clarinet Concerto, K. 622* and *Sinfonia concertante, K. 297b.* Sabine Meyer, et al. EMI Classics, 1990. Compact Disc.

Mozart, Wolfgang Amadeus. "Adagio, Serenade No. 10, K. 361 (370a)." *Mozart: Serenade No. 10.* H. Robert Reynolds. Koch International Classics, 2007. Compact Disc.

Mozart, Wolfgang Amadeus. *Mozart: Great Mass in C*. John Eliot Gardner, et al. Philips, 1990. Compact Disc.

Mozart, Wolfgang Amadeus. *Mozart: Requiem*. John Eliot Gardner, et al. Philips, 2005. Compact Disc.

Unit 9: Additional References and Resources

Landon, H. C. Robbins. *1971: Mozart's Last Year*. New York: Schirmer Books, 1988.

Mozart, Wolfgang Amadeus, and Spaethling, Robert. *Mozart's Letters, Mozart's Life: Selected Letters*. New York: W. W. Norton & Company, 2000.

Zaslaw, Neal. *The Classical Era: From the 1740's to the End of the 18th Century (Man & Music)*. London: Macmillan/ Prentice Hall, 1990.

Zaslaw, Neal. *The Complete Mozart: A Guide to the Musical Works of Wolfgang Amadeus Mozart*. New York: W. W. Norton & Co., 1990.

Contributed by:

Glen Scott Bersaglia
Assistant Director of Bands
University of Michigan
Ann Arbor, Michigan

Teacher Resource Guide

Bartók Variations

Timothy Broege
(b. 1947)

Unit 1: Composer

Timothy Broege was born in Belmar, New Jersey and as a child studied piano and music theory with Helen Antonides. He studied composition with M. William Karlins, Alan Stout, and Anthony Donato, piano with Frances Larimer, and harpsichord with Dorothy Lane at Northwestern University. He received a bachelor of music degree, with highest honors in 1969. From 1969 to 1980 Broege taught elementary school music in the public schools of Chicago, Illinois and Manasquan, New Jersey. He currently works as organist and director of music at First Presbyterian Church in Belmar, a position he has held since 1972, and organist and director of music at the historic Elberon Memorial Church in Elberon, New Jersey. Broege taught piano and recorder from 1985 to 1995 at the Monmouth Conservatory of Music in Red Bank, New Jersey.

Timothy Broege has composed more than sixty works for band that range from educational pieces to major staples in the wind literature. He appears frequently as a guest composer/conductor and clinician, and received the Edwin Franko Goldman Award from the American School Band Directors' Association in 1994. To honor his compositional career and contributions, Broege received the 2003 Award of Excellence from the New Jersey Education Association. He is a past-president of the Composers Guild of New Jersey, Inc., a member of the Organ Historical Society, and an affiliate of Broadcast Music, Inc. (BMI). In addition to his compositional activities, Timothy Broege is an active recitalist on early keyboard instruments and recorder, and maintains a teaching studio at his home in Bradley Beach, New Jersey.

155

Unit 2: Composition

Bartók Variations, written in 2003, is a Grade 2 work from Grand Mesa Music Publishers. The composition is a theme and variations, with the theme based upon Volume 1, No. 3, "Andante," from Béla Bartók's collection of piano pieces, *For Children*. Like many pieces in the *For Children* collection, the composition has the character of a Hungarian or eastern European folk song and should be performed with considerable expressive freedom as is found in all folk music. The melody is clearly stated in the opening measures, and is followed by three variations that focus on the various melodic, harmonic, and rhythmic features of the theme and its accompaniment. Scoring is for standard wind band; percussion scoring calls for timpani, crash and suspended cymbals, bells, chimes, triangle, tambourine, wood block, snare drum, and bass drum. The composition is approximately two minutes and forty-five seconds in length.

Unit 3: Historical Perspective

Béla Bartók (1881–1945) was perhaps the foremost twentieth-century representative of nationalism in music, and was also an inspiration to other nationalist composers. The son of amateur musicians, Béla Bartók studied piano and composition at the Budapest Academy of Music and later returned as a piano instructor. Bartók had a lifetime fascination with folk music, and along with fellow composer and friend, Zoltán Kodály, collected recordings of Hungarian folk music using an Edison cylinder. In the early 1920s Bartók's music was verging on an atonal style, but by the 1930s it took on a more neoclassical approach. The crises leading up to World War II forced Bartók to leave Hungary and settle in the United States, where he briefly held teaching appointments at Columbia and Harvard. His most notable pedagogic contributions were the teaching editions he made of the works of Bach, Haydn, Mozart, and Beethoven, and the pieces he composed for children. Bartók also made major contributions to the standard repertoire of the symphony, the concerto, piano music, and the string quartet.

For Children, written in 1908 and 1909, is a collection of eighty-five piano pieces based on Hungarian and Slovakian folk-tunes. Bartók revised the collection in the 1930s and 1940s, adding thirteen new pieces while reducing the total number to seventy-nine. Described as little teaching pieces for beginners, the pieces are a direct reflection of Bartók's interest in folk music. The melodies, in various modes, are coupled with simple accompaniments that preserve the original character of the music. Arrangements by Larry Clark, *Bartók Suite*; Walter Finlayson, *Three Pieces for Band*; and William Schaefer, *Four Sketches*, will provide additional opportunities for musicians and listeners to share in the beauty and richness of the folk song traditions found in the music of Béla Bartók.

Unit 4: Technical Considerations

Bartók Variations opens in 2/4 time and shifts to 4/4 time at the beginning of Variation 1. The tonality is centered in G minor but the final chord of the piece is G major. Staying true to the original piano piece, the opening andante tempo, quarter note=72, moves to a moderate allegetto in the third variation, quarter note=90, but always with considerable expressive freedom, as is indicative of folk music. The basic rhythmic challenges use combinations of whole, dotted half, half, quarter, and eighth notes. The percussion parts are not difficult, but require careful counting of rests to ensure a musically sound performance. The tambourine and snare drum parts require players to maintain an even eighth-note/quarter-note rhythm pattern and eighth note ostinato, respectively, with consistency of pulse at the *p* and *pp* dynamic levels.

Unit 5: Stylistic Considerations

A musically effective performance of *Bartók Variations* requires all wind players to understand legato, staccato, and tenuto styles and to cleanly articulate tongued and slurred eighth-note passages in the composition while negotiating leaps of a third or a fifth. Four-measure phrases are found throughout the work, while call-and-response patterns appear in the theme and all variations. Balance is an important performance aspect as students must be fully aware of the melody and its various manipulations, which are explored in each variation. Sustained voices must pay particular attention to dynamic levels and work to play lightly under the melody at all times. Writing for the percussionists is thoughtful, even graceful, and provides the appropriate colors and rhythmic direction in each variation.

Unit 6: Musical Elements

MELODY:

Timothy Broege derives the theme of *Bartók Variations* directly from Etude No. 3 from Volume 1 of *For Children*. Broege suggests playing a recording of the piano piece for the ensemble, or having someone perform the etude for the band, so the musicians can begin to understand the structure and flowing nature of the composition. The conductor may also wish to have the students sing the theme-and-variation melodies to help develop a lyrical style.

Although the melody is divided among different sections, it should be stressed that the melodic line be performed in a connected manner resulting in a "seamless" ensemble sound. With leaps of a third, fourth, and fifth in the various melodies wind players will need to adjust the air speed to maintain the melancholic character of each.

HARMONY:

The harmonic structure of this work is centered in G minor. Some chromatic writing appears as the second variation briefly moves away from G minor, but soon returns in the final variation.

Of interest is the final chord of the piece, as Broege chooses to end the work with a G major chord. The conductor can have the ensemble play the chord as written and then lower the third as a starting point for explaining major and minor tonalities to the ensemble.

RHYTHM:

The ensemble should easily understand the rhythms presented in *Bartók Variations*. The challenge will be in performing with the apposite "ebb and flow" that is found in folk music. Students should be comfortable playing the phrases in a variety of ways and, as an exercise, be encouraged to demonstrate their interpretations for the class. Following the lead of the conductor, the ensemble can use this work to further develop the concepts of musical sensitivity and interpretation.

TIMBRE:

The timbre and color of this work is representative of Timothy Broege's compositional style. His skillful orchestration is clear and never cluttered, but musicians must be sensitive to the role of the melody and the need for it to be heard at the softer dynamic levels. Broege cleverly presents the theme and variations in a variety of instrumental combinations, creating colors not typically heard in music at this grade level. The interesting percussion writing, while not overly demanding requires a light, precise touch to create the appropriate rhythmic presence and drive. The combination of musical independence and challenge creates an attractive piece that holds up to repeated rehearsals and performances.

Unit 7: Form and Structure

SECTION	MEASURE	EVENT AND SCORING
Theme	1–10	The first half of the melody is presented by the flute and oboe, and is passed to trumpet 1 in measure 5
	11–25	The theme is restated by the woodwinds and answered by trumpet 1 with tutti chordal accompaniment in the low winds; the opening section closes on a unison G

SECTION	MEASURE	EVENT AND SCORING
Variation 1	26–34	The rhythmic variation is introduced by the tambourine ostinato with the melodic material presented in a call-and-response manner by the lower and upper winds
Variation 2	35–42	The second variation begins with a new melodic pattern that is an inversion of the melody presented in measure 15; this section also serves as a transition between the first and third variations
Variation 3	43–55	The third variation begins quietly in the woodwinds and horns before the snare drum and selected winds begin an eighth-note ostinato that introduces a section of canonic imitation; the canonic imitation is initiated by the flutes and trumpet 1, followed by the entrances of clarinet 1 and alto saxophone 1; the third canon is presented by the low winds and appears as an augmented form of the original melody
Coda	56–62	The coda begins with a bold, dynamic statement, again in an augmented form, by the full band that *crescendos* to the final G major chord

Unit 8: Suggested Listening

Béla Bartók:
    Bartók Suite, arr. Larry Clark
    Dance Suite, for orchestra
    For Children, Volume I and II, for piano
    Four Sketches, arr. William Schaefer
    Hungarian Sketches, for orchestra
    Mikrokosmos, Volume II, *for piano*
    Three Pieces for Band, arr. Walter Finlayson
Timothy Broege:
    Jody
    Sinfonia VI, "The Four Elements"
    Sinfonia XVI, "Transcendental Vienna"
    Song with Variations
    Theme and Variations
    Train Heading West and Other Outdoor Scenes

Unit 9: Additional References and Resources

Boulden, George. Interview with Timothy Broege. May 21, 2007.

Broege, Timothy. Homepage. http://www.timothybroege.com (accessed April 21, 2007).

Camphouse, Mark, ed. *Composers on Composing for Band*. Chicago: GIA Publications, 2002.

Dvorak, Thomas L., ed. *Best Music for Young Band*. New York: Manhattan Beach Music, 2005.

Kvet, Edward J., ed. *Instructional Literature for Middle-Level Band*. Reston, VA: Music Educators National Conference, 1996.

Margolis, Bob, ed. *Best Music for Beginning Band*. New York: Manhattan Beach Music, 2000.

Miles, Richard, ed. *Teaching Music through Performance in Band*, Volumes 1–6. Chicago: GIA Publications, 1997, 1998, 2000, 2002, 2005, and 2006.

Miles, Richard, and Thomas Dvorak, eds. *Teaching Music through Performance in Beginning Band*. Chicago: GIA Publications, 2001.

Poultney, David. *Studying Music History*. Upper Saddle River, NJ: Prentice-Hall, 1996.

Salzman, Timothy, ed. *A Composer's Insight*, Volume 1. Galesville, MD: Meredith Music, 2003.

Contributed by:

George R. Boulden
Associate Director of Bands
University of Kentucky
Lexington, Kentucky

Teacher Resource Guide

Bells of Freedom

David R. Gillingham
(b. 1947)

Unit 1: Composer

Born in Waukesha, Wisconsin in 1947, David Ronald Gillingham was raised in a largely rural dairy land setting. He began piano study at age ten, and later taught himself to play the organ. By age twelve he was performing as a church organist. Participating in the local school band program, he emerged as an excellent performer on the euphonium.

David Gillingham attended the University of Wisconsin-Oshkosh, earning the bachelor of music degree in music education in 1969. Afterward, he was inducted into the U. S. Army as a musician, performing with the 266th Headquarters Army Band in Vietnam. Following military service, Gillingham returned to Oshkosh where he taught middle school band for four years. He returned to UW-Oshkosh for graduate studies, and was awarded the master of music in 1977. In 1980 Gillingham entered the doctoral program at Michigan State University, where he earned the doctor of philosophy degree in music theory and composition. His composition teachers and mentors include Roger Dennis, Jere Hutcheson, James Niblock, and H. Owen Reed.

Dr. Gillingham is an internationally recognized, award-winning, and prolific composer. He has written for various genres, but the majority of his compositions are for wind band, and it is in this area that he is most widely acclaimed. His works are performed frequently by professional and collegiate ensembles, as well as school bands.

Since 1984, David Gillingham has served on the faculty of Central Michigan University as professor of music. At CMU he has been the recipient of an Excellence in Teaching Award (1990), a Summer Fellowship (1991), a Research Professorship (1995), and recently, the President Research Investment Fund grant for his co-authorship of a proposal to establish an International Center for New Music at Central Michigan University. He is a member of ASCAP and the recipient of the ASCAP Standard Award for Composers of Concert Music from 1996 to 2005.

Unit 2: Composition

Bells of Freedom is a concert march of approximately four minutes duration, written expressly for beginning band and published by C. Alan Publications. The march gives young musicians a chance to explore and experience music on three different levels. First, the composer wrote the march with patriotic suggestions, borrowing melodic snippets of *The Star-Spangled Banner* to construct thematic material within the march's first, second, and final strains. Chimes, along with other standard military march percussion instruments, also add to the work's overall patriotic flavor.

Second, the march was intentionally composed with simplicity in mind, and allows young musicians to experience in music of the march, while remaining technically reasonable.

Finally, although the majority of Gillingham's compositions are designed for professional, collegiate, and/or advanced high school bands, *Bells of Freedom* introduces young people to a body of music composed by a highly significant and prolific composer, whose they will likely encounter again and again as they progress as band musicians.

Unit 3: Historical Perspective

Bells of Freedom was composed in 2001, and published by C. Alan Publications in 2002. While it is the only Grade 1 band piece Gillingham has written, his creative output totals well over seventy original compositions, the majority of which are for wind band. Given the stature and significance of the composer many other works for wind band, *Bells of Freedom* can be considered an excellent, if not vital entry point for young musicians into David Gillingham's music.

Unit 4: Technical Considerations

Bells of Freedom poses few technical challenges related to rhythm, range, or facility. However, there are a few notable exceptions, summarized by the composer in his own words:

There are a few issues that will make this march a bit more challenging than the standard fare of Grade 1 band works. First, there is a feature by the chimes. Though bells can be substituted, I strongly urge you to use the chimes, as the patriotic flavor of the work is much enhanced by this timbre. Consider featuring an older player on this part if there is not a percussionist who seems up to task for this part. Secondly, the range of the flute extends to the high C, which may be a note that has not been taught at this early stage, but certainly one in which the fingering can be easily learned. Thirdly, note the use of concert A-flat in measures 26 and 27 in the beginning and the addition of concert D-flat in measures 46, 49, 74 and 79. The A-flat is certainly not a new note, but its placement in the key of B-flat major is somewhat unusual. The D-flat, however, will be a new note for all involved.

—Notes by David Gillingham
from *Bells of Freedom* score

WINDS:

The requirement for flutists to play up to C6, and for the entire band to learn to finger and play concert pitches A-flat and D-flat have already been noted by the composer in the above information from the *Bells of Freedom* score notes.

PERCUSSION:

Beyond the challenge of the chime part, the conductor ought to consider other performance issues pertinent to the entire percussion section:

Percussion 1 – This part can be performed by a single player, or shared between two students if desired. The part requires a player to alternate between playing chimes and orchestra bells throughout. Whenever the player is required to change instruments, there is sufficient time (rests) in between passages to move from one instrument to another, and thus cover the part alone. However, given the difficulty level of the chime part in particular, the overall performance might be more secure with one player on chimes and the other on bells. Further, more students can be involved by using two players on this part. If the chime part proves too difficult, the composer suggestion to enlist an older player may be a wise and practical solution. A final consideration, because of the significant height of most chimes, some younger players may not be tall enough to effectively play the instrument.

Percussion 2 – This part can be played by a single player, or shared among three performers, if desired. Three instruments are included in the part: triangle, crash cymbals, and xylophone. While there is ample time during rests for a single player to move from one instrument to another, sharing the part between two or three players will likely ensure greater performance security and allow for increased student participation.

Percussion 3 – This part calls for snare drum only. However, the conductor may consider having the part doubled to allow for increased student participation, provided that this does not over-balance the rest of the ensemble. Tripling or quadrupling the snare drum part among three or four players is not recommended. The part requires the ability to perform alternated sixteenth-note passages and single flams. Neither rolls, nor other more technically advanced rudiments are ever called for in this work.

Percussion 4 – Three instruments are included in the part: tom-tom, bass drum, and suspended cymbal. While there is ample time during rests for a single player to move from one instrument to another and cover the part without assistance, sharing the part between two, or among three players may ensure greater performance security and will allow for increased student participation.

A final technical consideration has to do with the work's overall duration. The performance of *Bells of Freedom* requires the beginners to play for four minutes at one sitting. Compared to other shorter pieces typical for this age group, the longer duration will likely challenge youngsters with a prolonged mental concentration and physical endurance beyond that which they may be typically accustomed.

Unit 5: Stylistic Considerations

Clear, uniform articulations are a stylistic necessity for the performance of any march, and *Bells of Freedom* is no exception. However, since the piece is rhythmically simple and technically straightforward, younger players can easily attain clarity and uniformity of articulation and style. Sections containing pitches of longer duration, such as those found in the Trio, provide contrasting stylistic concepts, such as marcato vs. legato, to be learned and performed from section to section.

Unit 6: Musical Elements

MELODY:

Because the composer borrows from *The Star-Spangled Banner* for the melodic ideas in the march first, second, and final strains, the primary passages are predictably tonal and recognizable. Thus, the melodies throughout are not only obvious, but easily performable.

HARMONY:

Bells of Freedom is a clearly tonal work, grounded primarily in the key of B-flat major during the march's first half (Intro, First, and Second Strain); and primarily in E-flat major during the second half (Trio, break strain, final strain, and coda). Occasionally, flatted sevenths are employed for quick and brief modulations to the IV chord, such as in the Trio at measures 74 and 75. The break strain is written in C minor, the relative minor key of E-flat major, but soon modulates back to the Trio's home key. Tension is created by the occasional use of unresolved seconds and/or ninths against the primary tonic chord in the first and last strains.

RHYTHM:
The predominant rhythms found throughout include quarter, half, dotted-half, and whole notes. Eighth notes appear sparingly, in simple and straightforward constructions. Articulation is required for the majority of the work, since slurs are seldom used, and when they do appear they never contain more than two notes at a time. Therefore, the piece teaches youngsters to master contrasting yet technically simple styles of articulation.

TIMBRE:
Bells of Freedom is comprised of fuller band scoring for the preponderance, ensuring confident sonorities and ensemble security. The piece features percussion, the chimes in particular, in short exposed passages, to which the winds respond in full.

Unit 7: Form and Structure

Bells of Freedom follows a typical march structure. It contains an Intro, First Strain, Second Strain, Trio Introduction, Trio, Break Strain, and Final Strain. However, the phrase lengths are not always symmetrical, and the march concludes with an extended Coda. A snapshot of the march's overall form is:

SECTION	MEASURE	PRIMARY KEY CENTER
Intro	1–8	B-flat major
1st Strain	9–20	B-flat major
2nd Strain	21–34	B-flat major
Trio Intro	35–38	Transitional
Trio	39–58	E-flat major
Break Strain	59–66	C minor
Last Strain	67–84	E-flat/A-flat/E-flat major
Extended Coda	85–104	E-flat major

A more specific outline of form, events, and scoring follows:

SECTION	MEASURE	EVENT AND SCORING
Intro	1–8	Chimes, snare drum, tom-tom, and triangle present the opening three measures; all wind sections, except trumpets, join in measures 4 and 5, presenting a repetitive four-note rhythmic pattern (quarter – two eighths – quarter) that begins on beat three of each measure, and moves to beat one of the next; the four-note pattern becomes varied when it begins on beat 2 (two eighths – quarter – quarter)
First Strain	9–20	As the simple rhythmic pattern based on unison B-flat pitches first established in measure 5 continues, the trumpet section introduces and performs the melody; this is a clearly recognizable melody, as it is borrowed from the opening phrase of *The Star-Spangled Banner*; flutes and oboes occasionally reinforce the ongoing rhythmic pattern played by the rest of the band, but the flutes, on high C, add a kind of major-second/major-ninth tension to the overall sonority; the phrasing structure of the first strain is not symmetrical; rather, the measures group themselves as units of five, four, and three
Second Strain	21–34	This section begins with a more legato milieu and lighter overall texture, as the woodwinds and bells assume the unison melody, while brass remain silent during the first four measures; like the first strain, the second strain woodwind melody also presents material borrowed from *The Star-Spangled Banner*, this time based on the original's "rockets red glare" phrase

SECTION	MEASURE	EVENT AND SCORING
Second Strain	25–28	Trumpets reinforce the woodwind melody as the remainder of the brass section strengthen the texture and energize the phrase with three-note (two eighths – quarter) rhythmic punctuations derived from material used in the first strain; together, all voices *crescendo* over these four measures, and become even further energized in measures 27 and 28 by the snare drum sixteenth-note activity
Second Strain	29–32	These four measures contain a strong, stately reiteration of material from the first strain, namely a more assertive utterance of the "Oh Say, Can You See" phrase from *The Star Spangled Banner*
Perc. Reprise	32–34	Like the introduction, percussion instruments, unaccompanied by winds, are featured during these measures, where the chimes are again given predominance
Trio Intro	35–38	Similar to the five-note pattern first played by the winds in measure 4, simple unison B-flat pitches are presented in measure 35 and repeated in measure 36; these give way to sustained whole notes in measures 27 and 28, and finally resolve on a B-flat dominant seventh chord that puts in motion an expectation for the music to change key centers
Trio	39–46	As is typical of nearly all marches, the Trio section of *Bells of Freedom* contrasts conspicuously from the march's first half; first, the Trio is cast in a new key, E-flat major, written a perfect fourth higher than the original home key of B-flat major; second, the Trio is more legato, using slurred groups of notes (never more than two at a time), and other more sustained durations such as half, dotted-half, and whole notes; third, the Trio begins *piano*

SECTION	MEASURE	EVENT AND SCORING
		in all the parts except clarinet and bass clarinet; finally, the Trio's melody is played in unison by lower-voiced instruments (bassoon, bass clarinet, tenor sax, baritone sax, trombone, baritone, and tuba), and is harmonized at the third by low-register clarinets and alto sax; upper register flutes, oboes, and trumpets are omitted during the Trio's first six measures to soften the texture as the Trio begins; these voices, however, are added as bell tones in measures 45 and 46 before becoming melody with the rest of the band at measure 47; the Trio's first eight measures conclude with a V7/IV, stimulating modulation to A-flat major
Trio	47–58	A brief modulation to A-flat major occurs at measure 47, but then modulates back to E-flat by measure 51; measures 51–56 rise and fall dynamically before settling at measures 57 and 58
Break Strain	59–66	The "Sturm und Drang" typically associated with break strains is created by contrasts of key center (now in C-minor), dynamics (here abruptly marked to *forte*), and rhythms (in contrast to the Trio, constructed in vertically accented eighth and quarter notes); measures 65 and 66 set up the modulation back to E-flat major
Last Strain	67–74	Horns, trombones, and baritones present a sturdy and jubilant *fortissimo* melody while flutes, oboes, bells, and xylophone provide a simple yet musically interesting counter line of eighth notes, constructed and repeated five times as a *hemiola* over measures 67–70; the flutes, oboes, and bells, fortified by clarinets, alto sax, and trumpets, assume the melody in measures 71–74

SECTION	MEASURE	EVENT AND SCORING
Last Strain	75–84	The last strain's primary melody is reiterated, along with varied, yet harmonically interesting counter lines; increased rhythmic energy is produced in measures 79–84 by the repeated quarter-eighth-note rhythms played by the flutes and oboes on a unison B-flat
Transition	85–88	A dramatic cadential conclusion of the last strain merges with the beginning of these transitional bars, which essentially contain a derivation of the march's original percussion introduction; the chimes again predominate, and sternly reinforce tonic-dominant undulations of E-flat and B-flat major, respectively
Coda	89–93	Flutes, oboes, clarinets, alto saxophones, trumpets and horns assertively re-enter with the Coda material, which is based on the melody from the phrase "For the Land of the Free, and the Home of the Brave!"
Extension	94–104	Measures 94–98 feature percussion playing with great energy as the entire band dramatically sustains a seven-six suspension (concert A-flat), which finally resolves in measure 99; measures 99–102 feature even more dominant-tonic undulations reminiscent of a *Beethovenesque* extended coda, and lead to the final *forte-piano crescendo* of measures 103 and 104

Unit 8: Suggested Listening

Francis Scott Key/arr. Jack Stamp, *The Star-Spangled Banner*
Edwin Franko Goldman, *The Chimes of Liberty March*
John Philip Sousa, *The Liberty Bell March*

Unit 9: Additional References and Resources

Camphouse, Mark, ed. *Composers on Composing for Band.* "David Gillingham". Chicago: GIA Publications, Inc., 2002.

Conductor's Score Notes. *Bells of Freedom.* Greensboro, NC: C. Alan Publications, 2002.

Gillingham, David. *Bells of Freedom* score & audio samples. C. Alan Publications Web site: http://www.c-alanpublications.com/composers/gillingham-david.html

Gillingham, David. Composer's personal Web site: http://www.gillinghammusic.com

Miles, Richard, and Carl Chevallard, eds. *Teaching Music through Performing Marches.* Chicago: GIA Publications, 2003.

Contributed by:

David Martin Booth
Director of Bands
Wright State University
Dayton, Ohio

Teacher Resource Guide

Brother James' Air

James Leith Macbeth Bain
(b. 1860–1925)

arranged by Douglas E. Wagner
(b. 1952)

Unit 1: Composer

Very little has been written about James Leith Macbeth Bain, the composer of the hymn tune known as *Brother James's Air*. Since he was a spiritualist and humanitarian rather than a composer, there is no mention of him in music encyclopedias or dictionaries. An article entitled "Brother James and his Air" by Bernard S. Massey provides a wealth of information on what we would now call a "one-hit wonder."

Bain was born on November 21, 1860, in the picturesque village of Moulin, Perthshire in Scotland, about 70 miles north-northwest of Edinburgh. He was "a quiet and gentle soul with, it was said, the heart of a little child."[1] Some sources refer to Bain as a monk, but he was not one in the ecclesiastical sense. Instead he was "a mystical poet, writer, pamphleteer and faith healer."[2] Most of his books were on spiritualist themes and were published by the Theosophical Publishing House in London. Theosophy is less a religion than a state of mind. According to Pratt:

> The fundamental teaching of the ancient wisdom is the spiritual unity of all things...Rejecting the idea of a God existing outside nature, theosophy speaks of an all-pervading divine essence, an infinite ocean of consciousness, from which all things are born and to which they ultimately return. The human kingdom is one of the phases of experience that each god-spark must pass through during its long evolutionary journey through the worlds of matter.[3]

An early proponent of a healthy lifestyle, Brother James "was an ardent vegetarian and spent much time in the open air. In one of his many books, *The Barefoot League* (1914), he extolled the delights and benefits of walking barefoot whenever possible."[4] In the role of faith healer, Bain founded The Brotherhood of Healers in 1906 and "was frequently called upon to exercise powers of healing especially among the poor. The healing process involved singing to the afflicted—and no doubt his 'Air' was part of the repertoire for that purpose."[5]

Brother James passed away on September 19, 1925 at a garden party at the Kelmscott Children's Home in Wallasey, across the Mersey River from Liverpool. Bain had been living with his sister in West Kirby on the Wirral Peninsula where he would minister to the poor in the slums in and around Liverpool.[6] It was this ministry that earned him the name "Brother James."

The arranger of Brother James's simple tune is Douglas E. Wagner, a Chicago native and graduate of Butler University. He taught choir and hand-bells at North Central High School in Indianapolis for more than thirty years and was head of the Performing Arts Department. He has written more than 1,600 works for choir, concert band, orchestra, handbells, piano, organ, and voice.[7] His band arrangements of folk songs and hymn tunes are simple yet artistic in the use of countermelody, harmony and orchestration. They are playable by young bands but have a mature sound that makes them appropriate for high school, college and community bands as well. Wagner has arranged several lyrical works for band in the same style as *Brother James' Air*, including *O Tannenbaum, Slane* (Be Thou My Vision), *O Waly, Waly* (The Water Is Wide) and *Jasmine Flower*.

Unit 2: Composition

The hymn *Brother James' Air* is like its composer—quiet, gentle and childlike. The hymn tune is in an AAB form and its text is a rhymed and metered version of the Twenty-Third Psalm, found in *The Scottish Psalter*:

> The Lord's my shepherd, I'll not want. He makes me down to lie
> In pastures green: he leadeth me the quiet waters by.
> He leadeth me, he leadeth me the quiet waters by.
>
> My soul he doth restore again; and me to walk doth make
> Within the paths of righteousness, ev'n for his own name's sake.
> Within the paths of righteousness, ev'n for his own name's sake.

Yea, though I walk in death's dark vale, yet will I fear
    none ill:
For thou art with me; and thy rod and staff me comfort still.
For thou art with me; and thy rod and staff me comfort still.

My table thou hast furnished in presence of my foes;
My head thou dost with oil anoint, and my cup overflows.
My head thou dost with oil anoint, and my cup overflows.

Goodness and mercy all my life shall surely follow me:
And in God's house for evermore my dwelling-place shall be.
And in God's house for evermore my dwelling-place shall be.

In Wagner's arrangement, there is one note that is different from Bain's original. Following is the melody in solfeggio:

Bain: do-me-sol-do-sol-la-do-sol-fa-me-do-do-TI-do
Wagner:do-me-sol-do-sol-la-do-sol-fa-me-do-do-RE-do

The concert band arrangement uses the standard instrumentation but includes several doublings. There is only one clarinet and one trumpet part, neither of which divides. The horn part always doubles either alto sax or clarinet. Tenor sax, bassoon, baritone and trombone cover the tenor part and the bass part is played by bass clarinet, baritone sax and tuba. The percussion includes parts for chimes, bells, snare drum, bass drum, crash cymbals (one note four measures from the end), suspended cymbal and triangle. Some parts can be combined. The duration is about two minutes.

Unit 3: Historical Perspective

Massey relates the history of the hymn this way:

The first appearance of the famous "Air" seems to have been at the end of his [Bain's] book *The Great Peace* (4th edn, Theosophical Publishing Society, 1915). Here the tune is even more repetitive than the version now customary, since the first four bars do duty again at the end [AABA]. A four-part harmonization is provided but this is pretty basic. The piece appears under the name MAROSA, and the composer explains that it was named "after the seventh daughter of my friend Captain McLaren, whom I christened some years ago. The words are a version, slightly altered by me to suit the melody, of the old classic Shepherd-Psalm, that which I know of no more beautiful Hymn of Love."[8]

Brother James's Air would have probably remained an obscure hymn tune had it not been discovered by Gordon Jacob, who arranged it for unison voices and descant in 1932. "This setting soon became a runaway success with, it seems, almost every junior-school choir in the land. So Jacob, no doubt with an eye to his bank balance, also brought out versions for mixed voices (1934), SSA (1935) and Junior and SATB choirs combined (1958), to say nothing of instrumental arrangements. Indeed, he, not Brother James, has sometimes been credited as the composer."9

Unit 4: Technical Considerations

Wagner's arrangement of *Brother James' Air* is part of the *Belwin Beginning Band Series*. There are, however, some problems with trying to perform this with beginners. First, the hymn is in 3/4 time, which can be confusing for first year players, especially with the counterpoint involved. Second, there are a great many nuances throughout the piece: subtle dynamic swells, several tempo fluctuations (ritardando and *a tempo*), and the use of slurs and legato articulations. Third, the polyphonic texture, countermelodies, and lack of unison rhythms can be difficult for beginners. Four, the percussion writing provides atmosphere and color rather than a strict pulse with repetitive rhythms. The snare drummer must play a soft, sustained roll and sixteenth-note rhythms, and the other percussionists must be able to play isolated parts softly and tastefully and to wait for long stretches. Young percussionists will find this very challenging to their attention span.

On the easy side, ranges are within the bounds for first year players: Flutes play up to B-flat5, clarinets stay below the break and trumpets only go up to C5. The work is in B-flat major and accidentals are rare.

Unit 5: Stylistic Considerations

Style is the biggest challenge in *Brother James' Air*. The polyphonic texture, nuances in dynamics, tempo and articulation, and the sensitive percussion playing make this a very difficult piece for beginners. Directors should consider using this as a tone piece for more mature students as a respite from more demanding music, and as a beautiful interlude for the audience, possibly coupled with one of Wagner's other hymn tune arrangements mentioned above.

Unit 6: Musical Elements

MELODY:

The melody of *Brother James' Air* is simple and easy to hear. Players who do not have the melody could be directed to learn the tune by ear so eventually the entire band can play the melody together in unison. Directors could also provide the words from the Twenty-Third Psalm and have the band sing the tune.

HARMONY:

Wagner provides a rich harmony through the use of countermelodies, but an exercise in four-part chordal writing could be devised wherein students attempt to figure out what the basic underlying chords are, what the harmonic rhythm is and then write out a simpler hymn-style accompaniment to the melody.

RHYTHM:

If the piece is used with beginners, a rhythm sheet in 3/4 time using quarter- and eighth-note rhythms would be very helpful. Some of the instrument parts have an eighth-note rhythm pattern beginning on an upbeat in a few places, which first-year players do not normally encounter in their music.

TIMBRE:

Like the stylistic problems, the interplay between sections (especially phrases that elide or parts that move from melody to countermelody within a phrase) requires a mature control of tone and dynamics. Breathing exercises, including sizzling, will help students develop control, although it won't happen overnight.

Unit 7: Form and Structure

The form of *Brother James' Air* is rather straightforward: a four-bar intro followed by three statements of the hymn tune varied slightly by counterpoint, orchestration and embellishment. There is a four-bar bridge between each statement and a three-bar tag at the end. The artistry is not in melodic or formal development but in subtle variations that keep the ear listening and the mind interested.

Unit 8: Suggested Listening

Brother James's Air – hymn tune

Best Loved Hymns by the Choir of King's College, Cambridge, Stephen Cleobury, conductor (EMI Classics). A wonderful version for treble choir with harp accompaniment, and a great example of phrasing.

Ave Verum: Favourite Parish Anthems by the Clare College Chapel Choir, Timothy Brown, conductor (Guild GMCD–7109). Recording of the Gordon Jacob SATB arrangement.

The Oxford Book of Wedding Music by Jeremy Filsell, organ (Guild GMCD–7107). Recording of *Prelude on Brother James's Air* by Searle Wright. A contemporary treatment of the hymn tune.

Brother James's Air – concert band arrangement
    Recordings of other similar works by Douglas E. Wagner can be found at various Web sites including www.jwpepper.com and www.alfred.com:
        Jasmine Flower
        O Tannenbaum
        O Waly, Waly (The Water Is Wide)
        Slane (Be Thou My Vision)

Unit 9: Additional References and Resources

Massey, Bernard S. "Brother James and His Air." *Hymn Society of Great Britain and Ireland Bulletin* 6, No. 7, July 2001, 174–76.

Contributed by:

Donald Morris
Band Director, McClintock Middle School
Conductor, Charlotte Concert Band
Charlotte, North Carolina

---

1 Bernard S. Massey, "Brother James and His Air," *Hymn Society of Great Britain and Ireland Bulletin*, July 2001, 175.
2 Ibid.
3 David Pratt, "Exploring Theosophy," http;//www.theosophy.org (accessed May 30, 2007).
4 Massey, 174. for the complete text, see http://www.barefooters.org/key-works/barefoot_league.html.
5 Ibid.
6 Ibid., 175.
7 www.hopepublishing.com.
8 Massey, 175.
9 Ibid.

Teacher Resource Guide

Cahokia

Jared Spears
(b. 1936)

Unit 1: Composer

Jared Spears is professor of music emeritus at Arkansas State University in Jonesboro, Arkansas. He was born in Chicago, Illinois, in 1936, and received the BSE degree in music education from Northern Illinois University; the BM and MM in percussion and composition from the Cosmopolitan School of Music; and the DM in composition from Northwestern University. His teachers include Blyth Owen, Alan Stout, and Anthony Donato.

Spears taught theory, history, composition, percussion and band on all educational levels, from elementary school through college. After thirty-two years of teaching, he retired from Arkansas State University in May of 1999. He has maintained a heavy schedule of composing, guest conducting, and lecturing. He also serves as artistic advisor for the St. Louis Wind Symphony.

He is the recipient of numerous awards and citations including several ASCAP awards, the Faricy Award for Creative Music from Northwestern University School of Music, Citations of Excellence from the National Band Association, and the Award of Merit from the Arkansas Chapter of the National Federation of Music Clubs. He is a National Arts Associate of Sigma Alpha Iota and has been recognized in Outstanding Educators of America, International Who's Who in Music, and Who's Who in the World of Percussion-U.S.A. During his tenure at Arkansas Sate University, Spears received the University President's Award for Outstanding Faculty Member, as well as an appointment as a President's Fellow.

Spears has composed more than 250 original works for band, choir, orchestra, and chamber ensembles. Some of his better-known compositions include *Deo Gratsias*, *Wind River Overture*, *Spirit Canyon March*, and *Novena*.

Unit 2: Composition

Cahokia is a single-movement work, just over two minutes in length. From the program note of Jared Spears:

> *Cahokia* is a piece presenting musical snapshots of Cahokia, the most sophisticated prehistoric Indian civilization north of Mexico. Its remains, located a few miles west of Collinsville, Illinois at Cahokia Mounds State Historical Site, boast a city inhabited about A.D. 700 to 1400. At its peak the city covered six square miles with a population from 10,000 to 20,000 in extensive residential sections arranged around opened plazas.

Unit 3: Historical Perspective

Written in 2005, *Cahokia* is a dramatic piece for young musicians that is meant to musically reflect the images of war, peace, mystery and celebration one might associate with this ancient city.

Music honoring a people, a culture or an event is common in band literature, and often includes songs or compositional techniques borrowed from those sources. While little is known of the music of ancient *Cahokia*, the composer's dramatic use and combination of several compositional techniques all work together to create vivid images of this ancient Indian music.

Unit 4: Technical Considerations

The score to *Cahokia* includes the reference, "Music for Beginning Band," but this work would be well-suited for slightly more experienced musicians. This piece is cast in an ABA form in C minor and is marked "Allegro Drammatico" with a quarter-note marking of 120. It includes frequent dynamic contrasts from *crescendo*, *decrescendo*, and terraced dynamics. Passages of unison melodies and rhythms are contrasted with motives performed by one section in the band, while other sections play "responses" of those same motives in canon. Syncopation is included frequently, but is always supported by block scoring. Flutes and alto saxophones must be familiar with trill technique for concert G5.

Call-and-response techniques between unison or two-part wind writing and the percussion section also make this piece more challenging for beginning players. The percussion parts call for seven instruments (snare drum, bass drum, tambourine, timpani, triangle, suspended cymbal and bells)

and can be performed by five players. These parts are often independent of one another, and specific performance notations are included concerning mallet types and where to play on the drum or cymbal.

Unit 5: Stylistic Considerations

This piece includes ample opportunities for expressive playing. The dramatic quality of *Cahokia* can be captured with special attention to performing the composer's specific dynamic and articulation markings and the wide range of dynamic contrasts often occur quickly. Articulations, including staccato markings, accents, and slurs, change frequently throughout all instrumental parts, and when combined with the challenges of syncopation, can create interesting contrasts which are highlighted by the call-and-response compositional techniques.

The independent percussion parts require confidence from very young players, and are very important to capture the mood and style of this music.

Unit 6: Musical Elements

MELODY:
The majority of *Cahokia* is built around a diatonic, scale-like melody in C minor. Step-wise movement lends to the chant-like character of this modal melody. It is always marked *forte* and includes some accents and staccato markings.

The two brief contrasting melodies are very different in style. These lyrical melodies are *piano* and *mezzo-forte,* include many intervals of perfect fifths and minor thirds, and are always slurred. Passages of these contrasting themes incorporate the use of pentatonic scales, and hint at related keys of A-flat major and F minor.

HARMONY:
A large portion of the instrumental parts in *Cahokia* consists of unison writing across several octaves. Harmonic sections are completely diatonic, and only seven measures of the piece include passing chromaticism.

RHYTHM:
Cahokia is in 4/4 and is marked "Allegro Drammatico" (quarter note = 120). Rhythmic values are limited to quarter and eighth notes, with a few half and whole notes. Only the snare drum and timpani parts have sixteenth notes. A pair of two-measure passages in the woodwind and brass parts include basic syncopation.

TIMBRE:
With *Cahokia,* Jared Spears has provided an excellent teaching tool for young musicians to develop characteristic tone quality while performing a dramatic

piece of music. The easy unison melodies allow students to match pitch and tone quality, and the variety of dynamic contrast and articulations will make this an enjoyable piece for less-experienced players. Young percussionists will enjoy the independent parts and their central role in this composition.

UNIT 7: Form and Structure

SECTION	MEASURE	EVENT AND SCORING
Dramatic Opening	1–5	Five measures of alternating rhythmic statements between percussion and winds
Introduction	6–11	Introduction of main theme fragments by all winds, harmonized in thirds
Primary Theme	12–19	After an initial *forte* statement of the opening rhythm, the flutes and alto saxophones play the first statement of the primary melody, *piano*
Primary Theme	20–28	The primary theme is stated again from *forte* brass, with an added woodwind countermelody; cadences in C minor
Transition	29–33	Thinning texture includes a brief, descending pentatonic melody from flutes and clarinets, with low reed and low brass pedal C
Lyrical Theme	34–41	Lyrical *piano* theme and harmony from trumpets, answered in canon by low brass and low reeds
Lyrical Theme II	42–51	Second lyrical *piano* theme played in canon by clarinets, flutes, saxophones and horns; triangle and tambourine contribute to lighter texture before a *forte-piano* and *crescendo* lead to the return of the primary theme
Primary Theme	52–60	Similar to measure 20, with additional instruments and a rhythmically active pedal C; cadences with a sudden shift to A-flat major
Coda	61–65	Return of dramatic opening material with alternation of wind and percussion parts; concludes with syncopation in C minor

Unit 8: Suggested Listening

John Barnes Chance, *Variations on a Korean Folk Song*
Carlos Chávez, *Symphony No. 2, "Sinfonia India"*
Silvestre Revueltas, *Sensemaya*
Frank Ticheli, *Amazing Grace*

Unit 9: Additional References and Resources

Mick, Claudia. *Cahokia: City of the Sun*. Cahokia Mounds Museum
   Society, 1992.

Pauketat, Timothy R., and Nancy Stone Bernard. *Cahokia Mounds: Digging
   in the Past*. Oxford University Press, 1994.

Web sites:
   Cahokia Mounds Historic Site: www.cahokiamounds.com
   A Bibliography of Cahokia Studies:
      http://archaeology.about.com/cs/mississippian/a/cahokiabib.htm

Contributed by:

Christopher B. Knighten
East Carolina University
Greenville, North Carolina

Teacher Resource Guide

Canticle

Douglas E. Wagner
(b. 1952)

Unit 1: Composer

Douglas E. Wagner is a native of Chicago, Illinois and is an internationally recognized composer and arranger, holding undergraduate and graduate music degrees from Butler University. With thirty years experience as a high school music educator and administrator behind him, Mr. Wagner now devotes all of his time and energy to writing and editing. He is an ASCAP award-winning composer, an editor for a major publishing company, and he has served several denominations as a church musician. Mr. Wagner has more than 2,000 published titles, including original works and arrangements for choir, concert band, orchestra, hand bell ensemble, organ, piano, and voice.

Unit 2: Composition

Canticle is a work born from a fragment of a tune that the composer hastily jotted down in one of his sketch books and remained there untouched for quite some time. In the summer of 1995, Mr. Wagner was looking for a text for an original choral setting and happened upon the Shakespeare quote from *The Merchant of Venice* that appears on the cover of the full score.

"How sweet the moonlight sleeps upon this bank!
Here will we sit and let the sounds of music creep in our ears
Soft stillness and the night become the touches of sweet harmony."

William Shakespeare
The Merchant of Venice
Act V, Scene 1

The composer went back to the partial tune in his sketch book and set about to write a work for beginning band that simply mirrored the sentiment of this text. The work is a difficult Grade 1, requiring strong second-year players. The scoring is typical of beginning band instrumentation, but requires oboe and French horn players who can play independent lines. This work was published in 1996 and the duration is approximately two minutes and forty-five seconds.

Unit 3: Historical Perspectives

A *canticle* is a song or chant taken from biblical text. This work is based on the text taken from *The Merchant of Venice,* by William Shakespeare. It is believed that this text was written between 1596 and 1598, during the Renaissance period. Shakespeare shared this time period with people like Leonardo da Vinci, Michelangelo, Galileo, Christopher Columbus, Magellan, and Gabreli. Some of the musical characteristics of this period included the use of triple meter and the triad was the basic unit of composition.

Although this is an original, contemporary work and was not written to imitate the Renaissance style, it uses the compositional techniques of triple meter and the triad.

Unit 4: Technical Considerations

This work is playable by strong second-year players. There is a need for independent playing by the oboe and French horn. Ranges are comfortable for all instruments and clarinets stay below the "break." The work is written in E-flat major, but there are a few accidentals. The tempo is quarter note = 63. The meter is 3/4 throughout the work. The dotted-quarter note followed by an eighth note is a consistent rhythm in many of the parts. Unlike many other Grade 1 publications, the alto saxophone, tenor saxophone, and French horn often play independently and are not always scored together. This could present a challenge for many ensembles, but it is also a refreshing change. The oboe also does not have the typical doubling with the flute. The snare drum part should be marked "optional." It is included only for texture purposes and when used, its dynamic must remain well below the wind parts. The tuba has a low B-natural, which is often problematic, but it is doubled in the baritone saxophone and bass clarinet. At measure 33, the bass line appears only in the bass clarinet and baritone saxophone for four measures. This could be a problem for bands with incomplete instrumentation or weak players on those parts. Students will need to know which instruments have the melody throughout the piece.

Unit 5: Stylistic Considerations

This work helps young players to develop proper breath support, tone, and phrasing. Clearly marked, four-measure phrases assist the players with fitting these into a well-marked dynamic scheme. The composer indicates that the many *crescendo-decrescendo* wedges are to be considered subtle nuances that rise in their apex only one dynamic level. Smooth, well-supported tone is essential. The inclusion of the accelerando, ritard., a tempo, poco ritard., and Tempo I provide a wealth of opportunities for students to discover the stylistic nature of shaping the phrases musically, as well as dynamically.

Have students listen to recordings of hymns or chorales and play chorales and ballads to increase their understanding of the importance of shaping phrases.

Unit 6: Musical Elements

MELODY:
The opening phrase defines the melodic structure of this work. The melody is characterized by the use of the lower neighbor, the triad, and the diatonic movement within. This work does not follow the typical woodwind choir and brass choir concepts found in many beginning band pieces. As noted earlier, combinations of unlike instruments are often featured. Although the melody appears in a primary instrument, it is also doubled in fragmentary phrases in most voices throughout the piece.

HARMONY:
The use of the lower neighbor that was used in the melodic line, for example, E-flat to D-flat to E-flat and A-flat to B-flat to A-flat, also help to form the harmonic structure of this work. The structure of each phrase, I to V and I to IV, also contributes to the harmonic interest of this composition.

RHYTHM:
The rhythmic demands of this piece are limited. The most difficult rhythm is the dotted-quarter eighth figure. Students may be challenged by the overlapping rhythmic figures found throughout this work, but these are excellent for teaching rhythmic independence.

TIMBRE:
The greatest challenge will be blend, balance, and tone quality. Low wood-winds and low brass will need to be careful not to overbalance the moving woodwind and brass lines.

Unit 7: Form and Structure

SECTION	MEASURE	EVENT AND SCORING
A	1–8	Introductory material; melodic line appears in clarinet and horn voices initially, with overlapping fragments in the trumpet part based on a simple lower-neighbor motif; flute, oboe, and bells add a secondary line at measure 2, adding movement and harmonic support; low brass and low woodwinds briefly take the melodic lead before the upper wood-winds double it in measures 7–8; light percussion emphasize *crescendos* and cadence points
B	9–16	Main theme; an anacrusis is played by trumpet only one count before measure 9, and assumes the main melodic statement doubled only by the oboe in measures 15–16; subtle counterpoint occurs in the French horn and alto saxophone with tutti scoring minus the flute and clarinet; similar percussion minus the bells
	17–24	Trumpet continues the melody in measures 23–24, with the flute now playing the same supportive phrase the oboe had; the lower-neighbor harmonic phrase is passed back and forth between the low brass and low woodwinds and the French horn and alto saxophone voices and introduce the forthcoming bridge section; chimes enter at measure 17 with effective harmonic support

SECTION	MEASURE	EVENT AND SCORING
C	25–28	Clarinet assumes the melodic line without any doubling in the bridge or interlude section; texture is much lighter with only the alto and tenor saxophones and French horn offering harmonic support; triangle replaces chimes for a subtle rhythmic effect
	29–32	Clarinet continues melodically with the same background choir as measure 25; however, the flute answers with a line imitative of the opening fragment from measure 2
	33–38	The lower-neighbor phrases reappear and pass between the clarinet/trumpet and the flute, oboe, French horn, and bells; texture thickens gradually until all winds are tutti at measure 37, ending on the V chord at measure 38 with two fermatas and a caesura
A'	39–44	Transition of restated introduction with abbreviated cadence; Tempo I is marked with a recapitulation of measures 1–5 and an altered plagal cadence at measure 44 with another fermata
B'	45–52	Measures 9–16 are repeated with a second countermelody appearing in the flute and oboe voices; the bells join them at measure 49; the altered plagal cadence occurs at measure 52
Tag	53–56	This short, four-measure tag is more harmonic than melodic, moving from E-flat (I), to the lower neighbor D-flat and back to the tonic; the flute and oboe play a final melodic motif and are answered by the clarinet/trumpet voices; only bells appear percussively in the tag (with a cued chime tonic), which is marked poco ritard. at measure 55

Unit 8: Suggested Listening

James Curnow, *Renaissance Suite*
Calvin Custer, *A Renaissance Faires*
Elliot Del Borgo, *A Renaissance Couplet*
Theldon Myers, *Renaissance Dances*
Ken Singleton:
> *A Renaissance Festival*
> *A Renaissance Revel*

Unit 9: Additional References and Resources

Dvorak, Thomas L., Cynthia Crump Taggart, and Peter Schmalz.
> *Best Music for Young Band.* Brooklyn, NY: Manhattan Beach
> Music, 1995.

Kvet, Edward, ed. *Instructional Literature for Middle-Level
> Band.* Reston, VA: Music Educators National Conference, 1996.

Miles, Richard, and Thomas Dvorak, eds. *Teaching Music through
> Performance in Beginning Band.* Chicago: GIA Publications, 2001.

Contributed by:

Susan L. Taylor
Director of Bands
Anderson University
Anderson, Indiana

Teacher Resource Guide

Chippewa Lullaby

arranged by Anne McGinty
(b. 1945)

Unit 1: Composer/Arranger

Anne McGinty is one of the most prolific composers in the field of concert band literature. Her many compositions and arrangements for concert band, string orchestra, flute, and flute ensembles (more than 225 titles, all of which have been published), extend from the elementary through the professional level. More than fifty of these compositions were commissioned from bands in the United States.

Born in Findlay, Ohio in 1945, Ms. McGinty began her higher education at The Ohio State University, where Donald McGinnis was her mentor, band director and flute teacher. She left OSU to pursue a career in flute performance, and played principal flute with the Tucson (Arizona) Symphony Orchestra, Tucson Pops Orchestra, and in the TSO Woodwind Quintet, which toured Arizona under the auspices of a government grant. When she returned to college, she received her bachelor of music, summa cum laude, and master of music from Duquesne University, Pittsburgh, Pennsylvania, where she concentrated on flute performance, music theory, and composition. She studied flute and chamber music with Bernard Goldberg and composition with Joseph Willcox Jenkins

Ms. McGinty and John Edmondson formed Queenwood Publications in 1987 and were responsible for the creation, production, promotion, and international sales and distribution of Queenwood's catalog of concert band, jazz band and string orchestra music. They sold their company to the Neil A. Kjos Music Company in March 2002, and are writing exclusively for them under the Queenwood/Kjos name.

Ms. McGinty is a member of the American Society of Composers, Authors and Publishers (ASCAP) and has received annual composition awards since 1986. She received the Golden Rose Award from the Women Band Directors National Association and the Outstanding Service to Music Award from Tau Beta Sigma, a national honorary band sorority.

Ms. McGinty is also active as a guest conductor, clinician, and speaker throughout the United States and Canada. She has conducted regional and all-state bands, given clinics at many state conventions and universities on band performance, literature and emotions in music, and has given speeches at state and national conventions on many diverse topics, all of which are related to the performance and enjoyment of music and the values of music education. Her other interests include weight lifting, reading murder mysteries, learning to play the bagpipes, didgeridoo, and nurturing her two cats, Starz and Stripes.

One of Anne McGinty's goals, as stated in her myspace.com blog entry, "...is to provide a musical means for students and band directors to share their creative ideas about the interpretation and performance of a piece and to do my best to acquaint young instrumentalists with our folk song heritage so they in turn can pass it on to the next generation." In addition to *Chippewa Lullaby*, Anne McGinty's other arrangements of multicultural selections for band include: *African Folk Trilogy*, *African Folk Trilogy #2*, *American Folk Trilogy*, *Appalachian Folk Fantasy*, *Bartok: Folk Song and Dance*, *Canadian Folk Fantasy*, *English Folk Trilogy*, *Glory: An Indonesian Folk Song*, *Greek Folk Trilogy*, *Icelandic Folk Trilogy*, *Japanese Folk Trilogy*, *Kum Ba Yah*, *Russian Folk Fantasy*, *Scottish Folk Fantasy*, *Songs of the Emerald Isle*, and *Who Can Sail Against the Wind*.

Unit 2: Composition

Multicultural music education expert Dr. J. Bryan Burton, professor of music education at West Chester University in Pennsylvania, shared his thoughts and this native music with Ms. McGinty. Documented as "Lullaby No. 127," this simple melody was derived from the Chippewa Nation of North America's Native Peoples.

The intent of this melancholic song is for a mother to sing to her infant child who is in a swing or hammock. Often, this song would be accompanied by an older child singing in canon. The melody itself (pentatonic) is just four measures long (4/4 time).

The entire score is marked moderately soft, so as to represent a lullaby (not loud or brassy). Percussion instruments must play in a subtle manner. Conductors should encourage shaping of phrases, using only dynamic nuance. However, dynamic range should not extend past a *mezzo piano*. Teaching beginners to play with control in this narrow dynamic range, yet still give contrast to the phrases, will be an emphasis in preparing this selection.

Canonic and imitative entrances and lines are evident throughout. An ostinato appears in the lower voices and percussion, along with an original melody in the upper voices. The tempo changes, like the dynamics in this arrangement, are also quite subtle. The overall structure of this selection is theme and variations.

Duration of *Chippewa Lullaby* is about three minutes in length, with sixty-four measures, all in 4/4 time. Difficulty level is Grade 1.5, taking into consideration the reliance on section independence.

Chippewa Lullaby was published in 2002 by Queenwood/Kjos.

Unit 3: Historical Perspective

Chippewa Indians, also known as the Ojibwa, were one of the largest tribes north of Mexico, whose range was formerly along both shores of Lake Huron and Superior, extending across the Minnesota Turtle Mountains into North Dakota. They were settled in a large village at La Pointe, Wisconsin, about the time of the discovery of America. The Chippewa originally had territory in Michigan, Wisconsin, Minnesota, and North Dakota, and were part of the Algonquian Indians, which consisted of various groups of Native Americans who spoke similar languages. The Chippewas were closely related to the Ottawa Indians and Potawatomi Indians.

This lullaby bases its theme on the pentatonic scale. The tonal pentatonic scale occurs in the music of nearly all ancient cultures, such as Chinese, Polynesian, African, American Indians, Celtic, and Scottish. A number of Gregorian melodies are purely pentatonic as well.

Please see Unit 8 for suggested listening of parallel works for wind band.

Unit 4: Technical Considerations

Sound quality and tone management are key to performing this selection as the arranger intended. Students must be able to enter and exit phrases gently, and perform at a controlled dynamic level of *mezzo piano* or softer with a dependable legato style.

To assist with tone development, consistent warm-ups that include singing and long tones should be incorporated during rehearsals. Students ought to be encouraged to sing with good tone and intonation so that they can transfer these skills to their instruments.

For a developing instrumentalist, the dynamic level of *mezzo piano* is often difficult to play with control and consistency. The narrow and soft dynamics required in this piece can be established through use of imagery. Because this is a lullaby, and a mother is attempting to sing her child to sleep, the band's dynamic level should not wake the baby, but rather soothe the child. Additionally, students need to be aware not only of their own dynamic range, but also of how their dynamic fits within their section and the entire ensemble.

The concept of stagger breathing could be introduced or developed with *Chippewa Lullaby* so that phrases are extended (vs. choppy). Although phrases can last from five to nine measures, a planned breath could occur after about four measures, but this could be a stretch for many younger players. While planned breaths would work throughout, stagger breathing would give this piece a more peaceful effect, without interrupting the sound or melodic line. (If the mother stops singing, even for only an instant, the baby could awaken.)

Each instrument has its own challenges, however technical aspects of most of this selection fit well within the developing level of playing. The flutes will likely need to learn a new note: E-flat6. While the clarinets mainly stay in the *chalumeau* register, first clarinets need to play B-natural4 (over the break) for two measures. The clarinets need to play in the throat-tone register for several measures. Better intonation can be achieved on the throat tones with the right hand down (lowering the pitch if needed). Alto saxophones must play well in their lower range (D3) through B5. They will have to strengthen their upper range in tone as well as intonation as strong, firm embouchures are a necessity. Also in the alto saxophone part, the two whole notes on D5 sound better when the alternate fingering is used to bring the pitch down, as D5 is usually sharp on the alto saxophone. (Depress the low B key to lower the pitch on D5).

Trombones get the chance to work on their legato tongue technique, as four measures require some slurring. Overall, technical difficulties are not as challenging for the brass; however, they will be tested in the area of patience, as they perform on approximately 1/3 to 1/2 of the piece. Percussionists will need to learn proper performance techniques on the guiro, maraca, claves, triangle, and tambourine.

Chippewa Lullaby is based on a pentatonic scale. First presented in the key center of B-flat (B-flat, C, D, F, G), a key change to E-flat (E-flat, F, G, B-flat, C) appears at m. 25 and remains to the end. The meter of 4/4 is constant throughout. The pulse does vary however, with the tempo starting at quarter = 80, then quarter = 108, and back to quarter = 80.

Perhaps the greatest challenge of *Chippewa Lullaby* is the independent woodwind, high brass, and percussion parts. Unlike most young band scores, this arrangement does not heavily rely on the doubling of parts. Entrances are usually by an individual part (percussion) or by a section (flutes, clarinets, saxophones, trumpets). This is necessary to create the canonic and imitative effects throughout the selection. While there are just four measures (sixteen beats) of original melody, McGinty interweaves this melody, with new, complementing melody (usually changing the direction of the original melody, but staying within the pentatonic theme) and countermelody, which enhances the lullaby in this band setting. Because there are so many separate entrances, the conductor will find it difficult to cue each entrance, thus relying on the rhythmic security of the students.

Example 1: mm. 11–17

To strengthen independence within the ensemble, exercises should include scales with staggered entrances (allowing the band to play in thirds); as well as performing familiar rounds (such as *Row, Row, Row Your Boat* and *Frère Jacques*).

Rhythmically, this selection should not present a problem for developing players. Again, independent playing will be the chief concern, trying to maintain the written rhythm, played against other sections' rhythms.

Unit 5: Stylistic Considerations

Legato playing is key for this arrangement. Students must learn to play the correct articulations, but in a smooth, connected style.

While the entire score is marked *mezzo piano*, the conductor is encouraged to take some liberty with shaping phrases, allowing the natural rise and fall of the melodic lines. Keeping the lullaby idea intact is the primary concern. Percussionists are to sound as if they are "noises in the night," again, taking care not to wake the sleeping child.

Unit 6: Musical Elements

MELODY:

Anne McGinty has cleverly taken a sixteen-beat pentatonic melody and created an interesting and beautiful selection. While the pentatonic scale prevails throughout, it is interesting to note the inverted melodies, canons, and imitative lines. An ostinato appears in the faster section, presented by low brass, low reeds and the bells.

Example 2: Melodic theme

HARMONY:

The melodic line cadences on the tonic pitch (also the starting pitch). However, with overlapping entrances of melody, melodic fragments, and ostinato, the arrangement appears seamless and creates pleasing harmonies throughout. The treatment of the melodic line (original and newly created) is most apparent in the canonic sections, and this structure provides the harmony of the lullaby.

Texture is primarily polyphonic, which allows all sections to perform either the entire or portions of the melody.

RHYTHM:

There is never a complete rest in the entire piece. The meter (4/4) stays throughout, with two slight tempo changes. Never faster than an eighth note (quarter = 80; 108), rhythms are easily manageable.

TIMBRE:

Perhaps most interesting is the use of varied percussion instruments. Bells, guiro, maraca, claves, triangle, and tambourine are usually playing separately. Their role in this piece is to provide quiet sounds of the night. At the end of the selection, it might be appropriate to add a rain stick on the last measure.

In a young band arrangement, it is refreshing to hear individual sections (vs. tutti), and each student should feel that they are contributing an important part to this arrangement.

Unit 7: Form and Structure

SECTION	MEASURE	EVENT AND SCORING
Theme	1–11	Opening statement of theme; imitative and canonic entrances; woodwinds, percussion; key of B-flat major
Variation	12–24	Thematic variation; brass enter (exit at m. 18)
Variation	25–41	Thematic variation; some original melody; ostinato is added; woodwinds and percussion; brass enter at m. 28; tempo moves slightly faster; key change to E-flat major at m. 25
Theme/ variations	42–54	Thematic variation; imitative entrances; tempo slows to original tutti
Theme/ variations	55–64	Theme and variations; woodwinds, percussion, trumpets until m. 60

Unit 8: Suggested Listening

Other Native American works for wind band include:
Brian Balmages, *Chant and Savage Dance* (FJH Music)
Anne McGinty:
Kiva: Ritual and Ceremonies (Queenwood/Kjos)
Painted Desert (Queenwood/Kjos)

Other wind band works that make use of a lullaby:
Stephen Bulla, *An Irish Lullaby* (Curnow Music Distributors)
Michael Colgrass, *Apache Lullaby* (Colgrass Music)
Lawrence Moss, *Chinese Lullaby* (Northeastern Music)
James Swearingen, *A Child's Lullaby* (CL Barnhouse)
Other wind band works that employ the pentatonic scale:
John Barnes Chance, *Variations on a Korean Folk Song*
(Boosey & Hawkes)
Robert Garofalo/Garwood Whaley, arr., *Ahrirang*, (Meredith Music)
James Ployhar, arr., *Korean Folk Song Medley* (Belwin Mills)

Unit 9: Additional References and Resources

Anderson, William. *Multicultural Perspectives in Music Education*, 2nd Edition. Reston, VA: MENC Publications, 1996.

Bakan, Michael B.; Burton, J. Bryan; Obregon, Richad R.; Anderson, William M. (ed.); Moore, Marvelene C. (ed.). *Making Connections: Multicultural Music and the National Standards*. Reston, VA: MENC Publications, 1997. (Book and CD Set)

Campbell, Patricia Sheehan. *Music in Cultural Context: Eight Views on World Music Education*. Reston, VA: MENC Publications, 1996.

Campbell, Patricia Sheehan. *Music Resources for Multicultural Perspectives*. Reston, VA: MENC Publications, 1998. (CD)

Miles, Richard, and Thomas Dvorak, eds. *Teaching Music through Performance in Beginning Band*. Chicago: GIA Publications, 2001 (see composer Anne McGinty, Teacher Resource Guides)

Native American Facts for Kids
http://www.geocities.com/bigorrin/chippewa_kids.htm

Reimer, Bennett. *World Musics and Music Education: Facing the Issues*. Reston, VA: MENC Publications, 2002.

Teaching the Music of the American Indian. Reston, VA: MENC Publications. (Video)

The World Sings Goodnight, Vol. 1 and 2. (CD)
Lullabies sung in their native tongue from around the globe. Silver Wave Records, 1993, 1995.

Contributed by:

Linda A. Hartley
Professor of Music, Coordinator of Music Education
University of Dayton
Dayton, Ohio

Teacher Resource Guide

Courtlandt County Festival

William Owens
(b. 1963)

Unit 1: Composer

William Owens was born in Gary, Indiana, on January 22, 1963. He chose a career in music education with encouragement from his high school band director, Ann Betz, at Andrean High School in Merrillville, Indiana. He holds a bachelor's degree in music education from the VanderCook College of Music in Chicago. Upon graduation, he taught high school and middle school band in Brownsville (TX), Lubbock (TX), and the Dallas/Fort Worth metroplex. Mr. Owens is the winner of the ASCAPlus award and a two-time recipient of the Forrest L. Buchtel Citation for Excellence in Band Composition. Principal commissions include those from the California Band Directors Association, the Chicago Public Schools Bureau of Cultural Arts, the Florida Bandmasters Association, and the Texas University Interscholastic League. He is a member of ASCAP, the American Composers Forum (ACF), the Mansfield (TX) Wind Symphony, and the Texas Music Educators Association. Mr. Owens began composing in 1993 with support from his fellow band directors. Since then, he has written primarily for young band and has more than eighty published works for band including: *Plains West Concert March*, *Carpathia*, *Maesong*, *Kamehameha* and *Rock Springs Saga*.

Unit 2: Composition

Courtlandt County Festival was written in 2004. The title is fictitious, as it was written for a student of Owens whose middle name is Courtlandt. The piece is a Grade 1 difficulty and lasts about two minutes. The bouncy,

energetic first theme is followed by a lyrical second theme, and concludes with a recapitulation of the opening theme and a coda. The composer intends for his music to be enjoyable to both performers and listeners, and *Courtlandt County Festival* fulfills both of these intentions.

Unit 3: Historical Perspective

Courtlandt County Festival was composed in 2004 while the composer was teaching in the Dallas/Fort Worth metroplex. In that capacity he has regular, personal knowledge of the musical and technical abilities of middle school students. *Courtlandt County Festival* is the forty-seventh piece Owens has written since he began composing in 1993. Although he initially had no intention of becoming a composer, he has received encouragement and praise for his works from fellow band directors and mentors. His current output of more than 80 published works attests to his grasp of the musical and educational needs of beginning and middle school bands. *Courtlandt County Festival* successfully illustrates the delicate balance between repetition and variety that is essential to teaching young students. Although Owens has also written more difficult pieces, he is drawn to the challenge of writing beautiful and enjoyable music for young bands.

Unit 4: Technical Considerations

Courtlandt County Festival is in the concert keys of E-flat and B-flat major. The lyrical middle section modulates from concert E-flat to concert B-flat for seventeen measures before returning to the opening key. Concert D-flat is the only non-diatonic note. The slower B section is in 3/4 time (quarter note equal to about 86) while the beginning and end are both in 4/4 time at a bold march-like tempo. In addition to being slower, the middle section is also legato in contrast to the marcato boldness of the opening and closing statements. Rhythms consist of whole notes, dotted half notes, half notes, quarter notes, and no more than two eighth notes in a row with the exception of the percussion parts. There are no dotted eighth notes. The percussion parts contain the previous rhythms plus sixteenth notes, open and close rolls, and flams. Rhythms are all derived from the same duple eighth note pattern and demand attention to counting and provide pleasing musical variety as well. The percussion parts, while not technically challenging for this level, are written in an interesting and musically engaging manner, avoiding excessive repetition. Triangle and close snare drum rolls in the legato passages highlight the timbral changes in the winds. Range is not excessive for any instrument. Clarinets do not cross the break. Flutes and trumpets go no higher than concert B-flat4. Harmonies are diatonic with the exception of a flat major VII7 in the introduction.

Unit 5: Stylistic Considerations

There are few articulation markings in this piece; rarely are there more than two notes slurred at a time. Markings at the beginning of each section indicate the appropriate style. The first A section is marked "Boldly," while the concluding A section is to be played as marked at the Original Bright Tempo. The slower B section is marked Gently. These and the occasional marcato mark or slur are the only indicators of style. The composer refers to the opening material as "bounced and energetic" while the contrasting middle passage should be played "flowingly" to promote lyrical playing in young players. In the realization of this work, creating contrast between these two styles is important. The appropriate distinction between thematic materials is similar to that found in the opening movements of a Classical symphony by Haydn or Mozart. Dynamics range from *piano* to *forte*. The dynamics contribute to the style of the piece and provide an important educational goal for the students. Students should understand that, despite the marked dynamics, the melodic material and moving lines must always take precedence over accompanying harmonies.

Unit 6: Musical Elements

MELODY:
The two principal melodies are both diatonic. The first should be played in a bounced style with a light articulation and emphasis on the moving eighth notes. The second should be played smoothly with a slight stress on the first beat of each measure. Both melodies are primarily scalar but structurally use the interval of a perfect fourth. Each antecedent/consequent pair should *crescendo* to the middle of the phrase and *decrescendo* to the end of the phrase.

HARMONY:
The harmony is primarily diatonic with the exception of a major flat VII^7 in the introduction. It is based largely on tonic, dominant, and subdominant harmonies, often in root position. The texture is homophonic throughout with periodic timbral changes in scoring.

RHYTHM:
The opening and closing themes are in duple (4/4) meter while the lyrical middle theme is in triple (3/4) meter. Most of the rhythms are in unison with respect to melody and accompaniment, with no more than two different rhythms occurring at the same time. The complexity of the rhythm comes from the duple eighth-note groupings being placed on different beats in the measure. The melody provides many opportunities for developing rhythm-reading skills. The percussion parts are independent and rhythmically interesting. Open rolls should be used at the beginning and ending while close

rolls are appropriate in the lyrical section. Duple sixteenth patterns move around within each measure to add a pleasing variety to the snare drum ostinato. The bell part is often independent of the wind parts, requiring young percussionists to develop mallet instrument skills.

TIMBRE:

The dominant tone color in this work is tutti band. In some passages, however, the flutes are accompanied by lightly scored woodwind accompaniment. In the secondary theme, the clarinet melody is accompanied by saxophone and euphonium (cross-cued in the trombone and horn parts). The principal melodic material is always presented in unison to reinforce the importance and volume of the melody. The unison melodic passages can be used to develop pitch awareness, tone production, balance sensitivity and blend within each section and throughout the ensemble.

Unit 7: Form and Structure

Courtlandt County Festival is in a three-part ABA form. The concluding A section omits the secondary theme in favor of a coda, shortening the form slightly. The first A section consists of two themes, also in a three-part ABA pattern. The A theme is a simple, bounced melody of two four-measure antecedent/consequent phrases. The melody is first stated in the trumpets who are then joined by the full ensemble. The B theme is similar in character and rhythm, first played in unison by the clarinet section. They are joined by flutes, oboes, and horns and accompanied by the entire ensemble minus the trumpet section. The first A section concludes with a restatement of theme A. In the B section, the lyrical melody in triple meter is first heard in the flutes, with thinly scored woodwind accompaniment. The brass join the woodwinds for a restatement of the melody. A soft snare drum solo transitions to the recapitulation of the opening A theme, scored as before. The secondary theme from the beginning is replaced by a coda, which is based on the intervals and rhythm of the opening motive. A brief timpani solo brings the work to an exciting conclusion.

SECTION	MEASURE	EVENT AND SCORING
Introduction	1–4	Energetic duple meter melody in flutes, clarinets, and trumpets; tutti accompaniment
A	5–12	Theme A – lively pair of four-measure antecedent/consequent phrases with the melody in the unison trumpets with tutti accompaniment

Section	Measure	Event and Scoring
	13–20	Theme B – a pair of four-measure antecedent/consequent phrases with a softer secondary theme in unison clarinets joined later by all instruments except trumpets
	21–29	Return of theme A with a one-measure extension
B	30–44	Theme C – triple meter; a pair of eight-measure antecedent/consequent phrases in a slower, lyrical style; flute melody is thinly scored with woodwind accompaniment; entire ensemble joins for the second phrase the second phrase is highlighted by the snare drum transition
Transition	45–46	Quiet snare drum transition with a *crescendo*
A^1	47–53	Recapitulation of theme A; Secondary theme is omitted in favor of a coda
Coda	54–57	Tutti scoring based on fragments of theme A; timpani solo

Unit 8: Suggested Listening

Franz Joseph Haydn, Symphony No. 104
Wolfgang Amadeus Mozart, Symphony No. 38
William Owens:
> *American Landmarks*
> *Carpathia*
> *Maesong*
> *Rock Springs Saga*

Sergei Prokofiev, "Classical" Symphony

Unit 9: Additional References and Resources

Dvorak, Thomas L., Cynthia Crump Taggart, and Peter Schmaltz. *Best Music for Young Bands*. Edited by Bob Margolis. Brooklyn, NY: Manhattan Beach Music, 1986.

Contributed by:

John Wacker
Western State College of Colorado
Gunnison, Colorado

Teacher Resource Guide

Crossings in Time
Michael Sweeney
(b. 1952)

Unit 1: Composer

Michael Sweeney is a graduate of Indiana University where he studied music education and composition. He taught five years in the public schools of Ohio and Indiana, working with successful concert, jazz, and marching programs of all levels from elementary to high school. Since 1982, Sweeney has worked full time for Hal Leonard Corporation in Milwaukee, Wisconsin, and is currently director of band publications. In addition, he contributes as a composer and arranger in all instrumental areas. Sweeney is particularly known for his writing for concert and jazz bands at the younger levels, and has more than 500 publications to his credit. His works appear on numerous state contest lists, and are regularly performed throughout the world.

Unit 2: Composition

Written in the style of a tone poem and published by Hal Leonard Corporation in 2006, *Crossings in Time* is approximately three minutes in length. The work is scored for standard concert band instrumentation, and includes a part for "Convertible Bass Line." There are single parts for each instrument with the exception of clarinet (scored for three parts), and alto saxophone and trumpet (two parts each). Several of the low woodwind parts are cued for low brass. Percussion requirements are minimal, with parts for medium suspended cymbal, large suspended cymbal or gong, and bells, all of which could be covered by one performer.

The following program note was provided by the composer:

> All families experience change as our lives evolve and our relatives get older. This composition reflects the feelings and emotions resulting from events in my own family.
>
> In late November 2005, I drove across the country with my daughter as she relocated from Wisconsin to California. After dodging tumble-weeds and snowflakes over the plains, we stopped for a while in Colorado for an all too rare and brief visit with my aunt and uncle. Spending most of his time in a nursing facility, my uncle has defied the doctors' predictions of his imminent demise at the hands of Parkinson's disease and other ailments, but he continues to live on borrowed time. His older sister (my mother) is also in a nursing home, although in Indiana, and is unable to travel. Another sister is still further away in Connecticut and now with failing health of her own. The sad realization hit me that these siblings will likely not see each other again. As my daughter and I were leaving to continue our journey westward, I could sense the look in my uncle's eyes that said he did not expect to see us again either.
>
> After two more days on the road amid wide, open spaces and stunning scenery, we found ourselves on the crowded freeways nearing L.A. A short day of adjustment followed, then I prepared to head back to Wisconsin. I found myself on a three-hour flight covering roughly the same land that had just taken my daughter and I four days to cross by car, and with each passing mile I missed her more.
>
> Through time, our lives cross with one another, and our physical paths may lead us in opposite directions. But as long as we keep in our hearts and thoughts those we hold dear—we are never truly apart.

Unit 3: Historical Perspective

The tone poem is a type of program music based on an extra-musical idea. Especially popular with nineteenth- and twentieth-century orchestral composers, Franz Liszt is generally credited with the development of the genre. Descriptive in nature, these works are often inspired by a picture, poem, play, or scenery, although the subject is often converted into music without specific reference to the original inspiration. The title and/or program note provided by the composer usually identify the subject.

Unit 4: Technical Considerations

Technical considerations are at a minimum in this composition, which is excellent for teaching breath control and phrasing, as well as ensemble balance and blend. There should be few range or endurance issues for most students. Primarily written in 3/4, the easily manipulated transitions to 4/4 time provide an introduction to mixed meters. As the tempo ranges from quarter note = 76 to quarter note = 96, this element should also not present any real challenges to the young performer. The ensemble must, however, learn to move together and be flexible through the tempo adjustments for an effective and musical performance. There are no moments of pause, interruption of sound, or full-ensemble rests throughout the length of the work.

Unit 5: Stylistic Considerations

For an effective interpretation of this work, the ensemble needs to play expressively. The composer has included such phrases as "Dreamlike," "Push ahead," and "With urgency" to assist the performers in this task. The many subtle tempo changes indicated provide multiple opportunities for students to learn how to play in a rubato style. The work as a whole has a very reflective quality to it, and is reminiscent of music often found in contemporary film scores.

The following performance notes are provided by the composer:

This composition should be performed in a very fluid and connected style. In the sustained passages, have players stagger breathe as needed to maintain the extended phrases with no perceptible breaks. This work contains slightly unusual harmonies, and careful attention to balance and blend will be needed for the proper effect. There are two emotional and dynamic peaks—one at mm. 40–44 and a secondary peak at m. 60. Make sure both are approached by a gradual *crescendo* that is steady and controlled. Encourage your players to use good tone and balance at all dynamic levels. The percussion writing is very minimal but also very important. Throughout this work, the tempo should not be rigid. Use the indicated tempo changes as a guideline, and experiment with tempos that work with your particular ensemble.

Unit 6: Musical Elements

Crossings in Time allows students to explore and develop an understanding of the four main elements of music within a contemporary composition.

MELODY:

Using minimal melodic development, this work builds emotional intensity through changing textures and evolving harmonies. The layering of instruments, often with open intervals of parallel fourths and fifths, is prevalent. The composer frequently uses a pedal-tone effect, played by various instruments, to connect the melodic fragments and ensure continuous sound throughout the work. The one extended melody, found in the middle section of the piece, is shared among multiple instrument groups. By combining these short melodic fragments, students can learn how to construct a phrase.

HARMONY:

Although an E-flat major key signature is used throughout, the harmonic structure is much more contemporary in design. The tonal centers are primarily E-flat major and C minor, but the composer explores a harmonic language that continually evolves. In the middle section, the piece moves briefly to a contrasting tonal area, using D minor and B-flat major triads with extended chord tones (essentially C major triads) underneath the melodic material. The work then seamlessly transitions back to the harmonic structure found in the opening measures, prior to ending with a C major chord, implying a "Picardy third" effect for the listener.

RHYTHM:

With the emphasis more on the playing and layering of long tones in this work, there is little rhythmic variety. Quarter notes, half notes, and dotted-half notes are predominant. The few eighth-note passages, however, never group more than two eighths together at a time.

TIMBRE:

The majority of the ensemble plays throughout this short work, with the focus on blending and balancing the various timbres of the ensemble rather than exploiting individual voices or any particular combination of instruments. The percussion writing is very sparse. The primary color change in this work is created using dynamic contrast.

Unit 7: Form and Structure

SECTION	MEASURE	EVENT AND SCORING
Intro	1–8	"Dreamlike" (quarter note = 76); flute pedal tone with open interval chords in woodwinds; pedal tone moves to clarinets, and low brass are added to woodwind texture

SECTION	MEASURE	EVENT AND SCORING
A	9–16	"Dreamlike" (quarter note = 76); continuation and expansion of introductory material to set the style and mood
B	17–21	"Push ahead" (quarter note = 84); immediate tempo change with gradual *crescendo* as upper woodwinds play bell-tone chords
A	22–25	"Tempo I" (quarter note = 76); short restatement of introductory material, ending with a rallentando
C	26–43	"With urgency" (quarter note = 96); presentation of main melodic material, passed back and forth from alto saxophones and horns to flutes, oboes, and clarinets (and trumpets on the second statement); ends with a "broadening" of the tempo and *fortissimo* block chords from entire ensemble
A	44–55	"Tempo I" (quarter note = 76); return of introductory material with some expansion
B	56–60	"Push ahead" (quarter note = 84); restatement of transition material, however, bell-tone chords are now in saxophones and brass; ends with a ritard.
A	61–64	"Tempo I" (quarter note = 76); last statement of introductory material, with *diminuendo*
Coda	64–68	Ritard. clarinet pedal tone followed by long chord tones from the ensemble; last sound is an open fifth played by the bells

Unit 8: Suggested Listening

Claude Debussy:
    La Mer (1905)
    Prélude á l'Aprés-midi d'un faune (1894)
Paul Dukas, *L'Apprentisorcier* (1897)
George Gershwin, *An American in Paris* (1928)
Franz Liszt, *Les Préludes* (1848)

Ottorino Resphigi, *Pini di Roma* (1924)
Richard Strauss:
    Also sprach Zarathustra (1896)
    Ein Heldenleben (1899)
Piotr Ill'yich Tchaikovsky, *Romeo and Juliet* (1869)

Unit 9: Additional References and Resources

Menghini, Charles T. "*Imperium*." In *Teaching Music through Performance in Beginning Band*, Vol. 1. Edited by Richard Miles and Thomas Dvorak. Chicago: GIA Publications, 2001: 217–221.

Miles, Richard, ed. "*Ancient Voices*." In *Teaching Music through Performance in Band*, Vol. 1. Chicago: GIA Publications, 1997: 70–73.

Rehrig, William H. *The Heritage Encyclopedia of Band Music*, Vol. 3. Edited by Paul E. Bierley. Westerville, OH: Integrity Press, 1996: 768.

Web site:
    Hal Leonard Corporation: http://www.halleonard.com

Contributed by:

James Popejoy
Director of Bands
University of North Dakota
Grand Forks, North Dakota

Teacher Resource Guide

Crusade

Vince Gassi
(b. 1959)

Unit 1: Composer

Vince Gassi holds a bachelor of music education degree from the University of Western Ontario in London, Canada. After completing studies at the University of Western Ontario, he attended the Dick Grove School of Music, specializing in composition and arranging. He is a trumpet student of Claude Gordon.

Gassi has written for a variety of ensembles, including concert band, jazz ensemble, orchestra, woodwind and brass ensembles, and choral groups. Recently he has started writing music for television and film. In addition to his career as a composer/arranger, Gassi has taught instrumental music at the elementary and secondary school levels, and has conducted scholastic honor bands, community bands and musical theatre productions. He has taught privately, and is active as a clinician for workshops on brass performance and composition.

Currently, Gassi teaches instrumental music, music and computers, and musical theatre at Mary Ward Catholic Secondary School in Toronto, Canada.[1]

Unit 2: Composition

Written in 2006, *Crusade* is scored for beginning band and is approximately two minutes and ten seconds in length. The composer premiered this piece with the Mary Ward Catholic band in 2003. Given some of the technical demands of the piece, *Crusade* would fit well into a late-year concert program for a beginning band.

Unit 3: Historical Perspective

As a director, Gassi sought to compose a piece that was both enjoyable for his students and would address the technical and musical needs of the ensemble. The title of the piece stems from the composer's interest in a book he read involving the crusades of the eleventh and twelfth centuries; however, he does not relate any specific story to the piece.[2] The descriptive nature of the title, along with the interesting modality and dynamic contrast of the music, introduces students to program music. Students can create images, drama, and story lines to fit the music that is played.

Unit 4: Technical Considerations

Students must have knowledge of whole notes, half notes, and paired eighth notes in a variety of articulated patterns. Ranges are within the limits for a young group; however, flutes will be required to play D6 and E-flat6. In the opening six measures of the piece all of the parts have concert G-flat and D-flat at some point, with the exception of trumpet. Later the same pitches occur in mm. 41 and 42 in the bass clarinet, tenor saxophone, baritone saxophone, trombone, baritone, and tuba.

Percussion includes snare drum, bass drum, crash cymbals, gong, suspended cymbal, and timpani. This piece introduces students to instruments like the gong and timpani within a limited means. Students playing snare drum must have knowledge of flams and rolls, while students playing bass drum and timpani must be comfortable counting tied notes over bar lines.

Unit 5: Stylistic Considerations

The piece is comprised of many different articulations including slurs, staccato eighth notes, accents, and legato quarter notes. The conductor will need to address consistency of articulation throughout the piece. *Crusade* offers opportunities for dynamic contrast and growth of sound, especially through the many indicated dynamic markings. In mm. 22 and mm. 52 there is a *fp* marked on the *and* of beat four for the entire ensemble. Students will have to work not only on executing an accent on a weak beat, but also on mastering the *fp* articulation at the same time.

Unit 6: Musical Elements

MELODY:
Crusade is written in Dorian mode, which is reflected in the melodies throughout the piece. Students must be aware of the frequent accidentals. The opening motive consists of half note intervals of a fifth and fourth. Students should strive to play the half notes full value in two-bar phrases.

Throughout Theme A, all paired eighth notes are articulated with a slur and a staccato on the second note. The conductor should address this articulation to guarantee that students do not play the second eighth note too short. Theme B is stated by the full ensemble with the exception of percussion. This is a great opportunity to focus on consistency in articulating the tenuto and staccato markings. The stepwise motion of Theme C adds a nice contrast to the intervallic nature of the introduction.

HARMONY:
The use of modal harmony is prevalent throughout the work. The piece is written in the key of B-flat major, however is centered around C Dorian. By now students should be acquainted with the B-flat concert scale. To prepare students for the harmonic sounds of *Crusade*, the conductor can have them simply play a B-flat-concert scale, but starting on concert C. The presence of the concert A-flat and the use of half steps all lend themselves to modal harmony not typically found in music for young students. Gassi has found a way to use dissonant tones while remaining within the limitations of beginning students. The conductor will have to address these harmonies, especially between m. 58 through m. 67, for balance and intonation.

RHYTHM:
The opening introduction is marked quarter note = 116, while the body of the piece is marked quarter note = 138. At this tempo, the ensemble may have a tendency to rush. In particular, the sixteenth-note figures in the snare drum and the repeated quarter notes in the section beginning at m. 20 will both have a tendency to accelerate. All the rhythmic figures are within reach for this level of playing; however, the challenge comes from the different articulations each rhythm accompanies.

There is a hemiola in the opening four bars of the piece found in the timpani, which reappears in m. 58 in the timpani and in m. 60 in the bass drum. The timpani part is the only part that has written eighth rest/eighth note figures.

TIMBRE:
With any young group, great attention should be placed on good sound production, which leads to a characteristic timbre. Along with this idea, in *Crusade* the conductor should work on balancing the different melodic and rhythmic elements so that each timbre can come through the texture. For example, in m. 20 the fifth of the chord is present in second clarinet and horn. In m. 28 the alto saxophone and tenor saxophone state Theme A as before; however, the scoring and harmony change in m. 32. The unison concert C in mm. 8–9 and then in mm. 44–45 needs to be balanced to

accommodate the group instrumentation. Students must also strive to maintain appropriate timbre and balance throughout the many dynamic changes in the piece, especially the *fp* markings. Students will often arrive below the pitch when executing the *piano* element of a *fp*.

Unit 7: Form and Structure

SECTION	MEASURE	EVENT AND SCORING
Introduction	1–10	Half note motive with concert G-flat and D-flat; hemiola in timpani
Theme A	10–19	Ostinato 1 – clarinet and horn; Theme A in alto and harmonized at a third by tenor saxophones
Theme B	20–27	Theme B is a tutti statement, answered by percussion and timpani; *fp* in m. 22
Theme A	28–35	Ostinato 2 – clarinet; theme A – alto saxophone, flute and tenor saxophone, followed by a similar statement by flute, tenor saxophone and trumpet, but trumpet is harmonized at a fourth rather than a third; Ostinato 1: alto saxophone and horn
Theme C	36–39	Theme C; alto saxophone and trumpet; echoed in flute, clarinet, horn and bells
	40–49	Similar to introduction; low brass melody similar to mm. 1–2, percussion soli at mm. 46–49 similar to mm. 4–5 at m. 46 with added flams in snare drum
Theme B	50–57	Theme B is a tutti statement; *fp* in m. 52
	58–67	Building to the end, chromatic-concert D-flat, E, and A-flat; dissonant cluster at m. 67
Coda	68–72	Coda; melodically based on the third measure of Theme A, rhythmically based on Theme B

Unit 8: Suggested Listening

Elliot Del Borgo, *Modal Song and Dance*
Norman Dello Joio, *Scenes from "The Louvre"*
Vince Gassi, *Tsunami*
Gustav Holst, *The Planets: Mars*
Barry Kopetz, *Dorian Landscape*
W. Francis McBeth, *Chant and Jublio*
Robert W. Smith, *The Tempest*

Unit 9: Additional References and Resources

Alfred Publishing. Accessed 21 May 2007. http://www.alfred.com.

Gassi, Vince. *Crusade.* Van Nuys, CA: Alfred Publishing Co., 2006.

Gassi, Vince. Personal Phone Interview. 25 May 2007.

Ramsey, Darhyl S. "Beginning Band Goals and Objectives." In *Teaching Music through Performance in Beginning Band.* Richard Miles and Thomas Dvorak, eds. Chicago: GIA Publications, 2001.

Sadie, Stanley, and J. Tyrrell, ed. *The New Grove Dictionary of Music and Musicians.* London: Macmillan, 2001.

Contributed by:

Gina M. Lenox
Masters Conducting Associate
University of North Texas
Denton, Texas

---

1 Alfred Publishing. Acessed 21 May 2007. http://www.alfred.com.
2 Gassi, Vince. Personal Phone Interview. 25 May 2007.

Teacher Resource Guide

Danse Antiqua

Chris Sharp
(b. 1959)

Unit 1: Composer

Chris Sharp is a professional composer/arranger/orchestrator living in Gainesville, Florida. Mr. Sharp is currently published by the FJH Music Company, Inc.; his current output includes music for concert band and jazz band, and he is also developing materials in the area of jazz pedagogy. He has extensive experience as a professional trombonist, having served almost twenty years as a bandleader and sideman for The Walt Disney World Company. In addition, Mr. Sharp was a band director at West Orange High School in Winter Garden, Florida for four years.

As an arranger, he has provided music for many professional and scholastic groups including the Disney parks worldwide, Universal Studios (both Florida and California), and the Ringling Brothers and Barnum and Bailey Circus. He has also contributed pieces to several service bands, including the famed United States Air Force Airmen of Note, who recorded his arrangement of Duke Ellington's "Caravan" on their 1999 CD, *Invitation*.

Mr. Sharp studied at the University of Florida under Richard W. Bowles, Gary Langford, and Frank Wickes, and under Gary Lindsay, Ron Miller, Whit Sidener, and Alfred Reed while at the University of Miami. He is in constant demand as a clinician, having taught brass technique and composing/arranging in many different settings, including the Berklee School of Music in Boston. He has had compositions and arrangements performed at the prestigious Midwest Clinic in each of the last five years, and in 2005 and 2006 earned awards from ASCAP for sales of his published pieces.

Unit 2: Composition

Danse Antiqua is a single-movement piece composed in 2003 in tribute to Frank Erickson. This 68-measure work is considered to be a Grade 2 by The FJH Music Company, Inc. It is one minute and forty-eight seconds in length. Sharp writes:

> *Danse Antiqua* is a tribute to Mr. Erickson and the body of work he has provided. It mimics the form and harmonic style of some of his early works, giving it the feel of a Renaissance dance. This piece, like many of Erickson's works, was written to strengthen ensemble playing.

Unit 3: Historical Perspective

Frank Erickson was born on September 1, 1923 in Spokane, Washington. As a young child, he started his musical training first with piano studies and later he began to study the trumpet. Erickson's first composition for band was written when he was a senior in high school. During World War II, he arranged music for army bands, and afterwards studied composition with Castelnuovo-Tedesco. He received both his bachelor's and master's degrees in music from the University of Southern California, studying with Halsey Stevens. Erickson held teaching positions at the University of California at Los Angeles and San Jose State College. He died on October 21, 1996. Throughout his life, Erickson was a prolific composer with more than 250 published compositions and arrangements.[1] Sharp writes:

> Frank Erickson was a renowned composer of band music. He was one of the few significant writers whose focus was on younger bands; many of his best known works were written for easier grade levels. He spent many years devoting his finely tuned craft to providing meaningful compositions for these developing musicians.
>
> Mr. Erickson used many compositional techniques to give depth to his music while keeping it basic in its technical demands. Some became trademarks by which his pieces could be identified. For example, he often alternated between woodwind and brass passages. Also common was his use of hemiolas and a harmonic language that gave many of his pieces a Renaissance flavor. This, combined with his extensive knowledge of harmony (including jazz harmony), gave his music an unmistakable sound and feel.
>
> He was also adept at writing idiomatically for the instruments, anticipating and accommodating the usual pitfalls common to younger players. His knowledge of the individual characteristics of each instrument allowed him to create rich sonorities often making an inexperienced group sound much more mature.

Unit 4: Technical Considerations

Danse Antiqua is scored for full band: flute 1/2, oboe, bassoon, clarinet 1/2, bass clarinet, alto saxophone 1/2, tenor saxophone, baritone saxophone, trumpet 1/2, horn, trombone 1/2, euphonium (bass and treble clef), tuba, and percussion. The percussion includes timpani (without any pitch changes), snare drum, bass drum, tambourine, tom-toms, crash cymbals, and suspended cymbal.

The piece is in D minor and the melodic, harmonic, and natural forms of D minor are all used. Students should become familiar with all three scales to prepare for the accidentals that occur in their respective parts. The entire piece is in 3/4 time. The smallest subdivision of time for the wind players is eighth notes; however, some percussion parts subdivide into sixteenth notes. Range considerations include: D6 for flute 1; A5 for clarinet 1; E5 for trumpet 1; D5 for horn; and D4 for trombone 1.

Unit 5: Stylistic Considerations

Danse Antiqua is marked at quarter note = 132, and the tempo remains steady throughout most of the piece. The final statement of the A Section at measure 58 is marked "Broadly" and is preceded by a ritardando. This section requires musical pacing and direction as the coda of the piece at measure 66 has a molto ritardando which should not be approached too slowly.

Dynamic ranges extend from *mezzo piano* to *forte* with changes outlining the form of the piece. *Crescendos* appear only twice, in conjunction with the two ritardandos that occur toward the end of the piece. Students will need to focus as a group on making a difference in volume between *mezzo piano* and *mezzo forte*. The ensemble as a whole should focus on even growth of the *crescendos*.

Numerous expression markings are used to differentiate between the sections of the piece. Students need to understand the differences of playing staccato, accented, marcato, as well as slurred and legato. Particular care should be given to the ends of phrases and to playing full note lengths to provide smooth transitions between each phrase.

Unit 6: Musical Elements

MELODY:

Except for the introduction and coda, melodic material is presented in eight-measure phrases. Each new phrase is played by a different instrument grouping, and the melodic line is usually shared between at least two instrument voices. Transitions between phrases and instrument groups should be smooth, which can be accomplished by holding notes for full value, especially in the last measure of each phrase.

HARMONY:

Danse Antiqua is in D minor, with the tonality shifting between the melodic, harmonic, and natural forms of D minor. Students need to be comfortable with all three forms of D minor to navigate the accidentals throughout the piece. Sharp also makes use of secondary dominants and suspensions. Balances should be adjusted to hear these chord structures as well as the dissonance and resolution of the suspensions.

RHYTHM:

The rhythmic structure of *Danse Antiqua* is very straightforward for the wind players. Dotted-half notes, half notes, dotted-quarter, quarter, and eighth-note rhythms are most prevalent throughout the piece. Note values should be held full length, unless they are marked staccato. The percussion parts require the most amount of rhythmic independence. The timpani, snare drum, and tom-toms are often independent of each other, but the rhythmic figures will at times overlap for one or two beats. It may be necessary to work with the percussion separately to show the relationship between each of the parts, and then between the percussion and the wind parts. The percussion are required to play sixteenth-note rhythms and should be careful not to rush through those sections.

TIMBRE:

Sharp makes use of instrument choirs for the melodic material. Flute, oboe, clarinet, and trumpet are often combined together as one group, while alto saxophones, horns, and occasionally clarinets are combined as another. The low brass and low woodwinds are usually combined in the accompaniment. Balance within each choir as well as between each choir group is important so that all timbres and notes of the chord are heard. The most notable change in choir groupings occurs in the B section at measure 26, where the ensemble is grouped into a woodwind choir and a brass choir. Measures 50 through 57 will present a particular problem with balance in terms of range and rhythmic activity between the melodic line in the trumpet and the accompanying line in the upper woodwinds. The upper woodwinds need to carefully control dynamic levels and allow the trumpet melody to be heard.

Unit 7: Form and Structure

SECTION	MEASURE	EVENT AND SCORING
Introduction	1–5	Upper woodwinds and trumpets alternate opening melodic material with alto saxophones and horns
	6–9	Percussion only—all parts independent
A	10–17	First statement of A in clarinet, alto saxophone, and horn; quarter-note accompaniment in all other winds; no percussion
	18–25	Second statement of A in flute, oboe, clarinet, and trumpet; variation of quarter note rhythm accompaniment
B Antecedent	26–33	Legato woodwind chorale
Consequence	34–41	Trumpet melodic line with brass and tom-tom accompaniment
C	42–49	Melodic line in clarinet, alto saxophone and horn; second rhythmic variation of quarter-note accompaniment in low woodwinds, low brass and bass drum
	50–57	Second statement of C melody in trumpet; eighth-note accompaniment in upper woodwinds joins the quarter note accompaniment in low brass, woodwinds and bass drum
A	58–65	Full melodic line in upper woodwinds and trumpet; low woodwind and brass alternate between melodic rhythm, eighth-note accompaniment, and quarter-note accompaniment
Coda	66–68	Cadential extension of melodic line

Unit 8: Suggested Listening

Frank Erickson:
  Air for Band
  Balladair
  Black Canyon of the Gunnison
  Blue Ridge Overture

> *Buccaneer's Hornpipe*
> *Sonatina for Band*
> *Toccata for Band*
> Bob Margolis (after Gervaise):
> *Fanfare*
> *Ode and Festival*
> Chris Sharp:
> *Flying Colors*
> *Funtango*
> *Juju Dance*
> *Our Song Shall Rise*
> *Vikings Victorious*
> *Vision Quest*
> *Walden*
> *Windermere Overture*
> Tielman Susato/arranged by Curnow, *Renaissance Suite*
> Tielman Susato/arranged by Margolis, *The Battle Pavane*
> Orazio Vecchi/arranged by Daehn, *Fa Una Canzona*

Unit 9: Additional References and Resources

Hitchcock, H. Wiley, and Stanley Sadie, eds. *The New Grove Dictionary of American Music*. London: Macmillan, 1986.

Old Dominion University Libraries. "Frank Erickson Collection." Old Dominion University Libraries. http://www.lib.odu.edu/musiclib/contemporarymusic/frankerickson/biography.htm (accessed June 9, 2007).

Sharp, Chris. *Danse Antiqua*. Fort Lauderdale, FL: FJH Music, 2003.

Sharp, Chris. Email message to contributor. June 10, 2007.

Contributed by:

Jennifer Kitelinger
Doctoral Conducting Associate
University of North Texas
Denton, Texas

---

1 Raoul Camus, "Erickson, Frank," *The New Grove Dictionary of American Music*, ed. H. Wiley Hitchcock and Stanley Sadie (London: Macmillan, 1986), 2:56–57.

Teacher Resource Guide

Dimensions

Ralph Ford
(b. 1963)

Unit 1: Composer

Ralph Ford is the director of bands at Troy University. He also works as a staff composer and arranger for Belwin, a division of Alfred Publications, and has well over 130 publications for concert band, orchestra, jazz ensemble, and marching band to his credit. He has also composed and produced music for radio, television, and video productions. A Florida native, he received his degrees from Troy University and has been on the faculty there since 1986.

Unit 2: Composition

Dimensions is published by Belwin as part of their *Very Beginning Band* series. The work is sixty measures in length with an approximate performance time of two minutes. Other than an optional ritard. at the end, the tempo is constant throughout the entire work, marked as "Bold!" with a metronome marking of 132. Its spirit is that of a rousing fanfare, albeit for young band.

Unit 3: Historical Perspective

A great many works written for young band are in a contemporary, neo-Romantic style, and this is one such composition.

    Dimensions is Ralph Ford's first effort to write a work for Belwin's *Very Beginning Band* series. While he had composed other works for elementary band prior to this time, none have been at this level. Ford says that his goal was to write a composition that is technically as absolutely basic as possible but to make each individual part interesting so that students will enjoy playing the work.

Unit 4: Technical Considerations

This bold composition uses only six notes, and employs relatively long rhythmic note values. This results in a work that is not technically demanding, and is quite suitable for beginning bands. Instrumental ranges are well considered and extreme pitches are avoided. The clarinets do not go over the break and the highest note for the trumpet is a written A4.

One instrumentation issue that might cause a problem for some beginning bands: An important countermelody is written for horn (mm. 11–18). The part is also cued in the tenor saxophone, but the teacher could re-write it for another instrument should the band lack both horns and tenor saxophones.

Accurate interpretation of dynamics and articulations is an important goal when studying *Dimensions*. Many times the downbeat is staccato and the second beat is accented (see Figure 1), and these inflections are central to portraying the structure of the main theme. This is a great piece for teaching students about accents and staccato marks.

Figure 1

Generally the louder dynamic levels are not problematic, although Ford does use dramatic changes of volume to achieve contrast. The *fp* dynamic is employed several times (see mm. 9, 35, 37, 39) often followed by a *crescendo*, which may be a real challenge for some beginning bands.

A few specific rhythms might prove to be difficult for very beginning bands as well. The most obvious example is a tie over a strong beat in the countermelody found in measures 53 and 54, which could certainly pose a problem. One other figure is the syncopated rhythm found in the second measure in the percussion. Syncopation is a concept that might not yet be introduced when a piece of this difficulty level would be studied. This is not an insurmountable issue, however, because this single occurrence could be taught by rote or altered to a less difficult pattern (two eighths and a quarter, or two quarters similar to measure four).

As in a number of other works of this difficulty level, the quick tempo can be a challenge. If the piece is not performed at the indicated brisk tempo, the desired character of the piece might not be nearly as exciting. Obviously, much of the energy of the piece comes from its tempo.

Unit 5: Stylistic Considerations

As in most fanfares, the general style is one of confident energy. In *Dimensions* this is accomplished primarily through articulation, which is generally marcato or staccato. The consistently fast tempo throughout generates the stylistic vigor. Musical contrast occurs largely through dynamics, timbre and texture, and counterpoint. Percussion is often used to strengthen these contrasting elements.

Unit 6: Musical Elements

MELODY:

Melodic construction often begins by an ascending pattern of a major second, a minor third, and another major second. Sometimes the opening motive is then followed by a downward leap; other times the rising figure is followed by a descending scale (see mm. 1–4). Because the piece is so clearly rooted in B-flat, students would benefit from some preliminary work on the B-flat major scale, or at least the first six pitches.

Countermelody is often added to provide musical contrast. One such example is seen in the fifth measure where the flutes, oboes, clarinets, alto saxophones, and mallet percussion add somewhat disjunct counterpoint to the main theme presented in the brass.

HARMONY:

Harmonically, the composition is fairly basic. Given that there are no accidentals, the tonality stays pretty firmly linked to the home key of B-flat. Given the limitation of only six pitches, Ford does provide some moments of harmonic interest, especially with half cadences at various points.

RHYTHM

The entire work is in 4/4 meter. There are no eighth notes found in the wind parts with the exception of a single eighth linked to a tie in measure 34. The percussion part is more active with several eighth notes, including a syncopated figure.

A central feature of the work is a stress of the second beat in the measure (see Figure 1). Most normally in 4/4, the downbeat receives the greatest stress followed next by the third beat. Here it is the second beat that is the most important in the second measure of the main motive. This factor presents great potential for teaching students about the nature of meter.

Another commonly found rhythmic pattern is quarter-half-quarter, or short-long-short. This motive is good preparation for teaching the syncopated figure: eighth-quarter-eighth, also short-long-short.

TIMBRE

Both timbre and texture are central features of *Dimensions* in providing musical contrast. Ford often states a theme in a certain group of instruments and then restates it with added instruments. The beginning is an example. Trumpets, saxophones, horns, and trombones start the work. In the fifth measure, the remaining instruments enter with an expanded version of the original melody, beginning in measure 7 along with a new bass line and countermelody. The thinly scored second phrase begins with a duet between the horn and trumpet sections (both are cued in other instruments), and the upper woodwinds and mallet percussion are featured in the next phrase. Not unexpectedly, the work ends with the full ensemble.

The percussion parts are fairly basic, but include some colorful techniques such as the use of a metal scraper on a tam-tam.

Unit 7: Form and Structure

The work's musical structure might hold some of its greatest musical interest and significance. Given its very basic technical requirements, its structure is quite sophisticated. Teaching the concepts of restatement versus alteration of themes is certainly one potential educational goal.

Phrase construction is a central component of the structure. Normally, the phrases are clearly defined in units of eight measures, although twice with two-measure extensions (see next page). Each phrase can be further divided into semi-phrases of four measures each. Very often, Ford starts the second semi-phrase exactly like the first. However, in the third measure of this second semi-phrase, Ford uses some developmental technique (e.g., intervallic and/or rhythmic expansion, motivic variation) to change the structure, thereby providing variety. The very first phrase is a clear example. Except for instrumentation changes and the addition of counterpoint, measures 1 and 2 are identical to 5 and 6. However, instead of restating the opening motive as he did in the third and fourth measures, he alters both the melody and the rhythm and adds a two-measure extension. Instead of descending a fifth as he did between measures 2 and 3, he descends only a major second. The highest pitch is also introduced here (a concert G) creating the greatest melodic interest in this first phrase. The basic rhythm is elongated to half notes for the full ensemble and the percussion reinforces the overall rhythm instead of providing contrasting interjections as they did in the first semi-phrase. This technique is found repeatedly and is a clever approach to provide both unity and variety in a piece of this beginning level of difficulty.

There are seven phrases. Five are eight measures long and two (phrases 1 and 6) are ten measures, similar in structure to the other phrases but with two-measure extensions. Most of the phrases are quite similar in character except for the fifth, which provides contrast and the seventh, which is a coda.

SECTION	MEASURE	EVENT AND SCORING
Main Theme	1–34	
Phrase 1	1–10	(4 + 6 measures); serves as an introduction; primary motive in mm. 1–4
Phrase 2	11–18	(4 + 4 measures); begins like Phrase 1 but is developed starting in m. 12; thinner scoring throughout (trumpets and horns)
Phrase 3	19–26	(4 + 4 measures); similar to Phrase 2 but with a cadence in B-flat; like Phrase 2, scoring is thinner but here in woodwinds and mallet percussion
Phrase 4	27–34	(4 + 4 measures); very similar to Phrase 3 with tutti scoring and a more conclusive cadence
Interlude	35–42	
Phrase 5		Alternating two-measure figures between high and low instruments; different in character from the rest of the work
Main Theme	43–60	
Phrase 6	43–52	(4 + 6 measures); begins like Phrase 1 (mm. 1–8); final two bars differ
Phrase 7	53–60	((2 + 2) + 4 measures); coda

Unit 8: Suggested Listening

Beginning Music
    Larry Clark:
        Character
        Penta
    Ralph Ford:
        Cango Cave
        G-Force Five!
        Fire Caves of Golgathon
    Robert W. Smith:
        Liturgical Fanfare
        Tempest
    William Windham, *Vandivere Fanfare*

Advanced Music
    Ron Nelson, *Courtly Airs and Dances* (Movement 6)
    Ralph Vaughan Williams, *Flourish for Wind Band*

Unit 9: Additional References and Resources

Dunsby, Jonathan, and Arnold Whittall. *Music Analysis in Theory and Practice*. New Haven, CT: Yale University Press, 1988.

Green, Douglass M. *Form in Tonal Music: An Introduction to Analysis*. 2nd Edition. New York: Holt, Rinehart and Winston, 1979.

Hutcheson, Jere T. *Musical Form and Analysis: Volume 1 Basic Elements in Musical Form*. Boston: Allyn and Bacon, Inc., 1972.

Reed, H. Owen, and Robert G. Sidnell. *The Materials of Music Composition: Book I Fundamentals*. Reading, MA: Addison-Wesley, Publishing Company, 1978.

White, John D. *The Analysis of Music*. Englewood Cliffs, NJ: Prentice-Hall, Inc., 1976.

Web sites:
    Alfred (Belwin): http://www.alfred.com/
    Ralph Ford: http://www.soundofthesouth.org/Staff/ford_bio.htm
    Ralph Ford: http://spectrum.troy.edu/%7Eford/

Contributed by:

William Berz
Professor of Music
Mason Gross School of the Arts
Rutgers, The State University of New Jersey
New Brunswick, New Jersey

Teacher Resource Guide

Early One Morning

arranged by Duncan Stubbs
(b. 1961)

Unit 1: Composer

Duncan Stubbs was born in Stoke on Trent. He began his band career at age fourteen playing the bassoon and studied music performance at York University. Stubbs continued his education at Birmingham specializing in music education. His bassoon instructors included Michael Chapman, Andrew Barnell, and John Orford.

Mr. Stubbs joined the Royal Air Force in 1983 as a member of the Central Band. His interest in conducting led to work with several community bands in West London and in his hometown of Stoke on Trent. Following studies with Colin Metters at the Royal College of Music, Duncan was commissioned as director of Music Royal Air Force in March 1990.

He has been the director of music of both the Royal Air Force Western Band and the Band of the Royal Air Force College. Mr. Stubbs has earned an unprecedented six consecutive wins in the Boosey & Hawkes Inter Band Competitions and has also won the Cassel Cup four times. Squadron Leader Stubbs was appointed as director of music of the Central Band of the Royal Air Force in November 2000.

Duncan Stubbs has written music for bands and woodwind ensembles. Other band compositions and arrangements include:

Child's Play
Elegy on "Londonderry Air"
Fun of the Fair

The Last Lincolnshire Poacher
Three Carols from Olde England

All of Mr. Stubbs's compositions are available through Studio Music Publications.

Unit 2: Composition

Early One Morning was published in 2005 by Studio Music Company, London, England, under the *Simply Classics* editions. The work is a setting of the traditional British folk song of the same title and is listed as a Grade 1.5. Stubbs's setting uses standard band instrumentation with minimal percussion: suspended cymbal, glockenspiel, and triangle. All low brass and low woodwind parts are the same (bass clarinet, bassoon, baritone saxophone, trombone, euphonium, and tuba). Oboe, baritone saxophone, and horn in F parts are listed as optional. Stubbs has included cues for tuba, horn in F, alto saxophone, flute, oboe, bassoon, and bass clarinet. A treble-clef baritone part is included. The arrangement is marked Tranquillo and scored in cut time with a half note = 64. The 59-measure arrangement is approximately two minutes and thirty seconds in length.

Unit 3: Historical Perspective

Early One Morning is a British folk song that has been used or set by many composer/arrangers including Percy Grainger, Benjamin Britten, and Gordon Jacob. Grainger began work with *Early One Morning* in 1901 and in 1940 completed three settings. In 1950 Grainger scored the melody for Leopold Stokowski. Joseph Kreines used Grainger's 1940 and 1950 versions to craft a setting for band in his setting of *Two Grainger Melodies* (1988) (*Teaching Music through Performance in Band*, Vol. 1, pp. 210–213). Benjamin Britten scored the melody for voice and piano in 1957. Gordon Jacob uses the lyrical folk tune as material for the forth movement of his *Old Wine in New Bottles* (1960).

The text to this beautiful melody is:

> Early one morning, just as the sun was rising,
> I heard a maid singing in the valley below;
> Oh don't deceive me, Oh do not leave me!
> How could you use a poor maiden so?
>
> O gay is the garland, fresh are the roses
> I've culled from the garden to bind on thy brow.
> Oh don't deceive me, Oh do not leave me!
> How could you use a poor maiden so?
> Remember the vows that you made to your Mary,

Remember the bower where you vowed to be true;
O don't deceive me, O do not leave me!
How could you use a poor maiden so?

Thus sang the poor maiden, her sorrow bewailing,
Thus sang the poor maid, in the valley below.
O don't deceive me, O do not leave me!
How could you use a poor maiden so?

Unit 4: Technical Considerations

Technical demands on the ensemble are few. The challenge is to maintain a flowing legato style and balance throughout. Mr. Stubbs has used the quarter-note pulse and half-note movement to project the piece forward. The folk song melody and fragments of the melody used in the introduction, bridge, and coda are the main focus of the arrangement.

Unit 5: Stylistic Considerations

Attention should be placed on maintaining a quiet, simple, and lyrical style throughout. The focus on producing characteristic sounds in a balanced and blended ensemble is the key to success. *Piano* and *forte* are the only dynamic markings used for the setting. The *forte* section only lasts for six measures (measures 41–46) and ends with a *decrescendo* back to *piano* (measures 47–49).

The program notes read:

> The main aim should be always to keep the music gentle and flowing. While a quiet dynamic should be aimed for, this should not be a priority as quality of note production, ensemble and balance are more important. While the middle section is indicated at a louder dynamic, this is mainly to give the piece shape and the quality and blend of the overall sounds remains the priority throughout. All players should be encouraged to listen carefully to ensure the balance of parts is maintained.

To teach style, have students listen to examples of lyrical music and try to emulate the sounds on their instruments. Play recordings of band, orchestral and vocal examples of lyrical music for the ensemble. Several settings of the folk tune *Early One Morning* have been suggested at the end of this section. Have students sing the melody on neutral syllables or using the words provided in this section.

Unit 6: Musical Elements

MELODY:

The melodic material is the folk song melody *Early One Morning*. Fragments of the opening statement are used in the introduction and the closing section of the arrangement.

To help students understand the idea of balance, write out the folk melody for all instruments. Have the entire band play the folk tune in unison, then ask students to listen for the melody throughout the piece. Other activities may include having half the band sing the lyrics while the others play the melody. Focus should always be on producing characteristic sounds with excellent breath support.

HARMONY:

Early One Morning is set in the key of B-flat. Traditional tertian harmonies are used throughout the setting. An undulating half-note/quarter-note pulse gently rocks back and forth, creating a calming background for the melody. Chords change at a half-note pulse often with a sustained pedal in the low brass and woodwinds.

Students can create exercises that model the pattern used in the arrangement using the B-flat scale. In cut time beginning on B-flat, students play a four-measure pattern of quarter notes B-flat–C–B-flat–C–B-flat–C–B-flat–C and then resolve to two B-flat whole notes. Then students will repeat the pattern up the scale (C–D–C–D–C–D–C–D–C).

Stubbs uses accidentals to add color to the harmonic palette and to create a more interesting bass line. He doubles the altered pitches in measures 15, 16, 17, 18, 34, 35, 36, 45, 46. In measure 38 the only instrument that has the altered pitch (B-natural) is the second clarinet. The texture is thin, but directors should make sure the altered note is balanced and does not sound like a mistake.

RHYTHM:

Rhythms are simple and follow the frame of the folk tune melody. Stubbs uses whole notes, half notes and quarter notes in his arrangement. The setting is in cut time, and to teach students to play in this meter, have them play the first few measures in 4/4 time and then explain that the quarter notes in 4/4 time will be the subdivision of pulse for the faster cut time. In cut time the quarter notes become like eighth notes in 4/4.

Using the B-flat scale, students will play six measure patterns in cut time: two measures of whole notes, two measures of half notes, and two measures of quarter notes for each pitch up and down the scale. Make sure students are using a legato articulation. Vary the dynamics using conducting gestures, which will teach students to watch for changes in conducting style and aid in the *crescendo* and *decrescendo* in measures 25–28. In teaching *crescendos* and *decrescendos*, a numbering system can be helpful:

1 - *pianissimo*
2 - *piano*
3 - *mezzo*
4 - *forte*
5 - *fortissimo*

As the conducting gesture becomes larger, hold up the corresponding number of fingers in the left hand. Eventually replace the numbering system with a rising gesture in the left hand to symbolize a *crescendo*. In the right hand, concentrate on the joints used to create the gesture:

Fingers - *pianissimo*
Wrist - *piano*
Elbow - *mezzo-forte*
Shoulder - *forte-fortissimo*

TIMBRE:
Instrumental color is very important in this arrangement. The first melodic statement is a blend of flute, alto saxophone, and trumpet. Clarinet and alto saxophone play the first verse. Trumpet and oboe lead the chorus punctuated by glockenspiel and triangle at measure 21. The first time the tutti band plays is at measure 25. When the verse returns at measure 33 it is presented in the flutes. Measure 41 is the climax of the piece with tutti band and percussion playing a robust and rich *forte*. Stubbs ends the arrangement as he began with flute, alto saxophone, and trumpet. The setting is a mixture of blended sounds and delicate textures.

Unit 7: Form and Structure

Early One Morning is organized into five main sections: Introduction (mm. 1–12), Folk Song (mm. 13–28), Bridge (mm. 29–32), Folk Song (mm. 33–48), and Coda (mm. 49–59). Material from the opening statement of the folk song melody is used for the introduction, bridge, and coda. Other material used in creating form is the half note-quarter note "rocking" background. The overall dynamic is *piano* with the climax at measure 41–48 marked *forte*.

SECTION	MEASURE	EVENT AND SCORING
Introduction	1–12	Begins with "rocking" chords (mm. 1–4); statement of first two measures of the verse (mm. 5–8); echo statement of first two measures of the verse (mm. 9–12);
Melody	13–28	Verse – clarinet 1 and alto saxophone (mm. 13–20); chorus – oboe (clarinet 1 cue), trumpet 1 (mm. 20–24); at m. 25 – flute, oboe, clarinet, alto saxophone, tenor saxophone, and trumpet (mm. 25–28)
Bridge	29–32	Introduction material from mm. 1–4 with the addition of a flute 2 part
Melody	33–48	Verse – flute (oboe cue) (mm. 33–40); chorus – the climax of the piece is set at *forte* and has thicker scoring; the harmonic pulse is faster and the melodic material is harmonized; the melody appears at first in flute 1, oboe, trumpet, and tenor saxophone and harmonized with flute 2 and alto saxophone (mm. 41–44); in measures 45–46 the harmonized melody is scored for flutes, clarinets, alto saxophone; measures 47–48 are an augmentation of the last four notes of the melody from quarter notes to half notes and includes a *decrescendo* back to *piano*
Coda	49–59	"Rocking" chords statement from measure 1 (mm. 49–52); statement of first two measures of the verse from measure 5 (mm. 53–56); augmentation of the opening "rocking" chords material with a descending cadence in the alto saxophones (mm. 57–59)

Unit 8: Suggested Listening

Benjamin Britten, *Early One Morning*
Percy Aldridge Grainger:
    Early One Morning
    Two Grainger Melodies, arr. Joseph Kreines
Gordon Jacob, *Old Wine in New Bottles*
Pierre La Plante, *Early One Morning (English Country Settings II)*
David Mruzek, *Early One Morning March*
John O'Reilly, *Two English Dances*

Unit 9: Additional References and Resources

Aldrich, Mark. *A Catalog of Folk Song Settings for Wind Band.* Ft. Lauderdale,
    FL: Meredith Music, 2004.

Miles, Richard, ed. *Teaching Music through Performance in Band, Vol. 1.*
    Chicago: GIA Publications, 1997.

Miles, Richard, and Thomas Dvorak, eds. *Teaching Music through Performance
    in Beginning Band*, Vol 1. Chicago: GIA Publications, 2001.

Contributed by:

Craig V. Hamilton
Director of Bands
Ouachita Baptist University
Arkadelphia, Arkansas

Teacher Resource Guide

Fanfare for a New Age
Michael Story
(b. 1956)

Unit 1: Composer

Michael Story has quickly become one of the most prolific arrangers and composers for the marching band, concert band, and jazz band mediums. A native of Philadelphia, Pennsylvania, he earned his bachelor's and master's degrees in music education from the University of Houston School of Music, where he briefly served as assistant director of bands. Mr. Story has written band music for every age level, from elementary bands to professional ensembles such as the Houston Pops Orchestra. Many of his 750 compositions can be found through Warner Brothers/CPP Belwin Publications, Inc. and Alfred Publishing Co., Inc. Mr. Story is an active clinician with school bands in Texas and regularly presents workshops all over the United States.

Unit 2: Composition

Fanfare for a New Age was written in 2005. It is a single-movement composition approximately two minutes in length. The technical demands (range, endurance, and finger agility) indicate that this work was written for elementary band. The composer has written that "*Fanfare for a New Age* is designed as a concert, contest or festival opener." Mr. Story has composed numerous other fanfares and concert overtures, including *Contempo, Marchus Maxiumus, Azetc Dance, Christmas Fanfare* and *Prologue*.

Unit 3: Historical Perspective

A fanfare is defined by *The New Harvard Dictionary of Music* as "music played by trumpets or other brass instruments, sometimes accompanied by percussion for ceremonial purposes, especially to call attention to the arrival of a dignitary or the beginning of a public ceremony." Composers from Beethoven to Copland have used fanfares, either within their works or as separate compositions. Perhaps the most famous fanfares have been written in the twentieth century, including *Fanfare for the Common Man* by Aaron Copland and *Fanfare for a New Theater* by Igor Stravinsky.

Unit 4: Technical Considerations

This work is scored for traditional concert band, including separate parts for mallet percussion (xylophone and bells), timpani, snare drum, bass drum, suspended cymbal, crash cymbal, triangle and tom-tom. The composer specifically states that the tom-tom part should only be used if no timpani is available. The timpani part has one pitch change where a G must be tuned a major second lower to F. Important solo or supporting passages in the bass clarinet, bassoon, tenor saxophone and baritone saxophone parts are cross cued throughout.

Harmonically, this work is centered around C major and C minor. However, there are several borrowed chords that fall outside of these keys, including D minor, G-flat major and D-flat major. Measures 117–121 firmly indicate that the work ends in F major. Examples of triadic extension (non-dominant seventh chords), triads with added fourths and suspensions are also present.

Dotted eighth-note patterns are frequently found throughout as well as an extended articulated triplet passage beginning in measure thirteen. The instrumental ranges for the woodwinds are slightly larger than that of the brass. An optional passage is available to flute players at measure 106 for those who cannot play confidently above the staff. Alto saxophones and horns have the melody often in the middle of the work, spanning several leaps within the staff. Much of the melodic material is composed in five-measure phrases as opposed to two or four, as might be found in a "Classically" composed melody. Flute and oboe players must perform a half-step trill from C to D-flat in measure 113.

Unit 5: Stylistic Considerations

Use the opening, accented chords to teach balance (woodwinds to brass) as well as the weight and impact of the accents. The rapid articulation on repeated notes as well as use of staccato and tenuto at measure 13 requires students to develop and discern between several kinds of articulation. Proper blend and balance between the horns and saxophones as well as a smooth melodic line are important to providing contrast from the opening material. Several extended *crescendos* found in this work will require careful pacing, from soft to loud as well as from low to high, to be effective. Matching note lengths between flute, oboe, clarinet and snare drum at measure 92 is the key to establish clarity and rhythmic drive when the tempo accelerates. A proper balance at measure 96 when only the trumpets have the melody is critical to the success of this section.

Unit 6: Musical Elements

MELODY:
The main melodic material is found in the alto saxophone and horn, beginning with measure 37. This theme uses intervals from the various forms of the concert C-minor scale. Each melodic statement is five measures long, with occasional cadential extensions throughout.

HARMONY:
The opening chordal motive uses several types of triadic extensions, including non-dominant seventh chords and chords with added fourths. Most of the harmonies are generated from the key of C major and minor, but there are several borrowed chords from a variety of key centers. Several examples of suspensions are also used in this work.

RHYTHM:
There are several repeated dotted-eighth and sixteenth-note patterns as they comprise the first measure of the primary melodic material. In addition, there is an extended passage of articulated triplets beginning in measure 13.

TIMBRE:
This work explores many different instrumental combinations and balances. As previously mentioned, the "tall" opening chord needs to be balanced from top to bottom as well as between woodwinds and brass. Another challenge is to balance the primary melodic material as it is passed between different pairs of instruments.

Unit 7: Form and Structure

SECTION	MEASURE	EVENT AND SCORING
A	1–12	Opening chordal motive
	13–16	Transition – addition of percussion and triplet accompaniment in flute, clarinet, and xylophone

SECTION	MEASURE	EVENT AND SCORING
A	17–28	Opening chordal motive with triplet accompaniment
	29–36	Transition – percussion section
B	37–46	Theme in alto saxophone and horn; imitative interjections from bassoon, tenor sax, trumpet and euphonium; percussion material from mm. 29–36
B	47–51	Theme in flute and oboe with sparse woodwind accompaniment
B	52–58	Same scoring as mm. 37–46 plus bells and a cadential extension
B	59–68	Theme in flute and oboe with sparse woodwind and triangle accompaniment
B	69–73	Theme in trumpets/new accompaniment in flute and bells/chordal accompaniment in brass
B	74–79	Incomplete statement of theme-transition
A'	80–91	Two statements of opening chordal motive
A'	92–95	Transition/quarter note = 120; introduction of eighth-note accompaniment in upper woodwinds
A'	96–105	Two statements of theme in trumpets and bells/eighth-note accompaniment/chordal accompaniment
A'	106–110	Theme in flute, oboe, clarinet and bells/chordal accompaniment/shifting bass line
A'	111–116	Addition of trumpet to theme/cadential extention
Coda	117–121	Theme in augmentation/ascending scale derived from main theme

Unit 8: Suggested Listening

John Adams, *Short Ride in a Fast Machine*
Aaron Copland, *Fanfare for the Common Man*
David Diamond, *Heart's Music*
Karel Husa, *Smetana Fanfare*
Jack Stamp, *Gavorkna Fanfare*

Richard Strauss, *Vienna Philharmonic Fanfare*
Igor Stravinsky, *Fanfare for a New Theater*
Frank Ticheli, *Pacific Fanfare*

Unit 9: Additional References and Resources

Randel, Don, ed. *The New Harvard Dictionary of Music*. Cambridge, MA: The Belknap Press of Harvard University Press, 1986.

Web site: www.alfred.com/span_authors/dealer_html.cfm?lpage=story.html

Contributed by:

Jason Worzbyt
Associate Professor of Bassoon
Associate Director of Bands
Indiana University of Pennsylvania
Indiana, Pennsylvania

Teacher Resource Guide

Gathering in the Glen
Michael Sweeney
(b. 1952)

Unit 1: Composer

ASCAP award-winning composer Michael Sweeney is a graduate of Indiana University, where he studied music education and composition. He taught in the public schools of Ohio and Indiana for five years, where his teaching experience included working with successful concert, jazz, and marching programs at all levels from elementary to high school.

Since 1982, he has worked full time for Hal Leonard Corporation in Milwaukee, Wisconsin, and is currently director of band publications. In addition, he contributes as a composer and arranger in all instrumental areas. Sweeney is particularly known for his writing for concert and jazz bands at the younger levels, and has more than 500 publications to his credit. His works appear on numerous state contest lists and his music is regularly performed throughout the world.

Unit 2: Composition

Gathering in the Glen was published in 2002 as a part of Hal Leonard's *Essential Elements 2000* method book series. The piece is a medley of original and well-known Scottish folk songs, including "Scotland the Brave," "Loch Lomond," and "The Blue Bells of Scotland."

This Grade 1.5 piece is appropriate for beginning-level players and is approximately four minutes in length.

Unit 3: Historical Perspective

Traditional Scottish folk and dance music is one of the most recognizable international genres, having formed the basis for many settings of wind band, orchestral, and choral music. Among the common dances are lively jigs, reels, and strathspeys as well as flowing ballads, waltzes, and airs.

Composers and arrangers have long sought to imitate the tuneful melodies, modal harmonies, snappy rhythms, and vital timbres of Scottish folk songs, often turning to traditional instruments for inspiration. The bagpipe family is most closely associated with the music of Scotland, but it is not indigenous to the British Isles, having appeared throughout Europe, northern Africa, and South Asia prior to its arrival around the fifteenth century. The fiddle, harp, accordion, and tin whistle are other instruments commonly found in historical and current Scottish music.

Unit 4: Technical Considerations

Gathering in the Glen explores the key centers of B-flat major and E-flat major. The harmonic language is defined by a combination of common tertian and modal harmonies (mostly Mixolydian, created by the lowering of the seventh scale degree, a common Scottish tendency).

The technical demands of the music are interesting and challenging for beginners, with the majority of the rhythmic movement consisting of basic duple values at a slow and moderate tempi (quarter note = 104, 80, and 116). Ranges are standard, and parts contain both long, sustained lines in the ballads and perky rhythmic lines in the dances.

Percussion scoring in *Gathering in the Glen* includes triangle, snare drum, bass drum, crash cymbals, orchestra bells, and suspended cymbal, requiring a minimum of four players.

Unit 5: Stylistic Considerations

Successful performance of this piece requires the ensemble to stylistically navigate between the livelier dance styles of "Scotland the Brave" and "The Blue Bells of Scotland" (demanding lightness, space, and precise articulation) and the more lyrical and tender "Loch Lomond" and the original introduction (requiring sustained breath support, movement of the musical line, and dynamic contrast). Because of the imaginative scoring, students also have to concentrate on and contribute to the balance by making decisions about whether their part should be in the foreground, middle ground, and background of the music.

Unit 6: Musical Elements

MELODY:

Each section of *Gathering in the Glen* features a prominent tune set against a chordal accompaniment. The melodic material is tonal, with an occasional flatted seventh to add a modal flavor. Most of the melodic movement is scalar, with "Scotland the Brave" featuring a full arpgeggio as part of its structure. "Loch Lomond" is pentatonic.

HARMONY:

The harmonies in *Gathering in the Glen* are primarily major, with the aforementioned dabbling in Mixolydian mode, created by the flat seventh scale degree (a chordal substitution of VII for V). The frequent use of the open fifth (with no third) imitates the drone of the bagpipe.

RHYTHM:

Gathering in the Glen begins in 3/4 and is marked "Moderately" (quarter note = 104). In measure 10 the time signature switches to 4/4 for the remainder of the piece, with one 2/4 bar inserted in measure 45 (at the end of "Loch Lomond"). Measure 9 features a "Scotch snap" (eighth, dotted quarter), common to many Scottish folk songs.

TIMBRE:

The composer presents an interesting sound palette by using tutti scoring sparingly (only in the climactic portion of "Scotland the Brave" and in most of "Blue Bells of Scotland"). In a tip of the hat to traditional Scottish music, the clarinet and saxophone imitate bagpipe drones in the introduction, and the percussion section often mirrors the scoring of a pipe band.

Unit 7: Form and Structure

SECTION	MEASURE	EVENT AND SCORING
Introduction (original tune)		
	1–6	3/4, drone in clarinet and alto saxophone, original melody in flute
	7–10	Descending bass line joins melody, Scotch snap in m. 9
	10–12	Change to 4/4, Mixolydian chord progression (I6–VII–I), and pipe band percussion cadence

SECTION	MEASURE	EVENT AND SCORING
"Scotland the Brave"		
	13–21	Trumpet melody, open fifth drone in flute, clarinet, and saxophone; percussion playing on rims
	17	Addition of low brass and woodwinds on pedal B-flat
	21–25	Melody in clarinet, tenor saxophone, and horn; homophonic rhythmic accompaniment in flute, trumpet, low brass/woodwind, and percussion
	25–28	Trumpet melody returns with flute, tutti scoring, climactic section, cadence in B-flat major
	29–30	"Slowing," bridge to next section (modal A-flat major in trombone/euphonium with stacked B-flat, E-flat, F pyramid in trumpets, horns, and saxophones)
"Loch Lomond"		
	31–38	"Tenderly" (quarter note = 80), melody in flute and clarinet, pedal E-flat in tenor saxophone and trombone/euphonium
	34	Clarinet and alto saxophones join with counterline, triangle decorates
	39–47	Trumpet melody, counterpoint in saxophone and horn, chordal accompaniment in low brass/woodwinds and tenor saxophone
	45	2/4 bar inserted
	46–47	Echo of final phrase in flute and bells, cadence in unison E-flat
"Blue Bells of Scotland"		
	48–52	"March" (quarter note = 116); active snare drum passage with added bass drum; bass line enters at m. 50, leading to B-flat major
	52–55	Melody in alto saxophone, trumpet, and horn; dotted accompaniment in low brass/woodwind; active march percussion lines

SECTION	MEASURE	EVENT AND SCORING
	52–55	(Repeated section) flute, oboe, clarinet, and bells added on melody
	56–60	Melody in low brass/woodwinds, light eighth note accompaniment in clarinet, saxophone, trumpet, and horn; percussion out
	61–63	Final phrase of tune, melody in flute/oboe and trumpet; chordal accompaniment in tutti, march percussion returns
Coda	64–end	Snippets of different melodies heard in flute/oboe and trumpets; descending (modal) bass line and harmonies, rhythmic cadence on B-flat major

Unit 8: Suggested Listening

Malcolm Arnold, *Four Scottish Dances*
Howard Cable, *Scottish Rhapsody*
Peter Maxwell Davies, *An Orkney Wedding, with Sunrise* (orchestra)
Percy Grainger, *Ye Banks and Braes O' Bonnie Doon*
Clare Grundman, *An Irish Rhapsody*
Arthur Pryor, *Blue Bells of Scotland*
Frank Ticheli, *Loch Lomond*

Unit 9: Additional References and Resources

"A Guide to Scottish Music"
    www.musicinscotland.com/Scottish_Music.htm

Collinson, Frances. *The Traditional and National Music of Scotland*. London: Routledge and Kegan Paul, 1966.

Emmerson, George S. *Rantin' Pipe and Tremblin' String: A History of Scottish Dance Music*. London: Dent Publishing, 1971.

Farmer, Henry George. *A History of Music in Scotland*. Temecula, CA: Reprint Services Corporation, 1970.

"Music and Dance of Scotland"
    www.rampantscotland.com/music.htm

"Music in Scotland"
www.scotlandinternet.com/music.htm

Contributed by:

Scott A. Stewart
Emory University
Atlanta, Georgia

Teacher Resource Guide

Greek Folk Trilogy

arranged by Anne McGinty
(b. 1945)

Unit 1: Composer

Anne McGinty was born on June 29, 1945, in Findlay, Ohio. She received her bachelor of music from The Ohio State University and her master's of music from Duquesne University. McGinty has written compositions for concert band, orchestra, flute, and flute ensembles. She has more than 225 commissioned works ranging from Grades 1 to 6. In 2000, she commissioned *Hall of Heroes* for the Unites States Army Band and Chorus. In 2001 the United States Military Academy at West Point commissioned *To Keep Thine Honor Bright*.

McGinty began her career as the principal flutist with the Tucson Symphony Orchestra, Tucson Pops Orchestra, and TSO Woodwind Quintet. While pursuing her master's degree, she had the opportunity to study composition and theory with Joseph Willcox Jenkins. In 1987, McGinty and her husband John Edmondson opened Queenwood publishing company. They later sold the company to Neil Kjos in 2002.

Currently McGinty is active as a guest conductor, clinician, and speaker throughout the United States and Canada. She has contributed several works to the prolongation of folk songs and the importance of different cultures.

Unit 2: Composition

Greek Folk Trilogy is based on three folk songs from Greece. The first folk song, "Mount Agrafa," is the story of a man climbing a mountain as he dreams of his sweetheart. The second, "Kane Nanakia" (translated as "go to sleep" or "do sleep") is a lullaby, and the third song, "Beyond the Plain," describes what lies beyond the plain where the olive trees grow. This composition lists as a Grade 1.5. It is two minutes and five seconds long and in ABC form.

Unit 3: Historical Perspective

Folk songs are an important tradition to the people of Greece. They are often used to entertain children, guests, and to create dances. Note the use of the tambourine and augmented seconds in this composition as they are traditional aspects of this style of folk song.

The origin of the Greek folk song is traced back to the first centuries of Christianity. Ancient Greek tragedies and life experiences were passed down from generation to generation to preserve the Greek culture during the times of conquerors. The lute, tambourine, shawm, and drum were the primary folk instruments. Teachers would instruct pupils on the instrumental musical traditions of folk music. There were no books of these songs and pupils were expected to learn exactly what the teacher played or sung. Greek folk songs combine the unity of lyrics, music, and dance.

Unit 4: Technical Considerations

Greek Folk Trilogy uses the C minor and F minor scales. The minor tonality is disguised through the use of accidentals and the familiar key signature of E-flat major. Woodwind players must learn to play grace notes, as they appear several times. Players need to learn the following fingerings: flute=F-sharp and B natural; clarinet=G-sharp and C-sharp; saxophone=D-sharp and G-sharp; trumpet=G-sharp, F-sharp, and C-sharp; low reeds/low brass=D-flat concert. All of other fingerings can be taught through the B-flat and E-flat concert scales.

The ranges may be challenging for some players, but are well within the range for beginners. The flute ranges from G4 to D6 and is sometimes doubled by the oboe, which ranges from D4 to A5, deviating from the flute part as technical demands change. The first clarinets range from D4 to E5, crossing the break several times throughout; however, the second clarinets never cross the break. The first trumpets range from C4 to E5; the upper ranges of C5 to E5 can be challenging for the beginner. The second trumpets only range from C4 to B-flat4 which is a typical range. The saxophone (E4 to B5), French horn (C4 to B-flat4), Low Brass and low reeds (A1 to C4) are easily obtainable ranges for the beginner. There are five percussion parts: Snare drum, bass drum, tambourine, sleigh bells, and crash cymbals.

Rhythms consist of dotted quarter, dotted eighth-sixteenth, sixteenth notes, and off-beat playing.

Unit 5: Stylistic Considerations

Greek Folk Trilogy is written in four- to eight-measure phrases. It begins in 3/4, transitions to 4/4, and ends in 2/4. The opening statement is accented and the first section is dance-like; the second section is slow and lyrical, and the third section is written in a march style. Students will need to understand the differences between the sections of the composition to properly interpret the style of each.

In traditional Greek folk songs, the grace notes are stressed, off-beats are more important than down beats, augmented seconds are emphasized, and the tambourine is a key instrument.

Unit 6: Musical Elements

MELODY:

The melody is easily identifiable and transfers to various instruments. Students need to understand how the melody uses the minor scales. Mastery of the E-flat concert scale will aid in learning the relative minor scale.

1. Students play the E-flat major scale in half notes.
2. Students are then asked to start on the sixth note of the scale and play the scale in half notes.
3. Once they hear the tonality shift have them lower the sixth scale degree.
4. Once students understand the new tonality have them raise the fifth scale degree causing the Greek augmented second.
5. The instructor can make a chart on the board for each step of the process. It would be beneficial to transpose these scales for each instrument.
   a. E-flat–F–G–A-flat–B-flat–C–D–E-flat
   b. C–D–E-flat–F–G–A-flat–B-flat–C
   c. C–D–E-flat–F–G–A–B-flat–C
   d. C–D–E-flat–F–G-sharp–A–B-flat–C (melody appears in flute/oboe/clarinets first)
6. Ask students to identify the scale in their music.
7. Once they have mastered the scales they can be used with rhythm exercises.

The same process can be done for F minor.

HARMONY:

The chord progressions in *Greek Folk Trilogy* are very basic. Greek folk tunes are shaped around easily singable tonal centers. Students need to identify i–iv–v–vii chords, and can construct these chords using the minor scales chart.

1. Ask students to identify the first, third, and fifth degrees of a chosen scale.
2. Divide the instrument groups into three and assign one note to each group. For example, group I plays E-flat, group II plays G, and group III plays B-flat.
3. Ask students to listen for all three notes when they play the chord.
4. Then ask them to identify the fourth note of the scale. Assist them in building that chord. Do the same for the v and vii chords.
5. Once the students have their notes they can construct chord progressions. The instructor can use fingers to represent when the students change to any given chord to create different progressions.
6. Have students write down their notes for each chord so they can easily identify the number. Once they understand their part in the chord structure, switch the groupings so the students play a different part of the chord (extra time may be needed for this step).
7. Incorporate a rhythm of the day with a chord progression to facilitate mastery.

RHYTHM:
Rhythms can be taught during warm-up. The instructor writes an exercise encompassing some of the difficult rhythms in the composition on the chalkboard or on a handout.

1. Students verbally count the passage using a chosen counting system.
2. Write the counts or syllables under the note values as visual aids.
3. Students then play the passage on their instruments on a given pitch.
4. Students play the passage on each note of a given scale, in this case E-flat major, C minor, or F minor.
5. Students are asked to identify the rhythms in their music and give examples.

TIMBRE:
Each folk tune creates a different timbre. "Mount Agrafa" is a very emphatic and spirited section. In measures 9, 13, 17, and 21 the quarter note should be stressed and separated when leading to the next measure. The tambourine is the primary voice and is prominent even over the melody. The dynamics are extremely important and range from *p*, *mp*, *mf*, *f*. Intonation and tone quality should not suffer through the different ranges.

1. Explain the different dynamic ranges by writing them up on the board; *p, mp, mf, f.*
2. Play the C minor scale in whole notes. Ascending should be played *p* and descending should be *f.* The instructor can compare this to a roller coaster; the coaster creates suspense as it ascends and the thrill is experienced as it descends.
3. Ask for a group of eight volunteers. The first student begins by playing the first note, the second student joins in on the second note, the third student on the third note, continuing in this scale to build the dynamic. Students can hear the sound getting louder; then have them drop out one by one on the descent until one student is playing the final note.
4. Then ask students to play each whole note at a different dynamic, e.g., first note at *p,* the second note at *mp*, etc.

"Kane Nanakia" is a slow and legato section with thinner instrumentation. The woodwind choir and brass choir create two distinctly different timbres, and students need to learn how to play within a balanced ensemble.

1. Students in each choir should slur all of the notes in their two- to four-measure passage.
2. Build each section by having the bass line play first, harmonic line second, and melodic line third. For example, in measures 25–26 clarinets would play first, then the bells, then alto sax and flute.
3. Do the same for the brass choir.
4. Ask students to write in their music whether they are the bass line, harmonic line, or melodic line.

"Beyond the Plain" is in an aggressive, march-like style. The notes should be short and detached and the rhythms accurate.

1. Using the C-minor scale, ask students to play four quarter notes on each pitch ascending the scale.
2. Then have them play each quarter note as if it were an eighth note followed by an eighth-note rest. Explain the idea of staccato playing through this exercise.
3. Have students play measures 45–55 if they have an eighth note followed by an eighth rest only. Students should listen and match the length of the notes.
4. Repeat the process for the entire third section of the composition. Students playing the melodic line can do the same exercise as they pass and add on to the melody.

All three tunes should focus on good tone quality, intonation, rhythm, balance, blend, and dynamics. The best way for students to learn the timbre and style is through example. The instructor can demonstrate on a musical instrument. Also, recordings of Greek folk songs will aid in the development of the style and timbre of Greek music.

Unit 7: Form and Structure

Greek Folk Trilogy is written in a three-part form, ABC. Each contrasting section is a new folk song in a different key and key signature.

SECTION	MEASURE	EVENT AND SCORING
Introduction	1–8	C minor tonality in 3/4; flute/oboe/clarinet/alto sax with melodic line and descending augmented second; off-beat eighth notes created by trumpet/optional horn/tenor saxophone/tambourine; full bass line; snare/bass drum accent melody and off-beat patterns; bells reinforce chordal structure
"Mount Agrafa"	(tempo: quarter note = 112)	
"A" Theme	9–16	C minor tonality continues; flute/trumpet with the melodic theme; off-beat eighth notes created by clarinets/alto saxophone/optional horn/tenor saxophone; tambourine rhythm counters the melodic theme with full bass line; snare/bass drum continue to provide rhythmic stability of melody and bass; bells arpeggiate the chordal structure
"A" Theme	17–24	Thematic structure remains stable; chord progression changes slightly; transitions to 4/4 time and new key signature
"Kane Nanakia"	(tempo: quarter note = 76)	
"B" Theme	25–40	Key of F minor in 4/4
	25–26	Flute/oboe/alto saxophone with first thematic statement; clarinets harmonize a moving eighth-note countermelody; bells with arpeggiation of chord structure

SECTION	MEASURE	EVENT AND SCORING
	27–28	Trumpets harmonize the countermelody; optional horn/tenor saxophone/low brass/low reeds with the augmented second and chordal accompaniment
	29–30	Clarinets/alto saxophone harmonize the melodic theme while restructuring the melodic material
	31–34	Flute with harmonic material in a rhythmic augmentation of the theme; clarinets enter with melodic theme in a fugal style; bells provide arpeggiated chordal structure; sleigh bells add rhythmic structure
	35–36	Alto saxophone main theme; flute/oboe/clarinets harmonize countermelody
	37–38	Trumpets harmonize the countermelody; optional horn/tenor saxophone/low brass/low reeds with the augmented second and chordal accompaniment
	39–40	Flute/oboe/alto saxophone rhythmic augmented theme; clarinets with chordal accompaniment; snare drum rhythmic accompaniment
Transition	(quarter note = 112)	
	41–44	Time signature changes to 3/4; trumpets/low brass/low reeds play thematic material from introduction; snare/bass drum accompaniment; augmented second in the first trumpet
"Beyond the Plain" (quarter note = 120)		
Introduction	45–46	C minor key change; 2/4 time change; snare drum theme (roll-off effect); trumpets/optional horn/tenor saxophone/low brass/low reeds/bass drum focal emphasis of downbeat
"C" Theme	47–54	Clarinet theme passes to trumpet; full band focal downbeat
	55–62	Flute/oboe/clarinet/alto saxophone theme in chords; bells/tambourine rhythmic accompaniment

SECTION	MEASURE	EVENT AND SCORING
Codetta	63–72	Full band (adding crash cymbals); C theme passes in augmented rhythm; off-beats/ sixteenth notes/dotted eight-sixteenth rhythms

Unit 8: Suggested Listening

Franco Cesarini, *Greek Folk Song Suite*
Paul Curnow, *Marche of the Titans*
Anne McGinty:
    African Folk Trilogy
    Greek Folk Trilogy
    Metron Overture
    Russian Folk Trilogy
Jan Van der Roost:
    Artemis
    Postcard from Greece

Unit 9: Additional References and Resources

Alevizos, Ted and Susan, ed. *Folksongs of Greece*. New York: Oak Publications, 1968.

Apel, Willi, ed. *Harvard Dictionary of Music*, 2nd edition. Cambridge, MA: Belknap Press of Harvard University Press, 1972.

McGinty, Anne. E-mail correspondence with Katrina Davilis, May 2, 2007.

Miles, Richard, and Thomas Dvorak, eds. *Teaching Music through Performance in Beginning Band*. Chicago, IL: GIA Publications, 2001.

Web site:
    http://www.helleniccomserve.com/musichistory.html

Contributed by:

Katrina Lyn Davilis
Director of Bands
Music Department Chairperson
Thoreau Middle School
Vienna, Virginia

Teacher Resource Guide

Incantation and Ritual

Brian Balmages
(b. 1975)

Unit 1: Composer

Brian Balmages is an active composer, conductor, producer, and performer. His fresh compositional ideas have been heralded by many performers and directors, resulting in a high demand of his works for winds, brass, and orchestra. He received his bachelor's degree in music from James Madison University and his master's degree from the University of Miami in Florida. Mr. Balmages's compositions have been performed worldwide at conferences including the College Band Directors National and Regional Conferences, the Midwest Clinic, the International Tuba/Euphonium Conference, the International Trombone Festival, and the International Trumpet Guild Conference. His active schedule of commissions and premieres has incorporated groups ranging from elementary schools to professional ensembles, including the Baltimore Symphony Orchestra, the Miami Symphony Orchestra, the University of Miami Wind Ensemble, and the Dominion Brass Ensemble. Among the professional artists who have commissioned him are: James Jenkins, Principal Tuba of the Jacksonville Symphony; Lynn Klock, Saxophone Performing Artist for Selmer; Arthur Campbell, Clarinet Performing Artist for Leblanc; and Jerry Peel, Professor of Horn at the University of Miami. He has also had world premieres in prestigious venues such as Carnegie Hall, along with numerous performances abroad.

As a conductor, Mr. Balmages enjoys engagements with numerous honor bands, university groups, and professional ensembles throughout the country. Guest conducting appearances have included the Midwest Clinic, College

Band Directors National Conference, Mid-Atlantic Wind Conductors Conference, and the Atlantic Classical Orchestra Brass Ensemble.

Currently, he is director of instrumental publications for The FJH Music Company, Inc. in Fort Lauderdale, Florida, where he oversees all aspects of the instrumental program related to works for concert band, jazz ensemble, and orchestra.

Mr. Balmages studied trumpet with James Kluesner, Don Tison, and Gilbert Johnson. He is a freelance musician and has performed with the Miami Symphony Orchestra, the Florida Chamber Orchestra, Skyline Brass, and the Henry Mancini Institute Orchestra. He resides in Baltimore with his wife, Lisa and son, Jacob.

Unit 2: Composition

Notes from the composer:

> *Incantation and Ritual* is reminiscent of an ancient tribal gathering. It opens with a slow mysterious melody that should sound like a soft chant. The occasionally repeated percussion sounds break the calm atmosphere then retreat back into the texture. The ritual section is characterized with great fire and energy supported by a wealth of percussion.

Unit 3: Historical Perspective

Incantation and Ritual was commissioned by Melodie Shamp and Katye Clogg, directors of the East Stroudsburg (PA) Area School District fifth grade bands. The premiere was March 9, 2004 at the East Stroudsburg Area School District Festival, conducted by the composer. Through *Incantation and Ritual*, Mr. Balmages has attempted to create a work like the John Barnes Chance *Incantation and Dance*, but for younger, less-experienced players.

Unit 4: Technical Considerations

The FJH Music Company, publisher of the work, grades *Incantation and Ritual* as a 1.5. Written with a young band in mind, all parts lay extremely well on the instruments, and ranges are consistent with the abilities of most students in their first years of study.

The score calls for two clarinet parts and two trumpet parts. All other instruments have one part each, but the trombone and alto saxophone parts split in divisi lines in several passages. Percussion parts include bells and percussion 1–3. The third percussion part is optional, but will add style to the work as it calls for interesting color instruments.

Harmonically, *Incantation and Ritual* explores basic minor tonalities, and remains consistently in the home key. Accidentals are rare and are generally used as passing tones. Rhythmically, the work calls for no division smaller than the eighth note. Beats one and three are strongly emphasized, with only the occasional juxtaposition of eighth notes across different beats. There is no syncopation in the work. The time signature of 4/4 is used throughout; the tempo for "Incantation" is quarter = 84 and "Ritual" is quarter = 158.

Unit 5: Stylistic Considerations

Incantation and Ritual gives the conductor of a beginning band the chance to teach two contrasting styles. The "Incantation" section demands a lyric approach in the quiet dynamic ranges. The detached, staccato articulation marking is employed only rarely and the dynamics are indicated *piano* and *mezzo piano*. The "Ritual" portion of the work requires a quite opposite approach. To successfully realize the dance-like qualities of this music, the ensemble must maintain clear and separate articulations, and expand the dynamic range from *piano* to *forte*. However, the composer never asks for a *fortissimo* dynamic. The "Ritual" should remain light, even at its strongest dynamic marking (*forte*). The composer offers the following:

> Use the opening as a vehicle to teach sustainment to younger players. Students should sustain all whole notes their full value, especially when flutes and clarinets take a breath in measure 2. The entire opening is extremely legato. Beginning in measure 16, work with students to gradually increase air flow for an even *crescendo* into measure 20. In the ritual section, all notes should have some lift, but make sure there is a difference in length between quarter and eighth notes.

Unit 6: Musical Elements

MELODY:
Incantation and Ritual uses two thematic fragments as the basis of the work. The "Incantation" theme appears in the upper woodwinds at the outset, and reappears near the work's conclusion. The "Ritual" theme appears in measure 12, and reappears throughout the work in a few permutations. These permutations of the thematic material provide exciting teaching opportunities.

HARMONY:
Incantation and Ritual explores basic minor tonalities, and remains consistently in the home key. Accidentals are rare and they are generally used as passing tones.

RHYTHM:

Rhythmically, the work calls for no division smaller than the eighth note. Beats one and three are strongly emphasized, with only the occasional juxtaposition of eighth notes across different beats. There is no syncopation in the work. Time signature stays 4/4 throughout; the tempo in "Incantation" is quarter = 84 and "Ritual" is quarter = 158.

TIMBRE:

In the most general terms, the "Incantation" section of the work calls upon the most beautiful dark woodwind timbres. In contrast, the "Ritual" section relies more heavily on the brass (still dark and beautiful) and tribal percussion sounds. The short development-like section provides interesting "call-and-response" writing between these two sonorities, and the conclusion of the work generates its strength from the forces of the tutti band.

Unit 7: Form and Structure

SECTION	MEASURE	EVENT AND SCORING
"Incantation"	1–11	Quarter note = 84; mysterious introductory material in C minor; "Incantation" theme acts as melodic foreshadowing of "Ritual" theme
	12–19	"Ritual" theme appears in low brasses and reeds; orchestration, texture, and harmony builds toward arrival of "Ritual" section at measure 20
"Ritual"	20–25	Quarter note = 158; arrival of "Ritual" section; ostinato pattern in eighth and quarter notes sets the stage for the theme in the new tempo
	26–34	Theme appears in trumpet, juxtaposed with ostinato figure from previous measures
	34–37	Percussion duet in clave and tambourine creates an interlude with tribal qualities
	38–53	Brief development section; theme evolves by way of harmony, augmentation, and use of call-and-response type orchestration
	54–61	Quasi recapitulation; theme returns in alto saxophone and horn; ostinato figures appear in similar fashion at m. 26

SECTION	MEASURE	EVENT AND SCORING
	62–70	Final appearance of the "Ritual" theme; this time it is juxtaposed with the "foreshadowing" material from the introductory measures
	71–end	Brief codetta builds harmonic and rhythmic tension to the end

Unit 8: Suggested Listening

Brian Balmages:
    Chant and Savage Dance
    Kilauea (The Volcano's Fury)
John Barnes Chance, *Incantation and Dance*
Silvestre Revueltes, *Sensemaya*
Igor Stravinsky, *The Rite of Spring*

Unit 9: Additional References and Resources

Beckwith, Carol, and Angela Fisher. *African Ceremonies*. New York: Harry N.
    Abrams, 1999.

Kopetz, Barry. "An Analysis of Chance's Incantation and Dance."
    The Instrumentalist, October 1992.

Web sites:
    www.brianbalmages.com
    www.fjhmusic.com

Contributed by:

Daniel A. Belongia
Assistant Professor of Music
Assistant Director of Bands
Illinois State University
Normal, Illinois

Teacher Resource Guide

Journey Down Niagara

Chistopher Tucker
(b. 1976)

Unit 1: Composer

Christopher Tucker was born and raised in Texas, and earned a bachelor of music degree cum laude in music composition from the University of North Texas, studying with the late Martin Mailman. He received the master of music from the University of Texas at Austin, as a composition student of Dan Welcher and Donald Grantham. His interest in writing for wind band has led to a number of commissions and awards, including first place in the 2001 Biennial CBDNA Young Band Composition Contest for *Americans Lost*, and the 2003 CBDNA YBC award and the 2004 Claude T. Smith Memorial Band Composition Contest award for *Twilight in the Wilderness*. As a music copyist, he has worked with Daron Hagen, William Latham, and Joan Tower. He has served as a music editor for the "Forgotten Songs of Sousa" project, as well as Director of Artistic Administration for the Lone Star Wind Orchestra. His prolific compositional output, as well as further biographical information, may be found at www.tuckermusicworks.com.

Unit 2: Composition

Completed in September 2005, *Journey Down Niagara* was premiered by the Lake Travis Middle School Symphonic Band of Austin, Texas on May 26, 2006. The piece is dedicated to the composer's wife, Kimberly Joan Tucker. In May 2007, a companion piece, *Serenade at Prospect Point*, received its premiere performance.

This Grade 1+ symphonic band work is ninety-five measures in length, and approximately three minutes and thirty seconds in duration. *Journey Down Niagara* is published by Southern Music Company, and was recognized as the third-prize winner in Category One of the 2006 Manhattan Beach Music (MBM) Frank Ticheli Composition Contest. The composer provides insight into *Journey Down Niagara* in program notes found in the full score:

> *Journey Down Niagara* was inspired by a trip to Niagara Falls, Ontario with my wife Kimberly. Celebrating our one-year wedding anniversary, we experienced the Maid of the Mist, White Water Walk, Journey Behind the Falls, as well as the falls themselves. The work attempts to musically capture the essence of those experiences. The work begins with a short introduction inspired by a ride to the Horseshoe Falls on the "Maid of the Mist." The mist comes in short, drenching waves. "White Water Walk" makes up the first main statement with its disjunct and jagged musical gestures. Trillions of gallons of water are forced downstream from the falls through narrow and deep depressions. The result is one of the wildest and most relentless stretches of white water in the world. A brief interlude follows with a roaring sound in the percussion. The reverberation heard while experiencing "Journey Beyond the Falls" is not only heard but also felt. The "journey" in this work concludes with a broad overlook of "Niagara Falls," full of spirit and majesty.

Unit 3: Historical Perspective

For hundreds of years, composers have used imagery, programmatic elements, geographical locations, and folklore to musically bring a visual idea to life. In *Journey Down Niagara*, listeners and performers can navigate the mighty Niagara River as it winds its way through and over the three awe-inspiring falls that comprise the waterway shared by Niagara Falls, Ontario, Canada, and Niagara Falls, New York, USA.

The Niagara Falls area is a legacy of the last Ice Age, nearly 18,000 years ago, and is located 120 kilometers south of Toronto. The three distinct waterfalls, the Canadian Horseshoe Falls, the American Falls, and the Bridal Veil Falls, straddle the United States-Canadian border, and attract more than 12 million visitors each year. Niagara Falls is the second largest falls on Earth behind southern Africa's Victoria Falls, and is the largest producer of electric power in the world.

Journey Down Niagara musically explores four attractions visited by the composer: "Maid of the Mist," "White Water Walk," "Journey Behind the Falls," and the "Niagara Falls." "Maid of the Mist" represents the white, double-decker, diesel-powered riverboats that transport visitors within a few

yards of the base of the American and Horseshoe Falls. In service since 1846, these boats can carry up to 600 passengers to view the 170-foot tall falls from a truly stunning vantage point. The newest boat, the Maid of the Mist VII, made its debut in 1997, continuing the legacy of the ship's motto, "Explore the Roar."

"White Water Walk" is a boardwalk located along side the swiftly moving rapids of the Niagara River. Trillions of gallons of water are forced through a narrow passageway where visitors literally walk just feet from the powerful natural wonder.

"Journey Behind the Falls" allows its guests to ride an elevator carved through solid bedrock 150-feet below to tunnels leading behind the Horseshoe Falls. The adventure of experiencing the gentle mist and thunderous roar of the falls cascading from thirteen-stories above also includes a complimentary biodegradable rain poncho for visitors.

The Niagara Falls themselves are one of the world's most unique and widely recognized icons. The history of the Great Lakes Basin, the melting waters that formed them over 6,000 years, and the magnificent geological creation of the three towering falls make it one of North America's natural wonders.

Unit 4: Technical Considerations

Journey Down Niagara may be performed with a minimal number of players, twenty-three, but will work well with additional players on each part. The suggested instrumentation, and number of parts, includes: 2 flutes, 1 oboe, 2 clarinets, 1 bass clarinet, 1 bassoon, 1 alto saxophone, 1 tenor saxophone, 1 baritone saxophone, 2 trumpets, 1 horn, 2 trombones, 1 euphonium, 1 tuba, and 6 percussion. Bassoon, horn, and euphonium, instruments not as commonly found in beginning ensembles, have their parts doubled in other voices throughout.

A few special percussion effects are important to creating the dramatic rush and roar of the swift-moving water. Tam-tam (gong), chimes, timpani, tom-tom, wind chimes, and xylophone are required, along with the standard orchestra bells, bass drum, suspended cymbal, snare drum, and triangle. There are two separate xylophone parts, but these may be played on one keyboard with minimal revoicing.

Unit 5: Stylistic Considerations

The work makes use of large, full chords, accented notes and figures, descending patterns, wide dynamic swings, and creative percussive timbres in its programmatic agenda. *Journey Down Niagara* allows ensembles to explore the different styles needed to musically depict the events and places, making it important to experiment with different balances and combinations of percussive voices in representing the roaring sound of the falls. An equal balance between the rolling bass drum, suspended cymbal, rolling timpani, and tam-tam should provide the desired effect.

Unit 6: Musical Elements

Although short in duration, the work does provide the several different fundamental musical terms and techniques worthy of further discussion.

MELODY AND HARMONY:
Crafted around the key of B-flat, the piece features one melodic section, bookended by sections of chordal clusters, accented punctuations, and descending patterns that stem from the opening harmonic statement, B-flat–F–E-flat.

RHYTHM:
Eighth, quarter, half, and whole notes are used, and no dotted figures are found. *Journey Down Niagara* affords students the chance to explore fermatas, tempo changes, 2/4 and 4/4, as well as two measures where bells and chimes encounter contemporary notation in the form of sound boxes played at tempos chosen by the performer.

TIMBRE
Changing timbres effectively provide variety to the scoring, which includes passages of tutti playing as well as areas of like-timbre color (notably percussion and woodwind).

Unit 7: Form and Structure

SECTION	MEASURE	EVENT AND SCORING
Introduction	1–10	"Maid of the Mist"; chord clusters; percussive swells; non-traditional percussive notation in sound boxes
A	11–46	"White Water Walk"; 4/4; quarter = 152; pointed accents; descending, legato patterns; use of *fp*; wide dynamic ranges
Interlude	47–52	"Journey Behind the Falls"; 4/4; fermatas; large dynamic swell
B	53–82	"Niagara Falls"; main theme; quarter notes and half notes with chimes and bells; wind chimes

SECTION	MEASURE	EVENT AND SCORING
Coda	83–95	Return to "A" section material; *subito piano*

Unit 8: Suggested Listening

Christopher Tucker:
> *Americans Lost*, Kt 4
> *Journey Down Niagara*, Kt 12/4
> *Twilight in the Wilderness*, Clarence, NY: Mark Masters, 2005. 6150–MCD.
> *Winds of Enchantment*, Kt 12/1

Pierre La Plante, *American Riversongs*

Unit 9: Additional References and Resources

Christopher Tucker. Interview with composer via email, May 26, 2007.

Web sites:
> www.tuckermusicworks.com
> www.niagaraparks.com
> www.niagarafallslive.com

Contributed by:

Glen J. Hemberger
Director of Bands
Southeastern Louisiana University
Hammond, Louisiana

Teacher Resource Guide

Little Brazil Suite
Andrew Balent
(b. 1934)

Unit 1: Composer

Andrew Balent is a leading composer and arranger of educational music with more than 500 published compositions and arrangements for band, orchestra, chorus, and instrumental ensembles. Although his published works are written for all levels, he has specialized in music for young musicians and has received more than twenty ASCAP Special Awards for composition. Mr. Balent received both his bachelor of music and master of music degrees from the University of Michigan and taught in the elementary through high school levels for thirty years in Michigan. Mr. Balent has been a clinician and guest conductor in forty-five states, as well as in Canada, Europe, and South America. He is currently on the Sudler Cup selection committee for the John Philip Sousa Foundation and has served two terms on the Board of Directors of the National Band Association. Mr. Balent holds memberships in MENC, MSBOA, WASBE, and Phi Mu Alpha.

Unit 2: Composition

Mr. Balent has been a frequent guest conductor in Brazil and it is from these trips that he developed a keen interest in Brazilian music. From his travels as a guest conductor in Brazil Mr. Balent decided to write a Grade 1 piece to share the types of Brazilian music he heard while in that country with very young bands. The result is a suite comprised of three contrasting traditional Brazilian children's folksongs: "Marcha, Soldaro!" (March, Soldier), "Capelina de Melao" (Little Chapel of Melon) and "Ciranda, Cirandina," a popular children's circle dance. *Little Brazil Suite* gives educators a wonderful opportunity to introduce students to the culture of Brazil, South America's largest country. Andrew Balent also has two other published works inspired by Brazilian music, *Brazilian Reflections* and *Brazilian Children's Song*.

Unit 3: Historical Perspective

A large portion of the wind band repertoire is derived from folk songs from around the world. Some of the most well-known works are the compositions of Ralph Vaughan Williams and Percy Grainger. Brazil is a country rich with a folk-music tradition and some of these traditional Brazilian folk melodies served as the inspiration for the composition.

The folk music of Brazil has been strongly influenced by African rhythms and European forms. The Brazilian music has developed over 500 years into its own original styles and forms. Some of the most popular styles are the *choro*, *frevo*, and probably the most popular, the *samba*.

Unit 4: Technical Considerations

The instrument ranges and rhythms are well within the capabilities of most first year bands. In "Marcha, Soldaro!" the tempo may be adjusted if necessary. It is acceptable to play the piece a little slower than marked if that works better for the group, but the indicated tempo is preferred. The quarter-note accompaniment at the beginning should be played with separation. In "Capelina de Melao" the style should be performed in a smooth, legato manner with attention to dynamic control. In "Ciranda, Cirandina" as in the first movement, the tempo used will depend on the ability of the group. Students should perform this with a steady tempo throughout, always with excitement and enthusiasm.

Unit 5: Stylistic Considerations

The only articulation markings found in the work are staccatos and accents. The conductor should insist that the movements "Marcha, Soldaro!" and "Ciranda, Cirandina" be performed with a good solid articulation and energetic style. Percussion play an important role in Brazilian music and the percussionists should play strong, yet balanced with the winds.

"Capelina de Melao" should contrast the outside movements with a very smooth, legato style. Careful attention should be given that the dynamics are well controlled. Percussionists should work to play in a much lighter style than what has been demanded in the outer movements of the piece.

Unit 6: Musical Elements

MELODY:

I. "Marcha Soldaro!"

The melody is presented three times, first in the trumpets in measure 5 then measure 13 in the woodwinds and horns. A third incomplete statement of the melody, in which Balent augments the rhythms to twice their original value, occurs in the low brass and woodwinds.

II. "Capelina de Melao"

The movement should be played in a sustained, lyrical style. The eight-measure melody is stated twice, first by alternating between the upper woodwinds and upper brass at measure 5, and second at measure 13 with similar instrumentation, all tutti throughout the full melodic statement. The movement requires students to use a legato tonguing style and proper breath control. Pay careful attention to the balance between various instruments in the first statement of the melody. The expressiveness in the musical line is also of importance.

III. "Ciranda, Cirandina"

In this short, 25-measure movement Balent states the eight-measure melody two times. The first movement is scored in the upper wood-winds and the second statement begins with the low winds and for four measures and the last four measures back in the upper woodwinds.

HARMONY:

The harmonic structure of all three movements is very basic using primarily tonic and dominant chords. The first and second movements are in B-flat major with the last movement in E-flat major.

RHYTHM:

The meter of all three movements is 2/4 time. Rhythms are basic and the eighth-note subdivision is used throughout. There is very little rhythmic independence in the work.

TIMBRE:

Variations in tone color are limited to the changes between the woodwinds and brass. The use of percussion is very traditional and, when the bells are used, they always double the flute parts. Careful attention should be given to the pitch between the bells and the flutes.

Unit 7: Form and Structure

SECTION	MEASURE	EVENT AND SCORING
I. "Marcha, Soldaro!"		
Introduction	1–4	B-flat major; the theme is stated in the clarinets, saxophones and low brass
1st statement of melody	5–12	B-flat major; the theme is stated in the trumpets
2nd statement of melody	13–20	B-flat major; the theme is stated in the flutes, clarinets, saxophones, horns and bells
3rd statement of melody	21–28	B-flat major; the theme is an incomplete statement and is presented in the bass clarinet, baritone saxophone and low brass
Coda	29–32	B-flat major
II. "Capelina de Melao"		
Introduction	1–4	B-flat major; low winds and trumpets
1st statement of melody	5–12	B-flat major; the theme is stated in the flutes, trumpets, saxophones and horns
2nd statement of melody	13–20	B-flat major; the theme is stated in the flutes, oboe, clarinets, saxophones, and trumpets
Coda	29–32	B-flat major
III. "Ciranda, Cirandina"		
Introduction	1–2	E-flat major
1st statement of melody	3–11	E-flat major; the theme is stated in the flutes, clarinets, saxophones and trumpets
2nd statement of melody	12–17	E-flat major; the theme is an incomplete statement and is presented in the bass clarinet and low brass
Transition	18–21	E-flat major
Coda	22–35	E-flat major

Unit 8: Suggested Listening

Various selections from the compact discs of the Brazilian National Wind

Orchestra, Dario Sotelo, conductor. Conservatory of Tatui, Tatui, Sao Paulo, Brazil.
Heitor Villa-Lobos:
  Bachianas Brasileras, No. 4
  Bachianas Brasileras, No. 5

Unit 9: Additional References and Resources

Dvorak, Thomas, Cynthia Taggart, and Peter Schmalz. *Best Music for Young Band.* Bob Margolis, ed. Brooklyn, NY: Manhattan Beach Music, 1986.

Garafolo, Robert. *Instructional Designs for Middle/Junior High School Band,* Unit I. Fort Lauderdale, FL: Meredith Music Publications, 1995.

"The Basic Band Curriculum: Grades I, II, III." *BD Guide,* September/October 1989, 2–6.

Contributed by:

Mark Whitlock
Director of Bands
University of Minnesota–Duluth
Duluth, Minnesota

Teacher Resource Guide

Maesong

William Owens
(b. 1963)

Unit 1: Composer

William Owens grew up in Gary, Indiana. He graduated from VanderCook College in Chicago, with a bachelor's in music education. He is an active clinician and guest conductor and has published more than eighty pieces for both middle and high school concert bands, ranging from teaching and novelty selections to festival selections and commissioned pieces. Owens is the winner of the ASCAPlus award and a two-time recipient of the Forrest L. Buchtel Citation for Excellence in Band Composition. Professional memberships include the American Society of Composers, Authors, and Publishers, the American Composers Forum, the Historically Black Colleges and Universities National Band Directors' Consortium, the Mansfield (TX) Wind Symphony and the Texas Music Educator's Association. His compositions are published by FJH, RBC, and TRN Music Companies.

Unit 2: Composition

William Owens's *Maesong* is subtitled *For Georgia*. It is dedicated to his wife, Georgia, whose middle name is Mae. Of this piece, Owens said "I wanted to write a very lovely piece for my very best friend in the entire world."[1]

Approximately three minutes in length, this ballad has a poignant melody that will be memorable for students and audiences alike. Any level of ensemble would find *Maesong* a welcome addition to their concert repertoire. Limited technical demands allow young bands to concentrate on balance, blend, and expressive playing.

Music educators need to motivate students to connect to the literature that they rehearse and perform. These connections result in "teachable" moments and meaningful performances. An introduction to this selection could include questions leading to the personalization of this piece. Appropriate questions would include "Have you ever performed for your family members?" or "Think about your best friend. How could you show that person they are appreciated?" or "Do you and your friends have a favorite song?" A properly led discussion could include many answers from students, and allow for comparisons to the origin and structure of this piece. Adolescent students would certainly be interested in comparing melodic material and compositional techniques to their peer or family relationships. Music is an outlet for emotion, and *Maesong* can have personal meaning for every member of an ensemble.

Unit 3: Historical Perspective

"Music is the shorthand of emotion," said ancient Greek philosopher Plato. Throughout history, music has been written about friendship and love, admiration and heartbreak. Not only is *Maesong* a lovely piece, but it can be seen as an analogy for relationships from beginning to maturity.

Unit 4: Technical Considerations

The woodwind and brass parts are scored for a standard middle school or junior high ensemble: Flute, oboe, 1st and 2nd clarinet, bass clarinet, bassoon, alto saxophone, tenor saxophone, baritone saxophone, 1st and 2nd cornet, horn, trombone, euphonium B.C. or T.C., tuba, timpani, and suspended cymbal. The timpani and the suspended cymbal parts make a brief appearance to emphasize the *crescendos* into the *forte* phrase and key change.

Maesong begins in the key of concert E-flat. There are no accidentals with the exception of measure 32, when the piece modulates to concert-B flat. Students will need technical proficiency in concert E-flat and B-flat in preparation for this piece.

In younger ensembles, give careful attention to the pitch accuracy of the 1st and 2nd trumpet parts. In measures 37 and 45, the flute, 1st clarinet, and 1st trumpet all have a high concert D that needs to be produced consistently and free of tension, which will be a developing skill in some students. This note is naturally flat on all three instruments, but in varying degrees.

The only meter is common time (4/4). Rhythm issues should be few to none; however, developing musicians may allow slurs to detract from their rhythmic accuracy.

There is a molto ritardando and a poco ritardando, both of which end in fermatas. Students need to watch the director carefully so as to move with precision in both instances. Rehearsing tempo changes and transitions without allowing the students to look at the music is a technique that can make an immediate improvement. Establish a technique to end a note for the proper release of the fermata notes. This technique should be addressed from the first day of beginning band; the embouchure must stay set even after the sound stops, and the air should maintain speed and pressure through the release. The conducted release of both fermatas should be very clear and concise for younger ensembles.

Unit 5: Stylistic Considerations

This ballad is legato in style, with clearly marked slurs, *crescendos*, and *decrescendos*. Rehearse staggered breathing to maintain the sostenuto style.

One of the suggested listening pieces for *Maesong* is a movement from a Bach cello suite. Listening to a string performance can initiate a guided conversation about the weight and direction of certain notes, as well as the continuous, legato sound needed to play this ballad. Borrowing a string instrument or string player to demonstrate the weight and speed of drawing a bow across the strings is an excellent visual for students as they learn to shape phrases.

When addressing the characteristic articulations of this piece, students must master the precision of slurs. Slurring one extra note before or after the curved line can cause a lack of clarity. Rehearsal facilities or constant full ensemble playing can cause extra slurs to "hide" and then remain for a performance. Students need to be reminded to practice articulation properly, and individuals and sections need to be heard to determine uniformity.

Unit 6: Musical Elements

MELODY:
The main melody is heard with minor variations each time. It is also reminiscent of *Loch Lomond*, a Scottish Folk Song with similar intervals and step-wise motion.

All students should understand their part's relationship to the melody; countermelody or harmony. Seeing the score helps musicians understand their role. Allowing every student to hear and play the melody to better connect with the emotional content in this piece. One could draw the following comparisons and teach music theory simultaneously.

MEASURE	MELODY	ANALOGY
1–8	Simple version in alto saxophone and clarinet	First impression of someone; a V cadence sounds like there is more music to come, a relationship is beginning

MEASURE	MELODY	ANALOGY
9–16	Passing tones are added	Get to know more about this new acquaintance
17–24	C minor dominates but V chord does not become major Flute presents "B" melody, and trumpet answers	Sounds sad—perhaps a separation or conversation from far away, but feelings are reciprocated
25–32	Original melody in clarinet only, plus flute/oboe	Original interest remains and is enhanced by knowing this person better
33–40	Key change mezzo forte, entire band for first time	Life is changed, introduce this special person to friends and family
41–46	Only forte section in piece	Life together, life gets better and years pass
47–50	End of main theme simplified, back to alto sax and clarinet	Always remember that first meeting and the beginning of a lifelong relationship

HARMONY:

The harmony is E-flat major, and is established by the tonal melody with lower-voice accompaniment. There is one eight-measure phrase in C minor, which returns to E-flat major before modulating and ending in B-flat major.

This composition allows the accompanying low reed, horn and low brass voices to assist with the sostenuto quality and forward motion of the eight-measure phrase. Notice the tenor saxophone quarter notes at the half cadence in the fourth measure. Owens has specifically placed a *crescendo* into measure 5 where young players would want to breathe and possibly "chop" the dotted-half note. The low voices have the important job of propelling this measure forward with ascending quarter notes.

Example 1: *Maesong*, measures 1 to 6

RHYTHM:

The dotted quarter/eighth note is present in the flute, oboe, clarinet, alto saxophone, and trumpet. This rhythm will most likely be well-established by a group performing *Maesong*, but if dotted quarter/eighth note is a new figure for a class, consider teaching it to everyone at the same time. Students must see the rhythm, echo the rhythm, dissect the rhythm, and then demonstrate mastery.

Example 2: *Maesong*, Clarinet, measure 5

1. Perform the rhythm for the class.
2. Explain the "50% more free" dot.
3. Count the rhythm for the class. Make sure to give a slight visual or verbal cue for where beat two is: "One un and three four and" or if clapping, squeeze hands together on beat two.
4. Figure out together, "Where did beat two go?"
5. The class counts the rhythm together.
6. Check individual mastery by hearing individuals or small groups play or count.

Students should practice this rhythm on different pitches, and be able to identify it next time they listen to their favorite popular tune. Directors should be prepared to review the dotted-quarter/eighth note if it is still a new concept.

There are several measures with rhythmic independence between the 1st and 2nd trumpet or clarinet parts, but the differing rhythms in the 2nd part are found in the accompaniment voices also. Rhythmic precision will be tenuous if the vertical alignment of dotted-quarter/eighth/quarter notes and the accompanying half notes do not arrive at beat three together. Precision can be established for a young ensemble through a solid rhythmic foundation.

TIMBRE:

The timbre of *Maesong* is dominated by the clarinet and alto saxophone in the beginning. The darker-toned instruments accompany—clarinet, low reeds, horns, and low brass. The brighter-toned instruments are not present during the first two sections, allowing for a warm, rich ensemble sound. Dynamics are well marked for ensemble balance.

Unit 7: Form and Structure

SECTION	MEASURE	EVENT AND SCORING
A	1–8	First statement of theme by alto saxophone and clarinet; accompaniment is low reeds, horn, and low brass
A'	9–16	Second statement of theme by clarinet and alto saxophone, with several passing tones added; accompaniment is low reeds, horn, and low brass
B	17–20	Flutes enter with second theme in C minor; accompaniment is clarinet, bass clarinet, and alto saxophone
	21–24	Trumpets continue second theme; accompaniment is low reeds, horn, trombone and euphonium
A"	25–28	Clarinet returns with the first melody, along with a return to E-flat major; accompaniment is low reeds, horn, and low brass
	29–32	Flute and oboe join the clarinet; accompaniment remains the same
A'''	33–40	Trumpets add to existing melody; thicker texture heard due to scoring of full ensemble and divisi trumpet and clarinet parts; key signature modulates to B-flat with entire ensemble playing *mezzoforte*; accompaniment is low reeds, horn, and low brass

SECTION	MEASURE	EVENT AND SCORING
A''''	41–45	A *crescendo* in measure 40 leads to *forte* section; flute, oboe, 1st clarinet and 1st trumpet still have the melody; accompaniment is low reeds, horn, and low brass
	46	Climax of the piece with a molto ritardando and fermata
Closing	47–50	A return of the clarinet and alto saxophone to conclude; accompaniment is low reeds, horn, and low brass

Unit 8: Suggested Listening

Johann Sebastian Bach, *Suite for Solo Cello, No. 1, in G Major, BWV 1007: Prelude*

Larry Daehn, *Country Wildflowers*

William Owens, *The Southern Dawn*

Robert Sheldon, *In the Shining of the Stars*

Thomas Tyra, *Two Gaelic Folk Songs*

Unit 9: Additional References and Resources

Fisher, Dennis, Associate Director of Bands, University of North Texas. Band Clinic with the King George Middle School Symphonic Band, December 8, 2006, King George, Virginia.

Froseth, James. *Introducing the Instruments*. Chicago: GIA Publications, 1977, 5.

Pearson, Bruce. *Standard of Excellence*, Book 1. San Diego, CA: Neil A. Kjos Music Company, 1993, 34.

Contributed by:

Catherine R. Fisher
Band Director
King George Middle School
King George, Virginia

---

1 The author would like to thank William Owens for his enthusiastic support of this article. (Phone interview with the composer, 8 May 2007).

Teacher Resource Guide

"March of the Brigadier Guards" from *Iolanthe*

Sir Arthur Sullivan
(1842–1900)

arranged by Bruce Pearson
(b. 1942)

Unit 1: Composer/Arranger

Bruce Pearson was born in 1942 in Minneapolis, Minnesota. His father, who had served in the Navy, took Bruce to see the Navy Band when they came to town on national tours. While at these concerts, Bruce's father would ask, "How do you like my band?"[1] These concerts, along with his mother's interest in music influenced Bruce to join the school band.

Bruce started out playing clarinet, but a football accident cost him two of his front teeth (which remained out for over two years), forcing him to switch to the bass clarinet. He later learned saxophone and flute and began playing professionally.

In 1963, while a senior at St. Cloud State University, he started a band program in a nearby town. After one year there, and following another two-year teaching position in northern Minnesota, he moved to Elk River where he would remain for the next twenty-four years. While at Elk River he taught elementary, junior high, and high school band and began to write his first method book, *Best in Class*, which was published by Kjos in 1982.

His second method book, *Standard of Excellence,* was released by Kjos in 1993. His method books, arrangements, and compositions for young band have placed Mr. Pearson's works in virtually every band hall across the United States.

Mr. Pearson has twice been nominated for the "Excellence in Education Award," and was honored as "Most Outstanding in the Field of Music" for the State of Minnesota. In 1998, he was awarded the prestigious Midwest Band and Orchestra Clinic "Medal of Honor."

He holds the bachelor of science degree from St. Cloud State University, the master of arts degree from the University of Northern Colorado, and has done doctoral studies at the University of Minnesota.

In addition to two university teaching positions (Northwestern College and Bethel College—both in St. Paul, Minnesota) he has conducted and lectured in all fifty states, the Pacific Rim, the Orient, Europe, Mexico, and Canada.

Unit 2: Composition

Sir Arthur Sullivan (1842–1900) was one of Britain's most famous composers. His father was bandmaster at the Royal Military College in Sandhurst, and young Arthur first began singing as a choirboy at Chapel Royal. He was formally trained at the Royal Academy of Music and later at the Leipzig Conservatory alongside classmate Edvard Grieg.

Sullivan had many famous friends including writers Alfred Lord Tennyson, Charles Dickens, and George Grove (author of the *Grove Encyclopedia of Music and Musicians*).[2]

Some of Sullivan's best known works include incidental music for Shakespeare's *Tempest, Henry VIII, McBeth,* the opera *Ivanhoe,* and the hymn *Onward Christian Soldiers.* He later collaborated with William S. Gilbert to write many famous operettas (or comic operas) including *Pirates of Penzance, H.M.S. Pinafore, Iolanthe,* and *The Mikado.* The Savoy Theater in Westminster, London, was built for the express purpose of staging Gilbert and Sullivan productions.

Iolanthe is a fairy who was banished for marrying a mortal. Her son, Strephon is half fairy/half mortal and loves a shepherd girl, Phyllis. Because Phyllis is beautiful, several members of the peerage (lower nobility) seek to marry her. "March of the Brigadier Guards" was written for the arrival of these noblemen in the operetta. Strephon's request to marry Phyllis is rejected by the peers (who want her for themselves) and the boy seeks advice and consolation from his mother, Iolanthe. Phyllis sees this meeting with the youthful Iolanthe and thinks that Strephon has betrayed her.

The operetta is filled with conflicts between the peers, fairies, Strephon, Phyllis, and the Queen of the Fairies—who sentences Iolanthe to death for having married a mortal. In the end, however, the Queen decrees that fairies and mortals can marry and spares Iolanthe's life. Mortals and fairies unite for a happy ending.

Unit 3: Historical Perspective

Orchestral transcriptions have been popular programming for bands since the time of the American Civil War (1861–1865).

When John Philip Sousa (1854–1932) first became conductor of the United States Marine Band in 1880, his first two goals were (1) to invite the finest musicians to join the band, and (2) to begin building a library of music that would permanently belong to the band. (Many previous directors brought their own limited libraries to the post, and upon leaving the band, took the music with them). Among the works Sousa purchased were transcriptions of popular orchestral works from the catalogs of major European publishing houses.

During the late nineteenth century, the bulk of literature that bands played consisted of marches, popular tunes (like "Dixie" and "Camptown Races") and transcriptions of orchestra music—particularly that taken from opera.

Sousa enjoyed the works of Gilbert and Sullivan and studied them carefully when writing his own operettas. One of his early marches, *Mikado*, was based on themes from the Gilbert and Sullivan operetta of the same title. Sousa had several Gilbert and Sullivan piano and vocal scores in his personal book collection and even penned an arrangement, "Selections from Pirates of Penzance," which remains in the Marine Band Library to this day.[3]

Unit 4: Technical Considerations

Ranges in this Grade 1.5 work are moderate for all instruments. Two flute parts are provided with the first flutes playing no higher than C6. The oboe part doubles the first flute at the octave. Three clarinet parts are provided with the firsts playing no higher than G5. Two alto saxophone parts are provided with firsts playing no higher than A5. All low reed parts double the tuba part.

Three trumpet parts are provided with the firsts playing no higher than D5. Two horn parts are provided with firsts playing no higher than C5.

The trombone part often doubles the baritone part. However, Mr. Pearson has carefully scored several short, independent moments (no longer than two measures each) for the trombones. The baritone part consistently doubles the tuba part at the octave.

There is a full complement of percussion parts including: Timpani (F and B-flat only), bells (which double the first flute part), crash cymbals, snare drum, and bass drum.

All students should be reminded of the pitch tendencies for their instrument including: throat tones in the clarinets (generally sharp); C-sharp5 (generally flat), A5 (generally sharp), and D5 (generally sharp) for saxophones; D5 (which is flat) and D4 (which is sharp) for trumpets.

Many directors seek to integrate basic theory instruction with method book studies and literature performance. *March of the Brigadier Guards*, which contains many accidentals, is perfect for reinforcing student knowledge of the piano keyboard including:

(1) The names of the piano keys (white and black)
(2) The function of sharps, flats, and naturals
(3) The spelling of enharmonics
(4) The spelling of half steps and whole steps
(5) The rule of accidentals

Unit 5: Stylistic Considerations

All brass fanfare figures must be played in a regal, marcato style. Long tones (half notes, dotted-half notes, whole notes), and tied-note values must be counted carefully and held for their full duration. Breath impulse counting is strongly suggested for these figures. Accents, which appear throughout the piece, must also be played with breath impulse support with a slight spacing between each note.

Remind students that the many *crescendos* that appear on long tones are most effectively played by starting "softer than seems necessary" and growing through the entire duration of the note.

Tongue/slur combinations appear on groups of four eighth notes throughout the work, and follow two patterns: (1) tongue/slur/tongue/tongue, and (2) tongue/slur/tongue/slur. One effective means of playing tongue/slur figures is to have the students articulate "tah-lah" for each tongue/slur combination.

To maintain a majestic tempo, students should think of this as a royal processional (which it is in the opera). Eighth-note pairs cannot be rushed and should be played with a steady foot tap. Students may also want to align the word "e-ven" with the down-up motion of the foot tap.

Percussion must use restraint when playing the eighth note-two sixteenth figure that appears frequently in their parts. Many young percussionists tend to rush the two sixteenths, which will push the overall tempo.

Unit 6: Musical Elements

MELODY:
The regal fanfare (theme one) and stately second theme must be played majestically, with all players carefully matching note length and style. Eighth-note pairs (often beamed in groups of four) must be played with a short air stream (tongue up behind the top teeth or at the tip of the reed), using even division of the beat (initially with a foot tap), and placing space between each note.

Remind students that accidentals last for only one measure unless they appear in the key signature or the note is tied across the barline. In this case, the accidental "dies at the end of the tie."

Students should also play non-key signature accidentals louder than the other notes in their parts. Explain that composers write melodies using the eight notes of a scale, but in special circumstances, they use notes outside the scale (written with accidentals) to create more exciting melodies and harmonies.

HARMONY:

The chordal structure of this work is tertian, but tonal centers change in transition/development sections through sequences. Students must listen carefully to the vertical tuning and balance of these sonorities. Sustained major chords require students playing the third to lower the pitch of their note slightly for the best ensemble tuning.

RHYTHM:

March of the Brigadier Guards is written in 4/4 time and contains no tempo changes.

The following rhythm figures are found in the wind parts: whole note, dotted-half note, half note, quarter note, dotted-quarter/eighth note, eighth note pair, eighth note/eighth rest, whole rest, half rest, and quarter rest.

The following rhythm figures are found in the percussion parts: quarter note, eighth-note pair, eighth note/two sixteenths, nine-stroke roll, (quarter-note roll with a quarter note release), seventeen-stroke roll (half-note roll with a quarter-note release), and thirty-three stroke roll (whole note with a quarter-note release).

All parts include eighth notes beamed in groups of four. Students should be reminded that these are counted as two consecutive pairs of eighth notes (1 + 2 + or 3 + 4 +).

The dotted-quarter/eighth note figure is difficult for some students to understand. Try counting this figure using the phrase, "One the dot is two — And" with a steady foot tap. This will ensure that the dotted-quarter note is held for its full duration and the single eighth note falls accurately on the "and" of the beat. This counting may prove to be a tongue-twister for some students at first, but after a few tries, everyone should become comfortable with it.

Finally, remind students that the eighth note/eighth rest figure is counted, sounds, and should be played like a staccato quarter note.

TIMBRE:

A pyramid balance with higher voices listening down and playing just under the lower voices will produce a dark, late nineteenth century orchestra sound befitting this work. At times, high brasses and woodwinds may need to play out to yield more brilliance to a phrase or motive.

Unit 7: Form and Structure

The work is largely in the key of B-flat major and the two themes (theme one being a fanfare figure) are contrasted by transitional and closing material. Teachers should be cautioned that, while this piece is highly playable by younger bands, the transition (developmental) sections of the work include many accidentals and require students listen to and tune carefully as tonal centers change. With the exception of the fanfare figure, the entire piece is played by full band. A basic outline of the piece is as follows:

MEASURE	EVENT AND SCORING
1	Introductory fanfare (theme one) – stated in unison by trumpets and trombones. The response that follows is played by harmonized full band
10	Theme two – introduced by harmonized full band
16	Transition – harmonic instability begins and moves through Dm(vi), FM(V), and eventually returns to B-flat major(I)
26	Theme two – returns and is stated by harmonized full band
30	Transition – highly developmental and contains fragments from the fanfare and theme two with some motivic transformation
34	Transition continues with sequence – moving the band through the tonal centers of E-flat, F, G-flat, and B major (although the B major segment is spelled enharmonically using G-flat in place of F-sharp and, in the G-flat section, B in place of C-flat)
52	Retransition – begins a sustained dominant presence (F)
54	Return to home key of B-flat major
55	Final statement of fanfare
64	Final statement of theme two
68	Brief sequence (up a M2) of theme two played by the full band
72	Closing material begins

Measure	Event and Scoring
80	Fragments of fanfare and theme two – motivically transformed and worked into closing material
90	Fine

Unit 8: Suggested Listening

Arthur Gilbert and George Sullivan, *H.M.S. Pinafore*
George Frederick Handel, *Music for the Royal Fireworks*
Gioacchino Rossini, *Overture to William Tell*
Dimitri Shostakovich, *Finale from Symphony, No. 4*
Arthur Sullivan, *Pineapple Poll Suite*
Franz von Suppé, *Overture to Light Cavalry*
William Walton, *Crown Imperial Coronation March*

Unit 9: Additional References and Resources

American School Band Director's Association. *The ASBDA Curriculum Guide*. Pittsburg, PA: Volkwein Bros., 1973.

Battisti, Frank L. *The Winds of Change: The Evolution of the Contemporary American Wind Band/Ensemble and its Conductor*. Galesville, MA: Meredith Music, 2002.

Benjamin, Thomas, Michael Horvitt, and Robert Nelson. *Techniques and Materials of Music*, 7th ed. Belmont, CA: Thomson Schirmer, 2007.

Bonds, Mark Evan. *A History of Music in Western Culture*, 2nd ed. Upper Saddle River, NJ: Prentice Hall, 2006.

Garafalo, Robert. *Blueprint for Band*. Fort Lauderdale, FL: Meredith Music Publications, 1983.

Hansen, Richard K. *The American Wind Band: A Cultural History*. Chicago: GIA Publications, 2005.

Harris, Eric L. *Fundamentals of Music Theory for the Wind Band Student*, Workbooks 1–3. Huntersville, NC: NorthLand Music Publishers, 1999–2005.

Holden, Amanda, ed. *The Viking Opera Guide*. London, England: Penguin Books Ltd., 1993.

McBeth, William Francis. *Effective Performance of Band Music*. San Antonio, TX: Southern Music Company, 1972.

Merryman, Marjorie. *The Music Theory Handbook*. Fort Worth, TX: Harcourt Brace College Publishers, 1997.

Middleton, James, Harry Haines, and Gary Garner. *The Band Director's Companion*. San Antonio, TX: Southern Music Company, 1998.

Randel, Don Michael. *The Harvard Concise Dictionary of Music and Musicians*. Cambridge, MA: The Belknap Press of Harvard University Press, 1999.

Waguespack, Gerald E. "A Review of Grade One Band Literature Found on the University Interscholastic League List of Prescribed Music for Band." Ph.D. diss., The University of Southern Mississippi, 2000.

Wright, Craig, and Bryan Simms. *Music in Western Civilization*. Belmont, CA: Thomson/Schirmer, 2006.

Contributed By:

Eric L. Harris
Associate Director of Bands
Tennessee Technological University
Cookeville, Tennessee

---

1 Bruce Pearson. Telephone conversation, May 21, 2007.
2 Jon W. Finson. *Nineteeth Century Music: The Western Classical Tradition*. Upper Saddle River, NJ: Prentice Hall, 2002.
3 MGySgt Michael Ressler. Chief Librarian, The United States Marine Band, "The President's Own." Telephone conversations, May 21, 2007.

Teacher Resource Guide

May Day in Red Square
Christopher Prentice
(b. 1978)

edited by Barbara Lambrecht
(b. 1943)

Unit 1: Composer

Christopher Prentice, a native Texan, was born in 1978. His compositions and arrangements for concert band have been performed in Texas, New Mexico, and Washington, DC. Prentice was a Texas All-State horn player at Coronado High School in El Paso, where he studied with Richard Lambrecht. He performed twice at the Midwest Clinic in Chicago as part of the Coronado High School Orchestra. Prentice majored in theatre at Southern Methodist University and is an alumnus of the Santa Clara Vanguard Drum and Bugle Corps (1999). He currently resides in Chicago, Illinois where he is an actor and producing artistic director of Signal Ensemble Theatre.

Unit 2: Composition

Christopher Prentice composed *May Day in Red Square* in 2006. The piece was inspired by the composer's performance with the first American band to march in Red Square since World War II. Prentice was drum major of the Coronado High School band, which he conducted in Moscow's Red Square during May Day celebrations in 1996. The piece evokes the grandeur and magnitude of the 800-year-old city of Moscow. It is meant to depict the many sights of Moscow, from the stately Kremlin to the ornately beautiful Saint Basil's cathedral. The opening theme is a heavy dance that contrasts with the light, hymn-like body of the work. Published by TRN, the 66-measure piece

is approximately two minutes and eighteen seconds in length. *May Day in Red Square* was performed at the Midwest Clinic in Chicago, Illinois, in December of 2006.

Unit 3: Historical Perspective

Red Square (*Krasnaya ploshchad*) in the heart of Moscow was named not only for the color of the bricks that line it, but because the Russian word *Krasnaya* literally translates to either "red" or "beautiful." The word was originally applied to the beautiful Saint Basil's Cathedral, located at the southern end of Red Square, and was subsequently transferred to the nearby square. Red Square is surrounded by some of the most well-known landmarks in Russia—Saint Basil's cathedral, the Kremlin, and Lenin's mausoleum where the embalmed body of Vladimir Ilyich Lenin's body is displayed. The square was originally covered with wooden buildings, but was cleared after Ivan III's edict in 1493 to reduce the danger of fires. The newly cleared area eventually became Moscow's primary marketplace. Later it was used for public ceremonies and the occasional coronation of a Russian tsar. The square has been gradually built up and is now used for official ceremonies. During the Soviet era, the square maintained its significance, becoming the main square in the life of the new state. It was the official address of the Soviet government and was the renowned location for military parades. The square itself is more than 500,000 square feet of open land.

Unit 4: Technical Considerations

The work's introduction begins in concert E-flat major and then moves to the relative key of C minor, where it remains for the duration of the piece. There are few accidentals and the most difficult rhythmic patterns combine eighth and quarter notes. Written in 4/4 meter, the tempo changes from maestoso in the beginning, to allegro at the melodic entrance. Melodic themes are usually written in unison voicings. Dynamic contrasts are used throughout the piece and articulation markings are prevalent, especially the use of legato and staccato. The basic percussion writing requires only basic quarter note/eighth note rhythms and half note rolls. Instrument ranges are not extensive, and are easily accessible to young players.

Unit 5: Stylistic Considerations

The program note states that the piece "is a musical rendering of the Russian ethos." The programmatic piece is meant to bring images of Red Square to the musicians' and the listeners' minds. The introduction is marked "maestoso" and *forte* for the first two measures and concludes with a fermata. The key then changes to minor, and the dynamic to *piano*, for the last two measures of the introduction. This type of contrast continues throughout the piece: loud vs. soft, staccato vs. legato. There is ample opportunity for young players to develop control over their instrument and to produce a quality tone at both ends of the dynamic and articulation spectrums. The changes in articulation and dynamics indicate the changes between sections of the piece.

Unit 6: Musical Elements

MELODY:

The melody is first introduced at measure 5, following a four-measure introduction. The entrance of the melody also marks the tempo change to allegro, which remains through the end of the piece. The main melody is first stated in a unison woodwind line at a soft dynamic. A simple brass accompaniment of off-beat staccato quarter notes marks the restatement of the melody at measure 13. The main melody is replaced by a second melodic idea at measure 21, but returns in measure 29, this time in the brass with woodwind accompaniment. The main melody is then rhythmically varied in measures 37 through 44. This variation augments the melody, using half- and note/quarter-note rhythms instead of the original eighth- and quarter-note patterns. Measure 53 marks the return of the original melody in the high woodwinds and high brass, accompanied by the low woodwinds and low brass.

The secondary melody, which was first introduced at measure 21, uses the flutes, clarinets, and alto saxophones to produce a simpler and gentler musical line than in the main melody. The trumpets, low woodwinds, and tuba provide a contrasting accompaniment to the melody, which is more rhythmic than melodic in nature. The secondary melody is replaced by the main melody at measure 29, but returns in a varied form at measure 45. This variation is legato and soft and once again provides a gentler side to the main melody, just as Saint Basil's Cathedral contrasts the Kremlin in Red Square. Measures 45 through 52 are the last we hear of the secondary melody.

HARMONY:

The introduction begins in E-flat major but moves to C minor by measure 3. The remainder of the piece is modal with the exception of a few instances, primarily at cadential points, where dominant-to-tonic relationships occur. The piece ends on the major tonic of the minor key.

RHYTHM:

The rhythm is uncomplicated, yet it is vital in identifying the main and secondary melodies. Rhythmic modulation is the primary technique used to vary both melodies in measures 37 through 52. The percussion parts effectively reinforce both melody and accompaniment parts in the various sections of the piece. The piece employs a quarter-note pulse throughout and requires only basic subdivision to help stabilize the beat. Otherwise, the basic melody lines of quarter and eighth notes may be easily rushed by young players. The piece is not meant to be played extremely fast; the allegro marking is secondary to the melodic components.

Timbre:

The composer moves the melody lines from part to part, using timbre to help delineate the sections of the piece. The mostly unison melody lines make good tone color and blend an important emphasis when teaching and performing this piece.

Unit 7: Form and Structure

Section	Measure	Event and Scoring
Introduction	1–4	Maestoso; E-flat major and *forte* in measures 1–2 transitioning through a fermata to *piano* and C minor in measures 3–4
A	5–12	Unison main melody introduced in the clarinets and saxophones; *mezzo piano* dynamic
A	13–20	Restatement of the main melody with added flute and brass accompaniment, *forte* dynamic; percussion provides rhythmic contrast
B	21–28	Introduction of secondary melody with rhythmic contrasts in the lower voices, trumpets, and percussion; *mezzo forte* dynamic
A	29–36	Return of main melody in the brass with woodwind and percussion accompaniment
A'	37–44	Variation on the main melody in the woodwinds, *mezzo piano* dynamic; clarinet eighth notes help fill in the missing melodic pitches and add motion
B'	45–52	Variation on the secondary melody, *mezzo piano* dynamic; snare drum adds motion and rhythmic stability

SECTION	MEASURE	EVENT AND SCORING
A	53–62	Main melody in high woodwinds/brass, accompanied by saxophones, lower voices, and percussion; *forte* measures 53–60; piano melody echo in measures 61–62
Conclusion	63–66	Melody echo that concludes on a C-major chord, *forte* dynamic

Unit 8: Suggested Listening

James Curnow, *Russian Folk Fantasy*

Works by Russian composers, such as:
    Sergei Prokofiev
    Dimitri Shostakovich

Unit 9: Additional References and Resources

Miles, Richard, and Thomas Dvorak eds. *Teaching Music through Performance in Beginning Band.* Chicago: GIA Publications, 2001.

Prentice, Christopher. Electronic mail correspondence with the composer. May 2007.

Prentice, Christopher. *May Day in Red Square.* Barbara Lembrecht, ed. Alto, NM: TRN, 2006.

Web site:
    TRN Music: http://www.trnmusic.com

Contributed by:

Kirsten Trachsel
Director of Bands
Boyd Independent School District
Boyd, Texas

Teacher Resource Guide

Midnight Mission

Brian Balmages
(b. 1975)

Unit 1: Composer

Brian Balmages was born in 1975 in Baltimore, Maryland. The son of an elementary school band director, Balmages learned to play trumpet at an early age before joining the fifth grade band, taught by his father, Fred. He continued to play trumpet through high school and learned to play piano by ear, composing songs that he would record rather than write down.

His composing on paper began in college as a music industry major at James Madison University, where he studied composition and film scoring with Robert W. Smith. His first commission for a band work was from the Columbia Concert Band, a community band directed by his father. Balmages earned his master's degree from the University of Miami (Florida).

Balmages has written works for band and wind ensemble, orchestra, and brass ensembles. His band works span grade levels from .5 to 5. His interest in writing music for beginners was spurred in part by his wife, Lisa, who is an elementary band teacher in the Baltimore public schools.

Balmages is currently the director of instrumental publications for the FJH Music Company in Fort Lauderdale, Florida, and lives in Baltimore with his wife and their son, Jacob.

His compositional philosophy can be found on his Web site:

As a composer, I used to write music only for advanced level ensembles. However, after marrying an elementary band director, and with the support of numerous friends, colleagues, and directors, I have found great joy and challenge in writing music for younger students along with my more difficult works. After all, the youngest of musicians are equally deserving of good literature and I can only hope that my music will inspire them the way I am inspired by a Mahler symphony.

Unit 2: Composition

"Midnight Mission" is the first movement of a three-movement suite entitled *Midnight Suite*. The work was inspired by the birth of his son and the memories and feelings that surrounded that event. The second movement, "Midnight Sky," is slow and lyrical like a lullaby, and the third movement, "Midnight Madness," is hectic and confused like late-night awakenings.

Of the first movement, the composer writes in the score:

> *Midnight Mission* is designed to reflect a late-night adventure in which people are heard sneaking around in search of their mission objective. These midnight spies encounter various obstacles during their search, some more comical sounding than others, though the entire piece has a very light-hearted effect, as it is meant to symbolize the childhood games many of us played as kids.

Written in the form of a theme with four variations, the piece introduces young players to the important concepts of staccato and dynamic contrast through a delightful and fun musical work. Remarkably, Balmages has created a very interesting work using only the first six notes that students learn (concert B-flat to G). The work is in C minor and lasts approximately a minute and a half at quarter note = 144.

Even though *Midnight Mission* is a beginning band piece, it is subtle, sophisticated, and well written and would be a fun piece for an older group to play, especially for a recruiting trip to elementary schools.

Unit 3: Historical Perspective

Balmages did not set out to write music for a spy thriller, but the music brings to mind a dark alley and fearful anticipation. From Henry Mancini's *Pink Panther* to Lalo Schifrin's *Mission: Impossible*, spy music is generally bluesy, clipped, dark and quiet, with a big accent somewhere in the middle. Balmages's work draws on this rich history, but uses materials accessible to middle school players. Students will already be familiar with the style used in this piece and will have fun trying to match the sound of the recording.

Unit 4: Technical Considerations

The technical materials used in *Midnight Mission* include only the first six notes taught in most band method books (concert B-flat to G); only whole, half, quarter, and paired eighth notes; and only *piano, forte,* and *mezzo forte* dynamic levels. The difficulty in making this piece work, though, is in getting students to play in the correct style, which is mostly staccato, and to play quietly. Some teachers may not even want beginners struggling with playing staccato until their tone production has matured. This work may be better suited to the beginning of the second year rather than the end of the first year, when students have a better grasp of proper tone production.

Accents are used as well as *crescendos,* although little dynamic subtlety is involved. Because the work is in C minor, the brass players, especially the tubas, use the sharp first and third valve combination quite a bit; check their intonation carefully.

The instrumentation consists of five basic parts: flute (oboe), clarinet (one part divided on occasion), alto sax (horn and tenor sax), trumpet (one part divided most of the time), and a bass line (bassoon, bass clarinet, baritone sax, trombone, baritone, and tuba).

The percussion writing is easy, but sophisticated for this level. The parts can be covered by five players on numerous instruments: xylophone, snare drum, bass drum, temple blocks, triangle, crash cymbals, and two well-placed vibraslap notes. The snare drum part includes flams but not sixteenth notes, and all players must play softly and tastefully.

To help students practice the staccato and dynamic markings, Balmages has included two supplemental lines at the bottom of the page, which he calls "Musical Jump Start." Number One focuses on soft, staccato playing and is marked "Soft and Sneaky." Students respond well to this because they have heard "sneaky" music in soundtracks.

Unit 5: Stylistic Considerations

As mentioned above, soft, staccato playing is crucial in *Midnight Mission.* Although young players, especially beginners, have difficulty practicing stylistic elements, they love trying to make this music sound "sneaky" and can hear whether they are successful or not. Play a professional recording of the piece so students can hear the proper sound of the staccato, then record the band and let them hear how well they can play the soft, staccato sections themselves.

Unit 6: Musical Elements

MELODY:

The melody is disjunct. It is made up of a three-note motif that Balmages varies throughout, using it in canon and in inversion, in slight rhythm alterations, and using it in new melodic settings. The melody occurs in several different instruments and is sometimes divided up between sections in the middle of the phrase. Students need to be told where the melody goes and to bring it out.

HARMONY:

The accompaniment is mostly staccato quarters with a tonic-dominant bass line. There are a couple of places where parts move quickly from a quarter-note accompaniment to the three-note motif of the melody. Students will need to be told to hold back on the quarter notes and bring the melody part out.

RHYTHM:

The only real rhythmic challenge occurs in the last two measures, where students often have trouble figuring out the interplay of the parts. Rehearse the three-note motif parts separately from the bass line until students are secure in their counting.

TIMBRE:

This is where the most work will be needed and why saving this piece for a more mature group could be a good idea. Beginners may have a hard time playing staccato with a clear, focused tone. In fact, some teachers may not want their beginners struggling with staccato until they can produce a consistent tone on longer notes. Once students can play with good tone, practice playing increasingly shorter notes, rather than starting with a short note that has no tone. When practicing the staccato, remind students that only the first microsecond of a note is heard and that a clear and clean articulation is necessary for a good-sounding staccato note.

Unit 7: Form and Structure

Midnight Mission is written in the form of a theme and four variations:

MEASURE	EVENT
1–2	Introduction
3–10	Theme
11–19	Variation 1
20–24	Interlude
25–32	Variation 2
33–36	Bridge
37–44	Variation 3 with added countermelody
45–52	Variation 4 (similar to Variation 1)
53–55	Coda

As noted above, Balmages develops the opening melodic motif very artfully, especially for such a brief work. After rehearsing the work for a couple of weeks, directors could play a musical game with the band to see if students can discover where and how the melody changes.

Unit 8: Suggested Listening

Students will enjoy listening to soundtrack recordings of music from mysteries, spy movies, and TV shows. A quick search of Amazon.com will uncover classics from the 1950s and 1960s including *James Bond, Mission: Impossible; Man from U.N.C.L.E.; Peter Gunn;* and *The Pink Panther*, plus lesser-known shows. Part of the lesson is to help students learn the value of playing the *style* of the music, first using music they know, then leading them into different classical styles.

Unit 9: Additional References and Resources

Balmages, Brian. Telephone interview by Donald Morris. May 2007.

Web sites:
    Brian Balmages at FJH Music:
        http://www.fjhmusic.com/composer/bbalmages.htm
    Brian Balmages:
        http://www.brianbalmages.com

Both Web sites include recordings by Balmages of his other works for band.

Contributed by:

Donald Morris
Band Director, McClintock Middle School
Conductor, Charlotte Concert Band
Charlotte, North Carolina

Teacher Resource Guide

Mountain Song

Jared Spears
(b. 1936)

Unit 1: Composer

Dr. Jared Spears is Professor of Music Emeritus at Arkansas State University in Jonesboro, Arkansas. Born in Chicago, Illinois, he received a Bachelor of Science in Education degree in music education from Northern Illinois University, the Bachelor of Music and Master of Music in percussion and composition from the Cosmopolitan School of Music, and the Doctor of Musical Arts in composition from Northwestern University. Some of his teachers include Blyth Owen, Alan Stout, and Anthony Donato.

Spears, who taught theory, history, composition, percussion, and band to students from elementary school through college, retired from Arkansas State University in 1999. During his tenure at Arkansas State University, Spears received the University President's Award for outstanding faculty member as well as an appointment as a President's Fellow.

Dr. Spears has composed more than 250 original works for band, choir, orchestra, and chamber ensembles. His music has been performed and record-ed worldwide, and he has conducted band festivals, camps, and clinics in Canada, Europe, and throughout the United States. He has appeared at sev-eral universities as a guest lecturer.

Unit 2: Composition

Mountain Song is a legato setting of the hymn tune "Protection," which appears in many hymnals in the twenty-first century. The following program note is published in the conductor's score:

Joseph Funk (1778–1862), who established the first Mennonite printing business in America, spent the majority of his life in Rockingham County, Virginia. He is best known as the compiler of collections of hymn tunes. The melody "Protection" first appeared in *A Compilation of Genuine Church Music* (1832). The melody is most frequently associated with the hymn *How Firm a Foundation*, which was included in a collection by John Rippon (1751–1836). The melody for *Mountain Song* is from the same era and tradition as the hymn tunes "Prospect" and "New Britain" (*Amazing Grace*).

Mountain Song was composed and published in 2006 by Great Works Publishing, Inc. and was recorded by The Baldwin-Wallace Concert Wind Ensemble, Laura Joss, conductor. The work contains forty-six measures and is approximately 2:20 in length.

Unit 3: Historical Perspective

The early American tune "Foundation," found in the metrical index as 11.11.11.11, appears as "How Firm a Foundation"; the text is based on biblical passages taken from II Timothy 2:19, Hebrews 13:5, and Isaiah 43:1–5. The verses are included here as a reference:

> How firm a foundation, you saints of the Lord
> Is laid for your faith in his excellent Word!
> What more can he say than to you he has said,
> To you who for refuge to Jesus have fled?
>
> Fear not, I am with you: O be not dismayed,
> For I am your God and will still give you aid;
> I'll strengthen you, help you, and cause you to stand,
> Upheld by my gracious omnipotent hand.
>
> When through the deep waters I call you to go,
> The rivers of sorrow shall not overflow,
> For I will be with you in trouble to bless,
> And sanctify to you your deepest distress.
>
> When through fiery trials your pathway shall lie,
> My grace all sufficient shall be your supply;
> The flame shall not hurt you; I only design
> Your dross to consume and your gold to refine.

The soul that on Jesus has leaned for repose
I will not, I will not desert to its foes;
That soul, though all hell should endeavor to shake,
I'll never, no never, no never forsake!

Unit 4: Technical Considerations

Students must be comfortable performing in both E-flat and F major and be able to read accidentals (sharp, flat, and natural signs). The range of the work is limited; trumpet never exceeds a C5, the trombone/euphonium a B-flat3, and the tuba a B-flat2. The horn range is one octave from C4 to C5. Clarinets have one note over the break, a B-natural4 in the section written in F concert.

Mountain Song includes extensive dynamic markings ranging from *piano* to *forte* as well as *crescendo* and *descrescendo*. The introduction is perhaps the most difficult to perform because the thickest texture (measures 6–7) requires the softest dynamic and has a written *descrescendo* from *f* to *p*. The composition includes a variety of articulations including tongued passages in a legato style, slurred passages, and accents, which may present challenges for less-experienced players.

The work uses standard instrumentation; the clarinet and trumpet sections are divided into two parts. The percussion requirements include bells, suspended cymbal, triangle, bass drum, and snare drum. The bell and triangle parts are crucial to a successful performance of *Mountain Song*.

Unit 5: Stylistic Considerations

The work can be used to develop tone quality and balance between melody, countermelody and bass lines. Although the work must be performed in a legato style with four-measure phrasing, no phrases or breath marks are indicated in the score. The absence of these markings provides the opportunity to teach score marking and to reinforce the importance of breath control and phrasing. To supplement study, students should listen to and perform Bach chorales, choral and instrumental, for both style and phrasing.

Unit 6: Musical Elements

MELODY:
The hymn tune "How Firm a Foundation" generally appears in hymnals in the key of A-flat major with a 2/2 time signature. *Mountain Song* was written in E-flat concert and a 4/4 time signature. The melody features a great deal of contrast between stepwise motion and melodic leaps.

Figure 1. *Mountain Song*, melody

The tune consists of four four-measure phrases, and each phrase begins on the anacrusis. There are two full statements of the hymn tune in the work. *Mountain Song* is excellent to use when working on phrasing and breath support.

A valuable exercise would be to provide the hymn tune to the entire ensemble to play and sing it as a unison etude. The director could also provide the harmony and bass lines and have students perform the hymn in smaller ensembles. Ensemble members should also be encouraged to learn other hymns from this era such as "Amazing Grace" and "It is Well With My Soul."

HARMONY:

Because of its chordal construction, there is a great deal of emphasis on the interval of a major third throughout the work. A variety of exercises where students construct and balance chords will assist in the development of tone and intonation. Beginning with a focus on the V–I cadential progression in the keys of E-flat and F major will assist in the rehearsal and performance of the work. The rehearsal process should also highlight the suspension found in measure 15 in the alto saxophone part.

RHYTHM:

Rhythms in the work focus primarily on quarter, half, and whole notes. Eighth notes are only used in the flute, oboe, and bell countermelodies and in the snare drum part.

The moderate tempo, quarter note = 80, requires less-experienced performers to develop subdivision skills. In addition, *Mountain Song* is excellent for developing appropriate note lengths, as some accompaniment patterns require a pitch to be sustained for a single quarter note; often, these notes are played far too short by young ensembles.

Figure 2. *Mountain Song*, tuba, measures 16–19

TIMBRE:

The introduction begins on beat three of measure 1 in the trumpet and saxophone, and all subsequent phrases begin on beat three. A strong breath before beginning each phrase is key to a correct entrance and clear tone.

Throughout the work, the melody passes throughout the ensemble. The textures vary greatly, from tutti section playing (trumpet and snare drum in measures 35–37), to chamber-like writing (flute, oboe, clarinet, and percussion at measure 8) to full ensemble (all woodwinds, brass, and percussion in measures 30–35).

Unit 7: Form and Structure

SECTION	MEASURE	EVENT AND SCORING
Introduction	1–7	E-flat major; melodic motive taken from first phrase of the hymn (a); shifting textures; authentic cadence in measures 5–6; dynamic energy includes a *diminuendo* from *forte* to *piano* (measures 6–7)
a, a'	8–15	Hymn tune first appears in clarinet; two four-measure phrases; countermelody with eighth notes in the flute and oboe; ostinato in bells and triangle
b', a''	16–23	Melody appears in trumpet (measures 16–19) and flute (measures 20–21)
Transition	24–29	Transitional passage; modulation from E-flat major to F major; *crescendo* through cadence to I chord in measure 30
a, a'	30–37	Grandioso; F major; full texture and *forte* dynamic; countermelody in flute, oboe, and bells
b	38–41	Third melodic phrase (flute and oboe); countermelody in clarinet; *subito piano*
a'''	42–46	Extended final phrase; perfect authentic cadence in measures 43–44; unison *forte* F concert pitch in measures 45–46

Unit 8: Suggested Listening

Jack Bullock, *Amazing Grace*
David Holsinger:
   A Childhood Hymn
   On a Hymnsong of Philip Bliss
   On a Southern Hymnsong
Claude T. Smith, *The Water Is Wide*
Frank Ticheli, *Amazing Grace*
John Zdechlik, *Grace Variants*

Unit 9: Additional References and Resources

Young, Carlton, R., ed. *The Book of Hymns*. Nashville, TN: The United
   Methodist Publishing House, 1979.

Weborg, C. John. *The Covenant Hymnal*. Chicago, IL: Covenant
   Publications, 1996.

Contributed by:

Wendy McCallum
Instrumental Music Education Specialist
Brandon University
Brandon, Manitoba, Canada

Teacher Resource Guide

Our Kingsland Spring
Samuel R. Hazo
(b. 1966)

Unit 1: Composer

Samuel R. Hazo resides in Pittsburgh, Pennsylvania, with his wife and children. In 2003, Mr. Hazo became the first composer in history to be named the winner of both composition contests sponsored by the National Band Association. He has composed for the professional, university and public school levels as well as writing original scores for television, radio, and the stage. In addition to original symphonic compositions, his works have been included in performances with actors Brooke Shields, James Earl Jones, David Conrad, and Richard Kiley. He has also written symphonic arrangements for three-time Grammy Award-winning singer/songwriter Lucinda Williams. Hazo has served as composer-in-residence at the University of Minnesota Conducting Symposium, and has also lectured on music and music education at universities and high schools internationally. Mr. Hazo has taught music at every grade level from kindergarten through college, including work as a high school and university director. Mr. Hazo was twice named "Teacher of Distinction" by the Southwestern Pennsylvania Teachers' Excellence Foundation. He received his bachelor's and master's degrees from Duquesne University and was awarded as Duquesne's Outstanding Graduate in Music Education.

Unit 2: Composition

Our Kingsland Spring is actually the first movement of Hazo's multi-movement work titled "A Georgian Suite." The Grade 2 work for concert band was commissioned by Elizabeth E. Taylor, District Band Chair for the Georgia Music Educators' Association District 8 Middle School Honor Band. The District 8 Honor Band premiered *Our Kingsland Spring* in 2004 in Kingsland, Georgia, conducted by the composer.

Unit 3: Historical Perspective

The composer writes:

> "*Our Kingsland Spring* was commissioned by my friend Elizabeth E. Taylor, District Band Chair for the Georgia Music Educators' Association District 8 Middle School Honor Band. It was premiered by this ensemble in Kingsland, Georgia in a wonderful festival for which I was invited to guest conduct. The students and their teachers were so enjoyable to be around that I decided on this title to commemorate our time together. *Our Kingsland Spring* was the final piece in our festival concert, which was actually held on the first day of spring in 2004."[1]

Unit 4: Technical Considerations

As with most Grade 2 compositions, *Our Kingsland Spring* does not present any technical issues that would prevent younger and developing bands from performing the work. Mr. Hazo states, "Because *Our Kingsland Spring* was written for young bands, I did as much as I could to repeat note patterns so that the students could get to the music making as soon as possible without having to learn a ton of finger stuff."[2] Instrumentation requirements are not excessive, and perhaps the most demanding need would be for oboists to play an exposed and extended melodic passage with the flutes early in the composition. A good saxophone quartet will clearly improve the performance of the passage beginning at measure 64, but cues are provided to assist younger bands through this section. Intonation, blend, and balance are extremely important in the softer and more exposed passages of the piece, as some sections of the composition are thinly scored and quite transparent. The entire work is scored in E-flat major, and the range, and other technical issues are appropriate for developing players and should not present any problems.

Unit 5: Stylistic Considerations

The vibraphone solo in the opening statement is light and dance-like in nature (with hemiola) and perhaps jazz elements can be conceptualized into the rhythmic flow of the "A" theme. The melodic passages throughout the work, and especially those in more exposed settings, must be extremely expressive, song-like, and heart-felt. *Our Kingsland Spring* is an excellent work for promoting lyricism and musicianship in developing bands. Chorale-style passages, along with beautiful tutti passages can certainly bring ensemble

lyricism and balance issues into perspective, and some exposed chamber-like passages promote musical sensitivity for soloists as well as supporting voices.

Unit 6: Musical Elements

HARMONY:
Harmonic properties are quite traditional and there are no major shifts in tonal center. Harmonic blend and balance are of paramount importance in this composition, and the conductor will have to devote a substantial amount of rehearsal time to these issues. Proper tone production and intonation are clearly essential for an effective harmonic presentation.

RHYTHM:
Simple yet musically effective rhythmic structures are used in both melodic and non-melodic passages. Melodic lines are flowing and tuneful, and such sustained lines must remain absolutely cohesive to communicate the musical materials in a unified manner. Some temporal flexibility is required toward the conclusion of the work, and the frequent changes between "double-time" and "half-time" throughout the composition should not be problematic. The opening vibraphone passage of three quarter-note chords followed by two dotted-half note chords requires careful subdivision.

TIMBRE:
Hazo provides a variety of timbral elements to establish the colorful sonic landscapes represented in *Our Kingsland Spring*. Isolated percussion statements, moderate dynamic shifts in solo and tutti passages, solo passages with small ensemble accompaniments, chorale-style passages as well as soft and sensitive chamber-like settings, and dramatic and powerful passages for the full ensemble are some of the settings that contribute to the timbre and color of this expressive work.

Unit 7: Form and Structure

MEASURE	EVENT AND SCORING
1–4	Introduction; light spirited rhythmic pattern in vibraphone establishes key of E-flat major; rhythmic style of vibraphone passage suggests light dance-like and jazz qualities; simple, sustained pedal voices provided by bass clarinet and tenor saxophone support the active vibraphone line

MEASURE	EVENT AND SCORING
5–20	First appearance of "A" theme: a simple and pleasant melodic statement in flutes, which is complemented with a continuation of the introductory materials
21–34	Repeat of "A" theme in flutes and oboes; counter-melodic materials scored for horns, alto saxophones, and clarinets; accompanying voices continue previous style with added euphonium, tuba (bass line) and timpani
35–41	Tempo shift to "half-time" marks the beginning of a bold and expressive "B" theme, represented by full ensemble scoring and melody in first flute, oboe, first clarinet and first trumpet; a slowing of the tempo at measure 41 signals a return to a new presentation of the "A" theme
42–49	A more elaborate variation of "A" theme returns in flutes at the original tempo, with stylistic and rhythmic support provided by the ride cymbal and timpani; very light scoring reestablishes the spirit and style of the opening measures
50–57	Repeat of the "A" theme variation in a full-winds setting; melodic materials presented in flutes, oboes, second clarinets, and first trumpets, with remaining wind instruments providing countermelodic and harmonic support
58–63	Return to double-time tempo and full ensemble scoring for "B" theme; lead soprano and alto register voices dominate the melodic scoring; with other voices providing continued harmonic and secondary melodic materials
64–71	Return to a very soft and serene "A" theme variation in saxophone choir; the melody, however, is not included in this variation
72–79	Continuation of non-melodic "A" theme variation, scored for full winds in a chorale-like setting
80–87	Intense and brilliant interlude, marked by more active percussion scoring, punctuated and robust chords in the brass and woodwinds, and colorful trills in the flutes and oboes
88–95	Final exuberant statement of the "A" theme
96–101	Return to double-time and final statement of the "B" theme in a full ensemble setting

Measure	Event and Scoring
102–112	Coda; return to original tempo and concluding materials based on fragments from "A" theme; Final five measures present a sequence of brilliant and captivating ensemble chords, concluding with a resounding E-flat major chord

Unit 8: Suggested Listening

Samuel R. Hazo:
>   *Air*
>   *Ascend, Rivers*
>   *In Heaven's*
>   *Perthshire Majesty*
>   *Voices of the Sky*

Unit 9: Additional References and Resources

Web sites:
>   www.samuelrhazo.com
>   www.halleonard.com

Contributed by:

John Cody Birdwell
Director of Bands
University of Kentucky
Lexington, Kentucky

---

1 Hazo, Samuel, *Our Kingsland Spring* (program notes), Hal Leonard, Milwaukee, WI, 2004.
2 Hazo, Samuel, electronic mail correspondence, June 3, 2007.

Teacher Resource Guide

Pioneer Songs
Larry Daehn
(b. 1939)

Unit 1: Composer

Larry Daehn, born in 1939, was raised on a farm near his birthplace of Rosendale, Wisconsin. He received a Bachelor of Arts in music education from the University of Wisconsin-Oshkosh (1964) and a Master of Science in teaching from the University of Wisconsin-Platteville (1976). Although he has directed elementary through high school bands, he spent twenty-seven of his thirty-five years of public school teaching at the New Glarus High School in New Glarus, Wisconsin.

Daehn was recognized in the 1971 edition of *Leaders in American Education*, and was recognized as Outstanding Bandmaster by Phi Beta Mu, Pi Chapter in 1988. An ardent Grainger scholar, he continues to conduct extensive research and has written several arrangements of that composer's melodies. In 2001 Daehn composed the *West Point Bicentennial March*, which was premiered by the United States Military Academy Concert Band from West Point at Carnegie Hall, and was recorded by the ensemble in 2002. Since the founding of Daehn Publications in 1988, Larry Daehn has devoted his time to composing/arranging and publishing quality repertoire for wind band.

Unit 2: Composition

Pioneer Songs was composed and published in 2003. The composition is less than two minutes and thirty seconds long, and is based on three well-known folk songs: "Down in the Valley," "Skip to My Lou," and "Cindy." The work

was first performed and recorded by the University of Wisconsin-Eau Claire Wind Symphony, Richard Mark Heidel, conductor. The challenge of the work is to create the two contrasting styles, the singing style of "Down in the Valley" and the dancing style of "Skip to My Lou" and "Cindy."

Unit 3: Historical Perspective

The United States has a rich history of folk songs, and each folk song has as many versions as it has had singers. Pioneer musicologist and folklorist John Avery Lomax contributed significantly to the collecting and classifying of thousands of American folk songs. John Lomax provided the following insight:

> The first function of music, especially of folk music, is to produce a feeling of security for the listener by voicing the particular quality of a land and the life of its people. To the traveler, a line from a familiar song may bring back all the familiar emotions of home, for music is a magical summing-up of the patterns of family, of love, of conflict, and of work which give a community its special feel and which shape the personalities of its members.[1]

Pioneer Songs includes three popular folk tunes from the nineteenth century: "Down in the Valley," "Skip to My Lou," and "Cindy" ("Git Along Home, Little Cindy").

The opening of the work features "Down in the Valley." The following quote describes the source of the melody and text of the tune:

> When a mountaineer from the Smokies was sent to the state pen at Raleigh for moonshining or bushwhacking, he suffered more than the other prisoners. He found himself trapped in the dark and narrow valley of the prison, shut away from the sky and the stars and the fresh sweet winds of his native hills. Lowland water tasted so stale and flat, lowland air felt so close and stifling, that a man couldn't enjoy himself down in the valley, even outside the jailhouse![2]

In 1948 Kurt Weill wrote an American folk opera of the same name, which received hundreds of productions in schools and communities throughout the United States. In 1951 the tune appeared in the movie *Along the Great Divide*; it resurfaced again in the 1952 movies *The Last Musketeer* and *Montana Territory*. This melody is also known as "Birmingham Jail," "Barbourville Jail," and "Powder Mill Jail." The first verse of text is as follows:

> Down in the valley, valley so low,
> Hang your head over, hear the wind blow.
> Hear the wind blow, love, hear the wind blow,
> Hang your head over, hear the wind blow.

Eight additional verses are available in Alan Lomax's collection *Folk Songs of North America.*

"Skip to My Lou" was popular at play parties, or social gatherings in the 1800s. The "play party" was a socially acceptable compromise to the square dance, a dance that was frowned upon by conservative Protestant pioneer communities. Because instruments were also not allowed, songs such as this that accompanied simple dance steps became a popular form of entertainment.[3] In a play party, couples held hands in a large ring and sang as they skipped around in rhythm; one boy in the center of the ring was left to choose a partner.

Sources document up to sixteen verses of the lilting "Skip to My Lou" tune. The following lines are an example of the chorus and one verse:

> Lost my partner, what'll I do? (3x)
> Skip to my lou, my darling.

> I'll get another'n prettier'n you (3x)
> Skip to my lou, my darling.

The word "Lou" means "sweetheart," and "loo" is the Scottish word for love. "Skip to My Lou" was featured in the popular Hollywood movie from 1944, *Meet Me in St. Louis.*

"Cindy" or "Git Along Home, Cindy" is thought to have originated around 1805. When the five-string banjo was introduced and made popular in mid-nineteenth century minstrel shows, it soon became a popular accompaniment instrument, rivaling the fiddle among folk singers of the Southern Appalachians.[4] "Cindy," a "part minstrel song," was conceived as both a song and a fiddle or banjo tune, suitable for a square dance or reel. The following is one version of the text for the first verse and chorus:

> You oughta see my Cindy,
> She lives away down South.
> An' she's so sweet the honey bees
> They swarm around her mouth
> The first I seen my Cindy
> A standin' in the door
> Her shoes and stocking's in 'er hand
> Her feet spread 'round the floor

> Git along home, Cindy, Cindy,
> Git along home, Cindy, Cindy,
> Git along home, Cindy, Cindy,
> I'll marry you someday.

At least another dozen verses are available in different publications.

Unit 4: Technical Considerations

The work requires students to perform in multiple keys, including F, B-flat, E-flat, and D-flat concert. Although only two key signatures are indicated in the score and parts, (B-flat and E-flat major), accidentals move the ensemble through the additional key areas. *Pioneer Songs* employs two tempos, quarter note = 80 in the opening 3/4 section and quarter note = 126 in the contrasting 2/4 section.

The work uses standard instrumentation; the clarinet section is divided into three parts, and the bassoon, alto saxophone, trumpet, horn, and trombone sections have two parts each.

The work teaches young musicians the opportunity to work on the balance between the melody, countermelody, and accompaniment. Balance concerns are also primary in transition areas such as measure 19, where moving lines in the low brass and low reeds require special attention. All instruments have technical challenges and each section is given significant melodic material.

Unit 5: Stylistic Considerations

The opening section of the work based on "Down in the Valley" requires slow, sustained playing. There are extensive dynamic markings provided in this section, especially *crescendo* and *diminuendo* passages. The symbols are not written out (*cresc.* and *dim.*), so students may want to mark them in their parts. The melody "Down in the Valley" demands both slurring and tonguing, and the articulations are carefully marked.

In the rowdier "Barn Dance" section, there are no slurred passages. Although there are no written staccatos, notes must be played in a slightly detached manner to achieve the desired style. The composer uses accents in the coda, from measures 86–92.

Unit 6: Musical Elements

MELODY:
The work contains no introduction, but begins with a simple statement of theme one, "Down in the Valley."

Figure 1. "Down in the Valley," Theme One, mm. 1–11

In this setting, the first presentation of "Down in the Valley" is written in three measure phrases with a truncated fourth phrase (3 + 3 + 3 + 2 in measures 1–11). Students should work to produce a rich, sustained tone and take quick deep breaths, as the breath points are very exposed. In the second statement of the theme, the phrases extend to four measures, and the bass line acts as both a harmonic foundation and as a countermelody.

Theme two, the contrasting triadic melody of "Skip to My Lou," requires students to negotiate melodic leaps and quicker rhythms.

Figure 2. "Skip to My Lou," Theme Two, mm. 35–41

The melody for "Skip to My Lou" first appears in the alto saxophones and trumpets in measure 27. During this first statement, Daehn uses a lowered seventh degree in the third measure of the tune, which places the melody in the Mixolydian mode.

The third theme, "Cindy," incorporates much more stepwise motion in the melodic line with an occasional melodic leap.

Figure 3. "Cindy," Theme Three, mm.54–71

Flute

Both "Down in the Valley" and "Skip to My Lou" begin on the downbeat, but Cindy begins on the anacrusis.

In *Pioneer Songs*, each folk song appears in a simplified form. These tunes could be introduced by rote, using more complex rhythmic structures. A second option would be to write out each tune using notational software so that every student, regardless of instrument, could study all three melodies. Encourage students to transpose the melodies for an additional challenge.

HARMONY:
The unison opening statement of the theme (measures 1–3) breaks into harmony in measure 4 and uses the interval of an open fifth in measures 4–6; the notes will have to be carefully balanced, particularly during the *diminuendo*. In the opening theme, the second and third clarinets and the horn will have to be heard in measures 10–11, or the melody line will be overshadowed by the rich harmonic line. The perfect fifth interval continues to be prevalent in "Down in the Valley" through measure 25. The perfect fifth interval is also extremely predominant in the accompaniment at measure 27 in the "Barn Dance" section. The pedal tones in the low reeds and low brass sustain B-flat and F concert.

The work employs a variety of suspensions. For example, the second and third clarinets, alto and tenor saxophones, and the horn have a pronounced suspension in measure 21 that needs to be carefully balanced.

The plagal cadence in B-flat major in measures 12–13 provides an outstanding opportunity for the ensemble to construct and isolate the IV and I chords and to focus on tone production and intonation. The strong authentic cadence points in measures 26–27 (ii–IV–V–I) and measures 53–54 that could also be isolated and rehearsed.

RHYTHM:

Because both 3/4 and 2/4 time signatures are used in *Pioneer Songs*, it will be useful to spend time teaching strong and weak beat structures for those time signatures.

It is essential that the ensemble establish a strong group pulse and subdivide, particularly in the 3/4 time signature of "Down in the Valley." This is especially important because the phrases often require shaping (*diminuendo* or *crescendo*), and these dynamic changes can create an unstable pulse in younger players. Figure 4 demonstrates the subdivision that must occur to develop a strong sense of individual and ensemble pulse.

Figure 4. "Down in the Valley," mm. 1–3

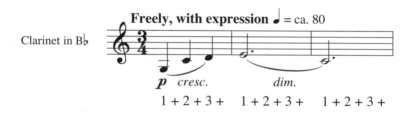

The three fermatas in measure 26 provide an excellent opportunity to work on following the conductor and rehearsing a variety of different releases.

The melody of "Cindy" includes extensive syncopated patterns, and the setting requires students to enter on the off-beats. Figure 5 demonstrates the rhythmic patterns that require these independent entrances.

Figure 5. "Cindy," mm. 72–76

The snare drum player is the only member of the ensemble who consistently maintains off-beat passages (measures 42–80). Divide the ensemble and have students alternate playing on and off the beat to reinforce

the concept and solidify the importance of the off-beat feel in the "Barn Dance" section.

By teaching these simple tunes by rote, students could be introduced to more complex rhythmic structures than those that appear in the composition. The folk-song melodies could introduce students to a complex rhythmic vocabulary that will be studied in subsequent works.

TIMBRE:

The clarinet section begins the work and the texture gradually increases to include all woodwinds and brass at measure 14. The percussion does not play in "Down in the Valley"; their first entrance is in measure 27. *Pioneer Songs* includes equally challenging parts for woodwind, brass, and percussion players. Every member of the ensemble has an opportunity to play both the melody and the accompaniment.

Unit 7: Form and Structure

SECTION	MEASURE	EVENT AND SCORING
"Down in the Valley"	1–11	First theme statement at quarter note = 80; 3/4 time signature; three measure phrases; B-flat concert
	12–13	Transition; plagal cadence
	14–26	Second statement of theme; full woodwind and brass scoring in four-measure phrases; ascending and descending accompaniment lines; phrase truncated; perfect authentic cadence (ii–IV–V–I)
"Skip to My Lou"	27–34	Marcato, a la "Barn Dance"; quarter note = 126; 2/4 time signature; eight-measure melodic phrase in B-flat concert Mixolydian (two four-measure sub-phrases)
	35–41	Statement two in the low reeds and low brass in F major (appearance of accidentals); phrase truncated by one measure (4 + 3)
	42–49	Statement three; modulation to D-flat major (again, no key signature shift, but appearance of accidentals)
	50–53	Transition; modulation to E-flat major in measure 54

SECTION	MEASURE	EVENT AND SCORING
"Cindy"	54–62	Theme three; four four-measure phrases that represent the melody's verse; melody appears in tenor saxophone, horn, trombone and passed to flute, oboe, clarinet, and trumpet; dense scoring, but light eighth-note accompaniment
	63–71	Four four-measure phrases (melody's chorus); melody in flute, oboe, clarinet, alto and tenor sax, trumpet, and horn
	72–79	Two four-measure phrases (verse); melody passed from low reeds and low brass to upper woodwinds and brass
	80–89	Chorus with phrase extension that acts as a coda; augmentation in measures 86–89; strong accents on beats one and two
"Skip to My Lou"	90–91	Theme two returns
	92	E-flat concert accented unison in low reeds, low brass, and percussion

Unit 8: Suggested Listening

James Curnow, *American Folk Song Suite*
Arthur Frackenpohl, *American Folk Song Suite*
Clare Grundman, *American Folk Rhapsody, No. 1, 2, 3, and 4,* (*Rhapsody No. 2* includes "Skip to My Lou")
Pierre La Plante, *Red River Valley*
Elie Siegmeister, *Five American Folksongs*
William Grant Still, *Folk Suite for Band*
Frank Ticheli, *Shenandoah*
Luigi Zaninelli, *Americana*

Additional works by Larry Daehn featured in *Teaching Music through Performance in Band* and *Teaching Music through Performance in Beginning Band* include:

> *As Summer Was Just Beginning*
> *British Isles Suite*
> *Country Wildflowers*
> *Nottingham Castle*
> *Song for Friends*

While I Watch the Yellow Wheat
With Quiet Courage

Unit 9: Additional References and Resources

Aldrich, Mark. *A Catalog of Folk Song Settings for Wind Band*. Galesville,
    MD: Meredith Music Publications, 2004.

Lomax, Alan. *The Folk Songs of North America*. Garden City, NY: Doubleday
    & Company, 1960.

Lomax, John A., and Alan Lomax. *Folk Song USA*. New York: New
    American Library, 1975.

Lomax, John A., and Alan Lomax. *American Ballads and Folk Songs*. New
    York: Dover Publications, 1994.

Ralph, Theodore. *The American Song Treasury*. New York: Dover
    Publications, Inc., 1964.

Contributed by:

Wendy McCallum
Instrumental Music Education Specialist
Brandon University
Brandon, Manitoba, Canada

---

1 Alan Lomax. *The Folk Songs of North America*. Garden City, NY: Doubleday & Company,
    1960, xv.
2 Lomax, 280.
3 Mark Aldrich. *A Catalog of Folk Song Settings for Wind Band*. Galesville, MD: Meredith Music
    Publications, 2004, 18.
4 Aldrich, 29.

Teacher Resource Guide

Pirate's Cove

Gene Milford
(b. 1946)

Unit 1: Composer

Gene Milford was born on July 1, 1946. A native of Canton, Ohio, he is a senior lecturer in music education at The University of Akron. He has also served on the faculty of Kent State University and Hiram College. Milford holds a Bachelor of Science in instrumental music education, a Master of Arts in music history, and a PhD in music education from Kent State University, where he was the recipient of a University Fellowship in 1998. He was an instrumental music educator for twenty-nine years, including twenty-three at Edgewood High School in Ashtabula, Ohio, where his bands performed at state and national conferences. Milford has served as a guest conductor, clinician, and adjudicator and presented clinic sessions at regional and national conferences. His articles on music education have appeared in *Triad*, *Dialogues in Instrumental Music Education*, *Contributions to Music Education*, and *The Instrumentalist*.

As a composer and arranger Milford has received numerous commissions, and was the recipient of a grant from the Ohio Arts Council. A number of his compositions appear on state required lists and are included in the catalogues of Alfred Publishing, Great Works Publishing, Heritage Press, Lorenz Publishing, and Ludwig Music. Milford's professional affiliations include the Ohio Music Education Association, where he has been a district president and on numerous committees at both the district and state level, the American School Band Directors Association, of which he was a state chair, the National Band Association, Phi Beta Mu, Phi Kappa Lambda, and the American Society of Composers, Arrangers, and Publishers, and has received an ASCAP Award each year since 2001.

Unit 2: Composition

Pirate's Cove was commissioned by the Champion (Ohio) Sixth Grade Band, Thomas Brucoli and Josh Cokrlic, directors. The work is dedicated to William Rasey, music educator and community leader. Regarding the programmatic inspiration for the work, Milford writes:

> *Pirate's Cove* is a short overture for young bands which captures the adventure, drama, and mystery of the legendary buccaneers as represented by the works of Robert Louis Stevenson and others.[1]

> I enjoy the writing of Robert Louis Stevenson, Walter Scott, and others. My then three-year-old grandson was developing an interest in pirate stories. I enjoyed watching Disney's movie version of *Treasure Island* with him. The melody at measure twelve is loosely based on the song "Yo, Ho, Ho, and a bottle of Rum" which is used in the movie.[2]

Pirate's Cove is seventy-three measures in length and approximately two minutes and forty-five seconds in duration. The work is scored for the traditional instrumentation of a beginning band, including flute, oboe, bassoon, clarinet 1 and 2, bass clarinet, alto, tenor, and baritone saxophone, trumpet 1 and 2, F horn, trombone, euphonium (with treble and bass clef parts included), and tuba. The percussion includes orchestral bells, snare drum, bass drum, wood block, crash cymbals, tambourine, suspended cymbal, and triangle and requires a minimum of five players. Published by Great Works Publishing in 2004, *Pirate's Cove* is exclusively distributed by Ludwig Music and designated a Grade 1 by the publisher.

Unit 3: Historical Perspective

As the title suggests, *Pirate's Cove* is a programmatic composition. However, rather than ascribing particular musical passages with specific programmatic events, Milford's piece instead evokes the spirit of the implied program. In *Pirate's Cove*, the composer alludes to the romanticized view of Caribbean pirates found in popular culture in the past century and a half.

In reality, piracy has had a long and storied history that goes back as early as the first commercial sailors of antiquity. The act of piracy is generally understood to be a robbery committed at sea by a group of individuals independent of a sovereign nation. Although they have existed in many forms throughout the ages, the traditional image of the pirate is that of the buccaneers, privateers, and pirates of the Caribbean Sea. Historians generally consider the "Golden Age of Piracy" in the Caribbean to be from the late seventeenth to early eighteenth centuries, when the Spanish Empire was in decline and before the British Empire flourished. Among the most famed and fabled of the pirates active during this period include Captain Henry Morgan, Stede Bonnet, Charles Vane, "Black Bart" Bartholomew Roberts, William Kidd, Anne Bonny, Mary Read, and last but not least, Edward Teach, the legendary "Blackbeard."

Although piracy exists in many forms even today, popular culture tends to romanticize and reference the image of the swashbuckling buccaneer of this golden age, as exemplified in the fiction writings of Robert Louis Stevenson. One of the most beloved of Stevenson's novels is the 1883 pirate adventure *Treasure Island*, which tells the story of Jim Hawkins and his adventures with Long John Silver and his crew. Another author, Rafael Sabatini, wrote two well-known books about pirates, *Captain Blood* in 1915 and *The Sea Hawk* in 1922. These tales and others have seen a multitude of incarnations, from various movie adaptations, to toys, and even to themed restaurants. The fictional, romantic view of the pirate has witnessed resurgence due in large part to the popular series of Disney films, *Pirates of the Caribbean*, based on the famous Disney theme park attraction of the same name.

The programmatic implications of *Pirate's Cove* present several cross-curricular educational opportunities. With careful planning and cooperation, concurrent units on Caribbean piracy can be introduced in other subjects. Colleagues in the history or geography department can address the historical role of the pirate. Additionally, teachers in the English and reading departments can teach units based on short stories or novels about, including those of Stevenson and Sabatini. Other cross-curricular activities might include the foreign language, math, science, and visual art departments.

Unit 4: Technical Considerations

One of the stated goals of *Pirate's Cove* is also one of its primary challenges. The piece introduces some meter changes, all with duple subdivisions: 2/4, 3/4, and 4/4. A simple method for teaching these multiple meters is to have students verbalize the beat count while the conductor alternates meters in a random order. Additionally, students can benefit from learning the basic conducting patterns to create tactile connections between the conducted meter and their music.

Only a few range concerns are present in *Pirate's Cove*. The allargando transitionary material in mm. 32–34 contains three such concerns: Written low F3 for bass clarinet, written low C4 for tenor saxophone, and written low F3 for F horn. The clarinet crosses the break into the *clarino* register to play written C6 only once, and trumpets are asked to play written C5 on only two occasions.

Students will benefit from scale work and can relate their familiarity with the E-flat major scale to the related key of C minor. An additional way to teach the two primary minor scales used in *Pirate's Cove* is to consider their modal relationship to the E-flat major scale, where C minor is the Locrian mode, or sixth mode, of E-flat major, and F minor is the Dorian mode, or second mode, of E-flat.

Some opportunities for independence exist in brief and thinly scored passages. Trumpets introduce the theme with only tambourine accompaniment and in several instances only one section plays the melody over a sustained harmonic accompaniment. The final statement of the main theme is a fragmentary occurrence in the codetta, which Milford suggests may be played as an optional flute solo.

The percussionists play an important part in *Pirate's Cove*. The section is required to play a range of instruments, including snare and bass drum, orchestral bells, wood block, crash cymbals, suspended cymbal, triangle, and tambourine. Milford insists in his performance suggestions that the tambourine part be played with an instrument that has a head, and the player should play it by striking the tambourine on the head. While the piece can be played with a minimum of five capable players who shift between a variety of instruments, there certainly are opportunities for many more percussionists to share playing duties by doubling or alternating passages.

Unit 5: Stylistic Considerations

In regard to style, the composer asks that "the opening allegro should be played in a marcato style, but measures 20–27 in a legato style for contrast." The B section is also in a contrasting legato style. To ensure that the contrast between these two divergent styles is evident, pay careful attention to the note length and articulation. Marcato style should be taught by discussing and demonstrating slightly detached note length and marked tonguing. The analogous syllable "tah" helps make the marcato articulation consistent. Emphasize connection of sound and lighter tonguing or "dah" in the legato passages. Contrast of style is also created by alternating dynamic indications of *forte*, *mezzo forte*, and *piano*.

Unit 6: Musical Elements

In electronic mail correspondence with the author, Milford expressed some general ideas regarding the musical elements of *Pirate's Cove*:

> It always seems to me that young instrumentalists enjoy playing melodies in minor keys; maybe they sound serious and important to young ears. Also, directors will enjoy the easy examples of mixed meters. I believe that it is important for each section to have important parts, usually melody lines. I also like to have opportunity to incorporate solo spots in young band pieces, though they are not marked, as it may turn some band directors away...In the case of

Pirate's Cove I would let different flute players have the opportunity to perform measures 70–72 alone.[3]

MELODY:

Melodic content is built around the minor mode. Generally presented in four-measure phrases, the simple melody should be easily retained by young ears. Mostly scalar in nature, the primary theme is identified by its opening ascending fifth that outlines the tonality. This is the largest interval in any of the thematic material, along with the occasional descending thirds and fourths.

HARMONY:

The harmonic content of *Pirate's Cove* is mostly in the minor mode. The introduction is centered around F minor, while the A section is firmly rooted in C minor. The indicated key signature of the piece is C minor, and while the pitch content never strays from this key signature, the harmonic areas do shift. An interesting aspect of the harmony is that, in spite of the fact that the tonality-implying third is often absent from the harmonic material, most of the harmonies give the impression of minor.

RHYTHM:

The most prevalent rhythmic challenge of *Pirate's Cove* is evident from the introduction—the presence of frequently changing meter. In his performance suggestions, Milford states that one of the primary goals of the piece is to introduce changing meters, and he accomplishes this by alternating 4/4, 3/4, and 2/4 meters. The marcato A section of the piece remains stable in common time, but the legato B section alternates 4/4 and 3/4 meters. The main melodic rhythm is comprised of quarter and eighth notes with an occasional half note on the cadence; accompaniment varies from marcato quarter notes to legato sustained notes. The two tempos of the piece, mm = 120 and mm = 60, are directly related with a 2:1 ratio, providing an opportunity to teach tempo changes by relating the half note of the first tempo to the quarter of the second.

TIMBRE:

The majority of *Pirate's Cove* is scored for the optimal range of the beginning player, so the conductor can expect clarinet parts written in the *chalumeau* register, and brass parts in the staff. The composer also includes some passages that are not scored for the entire ensemble to create interesting timbral combinations. For instance, only trumpets and tambourine are featured in the first statement of the primary theme at mm. 12–15. Another distinctive scoring choice is made in the B section of the piece, where the thematic material is traded off between brass and woodwind consorts.

Unit 7: Form and Structure

The overall form of *Pirate's Cove* is ABA' with an introduction and codetta. Both the A and B sections contain an antecedent-consequent phrasal and thematic relationship. The following overview provides more detail for each section of the piece.

Section	Measure	Event and Scoring
Introduction	1–11	Allegro maestoso, quarter note = 120; unison *forte* statement of introductory material in F minor and changing meter; flute and oboe join at m. 6 while harmony is produced through contrary motion in the lower and divisi voices; snare and bass drum interlude leads to the first statement of theme
A a	12–15	First appearance of primary theme in C minor scored for trumpets and accompanied by tambourine at *mezzo forte* dynamic; snare drum connects to second statement with a *crescendo* of eighth notes on beats 3–4 of m. 15
a'	16–19	Second statement of primary theme marked *forte* in flute, oboe, trumpets, and bells; quarter-note harmonic accompaniment
b	20–23	Expansion of the introductory material; becomes secondary thematic material, introduced by the alto saxophone with half-note accompaniment; *mezzo forte* dynamic
b'	24–27	Secondary material stated again by flute, oboe, and alto saxophone, once again accompanied by half note harmony; trumpet 2 shadows snare drum rhythm on concert E-flat
a'	28–31	Exact repetition of the primary theme from its appearance in mm. 16–19
Transition	32–34	Allargando transition material based on primary theme in eventual augmentation; *decrescendo* to next area

SECTION	MEASURE	EVENT AND SCORING
B c	35–39	Adagio misterioso, quarter note = 60; contrasting *legato* section derived from secondary theme in augmentation; *piano* melodic material first stated by clarinets with sustained harmonic accompaniment in winds and rhythmic material in suspended cymbal and woodblock
c'	40–43	Thinly scored repetition of B material by flute and oboe with sustained accompaniment by clarinet
d	44–47	New consequent material presented by trumpets and horn, accompanied by tambourine
d'	48–51	Echo repetition by flute, oboe, clarinet 1, and bells; clarinet 2 and alto saxophone provide sustained accompaniment with triangle
A'	52–53	Tempo I (quarter note = 120) return of A section; *forte* snare and bass drum interlude return to lead into the primary theme
a	54–57	Return of primary thematic material by flute, oboe, clarinets, and alto saxophone; accompaniment by low reeds, brass, and percussion
a'	58–61	Second statement of primary theme in exact repetition of original a' appearance
b'	62–65	Return of secondary thematic material in *forte* unison by bassoon, clarinets, bass clarinet, tenor and baritone saxophone, horn, trombone, euphonium, and tuba with snare and bass drum accompaniment
b	66–69	Rallentando; flute, oboe, clarinet, trumpet, and bells restate secondary theme with half-note accompaniment and crash cymbals
Codetta	70–73	A *tempo*; fragmentary statement of the primary theme by optional flute solo with triangle; percussion interlude in the penultimate measure leads to a unison C by the tutti ensemble to finish the piece

Unit 8: Suggested Listening

Gilbert, William, and Arthur Sullivan. *The Pirates of Penzance*. New York: G. Schirmer, 1986.

Hosay, James. *Swords Against the Sea*. Wilmore, KY: Curnow Music Press, 2001.

Roberts, John. *Swashbuckler*. New York: Carl Fischer, 2004.

Unit 9: Additional References and Resources

Miles, Richard, and Thomas Dvorak, eds. *Teaching Music through Performance in Beginning Band*, Volume I. Chicago: GIA, 2000.

Milford, Gene. *Pirate's Cove*. Grafton, OH: Great Works, 2004.

Sabatini, Rafael. *Captain Blood*. Teddington, UK: Echo Library, 2006.

Sabatini, Rafael. *The Sea Hawk*. New York: W. W. Norton, 2002.

Stevenson, Robert Louis. *Treasure Island*. New York: Signet Classics, 1998.

Contributed by:

Andrew Trachsel
Doctoral Conducting Associate
University of North Texas
Denton, Texas

---

1 Gene Milford, *Pirate's Cove*, Grafton, OH: Great Works Publishing, 2004), 2.
2 Gene Milford, e-mail message to author, June 1, 2007.

Teacher Resource Guide

Praises

Jared Spears
(b. 1936)

Unit 1: Composer

Professor Spears was born and educated in Illinois. He received his BSE in music education from Northern Illinois University; the BM and MM in percussion performance and composition from the Cosmopolitan School of Music. He eventually received the DM in composition from Northwestern University in Evanston, Illinois.

Professor Spears is retired from Arkansas State University in Jonesboro, Arkansas, where he taught for thirty-two years. His diverse background in teaching covers theory, history, composition, percussion, and instrumental music from the elementary to college levels. He is the recipient of the Citation of Excellence award from the National Band Association, and the Faricy Award for Creative Music from Northwestern University School of Music.

Unit 2: Composition

Composed in 2003, *Praises* is a spirited composition that is perfect for a beginning band concert. The thematic material is based on the E-flat major scale, and is very accessible for beginning bands. Praises is not technically difficult; however, it is imperative that the articulation markings and dynamics are closely followed. One of the most interesting aspects of this composition is the percussion writing. Each percussion part requires the player to play several percussion instruments, which is quite unusual for a beginning band composition.

Unit 3: Historical Perspective

While *Praises* is an original composition, it is based on a word that is familiar to most students. Webster's definition of praise is to commend, express approval, esteem, or commendation. This composition gives the teacher a reason to teach the meaning of praises and to challenge the students to find those in their lives who deserve to be praised, such as teachers, parents, historical leaders and community icons.

Unit 4: Technical Considerations

Praises is a solidly written Grade 1 composition. Professor Spears is aware of the many instrumentation issues that so many beginning band programs face. The composer has skillfully scored the bass clarinet, baritone saxophone, bassoon, trombone, baritone, and tuba in unison octaves. This allows bands with a relatively weak lower brass section to perform the piece and still have a solid bass presence. While the oboe part is often doubled by the alto saxophone, it is a stand-alone part for most of the composition. The sophisticated percussion writing is indicative of the composer's love and interest for developing percussion students as well rounded musicians. Unlike most Grade 1 literature, the percussion is not relegated to snare drum, bass drum, and cymbal. The mallet part accents and doubles the melody and the percussion 1 and percussion 2 parts both call for multiple percussion set-ups. The snare drum player may decide to use either natural or alternating sticking for this piece. However, the author would suggest using a paradiddle when possible for better phrasing of the sixteenth notes. Tessitura should not be a problem for the trumpets, as the highest note is a suggested E-flat. The first clarinets are required to cross the break.

There are no real difficult rhythmic phrases in this composition. However, the repeated section will need to be explained because there are three endings as opposed to the normal two endings, and some instruments play only once. The primary tonal center of the composition is E-flat major with occasional harmonic surprises at certain cadences. These harmonic surprises cause half steps to occur through out the composition.

Unit 5: Stylistic Considerations

Praises is an exciting composition that makes for an excellent concert opener. The composition should be performed much in the style of a traditional march. Careful consideration should be given to articulation, especially the accented notes. The conductor should emphasize the need for separation; however, the notes should not be played too short. The players should make a difference between the staccato and slurred articulations in the theme. Play recordings of famous marches to give students an aural image of the proper style.

Unit 6: Musical Elements

MELODY:

The melodic material of this piece is diatonic and it is extremely accessible for young students. The contour of the scale passages is excellent for teaching phrase shaping and dynamic contrast within the phrase. The second theme of the piece is also diatonic, but the articulation and dynamics are different. The interval of a fourth is introduced in the development section of the piece. While two measure phrases would fit the melodic structure of the composition, the author suggests playing four-measure phrases for a more continuous flow.

HARMONIC:

E-flat major is the predominant tonal center of the composition; however, the composer injects some deceptive cadences that make the piece more harmonically interesting to the listener. The brief departure into the C minor also gives a more sophisticated tonal structure for the listener and the performer. The concept of accidentals should be addressed before the preparation of this work.

RHYTHM:

The rhythmic language of *Praises* is extremely appropriate for this level of composition. However, counting rest and avoiding the temptation to rush may be a concern. Pay special attention to the rhythms in the obbligato flute and oboe parts so that students do not release them too soon. Rhythmic challenges in this composition are found primarily in the percussion section. Percussionists should have an understanding of eighth- and sixteenth- note subdivisions.

TIMBRE:

The homophonic texture of the composition renders a full band sound in the introduction. The lower winds are used primarily as accompaniment and to provide harmonic support. Give special care to the balance and articulation throughout the piece. In addition, sensitive playing is required of the percussionist throughout the composition.

Unit 7: Form and Structure

Praises is written in Intro–ABA–Coda form.

SECTION	MEASURE	EVENT AND SCORING
Introduction	1–8	Oblique unison scales in woodwinds and upper brass; accentuated by lower brass and percussion
Theme	9–21	Theme introduced by clarinets and accompanied by lower winds
Drum break	21	Snare drum break with syncopated bass drum and cymbals
Introduction material	22–32	Same as introduction
Development	33–43	New thematic material section with layering of voices; C minor tonal center
Recapitulation	43–55	Theme restated in clarinets with flute obbligato
Drum break	55	Snare drum break with syncopated bass drum and suspended cymbal
Coda	56–66	Same material as introduction

Unit 8: Suggested Listening

Anne McGinty:
Atlantis
Sea Song Trilogy

Unit 9: Additional References and Resources

Dvorak, Thomas L., Cynthia Crump Taggart, and Peter Schmalz. *Best Music for Young Band*. Edited by Bob Margolis. Brooklyn, NY: Manhattan Beach, 1986.

Kreines, Joseph. *Music for Concert Band*. Tampa, FL: Florida Music Service, 1989.

Contributed by:

Ricky L. Fleming
Director of Bands
Buffalo State College
Buffalo, New York

Teacher Resource Guide

Psalm 42

Samuel R. Hazo
(b. 1966)

Unit 1: Composer

Samuel R. Hazo's career as a music educator encompasses every educational level from kindergarten through post secondary. Long respected as a devoted teacher, he was named "Teacher of Distinction" by the Southwestern Pennsylvania Teachers' Excellence Foundation in two successive years (2003 and 2004). Having received both an undergraduate and master's degree from Duquesne University, Hazo also served on the Board of Governors in addition to being recognized as Duquesne's Outstanding Graduate in Music Education.

Hazo was the first composer to receive both of the National Band Association's sponsored composition prizes: The Merrill Jones (2001) and William D. Revelli (2003) Composition Contests. He continues to compose works for a broad spectrum of ensembles and artists, from public school to professional including original scores for radio, television and stage. Performed and recorded internationally, Hazo's works have garnered performances by the Tokyo Kosei Wind Orchestra, Birmingham Symphonic Winds (UK) and the University of North Texas. Many of his compositions have received premieres and performances at the Music Educators National Conference (state and national), the Midwest Clinic, Florida Music Educators Association Conference, World Association for Symphonic Bands and Ensembles Convention, National Band Association/Texas Bandmasters Association Convention, National Honor Band of America, College Band Directors National Association Convention as well as being featured on National Public Radio. In addition to his compositional output, he is an acknowledged contributor in a variety of educational settings, including

public schools, universities, and conducting symposia. Hazo is currently active as a guest conductor and clinician for the Hal Leonard Corporation and is a sponsored artist of the music software company, Sibelius Music Software. Recordings of his compositions are featured on both Klavier and Mark Records. Samuel R. Hazo remains a resident of Pittsburgh, Pennsylvania, with his wife and children.

Unit 2: Composition

Composed for ensembles of beginning ability and experience, *Psalm 42* is a single-movement work approximately two and one-half minutes in length. Dedicated to the McCurrie family of Upper St. Clair, Pennsylvania, Hazo recalled the performance of this psalm at a funeral mass dedicated to Gregory McCurrie. Stricken with the debilitating condition called Deletion 13-Q Syndrome, five-year-old Gregory finally succumbed to an unrelated heart condition. As Hazo describes, "Watching the McCurrie family raise Greg with an unfathomable number of challenges, and finally sharing their grief at his funeral, provided me with the opportunity to see people whose sense of love and faith were most deserving of admiration."

Psalm 42 was the first selection the congregation sang at the funeral. That melody left such an indelible mark on Hazo's psyche that he rescored the music for winds and subsequently performed it with his own school ensemble. Two of Gregory's brothers were members of the group that performed the winter concert premiere. This work attempts to embody the enduring nature of Greg's unconditional love and the abundance with which his two brothers, sister, and parents offered in return.

Unit 3: Historical Perspective

The *Book of Psalms* is perhaps the most significant source of text in music history. In their original Hebrew form, the psalms were not just poetry based on the principle of accentuation, but were conceivably songs with an instrumental accompaniment. The *Book of Psalms* contains 150 poems whose numbering system varies slightly between the Latin and English versions. Each psalm consists of several verses and two or sometimes three parts that may or may not be closely related. The psalms were employed as texts for the music of a variety of Christian Churches except for the Lutheran, whose music is derived from chorale texts.

Unit 4: Technical Considerations

The modest technical demands, key of F major, thin and full scoring, and limited range expectations create rewarding opportunities for expressive and artistic music making by young ensembles, yet this piece is worthy of performance by a mature ensemble as well. Interestingly enough, according to Hazo, "More high school and college bands have used the piece, either in a program or as a warm-up, than the elementary and middle school bands for whom it was written."

The initial trumpet solo is also cued in flute and violin (if strings are used). The percussion scoring is sparse: timpani, suspended cymbals, and glocken-spiel, all of which support and enhance the breadth of dynamic expression inherent in this piece. Except for the extended opening trumpet solo, the orchestration is tutti throughout. There are no rhythmic challenges beyond duplet eighth notes, and the 4/4 time signature remains intact throughout the prevailing chorale-like character of this work.

Unit 5: Stylistic Considerations

Although the sparsely scored introduction is in direct contrast to the full ensemble scoring in the second half, there are several opportunities for expansion and contraction of the time to capture the piece's expressive potential. The reflective folk-like quality of the melodic material requires sostenuto playing for both the solo and ensemble statements. Hazo dramatically increases the texture and harmonic tension in the build to the climactic section at mm. 26–27, and an appropriately paced *crescendo* certainly enhances this significant moment. As the only *ff* marking in the piece, a well-sustained tone and pitch control are imperative.

Unit 6: Musical Elements

Psalm 42 is scored for full concert band with divisi parts in B-flat clarinet and trumpet only. The limited percussion parts enhance the expressive elements of the work, especially the climax at m. 26. Clearly marked dynamics provide sufficient guidance regarding issues of balance. Psalm 42 offers a variety of subtle nuances, dynamic and textural contrast, predictable but rewarding voice leading and structural craft.

MELODY:
With a sense of simple beauty and an economy of ideas, Hazo has captured the essence of a traditional English folk song style. Melodic tessitura does not exceed an octave. Although initially stated in the trumpet I voice, the folk melody is also cued in flute and violin, but according to Hazo, not confined to these specific voices—an excellent opportunity for soloistic flexibility.

HARMONY:
The key center remains in F major throughout. The harmonic rhythm generally changes measure by measure while the internal voice leading of appoggiaturas and resolving ninths pervade the harmonic texture.

RHYTHM:

The rhythmic simplicity reflects the overall style and character of this folk song. Rhythmic patterns throughout the 4/4 meter are confined to whole, half, and quarter notes with the occasional duple eighth-note pattern.

TIMBRE:

The first half of the work presents the introductory trumpet solo and, except for m. 33, the second half calls for full tutti scoring. Melodic responsibilities are assigned to flute, oboe, clarinet I and trumpet I/II. The remainder of the scoring is dedicated to harmonic support and chorale-like voice leading. All voices fall well within beginners limited ranges.

Unit 7: Form and Structure

SECTION	MEASURE	EVENT AND SCORING
A section	1–16	Initial statement of folk theme in unaccompanied trumpet I (cued in flute and violin)
A' section	17–32	Restatement of folk theme by flute, oboe, clarinet I and trumpets I and II with full ensemble scoring and harmonies; the alto voice is scored for clarinet II and alto saxophone; the tenor voice is relegated to clarinet III, tenor saxophone and horn; the bass voice is scored in octaves in the bass clarinet, baritone saxophone, trombone, euphonium and tuba; string parts, if employed, follow a traditional four-part scoring paradigm
Codetta	33–36	Brief restatement of previous four measures in altered form and accompanying ritardando brings the work to a quiet conclusion

Unit 8: Suggested Listening

Fergal Carroll, *Psalm 8*
Samuel R. Hazo:
    In Heaven's Air
    Novo Lenio
    Perthshire Majesty
    Their Blossoms Down

Peter I. Tchaikovsky/Leonard B. Smith, *None but the Lonely Heart*
Frank Ticheli:
    An American Elegy
    Shenandoah

Unit 9: Additional References and Resources

Battisti, Frank. *The Twentieth Century American Wind Band/Ensemble*. Fort
    Lauderdale, FL: Meredith Music, 1995.

Randel, Don Michael, ed. *The New Harvard Dictionary of Music*. Cambridge,
    MA: Harvard University Press, 1996.

Slonimsky, Nicolas, ed. *Baker's Biographical Dictionary of Musicians*, 7th ed.
    New York: Schirmer, 1984.

The General Council. *The Hymnary of the United Church of Canada*.
    Toronto: The United Church Publishing House, 1930.

Web site:
    www.samuelrhazo.com

Contributed by:

Gordon R. Brock
Chair/Director of Bands
University of North Florida
Jacksonville, Florida

Teacher Resource Guide

Rising Star

Samuel R. Hazo
(b. 1966)

Unit 1: Composer

Samuel Robert Hazo has been a music teacher at every level from kindergarten through college. He received his bachelor's and master's degrees from Duquesne University, where he served on the Board of Governors and was named an Outstanding Graduate in Music Education.

As a composer, Hazo was the first to be named the winner of both composition contests sponsored by the National Band Association. He has completed works for professional, collegiate, and public school ensembles and has also written original scores for television, radio, and stage. His works have been performed and recorded worldwide, with premieres at the Midwest Clinic, College Band Directors National Association Conference, Music Educators National Conference, and the National Band Association/Texas Bandmasters Conference.

Hazo is a frequent guest conductor and clinician and was the composer-in-residence at the 2003 University of Minnesota conducting symposium, hosted by Craig Kirchhoff. He is a Hal Leonard Corporation clinician and is sponsored by Sibelius Music Software.

Hazo resides in Pittsburgh, Pennsylvania, with his wife and three children.

Unit 2: Composition

Rising Star was intended to let beginning players experience playing a lush chorale setting while keeping technical responsibilities at a minimum. This original composition uses only the first six notes learned by each instrument and note values are not smaller than a quarter note. *Rising Star* was written to teach beginners the concepts of independent moving lines, dynamic contrast, balance, and phrasing. It is a single-movement composition, approximately two minutes and forty-five seconds in length.

Unit 3: Historical Perspectives

Rising Star was commissioned by the Rising Starr Middle School Band and its director, Steven Tyndall, in Fayetteville, Georgia. The purpose of the commission was to present a new work for young and growing bands that did not necessarily sound like a piece for beginners.

Rising Starr Middle School premiered the work during their concert at the 2006 Western International Band Clinic in Seattle, Washington.

Unit 4: Technical Considerations

As stated earlier, each individual part of *Rising Star* uses the first notes learned in beginning band (concert B flat through concert G in all but the horn part, which uses concert F through concert A). There is an exception, however, in the first flute part, which uses the entire scale in two measures, requiring them to learn the fingering for A-natural.

The orchestration of this piece is more complex than most at this level, with seven independently moving wind parts and five percussion parts (snare drum, bass drum, suspended cymbal, bells, and timpani). The flute, clarinet, and alto saxophone parts are divided. For both reasons, students will have to work on counting and performing their individual parts, which may be moving in different directions or contain different rhythms than the student in the next section or chair.

Timbre changes in *Rising Star* are created by using changes in orchestration. These changes between smaller amounts of players and the full ensemble allow students to work on intonation, balance, and blend in various settings.

The dynamic range of the piece is *piano* through *forte*. The dynamic changes are uniform through the ensemble and incorporate four *crescendos*. No *decrescendos* are used, but there is a *subito piano* in measure 30.

Each melodic part is made up of scalar steps and leaps and includes several suspensions. The harmonic interest of the piece, although simple in note content, is created by these passing tones and suspensions. Good intonation and tone quality are necessary to create the appropriate balance and blend.

Additional information for conductors to consider is that the oboe, horn, and timpani parts are optional. The low brass and reeds are grouped as one voice throughout the piece, as are the horn, tenor saxophone, and second alto saxophone parts. Also, the composer mentions in the performance notes that conductors of very young musicians can cut measures 22 through 31 to make the piece more playable.

Unit 5: Stylistic Considerations

This piece requires students to work on smooth, legato playing. Students should strive to move their fingers quickly on note changes despite the slower tempo to improve ensemble clarity.

For the long, sustained phrases to be performed correctly, students will need to know how to use stagger breathing. Students need to be aware of phrase lengths and avoiding "unison" breaths to achieve the desired balance and blend. The long note values and phrases create opportunities to work on tone quality through proper air support and embouchure formation.

Every wind part incorporates slurring in most phrases; mainly slurs of two, three, and four notes. Directors should make sure that students understand and are interpreting articulation markings correctly. To improve understanding and performance, sing the articulations and have students imitate.

Unit 6: Musical Elements

MELODY:

Because each individual part (except for the first flute) consists of six notes and moves no faster than a quarter note, the melodic lines of *Rising Star* are limited. The first flute and trumpet parts have the majority of moving melodic lines.

Rising Star was composed in a chorale-like setting so most of the piece is tutti with seven voices moving in contrasting motion. These voices create a melodicism without one melody becoming the predominant theme.

HARMONY:

Although each individual part uses only six notes, the harmonies sound more complex through the use of passing tones, suspensions, and color chords. The use of up to seven moving parts creates thicker orchestration than is found most music written for this level. The composition is based mostly in B-flat major, with some phrases moving through the subdominant and dominant tonal areas.

RHYTHM:

The rhythm of the piece is the least complicated musical element. The meter of the piece is 4/4 with a metronome marking of quarter note = 80. Each part is made up of combinations of whole, half, and quarter notes; no voice plays any note value shorter than a quarter note.   Five fermatas are included and only the percussion, low brass, and low reeds play tied notes.

TIMBRE:

Because of the chorale-like setting, the timbre of *Rising Star* depends on the balance and blend of all of the voices. Timbre changes are mostly created by a change in orchestration or a change in ensemble note velocity. The best way to create the appropriate timbres is to listen for the moving line and adjusting accordingly.

The five percussion parts (snare drum, bass drum, suspended cymbal, bells, and optional timpani) add a great deal of timbre color. The snare and bass drum should be careful to not overplay the dynamics to avoid overbalancing the wind section.

Unit 7: Form and Structure

MEASURE	EVENT AND SCORING
1	Suspended cymbal roll
2–5	Tutti; flutes play quarter-note melody outlining area of B-flat major
6–9	Saxophones and horns accompany flute melody and clarinet countermelody
10–17	Tutti: contrasting movement between voices outlining area of E-flat major
18–21	Restatement of measures 2–5
22–23	Orchestration thins, 1st flutes begin half note ascension of B-flat major scale, 2nd flute and 1st alto saxophone create tension with major seconds
24	Low brass and low reeds enter on the third and ascend in half notes
25	Trumpets and 2nd flutes enter on the tonic and ascend in quarter notes while horns and saxophones descend in quarter notes
26–27	Tutti contrasting movement
28–29	Tutti half-note progression growing to *forte*
30–31	Orchestration thins, *subito piano* progression of "color chords" leading through E-flat to F
32–36	Tutti phrase at *mezzo-forte*, returns to B-flat major; suspensions create tension along with a *crescendo*
37–40	Tutti chorale at *forte* leading to the climax (half-note progression moving to a deceptive cadence on G minor 7)
41–42	Transition to resolution (F major)
43–50	Restatement of measures 10–17
51–53	Changing orchestration of three B-flat major chords at *mezzo-piano*

Unit 8: Suggested Listening

Larry Daehn, *As Summer Was Just Beginning*
Samuel R. Hazo:
    In Heaven's Air
    Rivers
    Their Blossoms Down
Hugh M. Stuart, *Hymn for Band*

Unit 9: Additional References and Resources

Hazo, Samuel R. *Rising Star*. Milwaukee, WI: Hal Leonard, 2006.

Miles, Richard, ed. *Teaching Music through Performance in Band*,
    Vol. 6. Chicago: GIA Publications, 2007.

Web site:
    www.samuelrhazo.com

Contributed by:

Andrea E. Brown
Director of Athletic Bands
Assistant Director of Bands
Austin Peay State University
Clarksville, Tennessee

Teacher Resource Guide

Russian Folk Dance
Elena Roussanova Lucas
(b. 1974)

Unit 1: Composer

Elena Roussanova Lucas is originally from Moscow, Russia. She began studying piano at the age of three and was accepted into the child prodigy music program at Central Music School in the former U.S.S.R. She later studied at the Tchaikovsky Conservatory of Music, Moscow, where she received the red diploma (summa cum laude) in composition, music history, music theory, and instrumentation. She studied composition with Tihon Khrennikov and Tatiana Choodova. Prior to that, she studied at the Ippolitov-Ivanov Music College/Academy of Music, Moscow, where she received a diploma in piano pedagogy and piano accompaniment.

Lucas is a member of the prestigious United Russian Composers Union. Her music has been performed by orchestras, bands, chamber ensembles and soloists worldwide, including: The Tchaikovsky State Orchestra of Moscow, the Radio and TV Orchestra of Moscow, the Dallas Brass, the Russian National Orchestra Brass Quintet, members of the Bolshoi Ballet, Ballet Lubbock and others. She has composed a variety of band and orchestra pieces specifically for young musicians.

She is active as a clinician/conductor and in 2003 presented a masterclass in composition at the Tchaikovsky Conservatory. As a pianist, Lucas has performed extensively in Moscow, the United Kingdom, The Netherlands, and the United States, winning first prize in a national piano competition in Russia, sponsored by the Russian Ministry of Culture, the Russian Academy of Music, and the Moscow National Institute of Music. Lucas currently teaches at Berklee College of Music and Boston University.

Unit 2: Composition

Russian Folk Dance was composed in 2004 and published by Alfred Publishing Company in 2005. Written in ABA form, the piece is based on original melodies and countermelodies that are passed throughout the different sections of the ensemble. Constructed in the keys of C minor and A-flat major, and containing a large stylistic vocabulary, *Russian Folk Dance* should be considered an advanced Grade 1 or Grade 2. It is approximately two minutes and thirty seconds in duration.

Unit 3: Historical Perspective

The folk dance is a type of dance that has developed without aid from choreographers, stems from traditional life, and is passed from one generation to the next. Folk dance melodies have permeated music throughout generations. Many composers have made use of Slavic folk tunes in their music, beginning with Franz Liszt and Mikhail Glinka, and continuing with a group known as *moguchay kuchka* ("the mighty handful") that included Mily Balakirev, Alexander Borodin, Cesar Cui, Modest Mussorgsky, and Nicolai Rimsky-Korsakov. Antonin Dvorak, Peter Tchaikovsky, Rheinhold Gliere, and twentieth-century composers Sergei Prokofiev, Dimitri Shostakovich, Bela Bartok, and Igor Stravinksky also used folk material within their compositions.

Lucas states that, among others, the works of Tchaikovsky and Prokofiev had a large influence on her development as a composer. Although the melodic material in *Russian Folk Dance* is entirely original, its harmonic and stylistic content is reminiscent of those used by the master composers. The work can introduce students to the works of the great Russian composers, as well as folk music and folk dance.

Unit 4: Technical Considerations

Russian Folk Dance presents several challenges for the young musician. However, these challenges can be used very effectively as teaching units within the composition. With an opening key signature of C minor, the piece shifts from natural minor to harmonic minor when the seventh scale degree is raised. The B section, while retaining the written key signature of the opening, is actually in A-flat major with the D-flat added as an accidental. As a result, the scales of C minor (natural and harmonic) and A-flat major should be taught and reinforced.

Presented in 4/4 with a metronome marking of quarter = 160 beats per minute, the piece, felt best in 2/2, contains a rhythmic inventory of half notes, quarter notes, and eighth notes. Brass ranges are within normal expectations for beginning band with the trumpets not exceeding C5 and the low brass not exceeding B-flat3. Woodwinds are also within acceptable ranges, with the clarinets having the largest range (written G3 to E-flat5). The clarinets are also expected to negotiate the break within rapid eighth-note passages on several occasions. The greatest overall technical demand falls to the flutes and clarinets. However, the low brass and low reeds are expected to perform eighth-note combinations as well, although not to the same degree as the upper woodwinds.

Articulation, note length, and style play a dominant role within the piece, as a large vocabulary of stylistic markings is employed. The work is voiced in typical beginning band fashion, with no divisi parts and with all winds playing the majority of the time. Bass clarinet and baritone saxophone double the tuba part and bassoon while tenor saxophone parts double the low brass with just a few exceptions. Percussion scoring includes bells, snare drum, bass drum and tambourine.

Unit 5: Stylistic Considerations

The style of a dance is determined largely by the tempo, meter, stylistic markings, and inflections within the phrase. Although the meter is 4/4, the feel is most definitely in 2/2. The dynamic spectrum ranges from *mp* to *ff* with very few *crescendos* or *decrescendos*.

The composer uses a stylistic vocabulary that will take time for younger students to master. The following markings are used extensively throughout the piece: tenuto, portato (a note length halfway between tenuto and staccato), staccato (at the end of a slur), accent, accent in combination with tenuto, and limited use of marcato accent. In order to effectively portray the character of the dance, take care to make distinct differences between the markings in terms of initial articulation, note length, and weight. Special attention should be given to the accented notes to ensure that they are created by an increase in the amount of air rather than the intensity of the articulation. It is also important to decrease the weight of the notes surrounding the accent to attain the dance feel.

Unit 6: Musical Elements

MELODY:

In keeping with the tradition of many Slavic folk tunes, the themes contain modal elements. The first theme in C-natural minor makes use of the flat seventh scale degree, which is later raised to create C-harmonic minor within the second half of the first A section. The theme then vacillates between C-natural minor and C-harmonic minor until the section concludes. The B section is in the key of A-flat major. Because the written key signature does not change, accidentals are present throughout many voice parts to facilitate this key change.

The melodic material is presented in a variety of instrument combinations and juxtaposed with countermelodies throughout. Melodies are mostly eight-bar phrases with clearly indicated breathing points. All wind instruments with the exception of the bass voices (bass clarinet, baritone saxophone, and tuba) have a melodic or countermelodic role at some point within the piece, allowing players to develop technique, as well as an understanding of melodic and phrasal components. In addition, the appropriate balance of melody and countermelody is an important concept.

Teaching Strategy: Isolate and rehearse each of the three scales used within the piece until they become second nature to the performers. Directors should also isolate each melody and countermelody in the piece so that students understand their musical role and the relative importance of their line within each section. The stylistic indications may be rehearsed very easily through the isolation of these lines. Close attention to each articulation, note length, and weight will be very important in providing clarity to each theme.

HARMONY:

Harmonies within *Russian Folk Dance* shift from minor to major and back to minor. Because the piece contains both major and minor keys, students must understand how the third scale degree changes a chord's quality. In addition, since the opening key of C minor shifts from natural minor to harmonic minor, students should know the construction of these scales, particularly the whole step/half step relationship within each scale. It is also important to note that, although the B section modulates to A-flat major, the written key signature does not change to include D-flat. Therefore, the understanding of the effect of accidentals on key signature is another important concept to learn.

Teaching Strategy: Three important concepts should be addressed during rehearsal time: 1) the role of the third scale degree in determining chord quality, 2) the construction of major and minor scales, and 3) the effect of accidentals within music.

The first concept of chord quality is easily accessed within the piece. To demonstrate the effect of the third scale degree upon tonality, simply have the students play their first note of measure 1 (that may be beat two for some instruments). Then, have those playing the minor third (trumpets) raise their pitch one-half step to create a major third. This could also be demonstrated by assigning students to a chord tone (root, third, fifth) in any key and then having those students playing the third move their note up and down to change the chord quality. The tuning of the major third and minor third could also be addressed at this time depending upon the level of the group.

A teaching unit on scalar construction provides a solid theoretical foundation as well as assistance in performing the piece. For *Russian Folk Dance*, it is important to teach the difference between the construction of the major and minor scale as well as the variants of the minor scale. Although the piece only contains natural and harmonic minor scales (raised seventh scale degree), the melodic minor scale (raised sixth and seventh scale degree) could be easily incorporated into the unit. With a correct understanding of whole step/half step relationships, the students should be able to build major and minor scales on any given starting pitch. A handout containing the following information could be useful in teaching this concept:

Major scale: whole step, whole step, half step, whole step, whole step, whole step, half step

Natural minor scale: whole step, half step, whole step, whole step, half step, whole step, whole step

Harmonic minor scale: whole step, half step, whole step, whole step, half step, minor third (one and one-half steps), half step

Melodic minor scale: whole step, half step, whole step, whole step, whole step, whole step, half step

A piano keyboard or other visual chart that shows these relationships would be useful in developing students' understanding.

The concept of an accidental's effect upon the note, the measure, and the key signature can also be taught while rehearsing *Russian Folk Dance*. While players must first understand how an accidental affects the note and the measure, it would also be helpful to show the correlation of the accidental to the key signature and, in this case, its relationship to the A-flat major scale.

Rhythm:
The 4/4 meter and tempo of quarter note = 160 is consistent throughout the piece, with the exception of a single two-measure ritard. However, the feel of the piece is most decidedly in 2/2 at half note = 80 beats per minute. The smallest rhythmic unit of the eighth note translates to sixteenth notes in the half-time feel. There are rhythmic challenges for all instruments with the exception of bass clarinet, baritone saxophone, and tuba. Due to the stylistic complexity of the melodic and countermelodic lines, rhythmic clarity will only occur when articulation, note length, and note weight are interpreted correctly.

Teaching Strategy: To develop pulse and aid with style, the 4/4 meter should be used only during the initial training period if needed, and students should begin to feel the music in 2/2 as soon as possible to place the proper emphasis within the phrase.

If the piece is initially taught in 4/4, it would be wise to set the metronome at half the desired speed using the eighth-note function to make beat one and beat three feel more prominent, which should develop the half-time feel more quickly. Conductors should still begin conducting in 2/2 and change the foot tap from quarter notes to half notes as soon as possible. This will be critical for those who have accompaniment parts such as quarter rest, quarter note, quarter rest, and quarter note.

TIMBRE:

Although the majority of the work is tutti scoring, there is a definite hierarchy within the vertical layers of the music. Most phrases have a melody, countermelody, accompaniment, and bass line. In addition, the combination of melodic instruments changes at the end of each phrase and sometimes within the phrase. Musical decisions regarding balance and blend of each individual line (melody, countermelody, etc.), and the balance of those lines within the overall phrase is, therefore, important. The difference in timbral construction of melodic and countermelodic lines between the phrases provides interest for the performer and listener alike.

Teaching Strategy: It is important that students understand their musical role within the phrase and their relative dynamic within their instrument group (voice part). A written handout defining melodic, countermelodic and accompaniment groupings such as the one contained within Unit 7 would help students' understanding. Class discussions regarding relative dynamic importance (balance) could then help to clarify each phrase. Students should make dynamic changes in their parts to correct the balance within each voice part. These changes should be based on the director's taste as well as the number of students in each section of the ensemble. Discussions regarding the difference between the terms balance (relative volume) and blend (fusion of tone qualities) would also be helpful in providing clarity.

Unit 7: Form and Structure

The overall structure of *Russian Folk Dance* is A–B–A.

SECTION	MEASURE	EVENT AND SCORING
Introduction	1–8	Harmonized melody in flute, oboe, clarinet and trumpet; all others play accompaniment

Section	Measure	Event and Scoring
A	9–16	Statement of Theme 1 (C-natural minor) in octaves by flute, oboe, and clarinet; trumpets tacet; all others play accompaniment
	17–24	Theme 1 continues with a slight variation; the melodic line is in the flute, clarinet, oboe, and trumpet in octaves for the first four measures and completed by the clarinet and trumpet; all others play accompaniment
	25–28	Four-measure extension of theme with melody in flute, oboe, and clarinet; others play accompaniment
	29–36	The modality shifts to C harmonic minor and the theme is varied more dramatically; melody in flute, oboe, clarinet, and trumpet with countermelody in alto and tenor saxophone, french horn, low brass, and bassoons; the bass line is provided by bass clarinet, baritone saxophone, and tuba
	37–40	The theme shifts back into natural minor; the melody is contained in the trumpet, low brass, and bassoon; upper woodwinds provide the countermelody; others play accompaniment
	41–44	The theme concludes with a return to harmonic minor and the melody is contained in the flute, clarinet, and trumpet while others shift to accompaniment
B	45–52	The B section begins with a key shift to A-flat major; the low brass and bassoon present a second theme with a complex countermelody contained solely in the flute; oboe, clarinet, and trumpet tacet; remaining instruments provide the accompaniment

SECTION	MEASURE	EVENT AND SCORING
	53–56	A second statement of Theme 2 occurs in the flute, clarinet and trumpet, and bells while a new countermelody is presented in the alto saxophone and horn with harmonization from tenor saxophone, low brass, and bassoon; others provide accompaniment
	54–60	The second half of the melodic phrase is completed by flute, clarinet, trumpet, and bells; all others provide accompaniment
	61–64	Theme 2 is varied with the low brass and bassoon presenting the melody and flute providing a countermelody; oboe, clarinet, and trumpet are tacet and remaining instruments provide accompaniment; these four bars lead to a *forte* culmination in measure 65
	65–68	The melody shifts from low voices to flute, clarinet, and trumpet as the full ensemble finishes the phrase
	69–72	The original second theme returns scored in similar fashion to measures 53–60 with the melody in flute, clarinet, and trumpet, and countermelody is presented in the alto saxophone and horn with harmonization from tenor saxophone, low brass, and bassoon; others provide accompaniment
	73–76	The flute, oboe, and trumpet complete the melodic phrase with others providing accompaniment; the tonality shifts in measures 75 and 76 along with a ritard. that sets up a return to the A section (C minor) at measure 9
A	9–16	Statement of Theme 1 (C-natural minor) in octaves by flute, oboe, and clarinet; trumpets tacet; all others play accompaniment

SECTION	MEASURE	EVENT AND SCORING
	17–24, 77	Theme 1 continues with a slight variation; the melodic line is in the flute, clarinet, oboe, and trumpet in octaves for the first four measures and completed by the clarinet and trumpet; all others accompaniment; all except flute and oboe arrive at whole-note G major (V) chord in measure 77 to set up the coda
Coda	78–85	Material from the introduction (measures 1–8) is restated; harmonized melody in flute, oboe, clarinet, and trumpet; all others accompaniment; final measure of phrase changed to provide conclusion

Unit 8: Suggested Listening

Orchestra:
Antonin Dvorak, *Slavonic Dances, Op. 46, No. 8*
Mikhail Glinka, *Ruslan and Lyudmila*
Elena Roussanova Lucas:
    Czar's Evening Waltz
    Persian Dance
    Prince Ivan and Vaselisa
    Russian Polka
Igor Stravinsky, *Petrushka*
Peter Ilyich Tchaikovsky, *Symphony No. 2, Op. 17 ("Little Russian")*

Concert band:
Ralph Gingery (arr.), *Two Russian Folksongs*
Reinhold Gliere/arr. Brian Beck, *Russian Sailor's Dance from The Red Poppy Suite*
Adam Gorb, *Yiddish Dances*
Elena Roussanova Lucas:
    Harvesting the Fields of Russia
    Tatarian Dances
Alfred Reed, *Armenian Dances, Part 1 & 2*
Nicolai Rimsky-Korsakov/arr. Leidzen, *Procession of the Nobles*
Dimitri Shostakovich/ed. H. Robert Reynolds, *Folk Dances*
Dimitri Shostakovich/arr. G. Duker, *Overture on Russian and Kirghiz Folk Songs*

Peter Ilyich Tchaikovsky/ed. Ray Cramer, *Dance of the Jesters from The Snow Maiden*
Jan Van der Roost:
   Balkanya
   Puszta

Unit 9: Additional References and Resources

Calvocoressi, M. D., and Gerald Abraham. *Masters of Russian Music*. New York: Alfred A. Knopf, Inc., 1936.

Kennedy, Michael, ed. *The Concise Oxford Dictionary of Music*, 3rd edition. Oxford: Oxford University Press, 1980.

Prokhorov, Vadim. *Russian Folk Songs: Musical Genres and History*. Lanham, MA: Scarecrow Press, Inc., 2002

Schimmerling, H. A. *Folk Dance Music of the Slavic Nations*. New York: Associated Music Publishers, Inc., 1951.

Contributed by:

Phillip L. Clements
Associate Director of Bands
Conductor, Symphonic Winds
University of Miami
Coral Gables, Florida

Teacher Resource Guide

Samurai

Barry Ward
(b. 1952)

Unit 1: Composer

Barry Ward received his bachelor of music education degree and a master of music degree in woodwind performance from the University of Southern Mississippi and completed additional graduate work in musicology at The Catholic University of America in Washington, DC. His career as a music educator spans three decades. Barry has been a member of the Arlington (VA) Symphony Orchestra for twenty years and maintains a private teaching studio for clarinet students. His recent interest in and focus on composition has resulted in more than twenty compositions for elementary and junior high bands. Barry was recognized in 2003 by the prestigious *Who's Who in Education* in the United States.

Unit 2: Composition

Samurai is a bold and colorful composition for standard concert band featuring the percussion section. Percussion scoring includes multiple woodblocks, gong or suspended cymbal, two bass drums, and bells. This composition is well within the abilities of first-year players. *Samurai* was published in 2004 by C. Alan Publications and is approximately two minutes in duration.

Unit 3: Historical Perspective

The title *Samurai* reveals a rich historical reference to the samurai warriors of twelfth century Japan. Samurai were members of an influential, hereditary warrior class that lived by a strict code of honor in feudal Japan. In traditional Japanese music, the use of drums is significant. The score reflects this with the use of multiple woodblocks at three different pitches, two bass drums, and suspended cymbal or gong. The Japanese percussion ensemble *Kodo* epitomizes this form of ceremonial music. *Kodo*, whose name means "heart beat," was founded in 1971 by Den Tagayasu. The ensemble consists of ten members who value and promote traditional Japanese music.

The use of modal harmonies and the pentatonic scale in *Samurai* is a reflection of the music of many non-Western societies. African, Asian, Polynesian, and the Native American Indian cultures base much of their music on the pentatonic scale. The pentatonic scale is made up of five tones —with no half steps in the note series. Various patterns and permutations are possible, which creates specific sound qualities. Thus, scales heard in Japan or China have the potential to sound quite different from one another.

Unit 4: Technical Considerations

The scale structure is pentatonic in nature. The concert key signature of three flats is used throughout the piece with raised pitches marked as accidentals. This gives *Samurai* a distinctly Eastern sound. The 4/4 meter is consistent and rhythms are simple. Tempo markings of allegro (quarter note = 120) and faster (quarter note = 132) may initially present a challenge. Articulations include accents, inverted accents, and the occasional eighth note slur. Establishing clarity of articulation and precision at the given tempos will present the greatest challenge for young ensembles. The tessitura is appropriate for all instruments. The highest note for trumpets is A4 and the clarinet part does not cross the break. The active and independent percussion part will engage young percussionists. Unison melodies, rhythms, and extensive part doubling make this an ideal piece for younger ensembles.

Unit 5: Stylistic Considerations

The overall articulation style in *Samurai* is marcato. The use of accents and the inverted accents bring out the ceremonial nature of this music. Pay careful attention to maintaining the length of accented notes and stress the concept of using the breath rather than the tongue to emphasize or give weight to the accents. Reaching a unified articulation style at the indicated tempos of a quarter note = 120 and 132 will challenge young players. Dynamic levels for the wind players range from *mezzo piano* to *fortissimo*. The percussion section encounters greater dynamic contrast with the recurring use of *sforzando crescendo*. The technique of *accelerando et crescendo* is used as a transitional device into the Faster section. The percussion interlude offers the greatest opportunity to exploit dynamic contrast, with each repeat of the phrase adding a new layer to the texture. Specific instructions to this regard are given in the score. Listening examples will enhance awareness of this style of music and the music of other cultures.

Unit 6: Musical Elements

MELODY:

Samurai introduces students to the pentatonic scale. In *Everyman's Dictionary of Music*, the pentatonic scale is defined as "a scale of five notes, any 'gapped' scale that omits two of the normal seven notes of the ordinary diatonic scale." This concept can quickly be represented at the keyboard by playing only the black keys. To actively involve the students, have them play only the first, second, third, fifth, and sixth scale degrees of any familiar major scale. The concert key signature of three flats in *Samurai* demonstrates this relationship with both major and minor keys. Have students play the pentatonic scale based on concert E-flat major, E-flat–F–G–B-flat–C. Then have students play the pentatonic scale based in the relative concert minor, C–D–E-flat–G–A. This pentatonic scale forms the basis of *Samurai*, with the exception of only one fourteen-measure section starting at measure 32. With few technical demands and the use of tutti unison melodies throughout, the conductor will have an excellent opportunity to stress a unified ensemble sound.

HARMONY:

The tonal center of this piece is C minor Dorian, which is suggested by the concert key signature of three flats. This modal scale results in a C–D–E-flat–G–A pentatonic pitch set. Introducing the structure of C minor Dorian scale to the ensemble will bring awareness to the raised sixth, which occurs as an accidental throughout the work. One can also reference the Dorian mode as a natural-minor scale with a raised sixth scale degree.

Mode	Spelling/Half Steps
Dorian	C–D–E-flat–F–G–A–B-flat–C
	2 3 6 7

The only exception to this harmonic structure occurs at measure 32 with a brief transition to the dominant G harmonic minor. The use of pentatonic modes is characteristic of traditional music throughout much of East and Southeast Asia.

RHYTHM:

A quadruple meter is used throughout *Samurai*. Rhythms in all wind and percussion parts are simple with no syncopation. Maintaining intensity and tempo throughout the composition may prove to be challenging for young musicians. Strive to develop independence between the wind and percussion sections as the parts do interact with and respond to each other to create the phrase. The rhythmic layers in the percussion interlude require specific attention.

TIMBRE:

Due to extensive tutti writing, the focus on timbre centers on blend and balance. Insist that students produce the best possible tone on their instrument at all times, for with this type of orchestration, young musicians have a tendency to overplay and distort the tone quality. At the section marked Faster at measure 32, the first statement of the theme is presented by woodwinds only. Two measures later the trumpets interject, adding the only brass color. This is an ideal time to teach the concept of blend, as the trumpet entrance should complement the tone color that has already been established by the woodwinds. With the entrance of the entire brass section at measure 39 we return to the full ensemble timbre that is present throughout *Samurai*.

The percussion interlude at measure 46 gives this composition a decidely Eastern quality. Discuss the proper performance techniques for striking the woodblocks and gong or cymbal to create maximum resonance. It should be noted that the bass drum parts require the beater handle to be struck on the rim of the bass drum. As previously mentioned, the role of drums and the tone color of wood on wood is a distinct feature of Japanese traditional music.

Unit 7: Form and Structure

SECTION	MEASURE	EVENT AND SCORING
A	1–8	C minor Dorian Ensemble statement of a theme – harmonic treatment
B	9–16	Ensemble statement of b theme – unison
C	17–20	Ensemble statement of c theme – unison
A	21–26	Ensemble statement of a theme – harmonic treatment
C	27–31	Ensemble statement of c theme with brass/woodwind exchange – unison

Section	Measure	Event and Scoring
B	32–45	G minor harmonic Ensemble statement of B theme with slight variation in melodic contour; woodwinds only with addition of trumpet in first phrase; second phrase; addition of full ensemble – harmonic
C	46–49	C minor Dorian; percussion interlude of C theme with optional repeat – unison
A	50–55	Ensemble statement of A theme – harmonic treatment
Coda	56–60	Ensemble statement of A theme – unison/harmonic

Unit 8: Suggested Listening

John Barnes Chance, *Variations on a Korean Folk Song*
Walter Cummings, *Gamelan*
Frank Erickson, *Japanese Fantasy*
Nancy Fairchild, arr., *Hotaru Koi*
Robert Garofalo and Garwood Whaley, arr., *Ahrirang*
Robert Jager, *Japanese Prints*
Francis McBeth, *Canto*
Bernard Rogers, *Three Japanese Dances*

Unit 9: Additional References and Resources

Blom, Eric. *Everyman's Dictionary of Music*. Revised by Sir Jack Westrup. London, Great Britain: JM Dent & Sons Limited, 1975.

Dearling, Robert, ed. *The Ultimate Encyclopedia of Musical Instruments*. London, Great Britain: Carlton Books Ltd., 1996.

Garofalo, Robert J. *Instructional Designs for Middle/Junior High School Band*. Fort Lauderdale, FL: Meredith Music Publications, 1995.

McBeth, W. Francis. *Effective Performance of Band Music*. San Antonio, TX: Southern Music, 1972.

Miles, Richard, and Thomas Dvorak, eds. *Teaching Music through Performance in Beginning Band*. Chicago: GIA Publications, 2001.

Miles, Richard, ed. *Teaching Music through Performance in Band*, Volume 5. Chicago: GIA Publications, 2004.

Ottman, Robert W. *Elementary Harmony*, 3rd edition. Englewood Cliffs, NJ: Prentice-Hall, Inc., 1983.

Web sites:
http://www.c-alanpublications.com
http://en.wikipedia.org/wiki/History_of_Japan#Feudal_Japan

Contributed by:

Sheryl A. Bowhay
Conductor
Edmonton, Alberta, Canada

Teacher Resource Guide

Scenes from Russia
Elliot Del Borgo
(b. 1938)

Unit 1: Composer

American composer Elliot Del Borgo was born on October 27, 1938 in Port Chester, New York. Del Borgo earned a Bachelor of Science degree (1960) from the State University of New York at Potsdam, a Master of Education degree (1962) from Temple University in Philadelphia, and a Master of Music degree (1962) from the Philadelphia Conservatory, where he studied composition with Vincent Persichetti and trumpet with Gilbert Johnson. In 1973 the State University of New York granted him a doctoral equivalency.

Early in his career, Del Borgo taught instrumental music in the Philadelphia public schools. He also served as a professor of music at the Crane School of Music at the State University of New York in Potsdam, where he held teaching and administrative positions from 1966 to 1995. During his tenure he became chairman of the Department of Theory, Literature and Composition. Del Borgo now holds the title of Professor Emeritus.

An award-winning member of the American Society of Composers, Authors, and Publishers (ASCAP), Del Borgo was commissioned to compose music for the 1980 Olympic Winter Games in Lake Placid, New York. He remains active as a consultant, clinician, lecturer, adjudicator, and conductor of bands and orchestras. In 1993, Del Borgo was elected to membership in the American Bandmasters Association.

Del Borgo's music represents more than 500 works for various media, and several different companies publish his music. He has composed hundreds of works for band along with numerous compositions for orchestra, string orchestra, solo winds, chorus, chamber ensembles, ballet, and songs. In addition, he has authored method and etude books, including *The Tonality of Contemporary Music*, *The Rhythm of Contemporary Music*, and *Modality in Contemporary Music*.

Unit 2: Composition

The melody on which *Scenes from Russia* is based is a well-known Russian folk song called *Polyushko-Pole* or *Meadowlands*, an English translation. According to the program note in the score, "This symphonic setting captures both the bleakness of the Russian landscape and the strength and determination of the people who live there."

   Scenes from Russia is part of the "Esprit Series" of the Focus on Fundamentals catalog from Curnow Music Press. The total time for performance is approximately three minutes and thirty seconds.

   Scenes from Russia is scored for at least one on a part: flute, oboe, bassoon, clarinet 1 and 2, bass clarinet, alto saxophone 1 and 2, tenor saxophone, baritone saxophone, trumpet 1 and 2, horn, trombone, euphonium (includes both bass clef and treble clef), tuba, mallet percussion part (bells and bass drum), timpani (two), percussion 1 (triangle, woodblock, tambourine, snare drum and bass drum), percussion 2 (field drum, suspended cymbals and tom-toms), and an optional piano accompaniment. Note: For the most part, the low brass and low woodwinds are playing the same bass line(s).

Unit 3: Historical Perspective

The words and music of *Polyushko-Pole* (*Meadowlands*) were thought to have originated during the years of the Russian Civil War (approximately 1918–1921). The Russian Revolution of 1917 had just ended and Czar Nicholas II, ruler of the Russian Empire, lost his throne. A Marxist political faction called the Bolsheviks (Communist Party) seized power under the leadership of Vladimir Lenin. From this takeover, many groups formed that opposed Lenin's Bolsheviks. A bloody civil war ensued, pitting the Bolsheviks's Red Army against a loose confederation of anti-socialist monarchists, bourgeois forces and, for a short time, foreign nations that were known as the White Army. Millions of people lost their lives in the war. The Red Army eventually triumphed, and the Soviet Union (USSR) was formed in 1922. The Communist Party reign lasted nearly seventy years until the USSR was officially dissolved in December 1991.

   During the time of the Russian Civil War, it is speculated that *Polyushko-Pole* was sung by the White Army first, but soon became so popular that the Red Army adopted it as one of their marching songs. It is a haunting, yet inspiring melody with a relentless energy and drive. One of the first-known recordings of this folk song was made by The Red Army Choir in the 1930s.

In addition to *Meadowlands*, *Polyushko-Pole* can be found under other titles including *Cossack Patrol*, *Song of the Plains*, *Oh My Fields*, and *Cavalry of the Steppes*. World War II dance-band leader Glenn Miller and his famous orchestra recorded the tune under the title *Meadowlands* (The Red Cavalry March).

The English translation of the text to *Polyushko-Pole* is below:

Meadowlands

Field, my field
my wide field...
There the heroes ride, hey, over the field,
hey, the heroes of the Russian army.

The girls are crying,
the girls are sorrowful today:
Their darling went away to the army,
hey, their darling went away to the army.

You girls, look here,
girls, wipe off your tears!
The louder let us sing our song,
hey, our pugnacious song.

We only see
a grey cloud:
The army of the enemy behind the forest
hey, the enemy's army like a cloud.

Unit 4: Technical Considerations

Scenes from Russia is written in 4/4 meter throughout with a concert key signature of two flats. The key signature does not change, and a G minor tonality dominates the majority of the work. The *cantabile* introduction begins with a pulse of quarter note = 76. The tempo shifts to a *con spirito* pulse of quarter note = 132 beginning in measure 22 and continues until the end.

Instrumental ranges are crafted for novice musicians. Melodic material appears in all areas: woodwind, brass, and percussion. There are two clarinet parts, and the second part stays below the break. The two trumpet parts are written for a range of less than an octave and do not go above C5. The scoring is well thought out, and is both polyphonic and homophonic. The percussion writing is well-constructed and challenging for this grade level, and employs several different types of instruments and sounds, independent lines, soli areas, and use of dynamics.

Unit 5: Stylistic Considerations

Most music can be cataloged as either "song" or "dance." This work encompasses both styles, starting with "song." Del Borgo suggests the opening be played in a "warm, cantabile style with emphasis on the flow of the melodic line."[1] It is important for young students to approach lyrical melodies as if they were actually singing words and phrases. In slow music, novice musicians have a tendency to clip note lengths and chop the ends of phrases when searching for a place to breathe, especially in transition areas. The conductor should dictate note lengths and releases, especially at the ends of phrases. Strive for quick breaths so as to not disturb the musical line. When two eighth notes are slurred together in slow music, care must be taken not to clip, or shorten, the second eighth note.

In addition, young musicians must continue to make good decisions when articulating notes, especially in lyrical sections. Using a "du," "da," or "doh" articulation when the music is not slurred might be helpful in legato passages that need to sound connected; avoid using a harsh "T" sound.

For the faster section of the work, articulations should not be too short, harsh, or heavy, and should portray the dance-like quality of the music. Using a "d" syllable word ("dit" or "da" or "du") for the non-connected notes may help create a lighter style. Also, in fast music, when two eighth notes are slurred together, you want to shorten/lighten and "lift" the second eighth note to avoid dragging it into the next beat. Accented notes (>) emphasize tone quality more than tongue. A "dah" or "doh" (low brass) articulation might help for young musicians when playing accented notes.

Unit 6: Musical Elements

MELODY:

There is one basic melody in *Scenes from Russia*. While the main theme is presented a number of times, it is not always articulated in the same fashion. The conductor and students may want to isolate the different melodic areas and compare them to one another.

Del Borgo did not use the folk song in its exact form, as seen below, which is shown in the same key Del Borgo uses (G minor) for *Scenes from Russia*. Del Borgo altered the melody slightly to fit within specific instrument ranges. The presence of both the raised and lowered seventh degree of the scale gives the melody a modal quality.

Example 1. *Polyushko-Pole* (*Meadowlands*)

To help students hear and play both the natural minor and harmonic minor scales, use a B-flat concert scale as part of the band's warm-up. Explain how the G minor scale is derived from the key signature of B-flat major. Have students write out a B-flat major scale, and write the scale degrees beneath each note. Next, have the students write out a G minor scale, beginning on the sixth scale degree in B-flat. Have students write another G minor scale with a raised seventh degree (F-sharp). For those students who have transposing instruments, they can duplicate the exercise in the appropriate key. Then students can play both types of G minor scales as a group. Directors may also want to discuss the history and importance of (church) modes, and their different pitch organizations. Each mode consists of seven notes with five whole steps and two half steps. Modal identity is determined by the placement of the whole and half steps. Most students have played modes whether they realize it or not. A "major" scale is the same as the Ionian mode, and the "minor" scale is the same as the Aeolian mode.

HARMONY:

The harmonic structure of the work is centered around the various major and minor tonalities from G minor. A good way for students to differentiate between major and minor tonalities is to identify the chord root, third, and fifth, both visually and aurally. Using the chalkboard or dry-erase board, show students two chords with similar roots and fifths. Then, add the third for both a major and minor triad. Play this same example on a piano, or better yet, a tempered pitch keyboard. (The placement of the third functions differently in major [sits lower] and minor [sits higher].) Then, have students sing the exercise: One third of the room sings the root, another third sings the fifth, and then the last third of the room sings the third—major the first time, then minor. Have students change chord roles so that everyone has a chance to sing each part. Subsequent discussions can lead into the overtone series and how it affects harmony, pitch, and tuning, and how mechanical tuners are not the best tools to use when tuning harmony. *Scenes from Russia* is full of perfect fifths, and is an excellent listening exercise for this important harmonic

combination. The melody also outlines the harmony and is another way for students to work on their listening and pitch-matching skills. Singing parts of the piece, especially the cadence areas, is an excellent tool as well and can help establish listening "ahead."

RHYTHM:
While the work uses two different tempos, there is nothing too rhythmically complex in the wind parts, although the percussion parts have a series of sixteenth-note patterns throughout the fast section. The challenge for the band will be to maintain a steady even pulse and subdivision within the slow and fast sections without either rushing or slowing down. Consider using a metronome in the early stages of preparation, and once students have established a good sense of internal pulse, turn off the metronome. Encourage students to match rhythm and style within their section, and then across the ensemble. They should also listen for how their particular rhythmic parts fit into the overall scheme.

TIMBRE:
There is no question that those bands we consider exceptional have acquired a basic understanding of good tone production. In addition, they perceive the mechanics of pitch matching (a continual decision-making process), and understand how to blend or fuse sounds together when required. Because there are no more than two parts within each section, and many times only one, there is quite a bit of unison playing in *Scenes from Russia*, which requires students to be discriminating listeners: to themselves, to those close at hand, and to those in the ensemble who have similar notes and passages. Consider isolating instrument families so students can hear one another better. Give students a sense of what they need to be listening for or to, as in notes that match a sustained harmony or outline a triad, notes that are not good on their particular instrument, notes that other instruments also have, etc. Always discuss the hierarchy of the melody; no matter what the dynamics may show, the melody must always be prevalent and played with good tone and support. Sections that require extreme soft or loud dynamics should be approached with extra care. Students should know what happens to their instruments at various dynamic levels when breath support is weak or forced. For example, when clarinets play softly, they have a tendency to play sharp, while flutes generally play flat. Always encourage students to produce "tone" over "tongue" in the faster passages, no matter how short the notes or phrase may look on the printed page. Good tone is essential always.

Unit 7: Form and Structure

MEASURE	EVENT AND SCORING
1–6	Quarter note = 76; eighth-note ostinato in clarinets; two-measure introduction followed by first half of melody in flutes; G minor
7–12	Second half of melody in trumpets; transition; C minor to G minor
13–16	Melody in low woodwinds and low brass; G minor
17–21	Second half of melody in woodwinds and trumpets; *mezzo forte decrescendo* to *piano*; G minor
22–27	*Con spirito* (quarter note = 132) snare drum solo (sans snares); tom-toms; G minor
28–35	(repeated) Dance-like version of main melody; melody in brass and lower woodwinds; spirited percussion parts; subito *forte*; G minor
36–39	Transition area; woodwinds and accented percussion; *fortissimo*; G minor
40–47	Continuation of transition material; tutti ensemble; polyphonic; *fortissimo*; G minor
48–54	Melodic rhythmic fragments in low woodwinds; low brass; transitional area; C minor to F major; *diminuendo* to *pianissimo*; percussion soli in wood-block and tom-tom rims; C minor to F major centricity
55–62	Melody in woodwinds; homophonic; light percussion accompaniment; F minor; *piano*
63–66	Transitional material; woodwinds; *mezzo forte*; G minor; *crescendo*
67–70	Continuation of transitional material; melody in trumpets; full ensemble; D major; *forte*
71–77	Melody in low woodwinds and low brass; full ensemble accompaniment; pesante and marcato; *fortissimo*; G minor
78–85 (end)	Melodic fragments finish out the work; full scoring; *fortissimo*; G minor; ends on a fermata (unison G) and percussion roll

Unit 8: Suggested Listening

Elliot Del Borgo:
Do Not Go Gentle into That Good Night
The Steppes of Russia
Glenn Miller Orchestra, *Meadowlands (The Red Cavalry March)*
Lev Knipper, *Symphony No. 4*, "To the Komsomol Fighters"
Red Army Choir, *Oh Fields, My Fields (Polyushko-Pole)*
Alfred Reed, *Russian Christmas Music*

Unit 9: Additional References and Resources

Del Borgo, Elliot. *Contemporary Rhythm and Meter Duets for Bass and Treble Clef Instruments*. Ft. Lauderdale, FL: Meredith Music Publications (Hal Leonard), 2000.

Del Borgo, Elliot. "More Views on Choosing Music." *The Instrumentalist*, Volume 52, No. 12, July 1998, 15.

Dvorak, Thomas L., Peter Schmalz, and Cynthia Crump Taggart. *Best Music for Young Band*. Brooklyn, NY: Manhattan Beach Music, 1986.

Miles, Richard, and Thomas Dvorak, eds. *Teaching Music through Performance in Beginning Band*. Chicago: GIA Publications,2001.

Miller, William. *Band Director Secrets of Success*. Edited by N. Alan Clark. Lakeland, FL: Aiton Publishing, 1980.

Rehrig, William H. *The Heritage Encyclopedia of Band Music*. Edited by Paul Bierley. Westerville, OH: Integrity Press, 1991.

Thurmond, James. *Note Grouping*. Detroit, MI: Harlo Press, 1982.

Vandercook, H. A. *Expression in Music*, revised edition. Chicago: Rubank, Inc., 1962.

Web sites:
http://www.kaikracht.de/balalaika/english/songs/poly_mel.htm
http://www.encyclopedia.com/doc/1O48RussianCivilWar.html
http://www.encyclopedia.com/doc/1B1–377337.html

Contributed by:

Linda R. Moorhouse
Associate Director of Bands
Louisiana State University
Baton Rouge, Louisiana

---

1 "Note to Conductor" from *Scenes from Russia* score.

Teacher Resource Guide

Shenandoah

Robert W. Smith
(b. 1958)

Michael Story
(b. 1956)

Unit 1: Composer

Robert W. Smith, a native of Daleville, Alabama, is one of America's most prolific composers today, with more than 600 publications for concert bands and orchestras. Smith's compositions range from music for professional bands and orchestras (United States Navy Band and the Atlanta Symphony) to music for beginning student musicians. In addition to Smith's output as a composer, he is principal conductor of the American Symphonic Winds and the American Festival Philharmonic Orchestra of Washington, DC., and he teaches in the music industry program at Troy University.

Robert W. Smith was recently appointed director of product development for the C. L. Barnhouse Company.

Michael Story is a native of Philadelphia, Pennsylvania, and received his musical training at the University of Houston, where he earned the Bachelor of Music and Master of Education degrees. Story has taught at the University of Houston School of Music, and he currently devotes his full attention to composing and arranging. Story has more than 500 published original works and arrangements, including works for concert band, jazz ensemble, and marching band. The majority of his published works are available through Warner Brothers/CPP Belwin Publications, Inc.

Unit 2: Composition

Shenandoah is one of nineteen collaborations by Smith and Story that accompanies the *Band Expressions* curriculum developed by the composers (curriculum by Alfred Publishing; companion pieces by Belwin Mills/Warner Brothers). *Band Expressions* is part of the *Expressions Music Curriculum*, a comprehensive music curriculum for grades K–8 that is based on the National Standards, and includes specific learning objectives that indicate skill development, comprehension, and critical thinking. The piece is approximately two minutes, thirty seconds in duration, and is at the Grade 1 level of performance.

Unit 3: Historical Perspective

The origins of *Shendandoah* are not clear, but the first appearance of the song in print was in an article titled "Sailor Songs" by William Alden, published in 1882 in *Harper's New Monthly Magazine*. It has been suggested that *Shenandoah* was a sea shanty, composed by sailors to coordinate the efforts of some of the sailors' duties on the ship. Others have suggested that it is of African-American origin, relating the story of the daughter of the Indian Chief Shenandoah, who was courted by a white Missouri river trader.

Unit 4: Technical Considerations

The scoring for *Shenandoah* follows the basic instrumentation for a beginning band, with only one part per instrument: flute, oboe, clarinet, bass clarinet, alto saxophone, tenor saxophone, baritone saxophone, trumpet, horn, trombone (with bassoon doubling), baritone, baritone TC, and tuba. Also included in the set are "world parts" for trombone in B-flat treble clef, horn in E-flat, trombone/baritone in B-flat bass clef, tuba in E-flat bass clef, tuba in E-flat treble clef, tuba in B-flat bass clef, and tuba in B-flat treble clef. Percussion scoring is for the following instruments: bells, wind chimes, triangle, suspended cymbal, and timpani tuned to B-flat and F, and an optional piano/keyboard part. All parts may be covered by a minimum of four players plus the keyboard player.

Ranges for each instrument cover the normal playing range for first-year players. Clarinets are not required to cross the break but must be able to play to low G3. Key signature remains constant, in the key of concert B-flat, and only the alto sax, horn, and trombone parts contain accidentals. The 4/4 time signature is constant throughout the piece, and tempo is set at quarter note = 80, with the second statement of the melody marked "slightly faster" and a ritard. at the end of the piece. Dynamics range from *piano* to *mezzo forte*, including the use of *crescendo* and *decrescendo* marks. Solo trumpet requires the use of straight mute.

Unit 5: Stylistic Considerations

The prevailing style of *Shenandoah* is a gentle, flowing legato. All parts make use of long slurs and phrase marks to create long lines, teaching young students to develop the phrase over multiple measures. When developing the phrase, encourage students to "play through the barlines" (without added emphasis on the downbeat) and to allow consecutive notes in a phrase to "touch each other" so there is no break in the sound.

Unit 6: Musical Elements

MELODY:
Shenandoah derives its melodic material from the well-known American folk song. The melody is presented twice in its entirety: The first presentation begins with clarinets followed by flutes, and the second presentation begins with the trumpets, and is later doubled by flutes and bells. There are no harmonic or rhythmic variations to the melodic material.

HARMONY:
The key signature for the entire arrangement is B-flat, and only moves away from the key a few times by layering an A-flat major chord over the B-flat root. Harmonic foundation for the melody is created both by the use of block chords as well as simple contrapuntal lines.

RHYTHM:
For the most part, rhythms are confined to those that do not require division of the beat: whole, dotted half, half, and quarter notes and whole, half, and quarter rests (solo trumpet has a few pairs of eighth notes). Countermelodies move in quarter notes against the long notes of the melody to create rhythmic energy and interest.

TIMBRE:
Shenandoah uses contrasting timbres in the two presentations of the traditional tune. The first "verse" is scored only for flute, oboe, clarinet, and alto sax, with a light percussion accompaniment, for a very transparent presentation of the theme. The second "verse" is a fuller, thicker scoring, using the full band for a dark, rich sound.

Unit 7: Form and Structure

SECTION	MEASURE	EVENT AND SCORING
Introduction	1–5	Full winds-percussion (B-flat major)
Section 1	6–23	First statement of melody (woodwinds with light percussion)
Transition	24–27	Full chordal scoring
Section 2	28–47	Second statement of melody (full brass/woodwinds with percussion)
Section 3	48–55	Coda; motive from intro

Unit 8: Suggested Listening

James D. Ployhar, *Shenandoah*
Robert W. Smith:
    Encanto
    The Great Locomotive Chase
Michael Story:
    Hudson River Sketches
    Sakura (Cherry Blossoms)
Frank Ticheli, *Shenandoah*

Unit 9: Additional References and Resources

Belwin-Mills Publishing Corp., Miami, Florida.

Web sites:
    http://www.robertwsmith.com/bio.html
    http://music.troy.edu/faculty_staff/rwsmith.html
    http://www.music-expressions.com
    http://lcweb2.loc.gov/cocoon/ihas/loc.natlib.ihas.20003152/default.html

Contributed by:

C. Kevin Bowen
Director of Bands
Wake Forest University
Winston-Salem, North Carolina

Teacher Resource Guide

Simple Song

Ralph Hultgren
(b. 1953)

Unit 1: Composer

Ralph Hultgren was born in Box Hill, Victoria, Australia, and now resides in Newmarket, Queensland, with his wife Julie and two of his five children. He began his professional music career as a trumpet player in 1970, and has performed with the Central Band of the Royal Australian Air Force, the Melbourne Symphony Orchestra, and the Australian Brass Choir. In addition to his freelance performing, he is currently Head of Pre-Tertiary Studies at the Queensland Conservatorium at Griffith University. Hultgren also conducts the Queensland Conservatorium Wind Orchestra, as well as lecturing in conducting and music education to both undergraduate and postgraduate students.

From 1979 until 1990, Hultgren was composer/arranger in residence for the Queensland Department of Education's Instrumental Music Program, where he produced 185 works. He is a founding member of the Australian Band and Orchestra Directors' Association (ABODA), as well as the World Association for Symphonic Bands and Ensembles (WASBE) where he is a member of the WASBE council and chairman of the WASBE Schools Network. In addition, he has received numerous awards to date, which include the Citation of Excellence from ABODA (1998), nominations for the "Sammy and Penguin Awards" for his television soundtracks, two Yamaha Composer of the Year Awards, and the Midwest Clinic International Award (2005).

Unit 2: Composition

Hultgren was once posed with a question from a colleague: "Why aren't there more slow pieces in 3/4 time?" This simple question led to the development of his *Simple Song*. According to the composer, this work reminds him of "making beautiful music" at a younger age.

The individual instrumental ranges are very friendly, and the slow legato style allows younger students to focus on producing the best possible tone. In regards to developing individual technique, young oboe players have a very good chance to succeed at playing the well-written part for the instrument. *Simple Song* can also be used as an effective warm-up to develop rubato phrasing, dynamics, chord sonorities, attacks and releases, ensemble balance and blend, and intonation. Within the individual parts, students frequently to play in tutti textures, as well as in highlighted soli passages. Although the piece is relatively short, the timing of each performance will depend on the tempo and interpretation of the conductor.

Unit 3: Historical Perspective

Simple Song is exactly what the title implies: a simple song. However, when compared to many previous trends in compositional style, this "simple" piece demands more sensitivity and a higher sense of musicality from the performers and conductor than similar pieces written in recent years. Some composers prescribe dynamics and tempo changes within a piece to instigate certain musical effects when they should instead rely on the musicianship of the ensembles for which they are writing. Some contemporary composers, such as Frank Erickson and Larry Daehn, have written similar works in this "simple" style to develop the musicianship of younger students. Representative works such as *Air for Band* and *A Song for Friends*, respectively, incorporate similar techniques that Hultgren has presented in his *Simple Song*.

Unit 4: Technical Considerations

Simple Song begins in 3/4 time with the tonality of C harmonic minor (strengthened by the appearance of B-natural). The meter is stressed by a strong tendency towards beat one of each measure, which should also create a naturally "flowing" texture from all instruments. The registers are easily managed by young embouchures and the sustained nature of the melody promotes good air support throughout the ensemble, although the isolated half notes at the ends of phrases may tend to be cut off by younger players who simply run out of air. The percussion scoring is somewhat sparse; however, it is tastefully placed within the ensemble.

Unit 5: Stylistic Considerations

The composer writes: "Don't allow the work to drag or rush, let it move comfortably...Make music is my only real wish." These are possibly the best recommendations any ensemble or conductor could receive. Intonation and balance are obvious points to consider; however, if great care is given to the overall smooth texture of the piece, many of the technical issues could resolve themselves. In addition, the style of the piece requires the performers to avoid repetitive two- and four-bar phrasing as well as breathing across the barlines whenever possible, emphasizing the smooth continuity.

Unit 6: Musical Elements

MELODY:

The piece opens with a four-bar introduction that contains material to be found later in the piece. The primary melody begins at measure 5. It might help students to hear the melody by itself, independent of the full ensemble sound, and then to sing the melody from a given pitch. By internalizing the melody away from the instrument the ensemble should be more aware of when the melody becomes fragmented later in the piece, which also helps the overall intonation and balance of the group.

Another way to develop sensitivity to the line is to have all the students learn and memorize the simplistic melody (some written transpositions may be required). After this is accomplished, conduct the melody in a variety of styles and tempos, asking students to play the melody based on the non-verbal gestures coming from the podium. This could easily turn into a "mimed rehearsal," where the conductor does not speak, but instead shows the intended effects through a variety of hand signals and body gestures. This would further reinforce the melody, and also get the students' eyes out of the music.

HARMONY:

Even though the piece is essentially in C harmonic minor, it temporarily moves to E-flat major in the B section at measure 21 through a phrase modulation. Numerous theoretical devices could be taught, but to keep things simplistic, it might be wise to focus on bigger concepts, such as the difference between major and minor chords.

In teaching basic chord structure to a younger ensemble, it is very easy to get lost in the theoretical aspects and confuse the students. Look at the blocked C major chord in the final measure (measure 66). Begin by explaining the concept of the root of the chord and have those instruments play that tone. Follow this with the explanation and playing of the fifth of the chord, then finally the third. In this case, the third is raised, creating the Piccardy third and a major tonality at a cadence, which ideally should be minor. Once students understand the parts of the chord, instruct those play-ing the third of the chord to play their tone one-half step lower. Another example of the major/minor concept would be simply that the minor tonality has a "sad" sound quality.

For more exercises, explore the score and highlight specific instances of major and minor block chords. Ask students to play the chord as an ensemble and then decide whether the chord is major or minor. Because *Simple Song* moves toward a major tonality in the B section, both chord types are in constant supply.

RHYTHM:

Simple Song should not pose any serious rhythmic concerns for the ensemble. The most rhythmically complicated figures are the ascending eighth notes within the first four bars. As stated earlier, this piece would be a good exercise in teaching rubato phrasing, as well as exploring different conducting gestures for appropriate articulations and releases.

Ask students to look at the final five measures of the piece, where the introductory material returns. A grand pause is implied in measure 65; try different release gestures at the end of m. 64 and ask students which release they thought was most effective. Coming out of the pause measure, try different attack gestures and question the ensemble as to which gestures they found most effective.

Understanding that a baton in motion should represent sound of some kind, encourage students to silently count through the grand pause measure without any kind of direction from the podium. In order for the ensemble to properly (and cleanly) articulate the final chord, they must first be able to collectively find the downbeat of the final measure without guidance. Once that concept is firmly in place, the conductor can explore ways to create more tension leading to the final resolution by slightly extending the grand pause, then simply give a preparatory gesture for the final chord.

TIMBRE:

One defining timbral characteristic of *Simple Song* is the use of the lower tessitura of all the instruments. In particular, the trumpets never reach C5, and the clarinets only cross the break momentarily in the return of the A section at m. 41. This rich sonority has a very large effect on the overall texture of the piece, and also doubles as a good exercise in air support in the lower registers.

Try recording the ensemble in rehearsal and have the students listen as a group. Afterward, ask the students to compare and contrast the first presentation of the melody at m. 5 with the return of the same material at m. 41. Hopefully they will be able to hear that, even though the melody is essentially the same, the sound is "happier" or "brighter" due to the use of a slightly increased register in the more prominent voices.

Looking specifically to the percussion, it might be interesting to try and combine the different sound qualities of the two triangle parts that begin at m. 41. The size of triangle used will have certain effects and colors, as well as the angle at which the triangle is struck. If the triangle is lightly struck with the beater parallel to the floor, a single tone will emerge from the instrument. However, if the triangle is struck with the beater at a 45-degree angle to the floor, a characteristic shimmer of tones will emerge. Ask the percussionists which sound they prefer based on what the ensemble is doing at that moment. Since their parts are relatively sporadic throughout, they will greatly appreciate the chance to contribute.

Unit 7: Form and Structure

SECTION	MEASURE	EVENT AND SCORING
Intro	1–4	C harmonic minor tonality is established through two repeated two-bar phrases
A	5–12	Cadence in C minor in m. 5; primary melodic material in upper woodwinds and trumpets
	13–20	A section is repeated with more instruments presenting the melodic material
B	21–28	Shift to E-flat major; fragmentation of primary melodic material
	29–40	Fragmentation continues; shifting back to C minor tonality
A	41–56	Cadence in C minor at m. 41; increased contributions from percussion
Coda	57–61	Fragments of primary melody return
	62–66	Intro material repeated; grand pause implied at m. 65, ensemble C-major chord (Piccardy third) at m. 66

Unit 8: Suggested Listening

Larry Daehn, *A Song for Friends*
Frank Erickson, *Air for Band*
Percy Grainger, *Irish Tune from County Derry*
David Holsinger, *A Childhood Hymn*
Ralph Hultgren, *Jessie's Well*

Unit 9: Additional References and Resources

Battisti, Frank, and Robert Garofalo. *Guide to Score Study for the Wind Band Conductor*. Fort Lauderdale, FL: Meredith Music Publications, 1990.

Brolga Music Publishing Company:
http://www.brolgamusic.com/index.html

Lisk, Edward S. *The Creative Director: Alternative Rehearsal Techniques*. Fort Lauderdale, FL: Meredith Music Publications, 1991.

Lisk, Edward S. *The Creative Director: Intangibles of Music Performance*. Fort Lauderdale, FL: Meredith Music Publications, 2000.

Neil A. Kjos Publishing Company:
http://www.kjos.com

Contributed by:

Michael Yonchak
DMA Candidate/Teaching Assistant
University of Kentucky
Lexington, Kentucky

Teacher Resource Guide

Siyahamba

arranged by Douglas E. Wagner
(b. 1952)

Unit 1: Composer

Douglas Wagner is a native of Chicago, Illinois. He received his undergraduate and graduate degrees from Butler University. After spending thirty years as a music educator and administrator, he now devotes his full concentration to composing, writing, and editing. Since 1973, Wagner has had 2,100 works published for various media including concert band, choir (sacred and secular), orchestra, handbell ensemble, instrumental solos, piano, organ, and voice. More than thirteen million copies have been sold worldwide. His compositions have earned awards from A.S.C.A.P. and have been heard on television, radio, and concert stages in the United States and at least twenty-six other countries.

Unit 2: Composition

Siyahamba is a traditional song of the Zulu people that originated in South Africa and was written during the apartheid movement. The text of *Siyahamba* repeats, "We are marching in the light of God, we are marching in the light of God." The song is included in many general music text publications and offers an opportunity to coordinate with elementary music specialists.

Douglas Wagner's arrangement of *Siyahamba* is a Grade 1 piece. The straightforward setting is only forty-six measures long. The ostinato bass line and energetic percussion provide the rhythmic drive to the accompaniment. Sustained chords fill out the harmonies and the melodic material is sometimes presented in a "call-and-response" manner characteristic of African music.

Unit 3: Historical Perspective

Apartheid was a law adopted in South Africa in 1948 that allowed racial segregation, even though it was present prior to that time. The South African government justified the apartheid by claiming that peace was only possible by separating all racial groups from each other. Many citizens of South Africa and other countries were against apartheid, which brought on numerous demonstrations, boycotts, strikes, and violence. In 1962, the United Nations General Assembly urged its members to break economic ties with South Africa until apartheid was abolished. South Africa began repealing its laws in the 1970s and 1980s, and in 1991, the last of South Africa's laws that formed the legal basis of apartheid was removed.

Siyahamba can be used to relate music to other cultures and periods in history; directors could coordinate and plan events with history teachers in conjunction with its performance.

Unit 4: Technical Considerations

Siyahamba is written in the key of E-flat. It is in 4/4 time throughout and maintains a steady tempo of a quarter note = 112. The melody and harmony are consistently diatonic. The trumpet is the primary melodic instrument; however, the upper woodwinds to carry the theme in some sections. The ascending major sixth in the melodic line can present a challenge for beginning trumpet players. Beginners may have a tendency to play an E4 when the music calls for a leap from C4 to A4 (see Example 2). The trumpet range is written up to C5. The sustained harmony parts require solid breath support while performing two-bar and four-bar phrases. Long-tone exercises will aid the players' development for these sections. The ostinato bass line calls for a steady tempo as well as a full, round sound on staccato articulations. The percussion parts introduce students to some instruments not often found in the beginning band repertoire. Parts are included for finger cymbals, tambourine, hand drums (either doumbeks, bongos, or congas), suspended cymbal, timpani, and bells. The hand drum part is the primary rhythmic vehicle in the piece, and the player should maintain a steady sense of tempo and possess an awareness of the other instruments in the ensemble.

Example 1. *Siyahamba*

Unit 5: Stylistic Considerations

Performers must approach *Siyahamba* with a knowledge of the folk song and the time period in which it became popular. The melody should be tuneful and clear with a sense of emotional determination. At the same time, there must be a steadiness that resembles the marching mentioned in the lyrics. The dynamics in the piece increase through each section, beginning *mezzo piano* and building to *forte*. One could think of this as watching a parade as it gets closer.

Articulation is limited to staccatos and slurs. The staccato markings appear only in the bass line until the full band's last note. The staccatos should be performed with a full sound but always with definite separation. Slurs are found in various parts and often with the interval of a descending third. These could be used to teach many aspects of slurring such as a steady air stream, evenness of fingers (woodwinds and horns), legato tonguing (trombones), and a quick slide (trombones).

Unit 6: Musical Elements

MELODY:

An important aspect of learning the melody is to familiarize the students with the original folk song. Singing the song is an effective way to learn the melody as is learning what the song is about. Since the trumpets carry a large portion of the melody, they need to be able to sing their parts. This will enable them to internalize the sound of the wide intervals, and in turn perform the melody more effectively.

Example 2. *Siyahamba*

HARMONY:

Siyahamba follows a simple harmonic structure typical of most folk songs. The A section follows a I–V–I progression while the B section uses V–I–V–I. Most of the harmony is carried by sustained whole notes and dotted half notes. Long-tone exercises are essential to help students produce a full sound for the duration of the phrase. With the simple harmonies and sustained pitches, balance between each chord tone can also be a focal point.

The harmony in the A section also introduces chords with a pedal bass note. Although the harmony changes from tonic to the dominant, the bass line remains persistent with its tonic pedal.

Example 3. *Siyahamba*

Alto Saxophone in E♭

Horn in F

Trombone

Tuba

RHYTHM:

Although the rhythms in *Siyahamba* are appropriate for beginners, there are several aspects that will further develop rhythmic understanding. The bass line (see example 3) includes a rest on beat two. Many beginners may have a tendency to skip the rest or to rush into beat three. This line is useful in developing a sense of the steady beat.

The melodic rhythm includes eighth notes (see example 4). In most eighth-note rhythms beginning students have encountered, the eighth notes are followed by a note on the downbeat. They may not be used to phrases that end on an upbeat. Precise counting in the last two measures of the phrase is important.

Example 4. *Siyahamba*

1   +   2   +   3   +   4   +

TIMBRE:

Blend and balance are main focal points throughout *Siyahamba*. The trumpets dominate much of the melody without any doubling in other instruments. Care must be taken to keep the supporting parts in the background. During the "call-and-response" sections, the scoring alternates between the trumpets and the woodwinds. Again, only a careful balance will produce the desired effect. The percussion section, with its use of hand drums, tambourine, and finger cymbals, adds colors associated with traditional African music.

Unit 7: Form and Structure

Section	Measure	Event and Scoring
Intro	1–6	Building of background material as the introduction, beginning with hand drums and finger cymbals in measure 1; adding tuba, bass clarinet, baritone saxophone in measure 3; finally adding sustained chords in clarinet, alto saxophone, tenor saxophone, bassoon, trombone and baritone in measure 5
A	7–14	Trumpet melody
B	15–22	Trumpet "call and response" with flute, oboe, clarinet, and alto saxophone
A	23–30	Clarinet and alto saxophone alternate melodic phrases with flute and oboe
B	31–38	Trumpet "call and response" with flute, oboe, clarinet, and alto saxophone
Coda	39–46	Tutti ending bringing together motives from the main themes

Unit 8: Suggested Listening

Heskel Brisman, *Uganda Lullaby*
James Curnow, *African Sketches*
Percy Grainger, *Lincolnshire Posy*
Anne McGinty, *African Folk Trilogy*
Vincent Persichetti, *Symphony No. 6, Op. 69*
Robert W. Smith, *Africa: Ceremony, Song, and Ritual*
John Philip Sousa, *Manhattan Beach March*
Ralph Vaughan Williams, *English Folk Song Suite*

Unit 9: Additional References and Resources

Alfred Publishing. "Douglas E. Wagner." http://alfred.com (accessed May 12, 2007).

Ambrose, Robert J. "Recent Developments in Band Literature." *Georgia Music News*, Vol. 63., No. 3 (Spring: 2003), pp. 49–52.

E-mail correspondence with the composer, May 21, 2007.

Miles, Richard, and Thomas Dvorak, eds. *Teaching Music through Performance in Beginning Band.* Chicago: GIA Publications, 2001.

Miles, Richard, ed. *Teaching Music through Performance in Band.* Chicago: GIA Publications, 1997.

Music Educators National Conference, Committee on Performance Standards. *Performance Standards for Music.* Reston, VA: Music Educators National Conference, 1996.

Wagner, Douglas E. *Siyahamba.* Van Nuys, CA: Alfred Publishing Co., Inc. 2006.

Contributed by:

Matthew G. P. Brunner
Associate Instructor, Department of Bands
Indiana University Jacobs School of Music
Bloomington, Indiana

Teacher Resource Guide

Skye Boat Song

arranged by John O'Reilly
(b. 1940)

Unit 1: Composer

John O'Reilly is one of the most-performed composers of band music in the world today. A recipient of numerous ASCAP awards, he has studied composition with Robert Washburn, Arthur Frackenpohl, Charles Walton, and Donald Hunsberger. Mr. O'Reilly graduated from the Crane School of Music, State University of New York at Potsdam. In addition, he received a master of arts in composition and theory degree from Columbia University. His years of experience teaching at elementary through college levels has provided him with insights to the needs of both students and educators. As co-author of *Accent on Achievement*, the *Yamaha Band Student,* and *Strictly Strings*, Mr. O'Reilly has made a major impact on contemporary instrumental music education. (from the Alfred Publishing Company Web site)

Unit 2: Composition

Skye Boat Song correlates with the *Accent on Achievement* series, Book One, Page 30. It is a Scottish air from the tradition of rowing songs, which were usually in compound meter to reflect the three-part motion of rowing (two counts for hitting and entering the water with a third count for bringing the oar forward again). The arranger heard this song while visiting Scotland and decided to arrange it so that young bands would have another piece with which to work on legato style.

   As with most folk songs, multiple versions of this melody exist, some with different words; for example, in Gaelic this melody was originally known as

"The Cuckoo in the Grove" and the two sections of the melody were reversed. The version of the song presented in this arrangement dates from the late nineteenth century and the first section is said to be an old sea shanty, while the second half was attributed to Annie MacLeod (Lady Wilson), who heard the tune while being rowed across Loch Coruisk (Coire Uisg, the "Cauldron of Waters"). She remembered fragments of the song and wrote them down to be included in a book she was writing with Sir Harold Boulton, who wrote the words that follow:

> Speed bonnie boat, like a bird on the wing,
> Onward, the sailors cry
> Carry the lad that's born to be king
> Over the sea to skye
>
> Loud the winds howl, loud the waves roar,
> Thunder clouds rend the air;
> Baffled our foe's stand on the shore
> Follow they will not dare
>
> *Speed bonnie boat...*
>
> Though the waves leap, soft shall ye sleep
> Ocean's a royal bed
> Rocked in the deep, Flora will keep
> Watch by your weary head
>
> *Speed bonnie boat...*
>
> Many's the lad fought on that day
> Well the claymore could wield
> When the night came, silently lay
> Dead on Culloden's field
>
> *Speed the bonnie boat...*
>
> Burned are our homes, exile and death
> Scatter the loyal men
> Yet, e'er the sword cool in the sheath,
> Charlie will come again.
>
> *Speed the bonnie boat...*

Unit 3: Historical Perspective

In 1689 King James II of Britain (and VII of Scotland) fled Britain in the wake of an army led by William of Orange. Supporters of King James, known as Jacobites, hoped to reinstate Catholicism as the national religion of Britain. The Jacobite court was exiled to Rome, from where several unsuccessful attempts to reclaim the British throne were launched. James II, his son James III, and his grandson Charlie (known as Bonnie Prince Charlie) all led armies from across the channel, but for various reasons all were unsuccessful.

It is Bonnie Prince Charlie's narrow escape from the Battle of Culloden during this last campaign in 1746 that is depicted in *Skye Boat Song*. Flora MacDonald helped Charles escape in a boat disguised as her spinning maid. While Charles did escape, he was never successful in regaining the throne for the Stuart line despite several attempts and support from numerous European states with strong ties to Rome.

Unit 4: Technical Considerations

The technical challenges of this three-minute work should be modest for most Grade 1 bands. It is in the key of F major and there are no accidentals or key changes, although the middle "B" section is in the relative minor.

Clarinets and trumpets both have two parts, and all the other instruments have one. The highest written notes for each part are as follows: flute–C6; clarinet I–C5; clarinet II–A5 (twice, with most of the part being below the break); alto saxophone–A5; trumpet (both parts)–D5; horn–D5; trombone/euphonium–A4; tuba–A3.

The percussion parts are few but important, using bells, triangle, and suspended cymbal in an integrated fashion. The piano reduction in the score may be useful during score analysis or rehearsal. Parts for non-standard instruments such as E-flat horn, bass and treble transposing parts for trombone, baritone, and tuba are also available via download.

Unit 5: Stylistic Considerations

Skye Boat Song belongs to the genre of folk songs known as "rowing songs" (known as *iorram* [and pronounced "irram"]), intended to regulate, reflect, or inspire the three-part motion of an oar or paddle being lifted, dropped, and pulled through water. This form is related to but distinct from other types of folk songs such as sea chanties (used primarily on merchant ships) and the larger category of work songs used to make jobs that require physical labor easier or more uniform. A simulation of the rowing action in rehearsal may be an extremely effective technique to determine the tempo and flow of the piece.

Skye Boat Song calls for a cantabile legato style that should be familiar to all musicians. The same singing style that is called for in classics of the band literature such as *Irish Tune from County Derry* and *Ye Banks and Braes O' Bonnie Doon* can be applied to this young band setting. While moderato is the only tempo or style term given, the conductor should feel free to approach the score with flexibility and fluidity in tempo, phrasing, and dynamics.

Every section of the band is given primary thematic material at some point in the piece. Additionally, the arranger has written interesting and meaningful accompaniment parts, which may require as much or more attention in rehearsal than the melodic lines.

The ending is of particular interest from the stylistic perspective; while the rest of the piece is comprised of four-bar phrases, this section contains several sequential two-bar phrases. The variety of choices this gives the conductor (e.g., how much of a break to take between phrases, whether or not to combine the two into a four-measure phrase, how much to ritard.) make this a section rich with artistic possibilities.

Unit 6: Musical Elements

MELODY:

The melody is the primary musical element of this piece, and careful analysis is important to an effective interpretation. The combination of steps and skips in the melody as well as an arch to the overall form are both important when considering interpretive elements. There are no accidentals and the overall range stays within an octave.

HARMONY:

The tonal center of F major should present no significant obstacles to young players and the harmonic treatment of the folk song setting is very traditional. The primary harmonic challenges of this piece may lie in measures 21–36 of the middle "B" section, as this is in the relative D minor. This stays in the natural minor, however, so there are no accidentals anywhere in the piece.

RHYTHM:

The most pressing rhythmic issues of this piece involve the 3/4 meter and the recurring dotted-quarter/eighth note figure. The rowing imagery of the words and the original folk song could be extremely helpful in teaching both the meter and the dotted rhythms.

TIMBRE:

The orchestrational variety in this setting is remarkable for this grade level. As stated elsewhere, all instrument groups play important thematic material at some point in the piece; there is enough textural transparency to achieve musically satisfying results with enough doubling of parts to maintain security. Horns are often coupled with woodwind parts, for example, and the only example of woodwind/brass block scoring occurs at the end of the "B" section (mm. 29–36) before the final statement of the theme. Dynamic markings in the piece never exceed *mezzo forte* and, if adhered to, should result in a restrained but satisfying performance.

Unit 7: Form and Structure

SECTION	MEASURE	EVENT AND SCORING
Intro	1–4	Primary motive introduced in flute/oboe, clarinet, alto saxophone, horn and bells
A	5–20	Setting of chorus (*Speed bonnie boat…*) in trumpets for first eight measures, joined by flute/oboe, alto saxophone, and bells for second eight
B	21–36	Setting of verse (*Loud the winds howl…*) in flute/oboe and clarinet for first eight measures, all brass in the second eight measures
A¹	37–50	Chorus melody is set in flute/oboe, alto saxophone, trumpet and bells; The second phrase is modified and repeated to the ending

Unit 8: Suggested Listening

Malcolm Arnold, *Four Scottish Dances*
Bruce Fraser, *King Across the Water*
Julie Giroux, *Culloden*
Clare Grundman, *Hebrides Suite*
Gustav Holst:
   Second Suite in F
   Somerset Rhapsody
Felix Mendelssohn, *The Hebrides, Op. 26 (Fingal's Cave)*
Ralph Vaughan Williams, *English Folk Song Suite*

Additionally, there are many recordings of *Skye Boat Song* by singers, bagpipers, and other instrumentalists including the King's Singers, Bob Sharples, and David Solley that would be well worth exploring for folk style and vocal inflection.

Unit 9: Additional References and Resources

Boni, Margaret Bradford, ed. *Fireside Book of Folk Songs.* New York: Simon and Schuster, 1947.

Collinson, Francis. *The Traditional and National Music of Scotland.* Nashville, TN: Vanderbilt University Press, 1966.

Email correspondence with the author, June 6, 2007.

Web sites:
     www.ibiblio.org/fiddlers/index.html (accessed May 20, 2007)
     www.scotshistoryonline.co.uk/charlieb.html (accessed May 27, 2007)

Contributed by:

Andrew Mast
Lawrence University
Appleton, Wisconsin

Teacher Resource Guide

Southern Chorale and March
Murray Houllif
(b. 1948)

Unit 1: Composer

Murray Houllif is a native of Woodbourne, New York. He holds degrees from the State University of New York at Potsdam and the State University of New York at Stony Brook. His teachers include Raymond Des Roches, Richard Fitz, James Petercsak, Sandy Feldstein, and Bey Perry. Having subsequently served as co-coordinator of percussion at North Texas State University in Denton, Murray has recently retired from thirty-two years as a band director and percussion specialist in the public schools of Smithtown, New York.

As a member of the percussion section of the Long Island and Nassau Symphonies, Murray has performed with Dave Brubeck, Marian McPartland, Itzak Perlman, Bryon Janis, Stanley Drucker, Julius Baker, Lynn Harrell, and Phil Smith. Murray currently performs with the Atlantic Wind Symphony as a freelance percussionist.

With more than 175 concert and pedagogic publications to his credit, Houllif has won the Percussive Arts Society Composition Contest two times and has written numerous articles for professional journals such as *Percussive Notes* and the *Music Educator's Journal*.

Unit 2: Composition

From the composer:

> I wrote the piece for my colleague, Gregory Dib, and his middle school band (Smithtown Sixth Grade Band) about 4–5 years ago (2003).

Having just retired as a middle school band director myself, I wanted to express a couple of things. I strived to make each part interesting, melodic, and hopefully, fun for the performers. I wanted instruments such as second trumpet, low brass and woodwinds, and percussion to play a vital role.

This piece is part of the publisher's "Pioneer" Band Series and is listed as a Grade 2 work. The piece is forty-six measures long and takes two minutes, fifty seconds to perform.

Unit 3: Historical Perspective

From the composer:

I have always been fond of music from the South. In fact, I play bluegrass guitar for my own enjoyment and truly love the music and culture which comes from that part of the country. So I started the piece with an "old-time" original chorale which included melodies and harmonies reminiscent of old Southern church music. I also included the element of syncopation which the African Americans brought to the music. The march came from the chorale melody and also, I think, I was inspired by the history as it relates to the Civil War. So you hear the "tramp, tramp, tramp" at the start of the march. There is also a kind of triumphant spirit in the march section.

Unit 4: Technical Considerations

The work is in the key of E-flat. For the winds, the fastest rhythmic duration is an eighth note; the piece contains some eighth-note scale passages. Percussion parts are well written for this level as there are appropriate contributions from the snare drum, bass drum, cymbal and tambourine. The snare drum part includes sixteenth-note and dotted sixteenth-note patterns, flams and rolls, the tambourine part contains a roll, and the bell part is written in thirds at times. The work includes a bit of syncopation in all parts including percussion. The work is scored as follows: flute (divisi at times); oboe; clarinet (divisi at times); bass clarinet; alto saxophone (divisi at times); tenor saxophone; baritone saxophone; horn (divisi at times); trumpet I; trumpet II (divisi at times); trombone I/II; baritone; tuba; percussion I (snare drum, bass drum, cymbals); percussion II (tambourine); percussion III (bells). There is no bassoon part, nor is there a timpani part.

Unit 5: Stylistic Considerations

The "Chorale" section of the piece is marked "*Andante*" (quarter note = 76) and should be performed in a chorale style, while remaining lyric, smooth, and sustained. The dynamic range is from *piano* to *forte*. Many stylistic teaching opportunities exist in the piece, as the work has both chorale and march settings. Take care to play in the appropriate styles, particularly on performing the phrases in the "March" section in a staccato, march-like manner. Discussion and analysis of both styles presented in the piece, along with representative listening examples, will be very beneficial to students when performing this work.

Unit 6: Musical Elements

MELODY:
The tonality of the work is in E-flat major and the piece is diatonic in nature. Rehearsing the E-flat scale, both on an individual and a group level, helps students develop a tonal concept of the piece. Directors may also want to analyze and identify instrument parts with primary melodic roles versus secondary roles in rehearsal. Discuss balance demands between the melodic lines and supporting material so that the listener is able to identify the melody throughout the piece, especially in the thicker textures of the work. Discuss also how call-and-response concepts relate to music of the South; this could be a valuable musical insight for students.

HARMONY:
Harmonies are generally triadic and diatonic in nature. The work uses tonalities of music from the South, bluegrass music, and marches. Discuss and analyze the differences between these styles, and provide representative listening examples and classroom activities.

RHYTHM:
A simple, 4/4 meter is used in the work. As stated earlier, the work contains several eighth-note, scale-like fragments. The snare drum part includes sixteenth-note and dotted sixteenth-note patterns. The rhythmic demands on the performer are appropriate and consistent with other quality works at this difficulty level.

TIMBRE:
The composer's mastery in writing for this level is evident in the work as he offers sounds reminiscent of quality works of the past. Houllif does an excellent job developing a variety of textures and timbres through various instrument combinations and groupings (i.e., call and response) for wind groups playing at this level.

Unit 7: Form and Structure

SECTION	MEASURE	EVENT AND SCORING
Chorale	1–4	Main theme is presented in clarinet and trumpet I with chordal accompaniment in low woodwinds and low brass; baritone part cued in the trombone part; dynamic level is *mezzo piano*; no percussion
	5–8	Restatement of main theme by flute, oboe, clarinet, trumpet and bells with tutti, chordal accompaniment; dynamic level is *mezzo piano*
	9–12	Second theme is presented in low woodwinds and low brass; chordal accompaniment in upper woodwinds and horn; dynamic level is *mezzo forte*; no percussion
	13–16	Second theme restated in contrary motion with flute, oboe, clarinet, bass clarinet, baritone saxophone, trumpet I, tuba, and bells; dynamic level is *forte*; chorale section ends with E-flat major, tutti fermata
March	17–20	Four-measure introduction to march section of piece; staccato quarter notes in trumpet, bass clarinet, and baritone saxophone parts with snare drum, bass drum, cymbals, and tambourine feature; dynamic level is *piano*
	21–24	Staccato, march-like figures in trumpet, snare drum and tambourine support the main theme presented in flute part; dynamic level is *mezzo piano*
	25–28	Staccato figures continue and are enhanced with chordal accompaniment in low woodwinds and low brass; main theme restated in upper woodwinds and bells; dynamic level is *mezzo forte*

SECTION	MEASURE	EVENT AND SCORING
	29–36	Third theme presented via syncopated call and response; Dynamics and scoring changes each measure as follows: m. 29–tutti/*forte* m. 30–woodwind choir/*mezzo forte* m. 31–tutti/*forte* m. 32–brass choir/*mezzo forte* m. 33–tutti/*forte* m. 34–percussion/*mezzo forte* m. 35, 36–tutti/*forte*
	37–40	Fourth theme stated in upper woodwinds and brass with bells; chordal and rhythmic accompaniment support melody in tutti scoring; dynamic level is *mezzo forte*
	41–44	Fourth theme stated in lower woodwinds and brass with minimal percussion accompaniment; dynamic level is *piano*
	45–56	Two-measure coda with ritard. and fermata; dynamic level is *forte*

Unit 8: Suggested Listening

Jerry Bilik, *American Civil War Fantasy*
Clare Grundman:
    American Folk Rhapsodies
    Kentucky 1800
Murray Houllif:
    A Cowboy Life
    A Summer Waltz
    Fanfare and Allegro
    Hot Cha-Cha
    McCoy's March
    Show-Down
Pierre La Plante, *American Riversongs*

Unit 9: Additional References and Resources

Houllif, Murray. Electronic mail correspondence with the composer. May 2007.

Miles, Richard, and Thomas Dvorak, eds. *Teaching Music through Performance in Beginning Band*, Volume 1. Chicago: GIA Publications, 2001.

Miles, Richard, ed. *Teaching Music through Performance in Band*, Volume 1. Chicago: GIA Publications, Inc., 1997.

Web sites:
Murray Houllif: http://www.murrayhoullif.homestead.com
C. Alan Publications: http://www.c-alanpublications.com

Contributed by:

Gene Bechen
Associate Professor of Music
Director of Bands
St. Ambrose University
Davenport, Iowa

Teacher Resource Guide

Star Voyage

Gene Milford
(b. 1946)

Unit 1: Composer

Gene F. Milford was born on July 1, 1946. This Canton, Ohio native is currently a senior lecturer in music education at The University of Akron. Prior to his appointment at the university, Dr. Milford amassed more than 30 years of experience as a public school instrumental music teacher. He spent 23 years at Edgewood High School in Ashtabula, Ohio, where he conducted bands that consistently received superior ratings at Ohio Music Education Association-sponsored events and performed at state and national conferences. Milford taught beginning band students in addition to his successes at the high school level.

Dr. Milford has a PhD in music education from Kent State University and was the recipient of a University Fellowship (1998). He has been a guest conductor, clinician, and adjudicator at contests and festivals throughout the state of Ohio, and his articles on music education have appeared in *Triad, Dialogues in Instrumental Music Education,* and *Contributions to Music Education.*

As a composer and arranger, Dr. Milford has received numerous commissions, was the recipient of a grant from the Ohio Arts Council (1995) and an ASCAP award, and he has works listed in the catalogs of Alfred Publishing, Great Works Publishing, Heritage Press, Lorenz Publishing, and Ludwig Music Publishing. Several of his compositions are currently on state required lists.

Unit 2: Composition

Star Voyage was composed in 2005. The composer describes it as "a contemporary concert overture that portrays the vast expanses of interstellar space and that quality of the human spirit which strives for an understanding of the universe." Approximately three minutes in duration, the composition begins with a statement of the essential motivic material (F, E-flat, A-flat; major second, perfect fourth). From this seed the rest of the work grows, as the basic motive travels through and is transformed by various environments.

Unit 3: Historical Perspective

Overtures as a musical form trace their origins to the beginning of the seventeenth century, when opera composers began to turn away from short prologues or flourishes in favor of more complicated introductory material. The first to standardize the form was Jean-Baptiste Lully, who established the French Overture style in his ballet *Alcidiane* of 1658. Alessandro Scarlatti subsequently introduced the Italian Overture style in his opera *Dal male i bene* of 1696. These contrasting styles existed side by side until approximately 1750, when the Italian style prevailed, given its relationship to the increasingly influential symphonic and sonata forms.

    The concert overture emerged as a form in its own right during the nineteenth century. Severing any connection to other material (operas, ballets, etc.), concert overtures began to fall into two general categories: Those in a single-movement sonata form, and those in a single free form, *Vorspiel* style.

    Star Voyage incorporates diverse elements from throughout the development of the overture form. Its basic tempo structure (slow, faster, slow) is reminiscent of the French Overture style. The somewhat imitative nature of the entrances in the middle section is characteristic of both the French and Italian styles, and the developmental treatment of the opening motive might be traced to the Italian or sinfonia style. The programmatic title resonates with the concert overture of the nineteenth century and calls to mind the descriptive labels of some of the earliest examples, e.g., *Roman Carnival Overture*, or *The Hebrides*.

Unit 4: Technical Considerations

Milford describes his compositional outlook:

> First, I am conservative regarding the technical level of works for young bands. I believe that as band literature provides a culmination and unification of learned musical skills and technical demands of performance, selections should be less than the level at which students

are working in method books and lessons. This allows the rhythmic and technical problems to be minimal, allowing students to concentrate on the many ensemble and musical requirements of performing in a group. Therefore, my approach to writing for beginning bands is to use limited ranges and rhythms while trying to provide some musical interest and opportunities for all players.

True to his word, Milford stays close to the staff with no leaps greater than a fifth. The winds' smallest note value is the eighth note, while the percussion must navigate an occasional group of sixteenths. However, the simple duple subdivision is in 4/4 meter throughout (with the exception of one 2/4 measure and one 3/4 measure). Of particular note is the fact that the percussion parts are an integral element even of the thinnest textures within the composition. The snare and bass drum parts function as the thread that links together all sections of the form.

Unit 5: Stylistic Considerations

In *Star Voyage*, Milford creates variety and contrast primarily through a colorful palette of articulations in combination with a terraced dynamic scheme. The composer specifically requests a general articulation style that is separated but has some resonance, within the category of "majestically." The percussion parts are carefully marked to indicate which tones are to ring, and the winds must interpret cap (^) and standard accents (>), as well as the occasional tenuto or slur. Given the composer's judicious placement of rests, careful attention to note releases proves to be as critical as distinguishing the initial articulations.

The four dynamic levels in the work (*f, mf, mp, p*) tend to alternate between loud and soft, rather than build or decay in increments. There are only three *crescendos* marked in the piece. This does not mean that the ensemble should fail to shape phrases as common sense and musicianship dictate. Rather, the composer has elected to provide a fairly Spartan template to enable the conductor and the ensemble to explore the myriad possibilities of inflection. The conductor must recognize that this score is meant to be a framework upon which to practice shaping phrases and building the larger form. Without this realization, *Star Voyage* is apt to be pedantic and one-dimensional rather than vibrant and flexible.

Unit 6: Musical Elements

MELODY:
The initial motive throughout *Star Voyage* is manipulated, using various compositional techniques such as inversion (m. 6), retrograde (mm. 26–27), transposition (m. 42, also retrograde inversion), and augmentation (m. 16).

Understanding the motive as a rhythmic construct (short, short, long), a sequence of pitches (F, E-flat, A-flat), and as a set of intervals (major second, perfect fourth) enables students to explore the music and track the motive and its component parts. Virtually every measure contains a piece of the main motive. The B section of the work provides fodder for a discussion of melodic form and phrasing, given its four component parts.

HARMONY:

The harmonic material in *Star Voyage* offers a rich context in which to discuss intervals, chords/clusters, resting tones, modes, and function. The main motive is presented in unison (with octave displacement), followed by a passage that builds a four tone cluster by stacking pitches on a common tone (mm. 4–7). The initial C functions as the "root" of the cluster, creating a I–V progression across the first phrase (mm. 1–7) and establishing F as the resting tone, or tonic, for the introduction. Given a key signature of two flats, students will be inclined to conclude that the piece begins in B-flat major. A discussion of resting tone and function will open the door to an understanding of the various modes (in this case, F Mixolydian) as they relate to familiar tonalities. The piece ends in B-flat major, exploring harmonic transitions, secondary dominants, and pivot chords along the way. The center of the B section is fertile ground as it uses E-flat major, G minor, and F major chords to move away from and back to B-flat major. The previously mentioned use of C as the dominant of F provides a foundation to understand how the piece ends up in B-flat major when the recapitulation of the A section is in F Mixolydian.

RHYTHM:

Although the rhythms in *Star Voyage* are quite simple, they provide a foundation for more advanced concepts such as augmentation and subdivision. The rhythmic structure of the piece, though uncomplicated, provides five distinct textural zones: Unison (mm. 1–3), additive (4–7), call and response (mm. 15–16, answered by m. 17), melody and accompaniment (mm. 26–33), and homophonic (mm. 34–37). These five areas enable students to practice the different modes of interaction fundamental to the ensemble experience.

TIMBRE:

Star Voyage reflects a traditional approach to orchestration for young bands. It is refreshing to note that the horn parts are distinct from the saxophone choir, and that the woodwinds and brass function both apart and in various combinations to broaden the spectrum of sonic possibilities. There are no unusual color combinations, although the composer employs a spectrum of articulations in the winds that helps to add interest (see Unit 5 earlier). The percussion provides the most in the way of timbral variance. The snare drum has passages with snares off to contrast the typical buzz, and the suspended cymbal player is called upon to use both yarn mallets and snare sticks. The piece calls for both suspended and crash cymbals in contrasting and appropriate roles, and the bell part separates from the xylophone part on occasion to blend more effectively with the winds.

Unit 7: Form and Structure

SECTION	MEASURE	EVENT AND SCORING
Introduction	1–13	Presentation of main motive (winds, first three notes); F Mixolydian; note inversion of motive in flute, m. 6
A	14–23	First melodic idea grown from main motive (see m. 16: motive in augmented note values); brass pass idea to woodwinds (m. 18); F Mixolydian
Transition	24–25	Shift to F major through C cluster in m. 23; F functions as dominant to impending B-flat major (m. 26)
B (a, a')	26–33	Second melodic idea (main motive retrograde, augmented rhythms); B-flat major; B melody includes four sub-phrases: a, mm. 26–29; a', mm. 30–33; b, mm. 34–37; a'', mm. 38–41; harmony of entire B section moves from B-flat major, through E-flat major, G minor, and F major before returning to B-flat major
B (b, a'')	34–41	New chorale-like material utilizing descending thirds in trumpets provides textural contrast as percussion drops out briefly
B'	42–49	B material in clarinets and trumpets with B-derived countermelody in flutes, oboes, and alto saxophones; accompaniment expanded to include full ensemble; four-part structure of B section is retained: a, mm. 42–45; a', mm. 46–49; b, mm. 50–53; a'', mm. 54–57

Section	Measure	Event and Scoring
	50–57	Return of chorale-like material with descending thirds in woodwinds rather than brass
A	58–66	Reprise of A material (see mm. 14–23). F Mixolydian
Closing	67–71	Introductory motive (original setting), followed by A material with percussion role inverted (answer rather than lead); final cadence: unison F to B-flat major

Unit 8: Suggested Listening

Related works for young band:
Warren Benson, *Ginger Marmalade*
Joel Blahnik, *Invention No. 1*
Timothy Broege, *Theme and Variations*
John Visconti (Elliot Del Borgo), *Space Echoes*
Chen Yi, *Spring Festival*

Model orchestral masterworks:
Ludwig van Beethoven, *Egmont Overture, Op. 84*
Hector Berlioz, *Roman Carnival Overture, Op. 9*
Johannes Brahms, *Academic Festival Overture, Op. 80*
Gustav Holst, *The Planets, Op. 32*
Felix Mendelssohn, *Hebrides Overture, Op. 26* ("Fingal's Cave")

Unit 9: Additional References and Resources

Boonshaft, Peter. *Teaching Music with Passion*. Galesville: Meredith Music, 2002.

Boonshaft, Peter. *Teaching Music with Purpose*. Galesville: Meredith Music, 2006.

Camphouse, Mark, ed. *Composers on Composing for Band*. Volumes 1–3. Chicago: GIA Publications, 2002, 2004, 2007.

Dvorak, Thomas, et al. *Best Music for Young Band* (revised edition). New York: Manhattan Beach, 2005.

Dvorak, Thomas, and Richard Floyd. *Best Music for Beginning Band*. New York: Manhattan Beach, 2000.

Hauswirth, Felix. *333 Selected Works for Wind Orchestra and Wind Ensembles, Grade 2–3*. Adliswil: Musikverlag Emil Ruh, 1998.

Lisk, Edward. *The Creative Director: Beginning and Intermediate Levels*. Galesville: Meredith Music, 2001.

Noble, Weston. *Creating the Special World*. Chicago: GIA Publications, 2005.

Salzman, Timothy. *A Composer's Insight*. Volumes 1–3. Galesville: Meredith Music, 2003, 2006.

Williamson, John. *Rehearsing the Band*. Cloudcroft: Neidig Services, 1998.

Contributed by:

Carolyn Barber
Director of Bands
University of Nebraska-Lincoln
Lincoln, Nebraska

Teacher Resource Guide

Starship

John O'Reilly
(b. 1940)

Unit 1: Composer

Composer and educator John O'Reilly's works are among the most frequently performed by bands today. In addition to the vast number of works by O'Reilly, he is also a co-author of *Accent on Achievement, Yamaha Band Students,* and *Strictly Strings* method books. He is recipient of numerous ASCAP awards and his teachers include Robert Washburn, Donald Hunsberger, Arthur Frackenpohl, and Charles Walton. O'Reilly is a graduate of the Crane School of Music, at the State University of New York, Potsdam, and of Columbia University, where he holds a master of arts in composition and theory. He is an elected member of the American Bandmasters Association and frequent clinician for honor bands throughout the world. He currently resides in Los Angeles, California, where he works as a senior editor for Alfred Publishing.

Unit 2: Composition

Written in 2006, *Starship* is part of the *Accent on Achievement* series for band. Described as a "bright and bold" overture, *Starship* offers many interesting harmonies and syncopated rhythms that provide a musical challenge for young musicians.

Unit 3: Historical Perspective

The overture is a common form used in music of many periods. With the rise of school band programs, overtures have often been employed as a compositional tool, allowing students to showcase multiple styles, speeds, and dynamic shifts. *Starship* is a great tool for teachers to show the above-mentioned concepts in action.

Unit 4: Technical Considerations

As part of the *Accent on Achievement* series, *Starship* corresponds with Book 2, page 24. This would be appropriate for any student completing their second method book. *Starship* has several syncopated eighth-quarter-eighth patterns as well as tempo and style changes. The writing is in a comfortable playing range for all instruments, including split trumpet and clarinet parts to accommodate students who have not developed a range above B-flat4. The composition is in 4/4 time and in the key of E-flat concert throughout.

Unit 5: Stylistic Considerations

O'Reilly uses great skill in crafting a balance between legato and accented sections to teach young players to play in an appropriate style. The smooth transitions and the use of allegro and andante tempo markings between sections allow directors to create a sense of finesse and teach students to watch the director for tempo changes.

Unit 6: Musical Elements

MELODY:
The melodic lines center around E-flat concert with no deviation or accidentals. Leaps of a perfect fourth and a major sixth, along with harmonization of the melodic line add extra contour to the line. O'Reilly also splits melodic ideas between voices to add additional flow in the legato melodies. Isolating the melodic line from the accompaniment may be useful in adding shape and dynamic contrast.

HARMONY:
Starship employs traditional chord structures but exposes students to some sounds not often found in E-flat major, including many seventh chords. This is especially true in the syncopated patterns. Traditional harmonies are used in new and exciting combinations. Isolate the harmonic line, especially the half notes in measures 34–38, to help students hear the harmonies and also work on tuning.

RHYTHM:
The rhythmic structure incorporates whole notes, half notes, quarter notes, and eighth notes. *Starship* makes liberal use of syncopated patterns such as the eighth-quarter-eighth pattern, and the dotted-eighth/sixteenth pattern

appears in the melodic lines as well. Battery percussion makes use of sixteenth-note combinations. Directors may want to have the band work on unison rhythmic patterns, especially the syncopated patterns, on a single concert pitch, which could be incorporated into a warm-up.

TIMBRE:

O'Reilly combines upper woodwind parts with trumpets, and unison low brass and woodwind lines to create traditional band colors. Saxophone, clarinet, and French horn parts are often scored together to counterbalance the upper woodwind/trumpet lines. The piece has five distinct percussion parts that add good colors and effects. Directors may want to experiment with seating arrangements to put like parts together to create sound blocks. Another option could be mixing like parts into separate sections to create a more balanced sound/color effect, but the seating is left entirely up to the discretion of the director.

Unit 7: Form and Structure

SECTION	MEASURE	EVENT AND SCORING
Introduction	1–9	Full band statement of theme; syncopated pattern; percussion transition
A	10–18	Main theme in upper voices, accompaniment in lower voices; first and second endings
A'	19–26	Legato countermelody in clarinets, saxophones and French horns, echoed by flute, oboe, and trumpet; low brass counterline
Transition	27–33	Full band return of introduction material, with ritardando and descending eighth notes in upper voices
B	34–48	Legato theme in flute, oboe, and trumpet half-note accompaniment; flute soli with trumpet answer
Introduction	1–9	Full band statement of theme; syncopated pattern; percussion transition
A	10–18	Main theme in upper voices, accompaniment in lower voices; first and second endings

SECTION	MEASURE	EVENT AND SCORING
A'	19–26	Legato countermelody in clarinets, saxophones and French horns, echoed by flute, oboe and trumpet; low brass counterline
Transition	27–28	Transition to Coda
Coda	49–52	Full band, return of original introduction; percussion has sixteenth-note patterns

Unit 8: Suggested Listening

James Barnes, *Westridge Overture*
John Edmondson, *Celebration for Winds*
Anne McGinty, *Windsor Overture*
John O'Reilly:
    A Shaker Hymn
    Chant and Canon
Jared Spears, *Star Flight*

Unit 9: Additional References and Resources

Miles, Richard, ed. *Teaching Music through Performance in Band.* Chicago: GIA Publications, 1997.

Miles, Richard, and Thomas Dvorak, eds. *Teaching Music through Performance in Beginning Band.* Chicago: GIA Publications, 2001.

O'Reilly, John. *Starship*, Van Nuys, CA: Alfred Publications Co, Inc., 2006.

Smith, Norman, and Albert Stoutamire. *Band Music Notes*, 3rd edition. Lake Charles, LA: Program Notes Press, 1979.

Contributed by:

Jeff Cranmore
McKinney High School
McKinney, Texas

Teacher Resource Guide

Storm Mountain Jubilee
Carl Strommen
(b. 1940)

Unit 1: Composer

Carl Strommen is a widely published composer and arranger whose works embrace a variety of genres: jazz, orchestra, vocal ensemble, instrumental solo/small ensemble, concert band, and piano. Strommen earned his BA in English Literature from Long Island University and his MA in music from City College in New York, New York. He studied composition with Stephan Wolpe and arranging with Rayburn Wright and Manny Album. Strommen currently teaches orchestration and arranging at the C. W. Post campus of Long Island University. Previously, he was the director of bands at Mamaroneck Public Schools in Mamaroneck, New York. His compositions are consistently recognized by ASCAP in the Standard Awards category, Strommen is also active as a clinician, lecturer, and guest conductor.

Unit 2: Composition

Although he is quite familiar with the Storm Mountains in the Western United States, Strommen feels the title, *Storm Mountain Jubilee*, connects the work more to bluegrass music rather than to a specific geographic location. The composer describes bluegrass as the "be-bop of country [with] its own groove and improvisatory style," saying it simply "feels good."[1] Strommen suggests directors listen to music of this genre to better understand the source material when constructing an authentic interpretation.

    Storm Mountain Jubilee is just under two minutes in length and is classified as Grade 1.5 to 2. The brevity of this work should not imply a lack of musical content. The marked tempo is quarter note = 200 for the entire piece (a cut-time approach is suggested in the score), and the composer actively changes style and orchestration from one section to the next to create variety within this brisk temporal framework. The formal structure begins and ends with an "A" section, and three additional sections (B–C–D) occur in the middle of the work. The repetition of sections and motivic ideas will promotes an efficient learning process and a secure student performance.

Unit 3: Historical Perspective

This work presents basic bluegrass elements in a contemporary concert band setting. Bluegrass is a style of American country music that grew in the 1940s from the music of Bill Monroe and his group, Blue Grass Boys.[2] Originating in the rural Southeast United States, bluegrass combines elements of dance, home entertainment and religious folk music.[3] Typically, a bluegrass band consists of four to seven individuals who sing and accompany themselves on acoustic string instruments.[4] As in jazz, alternating improvised solos are common in this genre. Bluegrass is generally in duple meter and emphasizes the off-beats. Tempos are relatively fast; a characteristically slow song is 160 beats per minute and a fast one is approximately 330 beats per minute.[5] Melodically, bluegrass music often employs pentatonic and diatonic scales. Rarely does the melody descend below the tonic, and the fifth scale degree is frequently a "duration tone" at the mid-point of a phrase.[6]

  Storm Mountain Jubilee adheres to several bluegrass characteristics with its lively duple meter, pentatonic melodies, an emphasis of the tonic pitch, and the potential for improvisation. A hymn-like presentation at m. 49 suggests the religious underpinnings of the genre, while student clapping and snare rim shots evoke the energy of a folk dance. The important off-beats in the accompaniment create the rhythmic bluegrass style throughout the work.

Unit 4: Technical Considerations

The harmonic focus of this piece firmly adheres to F major, and melodies most commonly outline F major diatonic or pentatonic scales. To develop the technical facility necessary for an effective performance, the director might have students determine the five notes used in the primary motive of the piece. The students could then create single-measure patterns using those five notes to develop proficiency with the leaps and steps inherent to that scale. Finally, the director could combine the patterns to create student-composed etudes. For example, the director might receive the following three patterns:

Example 1-a

Example 1-b

Example 1-c

The director could then compile them into an etude:

Example 2

Students will gain comfort and technical proficiency with "bluegrass" patterns and melodies through composition and performance.

To improve precision in rhythmically challenging sections, distribute specific motives from the piece in a non-pitched notation. For example, the melody from mm. 9–12, although notated in common time, implies 3/4 time in the interior measures:

Example 3

All ensemble members could perform this rhythm in conjunction with varying pitches and styles (perform all notes on a concert B-flat, superimpose ascending and descending F pentatonic or diatonic scales, clap, stomp, or break the parts into rounds). As students invent and practice varied repetitions of patterns found in the piece, they will be more comfortable when they encounter these motives in performance.

Unit 5: Stylistic Considerations

The primary stylistic issue beginners face stems from the performance of eighth-note/quarter-note patterns. A common obstacle arises when students fail to articulate, inadvertently rush, or use insufficient air when playing eighth notes. Students often over-correct by playing the quarter-notes that follow with a hard or heavy tongue. If this becomes the baseline stylistic approach, students will likely use a harder accent on the half notes as well, resulting in a sluggish melody that lacks phrasal flow and forward motion.

The director can correct this issue on two fronts: improve control of the muscles responsible for brisk tonguing and develop a habit of consistently increasing air speed when playing faster rhythms to facilitate clarity. Many method books provide exercises to improve the tonguing mechanics, such as scale patterns with changing rhythms that gradually increase in tempo or single-pitch exercises that start with quarter-notes and accelerate to eighths and sixteenths. Students often assume faster tonguing means harder tonguing; realistically, the opposite is true. When using such exercises, check individual sections to ensure that tongues are high in the mouth and air is passing freely regardless of speed or pattern.

In addition to developing fundamentally solid technique, encourage students to move more air through the instrument when playing faster notes. Younger players tend to "swallow" faster rhythms. Remind students to increase energy through eighth-note patterns and relax energy when arriving at quarter notes to discourage any unnecessary emphasis of longer notes (see Example 4).

Example 4
mm. 5–6, melody

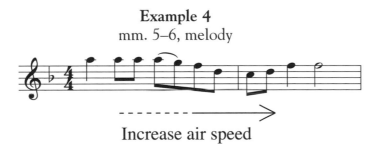

Increase air speed

Unit 6: Musical Elements

MELODY:
Due to the pentatonic underpinnings of the melodies in *Storm Mountain Jubilee*, melodic leaps of a third are rather prominent. When these leaps occur, remind students to increase air support on the lower note of the pair. If the motive is ascending, use more air on the first note to improve the accuracy of the second. Conversely, in a descending pattern, increased air toward the lower note promotes a fuller tone and discourages pinching.

HARMONY:

Although the tonic F major is structurally predominant, the composer maintains harmonic interest in a number of ways. First, the bass line is rarely static: Motion often alternates between the first and fifth scale degree or outlines chord tones in a walking-bass fashion. Furthermore, Strommen changes the texture from one section to the next, featuring upper woodwinds with accompaniment in the opening, abruptly dropping the accompaniment in section B, and presenting a full-ensemble chorale without percussion at m. 49.

Strommen approaches cadences stylistically to evoke a folk-music sound. For example, the walking bass in mm. 61–62 prepares a D7 chord as the dominant of a "ii" chord in F major. The following chord is actually a G9 chord, which serves as the dominant of a V in F major. Ultimately, a V7 (C7) follows to prepare the return to I (F major). Strommen, therefore, creates harmonic interest through a conventional circle-of-fifths preparation, and the resulting progression is familiar to most listeners.

RHYTHM:

Rhythm is a defining characteristic of the bluegrass style, and Strommen's authentic approach is structured in a manner that bolsters the ensemble's sense of security. When the melody is rhythmically active, the accompaniment and percussion clearly define the beat. When the percussion drops out (m. 49, for example), the ensemble plays a tutti rhythm, maximizing rhythmic integrity. The upbeat clapping at m. 38 serves as a rhythmic response to the percussion; in this section, Strommen suggests using any kind of additional percussion the director deems appropriate to improvise upon the clapping pattern.[7] The wood block is integral to establishing time for the ensemble and therefore requires special attention from both conductor and performer.

TIMBRE:

The homophonic sections of this piece feature melodic upper woodwinds. The conductor should emphasize the importance of appropriate dynamics in accompanying parts to allow the primary voices to emerge from the texture. The tutti chorale at m. 49 could reveal inconsistencies in precision. Students often think that slow music requires less precision, so the director must highlight the need to move fingers deliberately and in time when the ensemble is playing in a chorale style. One common method of drawing attention to precision is "bopping," or playing each note as short as possible while maintaining the notated rhythms of the chorale section (see Examples 5a–b).

Example 5a
Written:

Example 5b
Practice:

When "bopping," count off the ensemble, then stop conducting and allow them to perform the exercise without a conductor to develop the ensemble's internal sense of pulse. This skill is necessary to ensure precision in a legato or chorale style. Directors should encourage rhythmic precision regardless of style, articulation, or tempo.

Unit 7: Form and Structure

SECTION	MEASURE	EVENT AND SCORING
Intro	1–4	Establishes style; low voices and wood block
A	5–12	Theme 1; upper woodwind melody, bass, percussion
A'	16–23	Theme 1; trumpet/saxophone melody, low brass, percussion
Extension	24–25	Implication of 3/4 time
Transition	26–29	Chorale style; all winds, no percussion
B	30–37	Theme 2; upper woodwinds and trumpet unison; no accompaniment
B'	30–37 (repeat)	Theme; accompaniment and percussion added on repeat
C	38–46	Percussion feature; winds rest
C'	38–46 (repeat)	Wind players clap upbeats; improvisatory percussion if desired

SECTION	MEASURE	EVENT AND SCORING
Extension	47–48	Percussion only
D	49–64	Theme 3; winds and mallet percussion only; chorale style
A'	65–72	Theme 1 (as in mm. 16–23); trumpet/saxophone melody, low brass, percussion
A"	73–80	Theme 1; full band and percussion altered harmonic preparation for final cadence

Unit 8: Suggested Listening

Larry Blocher, *Bluegrass Moments*
Don Freund, *Jug Blues and Fat Pickin'*
Bill Monroe's Blue Grass Boys, *Goodbye Old Pal*

Unit 9: Additional References and Resources

"Authors and Clinicians," Alfred.com (Accessed 06 May 2007),
<http://www.alfred.com/span_authors/strommen.html>.

Rosenberg, Niel. "Bluegrass," *Grove Music Online*. L. Macy, ed.
(Accessed 01 May 2007), <http://bert.lib.indiana.edu:2100>.

Smith, L. Mayne. "An Introduction to Bluegrass." *Journal of American Folklore* 78, July-September 1965, 245–56.

Strommen, Carl. "Storm Mtn." Personal email (02 May 2007).

Contributed by:

Chad Nicholson
Associate Director of Bands
Colorado State University
Fort Collins, Colorado

---

1 Carl Strommen, "Storm Mtn.," personal email; 02 May 2007.
2 Neil Rosenberg, "Bluegrass," Grove Music Online ed. L. Macy; available from <http://bert.lib. indiana.edu:2100>; Internet; accessed 01 May 2007.
3 Ibid.
4 Ibid.
5 Ibid.
6 L. Mayne Smith, "An Introduction to Bluegrass," *Journal of American Folklore* 78 (July-September 1965): 245–56.
7 Carl Strommen, "Storm Mtn.," personal email; 02 May 2007.

Teacher Resource Guide

Symphony No. 15, K. 124, "Finale"

W. A. Mozart
(1756–1791)

arranged by Larry Daehn
(b. 1939)

Unit 1: Composer

Wolfgang Amadeus Mozart was born in 1756 in the town of Salzburg, Austria. Son of Leopold Mozart, an esteemed composer and violinist, Wolfgang was a child prodigy who began composing before he was five, and by this age had become a virtuoso on the clavier, harpsichord, organ, and violin. Publicly performing his own works (and others) by the age of six, Wolfgang was frequently tested by his appreciative audiences, at times reading concerti at sight, improvising variations, fugues, and fantasias, and accurately reproducing a work after hearing it only once. These performance tours his father had Wolfgang present were very beneficial during his impressionable years; he met important composers and performers and was exposed to different musical styles. Elements of those styles then appeared in his own compositions; some were used for a short time and then rejected, while others were absorbed into his distinctive musical style.is also included.

Mozart's own musical style is described and categorized as that of "absolute musicality." The works by many composers, either historical or contemporary, are autobiographical in a sense, and the hardships and disappointments that they have endured are reflected in their compositions. With Mozart, this was never a characteristic trait of his music. Although Wolfgang had many personal troubles during his lifetime, especially in the last ten years of his life, none of these troubles were reflected in his music. Like most great artists, Mozart lived his ideal life through his music, producing a world of great beauty. Composing came very easy to Mozart, and the speed and sureness of his creative power has been unrivaled by any other composer—past, present, or future. He usually composed the music in his mind first, even to the last detail, and writing it to paper was only a means of transferring the structure that was already, so to speak, before his eyes.

While many other composers during his time worked successfully under the patronage system, writing music for an aristocracy for whom the arts were a necessary part of life, Mozart was too strong-willed to endure comments and criticisms of the music he wrote. Mozart attempted this lifestyle for a short time, but in the late 1770s he quarreled with the archbishop of Salzburg, was dismissed, and in the last ten years of his life, established himself in Vienna to pursue the career of a free artist. Because worldly success depended on the support of the court, Mozart and his family spent these last ten years in financial hardship. At the age of 35, Mozart died from complications of rheumatic fever. Research differs in information, but many sources state that Mozart was buried in a pauper's grave in Vienna, and by the time this mistake was found, his body could not be located.

Unit 2: Composition

Mozart wrote approximately fifty symphonies during his lifetime, some of which are now lost. The development of his compositional skills and the changes in his musical style are seen clearly in his symphonies, for they evolved throughout almost all of his professional career. His symphonic style changed as his models changed: from J. C. Bach; to the Viennese school; to Sammartini and other Italian masters of the *sinfonia*; to Stamitz and the Mannheim school; and to Haydn.

Symphony No. 15, K.124 was written in 1772 while Mozart was still living in Salzburg, Austria. The purpose of the composition is speculative, but the piece is thought to have been written for a Lenten *concert spirituel* or the installation of Archbishop Hieronymus Joseph Franz.

The fourth movement, "Finale," exhibits a playful character and shows the influence of the Italian *opera buffa*. Mozart had traveled to Italy around this time period and was highly influenced by the light style and quality craftsmanship, with the bulk of their music aimed at entertainment.

The fourth movement, "Finale," is approximately two and one-half minutes in length and was arranged for band by Larry Daehn, owner and publisher of Daehn Publications in New Glarus, Wisconsin. To celebrate the 250th anniversary of the birth of Mozart, this arrangement was commissioned in 2005 by the Western Wisconsin Middle-Level Honors Band.

Unit 3: Historical Perspective

In the broadest sense, a symphony is a sonata for orchestra. The form is said to have directly descended from the Italian opera overture (termed *sinfonia*) that was in use during the last two decades of the seventeenth century. From the style changes and cross-currents characterizing the waning Baroque period (c.1600–1750) and the advancing Classical period (c.1750–1800), the symphony came into existence from several forms: the Italian opera overture, the trio sonata, and the Baroque concerto grosso. Characteristics from each of these forms helped to develop the internal details of structure, texture, style, and instrumentation of the symphony.

The classical symphony normally consists of four movements: an opening allegro first movement, sometimes with a slow introduction; a slow, lyrical second movement; a minuet and trio for the third movement; and a brisk and virtuosic fourth movement. The fourth ("Finale") movement is usually of a vivacious character, Allegro molto or Presto in tempo, written in either a rondo or a sonata-allegro form. This movement is usually lighter in style and character than the first movement and brings the cycle of the whole composition to a spirited ending.

Although Sammartini is credited with having written the first symphony (1734), Haydn is considered to have laid the foundation in the development of the symphony. Haydn wrote approximately 104 symphonies and highly influenced Mozart in this compositional form. From this influence, Mozart then continued to develop the symphony to an art of perfection, which influenced later composers such as Beethoven and Brahms, among others.

Mozart is said to have perfected such characteristics as presenting distinct opening ideas and closing material; the manipulation or development of motifs; and the standardization of techniques for transitions, harmonic motion, modulation, and orchestration.

Between 1772 and 1774, Mozart composed seventeen symphonies, which were written in either three- or four-movement structures. Composed in 1772, *Symphony No. 15, K.124* was thought to have been written for a Lenten *concert spiritual*, which is a series of public concerts that originated in France in 1725 and continued until the French Revolution in 1789. These concerts took place around Easter and were largely devoted to sacred music. The fourth ("Finale") movement is thought to have been influenced by the Italian *opera buffa*. The Italian *opera buffa* or "comic opera" began in the early 1700s and evolved out of the intermezzi that were performed between the acts of the Italian *opera seria* or "serious opera." The Italian *opera buffas* were remarkable for their liveliness and humor, for the highly developed comic character of the music, and for the ensemble finales.

Unit 4: Technical Considerations

The "Finale" from *Symphony No. 15, K.124* is scored for a full band with one part written for flute, oboe, bassoon, bass clarinet, alto saxophone, tenor saxophone, baritone saxophone, French horn, euphonium, and tuba, which is occasionally scored in split octaves. Two parts are written for clarinet, trumpet, and trombone. On one occasion, the low woodwinds have cues for low brass doublings to assist if needed. Percussion parts are written for two timpani (tonic and dominant, no re-tuning), snare drum, bass drum, and orchestra bells.

Written in 2/4 meter, the key to creating the lively and comical character of this fourth movement is performing the work in the prescribed tempo of Presto, with quarter note equaling 150–166 beats per minute. The main concern for students is to effectively maintain the tempo without rushing or dragging.

Students must have a technical, thorough understanding of the F major and C major scales, and for several measures in the piece, the C minor and C mixolydian scales. Accidentals are limited to the established harmonic progressions in those aforementioned key centers.

The primary rhythms are quarter notes, half notes, and eighth notes. Dotted-quarter/eighth note rhythms occur occasionally, as well as the syncopated rhythm of eighth note-quarter note-eighth note in one section toward the conclusion. Good preparatory work on the latter two rhythmic patterns helps students perform them properly and prevents rushing or dragging. Being able to properly subdivide the beat and play single eighth notes on the upbeat will help tremendously. Performers must be able to concentrate and play on alternating beats and measures against other instruments within the melodic or rhythmic parts of the work.

Trumpet range is conservative with the highest pitch being G5. Flute range is written predominantly above the treble staff, and clarinetists on both parts must be able to play across the break.

Unit 5: Stylistic Considerations

The "Finale" from *Symphony No. 15, K.124* includes distinctive stylistic elements. Crisp or "clean" articulations and, most importantly, a light or leggiero style is essential to the music of Mozart. The ability to preserve the energy, mood, and spirit of the original composition in this exciting wind arrangement needs to be the primary focus. By adhering to proper tone quality, phrasing, articulation, expression, and dynamics, the musical and emotional elements of the movement will be realized.

The style of Mozart is like no other composer in music history. His music requires a command of light/leggiero articulation, a buoyant quality in balance and tempo, and the ability to master and perform in a "clean," crisp manner that only Mozart can require. The teacher must be able to instruct how to play articulations in music originally written for strings on wind instruments.

Two dynamic levels are present throughout the composition: *piano* and *forte*. These two dynamic levels change *subito* from one phrase to the next. Student performers must be able to change between these dynamics effectively and must also realize that, whether playing at *piano* or at *forte*, the light articulation and buoyant style of the piece must remain. Intonation and tone quality must also remain constant from one dynamic level to another.

Unit 6: Musical Elements

MELODY:
For the majority of the work, the melody moves in a stepwise, diatonic fashion, particularly in the "A" sections. Leaps of a third or more are generally confined to motivic points in the melody, changes in texture/section, and the conclusion of the composition. The melody is very conjunct and sequential, especially in the "C" section. The melody appears in *hocket* on occasion.

HARMONY:
The work contains consonant harmonies of mostly triadic writing, with some seventh chords added at cadential points. Mozart stayed within those boundaries of the standard harmonies present during the Classical era. Some modulatory sections exist, but these transitional sections progress very quickly into another consonant key center. The key center of C mixolydian is present for a short while in section "C." One teaching concept/strategy is discussing the church modes and comparing these scales to the major and minor scales predominantly used in music of the Classical era.

RHYTHM:
The rhythmic content and predominant, underlying rhythm of the work is based on the eighth-note subdivision. The eighth note is present in the melodic content and rhythmic accompaniment. Rhythms alternate from measure to measure and from instrument group to instrument group in several sections or transitional phrases in the work.

TIMBRE:
The major timbral challenges arise in orchestrating the predominantly string piece for winds in this arrangement. While the main tone colors remain the same, the teacher should play a recording of the original composition for the students to compare the timbres and determine how to effectively replicate

this Classical-era symphony orchestra with a modern-day wind band. Effective playing of the leggiero style and articulations that Mozart has written will promote and affect the tone color of the ensemble. Timbre must also be addressed with the *subito* dynamic changes; these dynamic changes, in relation to breath control and support, will affect tone color and timbral clarity.

Unit 7: Form and Structure

The "Finale" of *Symphony No. 15, K.124* is written in rondo form, with the structure of ABACA/Coda.

SECTION		MEASURE	EVENT AND SCORING
A		**1–20**	
	a	1–10	Theme introduced; quarter-note and eighth-note rhythms predominate; F major
	a¹	11–20	Continuation of same scoring/restatement of material with cadence; whole section repeated back to beginning
B		**21–44**	
	a	21–28	Thinner texture with parts cascading among each other; style is now more lyrical, with new theme added in woodwind tutti; key center is modulatory, with hints of D minor
	b	29–36	Texture reverts back to that of A section with a similar theme in brass tutti; style back to light and buoyant; key of C major
Transition		37–44	Texture thinner with woodwinds alternating from measure to measure; eighth notes predominate
A		**45–64**	
	a	45–54	F major; material from A section (mm. 1–10) is restated verbatim
	a¹	55–64	Continuation and restatement from before (mm. 11–20); last two sections (B and A) are repeated
C		**65–84**	
	a	65–72	New theme and section begins in C minor for four measures, then moves to C major for four measures; lyrical style similar to section B; eighth notes and half notes predominate

SECTION	MEASURE	EVENT AND SCORING
b	73–80	Key changes to C mixolydian; style remains lyrical; texture thickens with theme alternating in woodwinds from measure to measure
Transition	81–84	Texture reverts back to that of section A; eighth notes and quarter notes predominate; key of C major
A	**85–104**	
a	85–94	F major; material from A section (mm. 45–54/1–10) is restated verbatim
a¹	95–104	Continuation and restatement from before (mm. 55–64/11–20); section is not repeated as before
Coda	**105–132**	
a¹	105–112	F major; syncopated rhythm introduced with underlying quarter-note accompaniment; predominant eighth-note and quarter-note rhythm follows
a¹'	113–120	Restatement of previous subsection
b	121–132	F major continues; eighth-note/ quarter-note rhythm continues; texture thickens as piece concludes

Unit 8: Suggested Listening

W. A. Mozart:
 Cosi fan tutte
 Eine kleine Nachtmusik, K.525
 Symphony No. 15, "Finale," K.124 (orchestral original)
 Symphony No. 20, K.133
 Symphony No. 25, K.183
 The Magic Flute
 The Marriage of Figaro
F. J. Haydn:
 Symphony No. 45 in F-sharp minor
 Symphony No. 46 in B major
 Symphony No. 49 in F minor

Unit 9: Additional References and Resources

Abel, Willi. *Harvard Dictionary of Music*. 2nd ed. Cambridge, MA: Belknap Press of Harvard University Press, 1972.

Grout, Donald Jay. *A History of Western Music*. 3rd ed. New York and London: W. W. Norton and Company, 1980.

Machlis, Joseph, and Kristine Forney. *The Enjoyment of Music*. 7th ed. New York and London: W. W. Norton and Company, 1995.

Mozart, Wolfgang Amadeus. Score program notes to *Symphony No. 15, K.124*, *"Finale."* Arranged by Larry Daehn. New Glarus, WI: Daehn Publications, 2006.

Stolba, K Marie. *The Development of Western Music: A History*. Madison, WI: Brown and Benchmark, 1994.

Contributed by:

Christian Zembower
Director of Bands
East Tennessee State University
Johnson City, Tennessee

Teacher Resource Guide

The Band in the Square on the Fourth of July

Pierre La Plante
(b. 1943)

Unit 1: Composer

Pierre La Plante, of French-Canadian descent, was born September 24, 1943. He received a Bachelor of Music Education and a Master of Music from the University of Wisconsin-Madison. In his undergraduate work he studied arranging with Jim Christensen, a prominent commercial arranger, composer, conductor, and music educator. La Plante taught classroom, vocal, and instrumental music at the elementary, secondary, and college levels for thirty-two years. He remains active as a bassoonist, performing with numerous ensembles including the Beloit-Janesville Symphony, Madison Wind Ensemble, Dubuque Orchestra, Madison Theatre Guild Orchestra and the Unitarian Society Orchestra. La Plante has composed several pieces for band, orchestra, choir, solo, and chamber music. He currently resides in Oregon, Wisconsin.

Unit 2: Composition

The Band in the Square on the Fourth of July is based on a late-nineteenth century patriotic song titled "There Are Many Flags in Many Lands." This popular patriotic song has been used in general music textbooks and on holiday celebrations such as Flag Day, Veterans Day, and Memorial Day. La Plante describes his instrumental setting as a slice of turn-of-the-twentieth-century Americana. La Plante explains his concept for the piece in a scenario based in part on one of his earliest recollections of a parade in Cedarburg, Wisconsin.

A small-town Fourth of July parade with bunting, banners, flags and school or town band approaching from the distance, becoming louder and louder until, at the loudest point, the band is directly in front of you. (You are standing on the curb on the same side as the bass drum and cymbals which, for a few seconds, overwhelm and drown out everything else around you.) Then the band passes by with the clarinets and flutes trailing behind, and all eventually fading away.

This work has a difficulty level of Grade 1 and is described as a patrol march with a duration of two minutes and fifteen seconds.

Unit 3: Historical Perspective

The march was purely functional in origin, designed to keep troops in step with a regular beat and a happy spirit. The modern band as we know it today came into existence during the time of the French Revolution. With this development the bands moved beyond performing military functions to presenting music for public occasions. The march also evolved to reflect the increased instrumentation and musical development of these bands. Several classifications of marches developed during 1876–1926, a time of great prosperity for American marches, to include the quickstep and the grand march. Another march form that evolved during this time was the paraphrase march, which involved adapting a well-known tune to the march style. One such paraphrase march was written during that time was *Revival March* (1876) by John Philip Sousa, which uses the well-known hymn "In the Sweet Bye and Bye."

The Band in the Square on the Fourth of July falls into the category of a paraphrase march. La Plante uses melodic material from the patriotic song "There are Many Flags in Many Lands" that seems to have first appeared in *The Child's Song Book for Schools and Home Circles* by Mary H. Howliston, published in 1888.

LINE	TEXT
1	There are many flags in many lands,
2	There are flags of many hue,
3	But there is no flag however grand,
4	Like our own red, white, and blue.
5	Say hurrah for our flag,
6	Our country's flag,
7	It's stripes and it's bright stars too.
8	But there is no flag however grand,
9	Like our own red, white, and blue.

The composer's score includes characteristic articulation and style markings, including accent, staccato, tenuto and marcato. La Plante has also written percussion parts in the traditional march style.

Unit 4: Technical Considerations

The Band in the Square on the Fourth of July begins in the key of E-flat major and moves to F major in the middle section. Accidentals occur in measure 38 during the transition to F major and also in measure 52 for first clarinet and second trumpet. Ranges of the instruments are well within the Grade 1 category. The highest note for clarinet and trumpet is C5. Most instrumental ranges remain within an octave to an octave and a half. There is a balance between unison and harmony throughout the piece, with some harmonized statements found later in the piece, including some brief divisi passages. These allow young players opportunities to develop some independence without weakening the orchestration. Variations of melodic, harmonic, and rhythmic elements provide compositional interest for players and audience. La Plante provides specific articulation markings including accents, tenuto, staccato, and slurs to aid in stylistic interpretation. With regard to rhythm, there is one syncopated, four-beat cell that is used four times. The composer provides cues throughout the piece where orchestration is limited to one or two sections of the band to provide security for pitch and balance if needed. In measures 24–28 the trumpet and French horn cues are provided in several parts to give the conductor the option of strengthening the orchestration; oboe and French horn parts are doubled throughout. Percussion parts are traditional for the march style, providing rhythmic drive and energy for the woodwind and brass parts. The score includes two snare drum parts that are basically identical, with the exception that one has rolls while the other does not. This additional version of the snare drum part provides more advanced students an opportunity to develop and build techniques for performing rolls. The score does not include a piano reduction.

Unit 5: Stylistic Considerations

The piece is marked Moderate March Tempo with quarter note = 108–116. Accent, tenuto, slur, and staccato markings are used consistently throughout the piece to define the desired style and phrase development. The march style is a strong tradition in the band literature. Ensemble unity, as well as interpretation of note length, articulation, and balance is crucial to the march style. Percussion parts play a vital role and can be used to help unify the woodwind and brass parts.

Unit 6: Musical Elements

The entire piece is a gradual *crescendo*-sustained *forte*-decrescendo that teaches students to pace the dynamics. Markings in the score and parts include *crescendo poco a poco, sempre crescendo, diminuendo poco a poco,* and marcato. Graphic representations for *crescendo* and *decrescendo* are also present. Dynamic markings include *pianissimo, piano, mezzo piano, mezzo forte, forte,* and *sforzando.* This march presents march style, syncopation, and key changes in a technical setting that allows students to execute these elements in a manner that goes beyond notes and rhythms.

MELODY:
The melodic material in this piece is based on the patriotic song titled "There Are Many Flags in Many Lands." La Plante uses the major keys of E-flat and F in this setting. The melody is first stated without any harmonization or wind-instrument accompaniment. The orchestration and rhythms vary with each successive use of melodic material.

HARMONY:
The tonal centers of this piece are E-flat and F major. The harmonic structure in this march is primarily triadic. A few passing and leading tones are present in more thickly orchestrated sections that teach young players how to stress and release particular pitches based on their harmonic function.

RHYTHM:
The basic rhythms for the woodwind and brass parts include whole, half, dotted-half, quarter, dotted-quarter and eighth notes. There is one four-beat syncopated pattern that occurs four times in the piece. The snare drum parts include combinations of eighth and sixteenth notes in addition to the note values mentioned above.

TIMBRE:
The orchestration of this march presents the melody in various instrumental combinations of for statements of including woodwinds, woodwinds + upper brass and low woodwinds + low brass. Dynamic markings and instrumentation used combine to propel the piece from the *piano* dynamic at the beginning to a *forte* section, then back to *piano*. This is meant to create the effect of a marching band coming down the street in a parade, passing by, and then moving farther and farther away. Players must keep air pressure and air speed focused, supported, and consistent in both soft and loud passages. Brass players should listen to and maintain a warm tone in the louder sections.

Unit 7: Form and Structure

Section	Measure	Event and Scoring
Introduction	1–4	Percussion cadence with snare drum and bass drum
Phrase A	5–8	The tonal center is E-flat major; melodic material comes from lines 1–2 of the song "There Are Many Flags in Many Lands" and is scored for flutes and clarinet 1–2; this material is cued for alto and tenor saxophones
Phrase B	9–12	Melodic material from lines 3–4; this phrase is scored for the same instruments as Phrase A, with the addition of tenor saxophone
Introduction	13–16	Percussion cadence with the addition of crash cymbals; there are some variations in rhythm
Phrase A	17–20	Melodic material is the same as the previous A phrases with the addition of oboe and alto saxophone; the remaining woodwind and brass instruments make their first entrance in this phrase as accompaniment and provide triadic harmony and rhythmic reinforcement for the percussion
Phrase B	21–24	This statement of Phrase B is the same as the previous one with the addition of full band accompaniment
Phrase C	25–28	Melodic material for Phrase C comes from lines 5–7; the melody is now scored for trumpet 1–2 and French horn with cues in clarinet 1–2 and alto and tenor saxophone
Phrase D	29–32	The material used in Phrase D comes from lines 8–9; the melody is stated by the flute, oboe, clarinet 1–2, alto and tenor saxophone, trumpet and horn, with accompaniment in all other wind parts
Introduction	33–38	Percussion cadence for snare drum, bass drum, and crash cymbals with variations in rhythm

SECTION	MEASURE	EVENT AND SCORING
Phrase A	39–42	Final statement of Phrase A from lines 1–2; accidentals for melody instruments occur in pick-up notes before measure 39 as a transition into the key of F major; melodic material is scored for flute, oboe, clarinet 1–2, alto and tenor saxophone, trumpet 1–2, and French horn; accompaniment in the wind parts doubles the quarter-note rhythm of the bass drum; off-beats occur in the snare drum part for the first time in the piece
Phrase B	43–46	The return of Phrase B from lines 3–4 includes the addition of rhythmic variation in measure 45 with the addition of eighth notes
Phrase C	47–50	This second statement of Phrase C has the mallet player switching from bells to xylophone; the melody is scored for low pitched instruments including bass clarinet, tenor and baritone saxophone, trombone, euphonium, and tuba
Phrase B	51–56	The final statement of Phrase B from lines 3–4 contains rhythmic augmentation in measures 53–56; as a result, this phrase is extended from four to six measures
Coda	57–66	The coda uses a melodic fragment from Phrase B with rhythmic augmentation to produce the fade-out effect; instrumentation is gradually reduced until the percussion are the only parts left in the final measure; low-pitched wind instrument cues are written in baritone saxophone, trombone, and tuba

References of melodic material from lines in "There Are Many Flags in Many Lands":

Phrase A: Lines 1–2
Phrase B: Lines 3–4
Phrase C: Lines 5–7
Phrase D: Lines 8–9

Unit 8: Suggested Listening

Edwin E. Bagley, *National Emblem*
Frank W. Meacham, *American Patrol*
John Philip Sousa, *Revival March*

Unit 9: Additional References and Resources

Miles, Richard, and Carl Chevallard, eds. *Teaching Music through Performing Marches*. Chicago: GIA Publications, 2003.

Goldman, Richard Franko. The *Golden Age of the American March*. New York: New World Records, 1976.

Contributed by:

Pamela Bowen Bustos
University of Wisconsin-Superior
Superior, Wisconsin

Teacher Resource Guide

Three Renaissance Dances

arranged by John Moss
(b. 1948)

Unit 1: Composer

A native of Benzonia, Michigan, John Moss is an experienced composer and arranger with several hundred published works to his credit. Born in 1948, he completed his undergraduate work in instrumental music at Central Michigan University and studied theory and composition at the graduate level at Michigan State University. He has worked as a public school band and choral director in addition to teaching theory at the university level in the state of Michigan.

Mr. Moss's original music has appeared in several documentary, educational, and promotional films as well as on the concert stage. He has received commissions from many notable ensembles including the Detroit Symphony Pops, the Canadian Brass, and the Detroit Chamber Winds. Many of his most recent commissions have been from school bands and orchestras. His arrangements have been used for musical revues, production shows, and marching band performances. He currently resides in East Lansing, Michigan.[1]

Unit 2: Composition

Three Renaissance Dances was composed in 2003 and is published by Hal Leonard through their MasterWorks series. The publisher lists the work as Grade 2. However, some technical aspects require Grade 3 abilities, such as ties across the barlines and delicate triangle and tambourine rolls. It should be noted that Moss's *Palestrina Suite*, written some three years later,

represents another outstanding arrangement of Renaissance music for young wind band.

The work consists of three very short movements (1:15, 1:14, and 1:13, respectively, totaling 3:42). The first movement, "Basse Danse," is based on a melody of Tielman Susato (ca. 1500–1560), one of the most well-known and prolific composers and publishers of the Renaissance. The second movement, "Volte," presents a dance by Michael Praetorius (1571–1621), a composer who chronologically straddled the time period between the high Renaissance and early Baroque. The third movement, written by an anonymous composer, bears the subtitle "The King's Pavane."

Unit 3: Historical Perspective

The piece is based on three Renaissance dances of very different character. The *basse danse* was the principal court dance of the late Middle Ages and Renaissance. Extremely popular during the fifteenth century, it disappeared after the middle of the sixteenth century.[2] This dance is typically in triple meter.

The *volte* was a dance of French origin that required the couples to dance closely together. It was this distinctive and shocking quality that may have led to its demise around 1610. The music for the volte was commonly written in 6/4, but the dance was usually interpreted as two bars of 3/4.[3] However, the metric accents would shift at times from two groups of three to three groups of two.[4]

The *pavane* was a court dance of the sixteenth and seventeenth centuries widely believed to be of Italian origin. Sedate in nature, it was often used as an introductory, processional dance.[5] The music for the pavane was generally in a duple meter and often contained the signature rhythmic ostinato of quarter note, eighth note, eighth note.

Unit 4: Technical Considerations

Three Renaissance Dances contains modal melodies and harmonic progressions. The first two movements are written in the key of three flats. The third movement has four flats, which may pose challenges to younger musicians. Once students can play the concert E-flat and A-flat major scales, the piece can be used as an excellent teaching tool to introduce modes. Simply have students start their scale patterns on different scale degrees, bearing in mind that some octave adjustments may be necessary, especially in brass.

The first movement is written in 4/4 time with a tempo indication of lively and a pulse of approximately 132 beats per minute. The second movement is marked *andante* in 3/4 time with a pulse of quarter note = 88.

The third movement is written in 2/2 time with a half-note pulse of 76 beats per minute. Conductors might consider beginning this movement by relaxing the tempo and having students think in 4/4 time. Students can then sizzle or clap their parts to solidify the rhythms without the challenge of actually playing the notes on the instrument. If possible, the conductor should eventually beat the movement in two to help maintain the character of the pavane.

Rhythmically, the piece presents only minor challenges. Aside from two sixteenth notes in the second movement, the fastest-moving rhythms are groupings of four eighth notes (slur two/tongue two) at quarter note = 152. The numerous quarter-note ties across the barline that change pitch on the subsequent and of count one are much more challenging to teach. One teaching strategy is to have students replace the sustained note with a tongued eighth note to encourage subdivision. Another is to have the students first clap, then sing, and finally play their part. While the goal is not to sing the exact pitches, students should strive to sing in a directionally accurate manner.

Although intended for young musicians, *Three Renaissance Dances* does present some performance challenges, especially in percussion. Six players are required to cover all of the parts with two players covering multiple instruments, although it is possible to disperse the parts among additional players if desired. A suggested part assignment chart for six players is as follows:

Player	Movement 1	Movement 2	Movement 3
1	snare drum	suspended cymbal	bass drum
2	tenor drum	tenor drum	tenor drum
3	triangle/suspended cymbal	triangle	triangle/ suspended cymbal/ finger cymbals
4	tambourine	tambourine	tambourine
5	bells	bells	bells
6	timpani	timpani	timpani

The tambourine rolls require great delicacy and are best played with the thumb, but this technique may be too advanced for younger players to execute. The player can use a shake roll instead, remembering to start and stop the roll with a tap. Another method, suggested by Professor Dennis Fisher who recorded the work, is to lay the tambourine flat on the table and perform a hand roll. The written dynamic changes can be accomplished by adjusting the position of the tambourine from head level (louder dynamics) to the waist (softer dynamics). In movement two, measures 9 and 10, the tambourine has staccato indications. The player may wish to dead stroke these notes by tapping the tambourine and then holding the hand or palm down on the head. Note that the tie into the roll in measure 9 is a misprint in the score and part.

If assigned to a single musician, the triangle/suspended cymbal/finger cymbal part requires the player to make quick changes between instruments; it also calls for triangle rolls at various dynamics. To execute these rolls, the young player can hold the beater vertically, place it inside one of the bottom corners of the triangle, and quickly move the hand back and forth. The angle of the beater will generate a very reasonable sounding roll. Generally, the player should hold the triangle with the hand to allow for the best possible projection and dampening capabilities. The triangle should be suspended from a stand only when the player has to move quickly between instruments.

The timpani part requires the pitches B-flat2 and E-flat3 for the first two movements and C3 and F3 for the third. If the player is skilled at tuning and the ensemble breaks between the second and third movements, the conductor may let the player tune the drums in performance. Another solution would be to use four timpani tuned accordingly: 20" at F3, 23" at E-flat3, 26" at C3, 29" at B-flat2. Remind the player that all four drums will ring sympathetically and to sure to dampen each drum after every gesture or place a timpani mute on the two drums that are not in use. Also, the conductor may wish to double check that the timpanist plays both open and single-stroked rolls.

The instrumentation of the piece calls for single flute, oboe, bassoon, horn, and trombone parts. The clarinet, alto saxophone, and trumpet each have two parts, although much of the trumpet writing is in unison. In an ensemble with several flute players, the conductor may consider assigning the majority of the players to the oboe part, which doubles the flute an octave lower throughout the entire piece. Note also the flute divisi in measure 33 of movement three.

The written ranges are modest on all instruments. Except for two occurrences of E-flat6, the flute range is quite limited, encompassing only a minor seventh, from D5 to C6. The written notes of the first clarinet stay within the treble staff throughout. While the difficulty of the clarinet part is limited in regards to range, the large number of throat-tone notes that are difficult to play in-tune and with satisfying tone quality. Dropping the right hand will almost certainly improve the tone quality and may help the pitch if these notes are sharp. The upper brass ranges are conservative with the highest written notes in trumpet and horn as D5 and C5, respectively.

From the standpoint of intonation, the written key signatures create mostly favorable pitches on each instrument. Some notable exceptions are as follows:

The written pitches in the French horn part straddle the range of notes

Instrument	Pitch(es)	Tendency	Possible Solution
clarinet	throat tones	sharp or flat	If G, G-sharp, A-flat and A are sharp, add the right hand.
alto saxophone	C-sharp5	very flat	Use the middle right hand side key or the first and third right hand side key or the octave key and third finger of the left hand.
trumpet	D5	flat	Use first and third valves (which will be sharp) and trigger the third valve slide out.
euphonium	C3	very sharp	Use fourth valve if possible.

typically played on the F side (F-sharp3 to G4) and B-flat side (pitches above G4).[6] The talented student with a double horn can learn the fingerings on both sides of the horn and then use whichever side is more in-tune for each particular note.

The piece provides many outstanding opportunities for students to develop their ability to tune major and minor chords. The conductor may wish to focus on certain chords in the warm-up and explain some or all of the following concepts relative to chordal tuning:

- Poor tone quality, blend, and balance all contribute to a chord sounding out of tune.

- When balancing a major or minor chord, generally, the root should be the loudest sounding note, followed by the fifth, then the major or minor third.

- Major thirds should be adjusted fourteen cents flat and minor thirds should be played sixteen cents sharp. If time or other factors do not allow for an explanation of cents, students can be told to play their major thirds slightly lower and their minor thirds slightly higher.

- If possible, students should identify which part of the chord they are playing and how they fit into the sound of the chord. For advanced ensembles, inverting the chord and listening to the color and balance change is extremely useful for teaching chordal tuning.

- Students should follow a three-step process for adjusting out-of-tune chords: (1) assume that you are the person who is out of tune (no small feat!); (2) play slightly softer and listen to the lowest-sounding instrument for pitch center; (3) make some kind of adjustment to try and make the pitch more in tune. Remind students that conductors do not always guess correctly when adjusting pitches. This may make them more willing to take chances when attempting to correct pitch.

Unit 5: Stylistic Considerations

When performing *Three Renaissance Dances*, the style of the original dance music must be considered. The piece requires players to play slurred, lightly tongued, staccato, legato and accented. Slur two/tongue two gestures are frequent in the first and third movements. Encourage players to shorten the second note to put some space on either side of the tongued notes. Students are likely to rush this figure; have the accompaniment players subdivide their long notes with steadily tongued eighth notes, and have those with the eighth notes tongue all four notes at first. Once students understand the need for subdivision and how their part works they can change back to their original part. Create warm-up exercises to teach slur two/tongue two patterns in the key of three and four flats, and have students think of the written accents as slightly weighted. Make sure that students are generating the accent primarily with breath rather than a hard tongue.

The dynamic capabilities of Renaissance instruments were more modest than modern instruments; therfore, dynamics should be somewhat reserved. With the exception of a single *piano* in movement two, the dynamics range from *mezzo piano* to *forte*, with a majority of the dynamics lying in the *mezzo* range. Make sure that the ensemble's *forte* is warm and blended. Bells should be played lightly with plastic mallets to balance the melody.

From the standpoint of phrasing, teaching opportunities abound in this piece. An excellent example of a balanced four plus four phrase is the A theme of movement three, while the B theme of movement two is an example of unbalanced or uneven phrasing. The conductor may wish to engage students in a discussion about how phrase lengths affect breathing. Since many young musicians breathe more often than is necessary, consider using a tutti section, perhaps measure 11 of movement two, to implement the following teaching strategy. Ask students to begin playing and to simply stop when they have run out of air. Students love the challenge of this "last person standing" game and tend to take deeper breaths and use their air more effectively.

Unit 6: Musical Elements

MELODY

The range of each of the melodies is very modest, staying within a major sixth in all movements. The melodies are primarily diatonic with accidentals appearing only to create leading-tone motion into cadence points (i.e., E-flats are often raised to E-natural just before an F major chord). Each melody hints at modality, but eventually resolves to either the major key represented in the key signature or its relative minor.

HARMONY:

The harmony throughout the piece is primarily modal. The recurring use of the lowered seventh scale degree in the first movement produces the borrowed chords of D-flat major and B-flat minor, which strengthen the modal feeling of the music. In the third movement, the F-minor tonality is strengthened by the use of the major V chord, C major. Suspension/resolution gestures abound, especially at cadence points. Make sure that the resolution note in 4–3 suspensions is lowered and soft enough to balance in the major chords.

RHYTHM:

The shifting metric feel of the volte, indicated with dotted lines within the measure, is an excellent example of hemiola. The dominant rhythmic challenge for young musicians is likely to be the recurring ties across the barlines (note the suggested teaching strategy described above).

TIMBRE:

In the Renaissance era, musical variety was usually not created by melodic or harmonic manipulation, but rather by alternating different choirs of sounds (high/low, loud/soft). In *Three Renaissance Dances*, Moss faithfully reproduces this important hallmark of the period by frequently alternating between woodwind, brass, and tutti colors. The most thinly scored section of the piece is the opening of the second movement, during which the flutes play unaccompanied.

Unit 7: Form and Structure

SECTION	MEASURE (PHRASING)	EVENT AND SCORING

Movement I: "Basse Danse"

Introduction	1–4 [4]	Key of three flats; percussion only; timpani B-flat/E-flat gives strong indication of dominant/tonic motion in E-flat major; strong duple feel
A	5–16 [12:3+3+3+3]	Written in 4/4 time but felt in three; the first three subphrases hint at G phrygian and D locrian while the final phrase cadences in E-flat major; harmony uses D-flat major chord frequently to "hide" leading tone motion of D to E-flat; scoring is nearly tutti for entire section
B	17–28 [12:3+3+3+3]	Shifting tonal centers; shifting tonal centeres; first subphrase closes in B-flat major with the melody providing the leading tone motion of A-natural to B-flat; second subphrase closes on F major with the melody providing leading tone motion, E to F, in that tonal center; third phrase is identical to the first; final phrase is identical to the final phrase of A theme, firmaly establishing E-flat major; shifting choirs of sound (brass-woodwind-brass-woodwind) on successive statements

427

Section	Measure (Phrasing)	Event and Scoring
B	17–33 [13:3+3+3+4]	Repeat of B theme with second ending; fourth subphrase presented in augmentation with full ensemble; final chord contains more thirds than fifths, which may make balance and tuning a challenge

Movement II: "Volte"

Section	Measure (Phrasing)	Event and Scoring
A	1–8 [8:4+4]	Key of three flats; melody strongly implies B-flat mixolydian; the only sixteenth notes of the piece occur in measure 3; movement opens with unison flutes in 3/4 time; in measures 3 and 4, the metric feel shifts to 2/4 but the written meter remains unchanged
A	1–10 [8:4+4]	Repeat of A theme with second ending; instruments added are oboe doubling the melody, clarinets providing harmony, and percussion providing color; section closes in E-flat major
B	11–20 [10:3+7]	First of two statements of the B theme; scored for middle and lower woodwinds, triangle, suspended cymbal, and tambourine; melody in unison between first clarinet and first trumpet; both melody and harmony hint at B-flat mixolydian until the final two measures which clearly establish E-flat major
B	11–22 [10:3+7]	Second statement of B theme with full ensemble; with the exception of the clarinets, the chord is scored exactly the same as final chord of movement one

SECTION	MEASURE (PHRASING)	EVENT AND SCORING
Movement III: "The King's Pavane"		
Introduction	1–4 [4:2+2]	Key of four flats; tambourine provides characteristic pavane ostinato rhythm of quarter note, eighth note, eighth note
A	5–12 [8:4+4]	Melody stated in first trumpet, harmonized by second trumpet and trombone; tonal center of F minor E-natural pitches create C major chords, strengthening the F minor tonality; upper woodwinds, tuba are tacet
A	13–20 [8:4+4]	Second statement of A theme with full instrumentation
B	21–28 [8:4+4]	Shift to A-flat major tonal center; first subphrase closes on E-flat, second on C major
B'	29–36 [8:4+4]	C major chord leads to D-flat major, the IV chord of A-flat major
B'	29–40 [10:4+6]	Second statement of B' theme with added countermelody in upper woodwinds; melody is augmented in last three measures and piece ends with a Picardy third, in F major

Unit 8: Suggested Listening

Wind band:
Thoinot Arbeau/Margolis, *Belle Qui Tiens Ma Vie*
Mark Camphouse, *Canzon, Fugato, and Hymn*
Norman Dello Joio, *Scenes from the Louvre*
Girolamo Frescobaldi/Slocum, *Toccata*
Kenneth Hesketh, *Danceries*
Gordon Jacob, *William Byrd Suite*
Robert Jager, *Colonial Airs and Dances*

William Latham, *Court Festival*
Bob Margolis:
 Fanfare, Ode and Festival
 Palestrina Suite
 Royal Coronation Dances
 Terpsichore
 The Renaissance Faire
Ron Nelson, *Courtly Airs and Dances*
Francis Poulenc, *Suite Francaise*
Mark Scatterday, *Renaissance Set I*
Tielman Susato/Dunningan, *Selections from "The Danserye"*
Tielman Susato/Margolis, *The Battle Pavane*
Fisher Tull, *Sketches on a Tudor Psalm*

Orchestra/Opera:
Benjamin Britten, *Gloriana*
Claudio Monteverdi, *Orfeo*
Ralph Vaughan Williams, *Fantasia on a Theme of Thomas Tallis*
Peter Warlock, *Capriol Suite*

Unit 9: Additional References and Resources

Blankenburg, Walter, and Clytus Gottwald. "Praetorius, Michael: Bibliography." *Grove Music Online* (2007), http://ezproxy.gsu.edu:2188/shared/views/article.html?section=music.222 53.8 (accessed May 5, 2007).

Brown, Alan. "Pavan." *Grove Music Online* (2007), http://ezproxy.gsu.edu:2188/shared/views/article.html?section=music.21120 (accessed May 5, 2007).

Colwell, Richard J., and Thomas Goolsby. *The Teaching of Instrumental Music*, 2nd ed. Englewood Cliffs, NJ: Prentice Hall, 1992.

Donnington, Robert. "Volta (i)." *Grove Music Online* (2007), http://ezproxy.gsu.edu:2188/shared/views/article.html?section=music.296 57 (accessed May 5, 2007).

Fabrizio, Al "Corky." *A Guide to Understanding and Correction of Intonation Problems*. Ft. Lauderdale, FL: Meredith Music, 1994.

Forney, Kristine. "Susato, Tylman: Bibliography." *Grove Music Online* (2007),http://ezproxy.gsu.edu:2188/shared/views/article.html?section= music.27146.3 (accessed May 5, 2007).

Hal Leonard Corporation, "Writer Profiles: John Moss," Hal Leonard Corporation, http://www.halleonard.com/biographyDisplay.jsp?id=165& location=BandOrchestra&subsite=subsite_band (accessed May 28, 2007).

Heartz, Daniel. "Basse danse." *Grove Music Online* (2007), http://ezproxy.gsu.edu:2188/shared/views/article.html?section=music.0224 2 (accessed May 5, 2007).

Library of Congress Music Division, "An American Ballroom Companion: Dance Instruction Manuals ca. 1490–1920," Library of Congress, http://memory.loc.gov/ammem/dihtml/diessay0.html (accessed May 29, 2007).

Montagu, Jeremy. *Timpani and Percussion*. New Haven, CT: Yale University Press, 2002.

Moss, John. *Three Renaissance Dances*. Milwaukee, WI: Hal Leonard, 2003.

Randel, Don. *The New Harvard Dictionary of Music*. Cambridge, MA: Harvard University Press, 1986.

1   Hal Leonard Corporation, "Writer Profiles: John Moss," Hal Leonard Corporation, http://www.halleonard.com/biographyDisplay.jsp?id=165&location=BandOrchestra&subsite=sub- site_band.
2   Daniel Heartz. "Basse danse," Grove Music Online (2007), http://ezproxy.gsu.edu:2188/shared/views/article.html?section=music.02242.
3   Robert Donnington. "Volta (i)," Grove Music Online (2007), http://ezproxy.gsu.edu:2188/shared/views/article.html?section=music.29657.
4   The program notes located in the score erroneously state that in the volta there are "occasional rhythmic shiftings from 1–2–3 1–2–3 to 1–2–3 1–2–3 . . ." It should read "1–2–3 1–2–3 to 1–2 1–2 1–2."
5   Alan Brown. "Pavan," Grove Music Online (2007), http://ezproxy.gsu.edu:2188/shared/views/arti- cle.html?section=music.21120.
6   The author recognizes that there are different schools of thought relative to where one should switch from the F to B-flat side of the French horn.

Contributed by:

Robert J. Ambrose
Director of Wind Studies and Ensembles
Associate Director, School of Music
Georgia State University
Atlanta, Georgia

Teacher Resource Guide

Two Appalachian Songs

arranged by Michael Story
(b. 1956)

Unit 1: Composer

Michael Story was born on April 27, 1956, in Philadelphia, Pennsylvania. He studied at the University of Houston, where he received bachelor of music and master of music degrees. After serving as assistant director of the Cougar Marching Band at the University of Houston from 1979–1981, he decided to devote his full attention to composing and arranging. Story has over 1,200 original works and arrangements in print for concert band, marching band, jazz ensemble, and orchestra, along with numerous solo books. Many of his compositions have been selected for state band contest lists. Michael Story has written extensively for college, high school, junior high school, and elementary school bands as well as for professional ensembles, including the Houston Pops Orchestra. Most of his works are published by Alfred Publishing Company, Incorporated, owner of CPP/Belwin, Warner Brothers (formerly Columbia Pictures Publications. A versatile writer and current editor for Alfred (Belwin), he is adept at focusing on the needs of the developing band. His works for young or inexperienced concert and marching bands, such as his *Big and Easy* marching band series, is designed to accommodate uneven instrumentation while maintaining a full band sound. Michael Story works regularly with school bands in Texas, and presents band workshops throughout the country. Although a young composer, he is already known as a dynamic and prolific writer and has been an industry leader for over 30 years. Mr. Story is also a composer/arranger/author with the *Expressions Music Curriculum*, the first-ever comprehensive K–12 music program. Michael Story currently resides is Houston, Texas with his wife and three children.

Unit 2: Composition

Two Appalachian Songs contains a pair of American folk songs in contrasting styles and settings. Written in 2005, the work contains two movements, "Once I Had a Sweetheart," and "Cindy." The first movement is very lyrical and provides ample opportunity for phrasing and musicality. The second movement is dance-like and incorporates several stylistic markings. Together, these movements provide a great contrast. This is the primary reason Mr. Story chose these particular works to arrange for beginning band. He enjoys folk music from different countries for its emotional content and ability to tell the story of its people. He is constantly searching for hidden gems among the folk genre to arrange for band.

Unit 3: Historical Perspective

The Appalachian mountain system runs parallel with the eastern seaboard of the North American continent and lies about 250 miles inland and includes the states of North Carolina, Tennessee, Virginia, and Kentucky. The inhabitants of these mountains are mainly of British descent—English, Scots, and Scot-Irish, their ancestors having left their native shores more than two hundred years ago. The people lived in primitive log cabins dotted along the banks of the rivers. They were nearly self-supporting, building their own log cabins, spinning and weaving the wool for their clothes and growing their own food. Their living was not luxurious, but they had leisure and they prized more than material comfort and possessions. Singing was a part of their every day life. People sang for their own enjoyment or for that of their immediate circle of friends and family.

The first movement of *Two Appalachian Songs* entitled "Once I Had a Sweetheart" was originally published in 1729 in Wright's *Compleat Tutor for Ye Flute* under the title of "Once I Had a True Love." The original composer of this work is unknown. This tune and another are given in Sedley's *The Seeds of Love*, published in 1967. Three texts grouped under the title "Red, White, and Blue" in the *Frank C. Brown Collection of North Carolina Folklore*, contain the theme "Once I Had a Sweetheart." The second of these texts, actually entitled "I Once Had a Sweetheart," supplied by Margaret Barlowe, a student at Appalachian Training College (now Appalachian State University), Boone, North Carolina, begins with this verse:

> I once had a sweetheart, but now I have none
> He's gone and left me and left me alone,
> But since he has left me, contented I'll be,
> He is loving another girl better than me.

These three texts dwell more on the inconstancy of men and less on the depth of the girl's sorrow, than the text stemming from the other tradition which follows:

> Once I had a sweetheart
> And now I have none,
> He's gone and left me
> To sorrow and moan.
>
> Last night in sweet slumber
> I dreamed I did see
> My own precious jewel
> Sat smiling at me.
>
> And when I awakened
> And found it not so,
> My eyes like some fountain
> With tears overflowed.
>
> I'll venture through England,
> Through France and to Spain;
> All my life I'll venture
> The watery main.

The second movement, "Cindy," a traditional 1800's banjo minstrel, reveals a story about a spunky and mischievous girl named Cindy. The composer of this work is unknown. The text of the song is as follows:

> You ought to see my Cindy,
> She lives a-way down south,
> And she's so sweet the honey bees
> All swarm around her mouth.
>
> Get along home, Cindy, Cindy,
> Get along home, Cindy, Cindy,
> Get along home, Cindy, Cindy,
> I'll marry you someday.
>
> The first time that I saw her
> She was standin' in the door,
> Her shoes and stockings in her hand,
> Her feet all over the floor.

Chorus

I wish I was an apple
A-hangin' in a tree,
And every time Cindy passed,
She'd take a bite of me.

Chorus

Unit 4: Technical Considerations

"Once I Had a Sweetheart" contains no great technical demands as it is a Grade 1 composition. Written in common time with a tempo marking of quarter note = 108, the entire movement is in D-natural minor. Legato playing from the entire ensemble is necessary to achieve the desired musical effect. In the dance-like "Cindy," also a Grade 1 composition, there are several rearticulated notes throughout in nearly every part. Written in common time, the tempo is marked at quarter note = 112, and the articulations need to be consistently clear and clean. The work begins with a pyramid effect which lasts for one bar. An interesting countermelody is found in the second statement of theme one in the horns and alto saxophones. Proper balance will need to be adhered to for this scoring to be effective. Although primarily in B-flat major, there are some accidentals in the countermelodic lines.

Unit 5: Stylistic Considerations

Throughout "Once I Had a Sweetheart," slurs and legato playing are incorporated. The entire movement is felt in a cantabile style and the expression and phrase potential is great. In the program notes on the score, Mr. Story indicates that adherence to the numerous articulations in "Cindy" is necessary for a musical performance. Even though there are a number of accented notes, a light style should be maintained throughout. The score is very clear about these contrasting articulations. There are also many subito dynamic contrasts throughout "Cindy" providing even more contrast from the linear first movement.

Unit 6: Musical Elements

Because of the linearity of the first movement, a great deal of expression and phrasing can occur. With the detailed stylistic markings of the second movement, it should be performed in a very light manner so the accented notes can dance out of the texture.

MELODY:

From measures 5–12 in "Once I Had a Sweetheart," the lush melody is given to the clarinets, which never play over the break. From measures 13–20, the trumpets have the melody in a very comfortable range from D4 to C5. The melody is always smooth and is often slurred. The melody in "Cindy" is first given to the clarinets from measures 3–6. From measures 7–11, the melody is found in the flutes, oboes, and clarinets. From measures 11–14, the trumpets and alto saxophones join the woodwinds with the melody. From measures 15–18, the flutes, oboes, and clarinets again share the melodic line. There is a very nice countermelody in "Cindy" scored in the alto saxophones and horns from measures 7–9 and 15–17 that adds yet another layer of interest.

HARMONY:

The harmony is treated in a linear fashion in both movements. Great independence of line is achieved by not having multiple parts in each instrument family. Greater detailed listening is achieved because each instrument family is playing the same part.

RHYTHM:

The rhythms used include whole notes, dotted half notes, half notes, quarter notes and eighth notes, along with the reciprocal rests. There are no rhythmic difficulties in either movement.

TIMBRE:

The timbre of "Once I Had a Sweetheart" is dark and sorrowful. The key of D-natural minor provides a rich pallet to sculpt meaningful phrases. The timbre of "Cindy" is very bright and light set in B-flat major in great contrast to the first movement.

Unit 7: Form and Structure

"Once I Had a Sweetheart" – entirely in D-natural minor

SECTION	MEASURE	EVENT AND SCORING
Intro	1–4	Introduction; flutes and bells with moving lines accompanied by alto saxophones; linear drones played by the low saxophones and low brass

SECTION	MEASURE	EVENT AND SCORING
A	5–8	Theme 1 stated by the clarinets accompanied by full ensemble playing whole and half notes
A	9–12	Theme 1 restated as above
B	13–16	Theme 2 stated by the trumpets with full ensemble accompaniment; counter-melody in flutes, oboes, clarinets, alto saxophones, and horns
B'	17–19	Theme 2 restated with a more thinly scored accompaniment incorporating tenor and baritone saxophones and low brass
Coda	20–24	Coda based on introductory material serving as a quasi recapitulation

"Cindy" – entirely in B-flat major

Intro	1–2	Introduction featuring an ascending pyramid effect; full ensemble; snare drum and bass drum
A	3–6	Theme 1 with melody in the clarinets; staccato accompaniment in the bass clarinet, tenor and baritone saxophone, low brass, and tambourine
A'	7–10	Theme 1' with the melody shared by the flutes, oboes, and clarinets; counter-melody shared by alto saxophones and horns; staccato quarter note accompaniment continues in bass clarinet, low saxophones, and low brass; woodblock is added
B	11–14	Theme 2 with melody in the trumpets, flutes, and oboes along with melodic fragments shared by the clarinets and bells; full ensemble; snare drum and bass drum are added (4 percussion parts)
B'	15–18	Theme 2' varied with countermelody in the alto saxophones and horns; full ensemble (5 percussion parts)
Tag Ending	19–20	Tag ending; variation of the introductory material

Unit 8: Suggested Listening

Michael Story:
- *Ayrshire Portrait* (Grade 1)
- *Between Wind and Water* (Grade 1)
- *Blue Mountain Legend* (Grade 2)
- *Land of the Rising Sun* (Grade 2)
- *Three American Sketches* (Grade 2)
- *'Twas in the Moon of Wintertime* (Grade 1)
- *Udala'm* (Grade 1)

Unit 9: Additional References and Resources

Alfred Publishing Company, *Michael Story*, 25 May 2007 http://www.alfred-publishing.com, (25 May 2007).

Folk Music Society, home page, 25 May 2007, http://www.lvfolkmusicsociety.org/cdsonglist.html, (25 May, 2007).

KIDiddles Song Lyrics, home page, 25 May 2007, http://www.kididdles.com/lyrics/c003.html, (25 May 2007).

Miles, Richard, ed. *Teaching Music through Performance in Band*, Vol. 4. Chicago: GIA Publications, 2002.

Rehrig, William H. *The Heritage Encyclopedia of Band Music*. Westerville, OH: Integrity Press, 1996.

Sandii Castleberry, "Acoustic Country and Bluegrass Bands," http://www.sandiicastleberry.com/Lyrics1.html, 25 May 2007.

Sharpe, Cecil, and Maud Karpeles. *Eighty Appalachian Folk Songs*. Winchester, MA: Faber Music Limited, 1968.

Smith, Norman E. *Program Notes for Band*. Chicago: GIA Publications, 2002.

Smith, Ralph Lee, and Pat Kuchwara. *More Dulcimer Old Time and Traditional Music*. Troubadour Music, Inc., 1975.

Story, Michael. Telephone interview by John Stanley Ross, May 31, 2007.

Story, Michael. *Two Appalachian Songs*. Miami, FL: Belwin-Mills, 2005.

The Lied and Art Song Texts Page, *Texts and Translations to Lieder*, 25 May 2007, http://www.recmusic.org/lieder/get_text.html, (25 May 2007).

Contributed by:

John Stanley Ross
Director of Bands
Appalachian State University
Boone, North Carolina

Teacher Resource Guide

Two Dances from "Capriol Suite"

Peter Warlock
(1894–1930)

arranged by Johnnie Vinson
(b. 1944)

Unit 1: Composer

Peter Warlock was a pseudonym for English composer, critic, and musicologist Philip Arnold Heseltine. Primarily a self-taught musician, Warlock briefly attended both Eton College and the University of London. After a short but artistically prolific period living in Ireland, Warlock returned to England and worked as the editor of the controversial magazine, *The Sackbut*. Upon being relieved of his editorial duties, Warlock returned to his hometown of Wales and eventually settled in Eynsford in 1925. From 1925 to 1929 Warlock lived a notorious lifestyle in which he had many run-ins with the local police. It was during this period that Warlock wrote *Capriol*, perhaps his best-known work. After struggling with fits of depression, Warlock died of gas poisoning at the age of thirty-six.

Unlike his British contemporaries Gustav Holst and Ralph Vaughan Williams, Warlock's primary output consisted of small-scale works such as songs with piano accompaniment. He was also a distinguished editor and transcriber of early music, with more than 570 published items. A prolific author and critic, Warlock wrote nine books, seventy-three articles, and fifty-one critical reviews.[1]

Capriol was arranged for young band by Johnnie Vinson. Vinson is the director of bands and professor of music emeritus at Auburn University in

Auburn, Alabama. He received the bachelor of science and master of education degrees from Auburn University and the doctor of arts degree in music theory from the University of Mississippi. Dr. Vinson is internationally recognized as an arranger and composer of music for bands with more than 350 works published primarily through the Hal Leonard Corporation. He has served as an adjudicator and clinician throughout the United States.

Unit 2: Composition

Peter Warlock first composed *Capriol* for piano duet in October 1926 and later arranged the piece for strings. Although there is also a full-orchestra arrangement, the string version is the most commonly played and recognized. The suite in its original form is six movements long and loosely based on melodies drawn from the dance treatise *Orchésographie* by Thoinot Arbeau (1520–1595). Vinson used shortened forms of the first and last movements in his band arrangement, using the string orchestra version as a reference.[2]

The first movement is forty-four measures long and the second movement is fifty-two measures. Performance time is approximately two minutes and twenty-two seconds. The arranger states that, although the score is labeled as Grade 1, he considers the piece to be slightly more advanced because the first clarinets play across the break.[3]

Unit 3: Historical Perspective

Capriol is loosely based on melodies that were present in Thoinot Arbeau's 1588 treatise on dance, *Orchésographie*. Thoinot Arbeau was the anagrammatic pen name of Jehan Tabourot, a sixteenth-century French cleric and author. Arbeau believed in the positive nature of dance and saw dance not only as a means for physical health, but also as an integral part of courtship. He wrote *Orchésographie* in the form of a dialogue between himself and a lawyer named Capriol (hence the name of Warlock's composition). In the text, Arbeau details most of the French social dance types of the period using his own dance tablature. His correlation of dance steps with popular music of the day is more precise than many sources from the sixteenth century.

Orchésographie is available in an English translation by Mary Stewart Evans through Dover publications. It contains detailed instructions as well as sketches of both dances used in Vinson's arrangement of *Capriol*: the Basse-Dance and the Mattachins (sword dance). Musical examples are also shown to help illustrate dances. These instructions can be used to teach the context of sixteenth-century music. Consider having someone demonstrate the dances, or have students learn the dances themselves to better realize the style of the music.

Dr. Vinson provides the following about the two movements used in his arrangement:

Basse-Danse – This dance was stately, and the feet were not raised but glided over the floor, hence the name. Warlock's music follows Arbeau exactly, but each repetition is harmonized and/or orchestrated differently.

Mattachins – The first half of the movement sets one of Arbeau's variants of the *Air des Bouffons*. Near the end are a series of discordant clashes which sound more like Bartók than a composer of English birth. (Warlock knew Bartók well, and admired his music.) Mattachins was a sword dance, and as such was very noisy!

Unit 4: Technical Considerations

Two Dances from "Capriol Suite" is a mature Grade 1 composition. It is scored for a young concert band: Flute, oboe (optional), B-flat clarinet 1/2, B-flat bass clarinet, bassoon, alto saxophone, tenor saxophone, baritone saxophone, B-flat trumpet 1/2, french horn (optional), trombone, euphonium, and tuba. The tenor and bass instruments are written in unison/octaves so that the bass line can be covered by any of these instruments, making the work more accessible to bands with incomplete instrumentation. Percussion is separated into three parts and includes: bells, snare drum (with snares off throughout), bass drum, tambourine, and triangle. Five percussionists are required to play all parts, although the arranger states that the parts were composed and added primarily to involve those players. The arrangement could be performed successfully without percussion.

The tonal centers are D Aeolian in the first movement and E-flat major in the second movement. All sections are required to play eighth-note rhythms in these scales. The brief dissonant sections are ideal for teaching non-tonal harmony to young students.

The movements remain in 3/4 and 2/4 throughout, with two measures of syncopation at the end of the second movement. Rhythms consist of quarter-note and two eighth-note combinations throughout the entire piece.

The first clarinets cross the break while playing melodic eighth-note patterns in both movements; clarinet two has less rhythmic responsibility and does not cross the break.

Range considerations include: C6 in flute one, F5 in clarinet one, D4 in alto saxophone, and D5 in trumpet one (this is always doubled in the flute or clarinet part).

Unit 5: Stylistic Considerations

The style of *Capriol* reflects Renaissance dance music. The melodic line should dominate throughout and the articulations should be lifted, not heavy.

Observe the articulations provided by the arranger to help the ensemble with stylistic unity. Use the example of strings bowing to give students a good visual demonstration of proper articulations.

Incorporating the articulations found in the piece into daily warm-ups will also help students grasp the style of the piece. Have the ensemble play a warm-up scale playing the rhythm of the first two bars in movement two on each note of the scale. Play the warm-up at the same tempo that they play the movement to help stabilize the tempo.

Play recordings of the string arrangement to give students a better understanding of the style of the piece. Suggested recordings are listed in Unit 8 of this resource guide.

Unit 6: Musical Elements

MELODY:

The melodies and basic structures are very similar to those printed in Arbeau's *Orchésographie*. The melody of the Mattachins is based on *Air des Bouffons*. All melodies are set up in eight-bar phrases and remain within the diatonic structure of the work with some chromatic alterations. The lower voices play contrapuntal lines in both movements. The quasi-drone and drum rhythm at the beginning of the Mattachins is derived from the melodic material of both movements.

HARMONY:

The first movement is harmonized in D Aeolian. The dissonance in measures 20 and 36 caused by the C-natural in the alto saxophone and horn are purposeful. Warlock chose to add the melodic dissonance and published it in his three separate arrangements of the piece. It would help to make students aware of the dissonance so that they do not mistake it as a wrong note.

The second movement is centered around E-flat major. The clashing of swords is represented in measures 45 through 50 when both the minor and major thirds of the chord are played simultaneously. Isolate the G-flat in the flute, oboe, and clarinet one to help players understand the dissonance. Have the ensemble play first without these groups, then have them join so that they hear how they fit into the chord. This also helps to balance the dissonance. Warlock's distinctive harmonic language is present throughout the suite and is an excellent tool for teaching young students about dissonant harmonies.

RHYTHM:

The first movement is in 3/4 time and the second movement is in 2/4 time. Players need to be able to play eighth-note rhythms at an allegro tempo. The tempo markings are given only as suggestions for younger players and are slower than performance practice standards. The arranger states that if the players are capable, the tempos should be taken much faster. Typical tempi for the string arrangement are quarter = 140–160 in the first movement and quarter = 160–180 in the second movement; the ensemble's ability level will dictate a suitable tempo.

The hemiola at the end of the first movement is emphasized by the accent mark on beat two of measure 38. Hemiolas are a distinguishing feature of some French folk dances and were typically used to create rhythmic variety at the ends of dances.

The syncopated rhythm in measures 49 and 50 of the second movement could confuse younger players. Incorporate these rhythms into daily warm-up routines (e.g., scales) to help students master and understand these rhythms.

TIMBRE:
The timbre is melodically driven. Instruments play in different groups and should try to match the tone color of the group in which they are playing. Be sure that students are aware of the other sections. The percussion should never be overbearing, but it should support the melodic lines.

Unit 7: Form and Structure

"Basse-Danse" is in binary form with a shortened statement of the A and B sections when they return at the end. Although the melodies remain the same, the harmonies change with each statement.

SECTION	MEASURE	EVENT AND SCORING
Movement I		
A	1–8	D Aeolian is the tonal center; clarinet 1 and alto saxophone play the melody
	9–16	Alto saxophone plays the repeat of the melody; this statement is harmonized differently than the first eight bars
B	17–24	The B theme is presented in the trumpets; clarinets, saxophones, and low voices answer in measure 18 in counterpoint; the melodic C-natural in alto saxophone and horn is a purposeful dissonance

SECTION	MEASURE	EVENT AND SCORING
A	25–32	A single *fortissimo* statement of the A section is given with the flute, oboe, and trumpet playing the melody; the lower voices are more active and the harmonies progress more quickly; auxiliary percussion enters at the recapitulation and signifies that the movement is coming to an end
B	33–40	the B theme is also shortened to a single statement and the counterpoint from the first statement returns; the dissonant C-natural is repeated in the alto saxophone and horn; the accent on beat two of measure 38 emphasizes the hemiola feel at the end of this section
Coda	41–44	Measures 41 and 42 are harmonically driven and there is one final statement of the counterpoint melody; the accents in the final two bars should be weighted but shorter than other accents in the movement
Movement II Introduction	1–4	The brief introductory rhythm stated in open fifths is derived from the melodic rhythm of both movements
A	5–12	The clarinet and trumpet melody in this section should be brisk and short; observe the written slurs and staccato articulations to assist with some of the technical difficulties the students may have
B	13–20	Clarinet 1 and trumpet 1 again state the melody; be sure that the countermelody eighth notes on beat two of measure 16 do not get lost in the texture

SECTION	MEASURE	EVENT AND SCORING
B	21–28	The repeat of the B section is characterized by the dynamic contrast the *piano* dynamic in measure 21 should be *subito*; be sure that students maintain the short articulations, even at different dynamic levels
A	29–36	A tutti statement of the A section is given at *forte*; students should not play too strongly as this is not the dynamic peak of the work
B	37–44	The full ensemble plays the third statement of the B section; the style of this section should still be light even when the dynamics reach *forte* and *fortissimo*
Coda	45–52	The ensemble plays an E-flat chord with both a minor and major third stated in the flute, oboe, clarinet 1, and trumpet 1; the dissonance represents the clashing of the swords at the end of the sword dance; be sure that students understand the dissonance so they can balance the chord evenly

Unit 8: Suggested Listening

Gordon Jacob (after William Byrd), *William Byrd Suite*.
    On *Altered States* by the North Texas Wind Symphony (GIA, CD-685)
Bob Margolis (after Claude Gervaise), *Fanfare, Ode and Festival*.
    On Resource Recording *Teaching Music through Performance in Band*, Volume 2, Grades 2 and 3, by the North Texas Wind Symphony (GIA, CD-446)
Bob Margolis (after Tielman Susato), *Soldier's Procession and Sword Dance*.
    On Resource Recording *Teaching Music through Performance in Band*, Volume 1, Grades 2 and 3, by the North Texas Wind Symphony (GIA, CD-418)
Tielman Susato, arranged by Patrick Dunnigan, *Selections from "The Danserye."* On 2003 WASBE featuring the Florida State University Wind Orchestra (Mark Custom Records, MCD-4737)

Peter Warlock, *Capriol*. On *English Music for Strings* by the Guildhall String Ensemble (RCA Victor, 7761–2-RC)

Unit 9: Additional References and Resources

Arbeau, Thoinot. *Orchésography*. Translated by Mary Stewart Evans. New York: Dover Publications, Inc., 1967.

Collins, Brian. *Peter Warlock: The Composer*. Brookfield, VT: Ashgate Publishing Company, 1996.

Copley, I. A. *The Music of Peter Warlock: A Critical Survey*. London: Dobson Books Ltd, 1979.

Kitelinger, Shannon. E-mail interview with Johnnie Vinson. June 2007.

Rushton, Julian. "Hemiola." In *Grove Music Online*, ed. L. Macy. New York: Oxford University Press, 2007. http://www.grovemusic.com (accessed June 5, 2007).

Smith, Barry. "Peter Warlock." In *Grove Music Online*, ed. L. Macy. New York: Oxford University Press, 2007. http://www.grovemusic.com (accessed June 5, 2007).

Sutton, Julia. "Arbeau, Thoinot [Tabourot, Jehan]." In *Grove Music Online*, ed. L. Macy. New York: Oxford University Press, 2007. http://www.grove-music.com (accessed June 5, 2007).

Warlock, Peter. *Capriol: Suite for String Orchestra*. London: Boosey and Hawkes, 1943.

Contributed by:

Shannon Kitelinger
Doctoral Conducting Associate
University of North Texas
Denton, Texas

1 Barry Smith, "Peter Warlock," Grove Music Online, ed. L. Macy. http://www.grovemusic.com (accessed 5 June 2007).
2 Johnnie Vinson, e-mail correspondence with the author, June 8, 2007.
3 Ibid.
4 Julia Sutton, "Arbeau, Thoinot [Tabourot, Jehan]," Grove Music Online, ed. L. Macy. http://www.grovemusic.com (accessed 5 June 2007).
5 Johnnie Vinson, e-mail correspondence with the author, June 8, 2007.
6 Brian Collins, *Peter Warlock: The Composer* (Brookfield, VT: Ashgate Publishing Company, 1996), 328–343.
7 Julian Rushton, "Hemiola," Grove Music Online, ed. L. Macy. http://www.grovemusic.com (accessed 5 June 2007).

Teacher Resource Guide
Üsküdar

arranged by Robert W. Smith
(b. 1958)

and Michael Story
(b. 1956)

Unit 1: Composer

Robert W. Smith was born in Alabama in 1958. He holds a bachelor's degree from Troy University and a master's degree from the University of Miami in Florida. He is a prolific composer and arranger with more than 600 published works to his credit including works for symphonic band, orchestra, marching band, drum and bugle corps, and solo genres. He has also appeared as a conductor and clinician throughout the United States, Canada, Japan, Europe and Australia and is the co-creator of the *Expressions Music Curriculum*. Currently, Mr. Smith is the director of product development for the C. L. Barnhouse Company and also Walking Frog Records. Additionally, he is on the music industry faculty at Troy University in Troy, Alabama.

Michael Story was born in Philadelphia, Pennsylvania in 1956. He holds bachelor and master degrees from the University of Houston. Well known for his works for ensembles of all levels including elementary, junior high, high school, collegiate as well as professional groups such as the Houston Pops Orchestra, Mr. Story has more than 1,200 published compositions and arrangements to his credit. His *Big & Easy Marching Band Series* has been an industry leader for thirty years. Currently, Mr. Story is the editor/producer for marching band publications with Alfred Music and is a composer/ arranger/author for the *Expressions Music Curriculum*.

Unit 2: Composition

Üsküdar was composed in 2005 and correlates to the *Band Expressions*™ Book One. The program notes included with the score state that the work "was crafted by drawing upon Middle Eastern sights and sounds for inspiration." This single-movement work is sixty measures in length and lasts approximately two minutes and fifteen seconds. The melodic material is presented in most all sections of the ensemble at some point during the work with the noted exception of the low brass and percussion. From a technical standpoint, most young groups should be able to perform the work by the time they reach the end of their first band method. The difficulties of this work lie in balancing the melody with the accompanying materials, performing the correct articulations, and improving the authentic feel of the percussion rhythms.

Unit 3: Historical Perspective

Mr. Smith states in the program notes provided with the score that "*Üsküdar* is a popular Turkish folk song named after a very important town in Middle Eastern culture and history. Every year the Turkish people going to Mecca for Hajj were sent from Üsküdar, now a suburb of modern-day Istanbul. On the first day of Spring, a procession begins leading to Mecca in commemoration of love and celebration of faith."

This arrangement is a great choice for a multi-cultural program. The combination of the sonorities, vocal effects and percussion instruments all help to provide a wonderfully authentic Turkish sound.

Unit 4: Technical Considerations

Üsküdar begins in the tonal center of C minor and changes to the dominant in measure 35 and returns to the tonal center of C minor in measure 49. The wind-instrument ranges are consistent with the requirements of a student who is concluding the first band method book. The percussion parts are more rhythmically challenging than the wind parts but, like the winds, are consistent with their method-book requirements.

Note that, when working out the percussion rhythms beginning in measure 17, the eighth-note and sixteenth-note combinations on the small bongo drum (or doumbek) and tambourine provide the both an implied speeding of the tempo and also the basis of the cultural flavor for the work. Take care that the tempo is consistent, the figures are clearly articulated, and the accented notes are performed in an appropriate manner.

Unit 5: Stylistic Considerations

There are two main style sections in this work. The work opens with the marking of *Mysterious* and the tempo marking of quarter note = 102–120 beats per minute. This opening section is marked "legato" and contains a combination of long tones and slurs that define the intended style. Measure 17 brings a new marking of "Joyous!" and the feeling of a faster tempo. There are no new tempo instructions, but the style and feeling of the tempo change are noted by the addition of the staccato eighth notes and the rhythmic ostinato in the percussion.

The opening phrase should be performed as legato as possible in the clarinets, and the "desert wind" vocal effect should be light and airy in regards to the texture. The staccato eighth notes should be very light, with weight given to the quarter notes in the "Joyous!" section. Additionally, sculpt the last four measures of the work with maximum dynamic contrast to provide an exciting conclusion.

Unit 6: Musical Elements

MELODY:
The opening melodic statement in the clarinet and bass clarinet is an augmented version of the main melodic statement found throughout the remainder of the work. The flute, oboe and bassoon echo this statement by soli clarinets, before the style change occurs in measure 17.

Once the style change takes place, the melody is predominantly found in small groups of either woodwinds or high and middle brass with the low woodwinds and low brass providing the harmonic accompaniment.

HARMONY:
The harmonic structure of this work is relatively easy to follow. It begins in the key of C minor and modulates to the dominant using accidentals in measure 35. The key of C minor returns in measure 49 and remains until the end of the work.

RHYTHM:
The work is in common time throughout and begins with a rhythmically simplistic theme that progresses into more elaborate rhythmic variations. Take care with the percussive interaction beginning in measure 17; the percussion instruments used here, specifically the small bongo drum (or Turkish doumbek if available), tambourine, and large concert tom provide the Turkish rhythmic and cultural flavor. Plan on spending some rehearsal time assisting the percussionists with these parts at first, as they are crucial to the overall feel of the work.

TIMBRE:

The timbres of this work change from the introduction to the main body of the work. A simple soli clarinet voice, including the bass clarinet opens the piece with an initial statement of an augmented version of the theme. The style and timbre change begin in measure 17 with the introduction of the main theme as the percussion instruments enter, playing rhythmic patterns indigenous to the Turkish culture.

Unit 7: Form and Structure

The form of this piece is a basic ABA structure with an introduction. The B section modulates into the dominant, and transitions back to the original tonal center of C minor with the return of the A section.

SECTION	MEASURE	EVENT AND SCORING
Augmented theme (Introduction)	1–8	Tonal center of C minor; tempo marked *Mysterious* with the quarter note = 102–120; initial statement of the augmented theme in clarinet and bass clarinet; the rest of the ensemble provides "desert wind" vocal effects by hissing in the first two and last two measures of this phrase; bells, wind chimes, and timpani provide some percussive coloring
Augmented theme	9–16	Flute, oboe, and bassoon join the soli clarinet line and repeat the augmented theme; bells, suspended cymbal, and timpani provide accompaniment
Transition (A Section)	17–18	Style marking changes to "Joyous!" The percussion rhythmic ostinato and the addition of staccato eighth notes in the winds imply a tempo increase; the alto saxophone, tenor saxophone, and French horn provide a rhythmic ostinato over a bass clarinet, bassoon, baritone saxophone, tuba and timpani repeated tonic-dominant quarter-note passage; the percussion enters providing the basis of the Turkish feel with the small bongo drum (or Turkish doumbek if possible), large concert tom, and tambourine performing an

SECTION	MEASURE	EVENT AND SCORING
		eighth-note and sixteenth-note combination that is more difficult than any of the wind parts throughout the entire work; the percussive voices must be heard clearly and distinctly
Main Theme	19–26	The main melodic theme is presented by the flute, oboe, and clarinet while the alto saxophone, tenor saxophone, and French horn continue to play the previous rhythmic ostinato; the bass clarinet, bassoon, baritone saxophone, tuba, and timpani continue the repeated tonic-dominant quarter-note passage; percussion continues previous ostinato
Main Theme	27–34	Main theme repeats with slight changes of pitch and rhythm; instrumentation stays consistent
Secondary Theme (B Section)	35–40	Tonal center changes to dominant through the use of accidentals; secondary theme is presented in oboe, alto saxophone, tenor saxophone, baritone saxophone, and French horn; the flute, clarinet, bass clarinet, bassoon, trumpet, trombone, baritone, and tuba provide harmonic support with long tones and tonic and (secondary) dominant chord tones; the percussion texture thins considerably for two measures and then returns to the previous ostinato
Secondary Theme	41–44	Flute and clarinet repeat the melody from the previous phrase; the harmonic accompaniment remains consistent, as does the percussion scoring

SECTION	MEASURE	EVENT AND SCORING
Transition	45–48	Transition phrase shifts the tonal center back to C minor; long tones in the flute, oboe, clarinet, alto saxophone, tenor saxophone, baritone saxophone, and French horn are added to tonic and (secondary) dominant chord tones in the bass clarinet, bassoon, trumpet, trombone, baritone, tuba, and bells; the percussion texture thins considerably for two measures and then returns to the previous ostinato
Main Theme (A Section)	49–56	The main melodic theme returns and is presented by the flute, oboe, clarinet, and trumpet while the alto saxophone, tenor saxophone, and French horn continue to provide the rhythmic ostinato from the previous main theme; the trombone and baritone provide a secondary melodic line; the bass clarinet, bassoon, baritone saxophone, tuba, and timpani continue the repeated tonic-dominant quarter-note passage; percussion continues the ostinato from the initial statement of this main theme
Closing Phrase	57–60	The closing motif is based on the transition from measures 45–48; the piece ends with a *crescendo* to a *fortissimo*, tutti rhythmic measure

Unit 8: Suggested Listening

Ludwig van Beethoven, arranged by James Curnow, *Turkish March*

W. A. Mozart, arranged by Robert Longfield, *Turkish March –*
   Rondo alla Turca from *Piano Sonata, No. 11*

William Owens, *At a Turkish Market*

Halsey Stevens, arranged by William Schaefer, *Ukrainian Folk Songs*

Unit 9: Additional References and Resources

Crocker, Richard. *A History of Musical Style*. New York, NY: McGraw-Hill, 1966.

Grout, Donald, and Claude Palisca. *A History of Western Music*. Fourth Edition, New York: W. W. Norton & Company, 1988.

Miles, Richard, ed. *Teaching Music through Performance in Band*. Volumes 1–6. Chicago: GIA Publications, 1996–2007.

Miles, Richard, and Thomas Dvorak, eds. *Teaching Music through Performance in Beginning Band*. Chicago: GIA Publications, 2001.

Pen, Ronald. *Introduction to Music*. New York: McGraw-Hill, 1992.

Randel, Don, ed. *The New Harvard Dictionary of Music*. Cambridge, MA: Belknap Press of Harvard University Press, 1986.

Smith, Robert W. Email interview with David Ratliff, May 3–5, 2007.

Story, Michael. Email interview with David Ratliff, May 3–5, 2007.

Web sites:
    http://www.robertwsmith.com
    http://www.alfred.com

Contributed by:

David Ratliff
Director of Bands
Madison Southern High School
Berea, Kentucky

Teacher Resource Guide

Ye Banks and Braes O' Bonnie Doon

lyrics by Robert Burns
(1756–1796)

composed by Mr. James Miller
(1788–?)

arranged by Michael Sweeney
(b. 1952)

Unit 1: Composer/Arranger

Although there is some argument as to the original composer of this tune, James Miller is recognized as the composer of this version of the air, which was later titled *Ye Banks and Braes O' Bonnie Doon*. While seeking the origin of the melody, for which he wrote his lyrics, poet Robert Burns wrote to George Thomson in 1794:

> Do you know the history of the air? It is curious enough. A good many years ago, Mr. James Miller, writer in your good town (Edinburgh), a gentlemen whom, possibly, you know, was in company with our good friend Clarke; and taling of Scottish music; Miller expressed an ardent ambition to be able to compose a Scots air. Mr. Clarke, partly by way of a joke, told him to keep to the black keys of the harpsichord, and preserve some kind of rhythm, and he would infallibly compose a Scots air. Certainty is, that, in a few days, Mr. Miller produced the rudiments of an air, which Mr. Clarke, with some touches and corrections, fashioned into the tune in question. (*Musical Times*, 1896)

Although controversial, Mr. James Miller (1788) is credited with composing the tune called *The Caledonian Hunt's Delight*. Robert Burns created his lyrics and gave the title *Ye Banks and Braes O' Bonnie Doon.*

Robert Burns was born in Alloway, South Ayrshire, Scotland in 1759. He is widely known as a poet and lyricist. He has been given nicknames such as "Rabbie Burns," "Scotland's favorite son," the "Ploughman Poet," and the "Bard of Ayrshire," in recognition of the fame and admiration for his work. More than five hundred poems are attributed to Burns. Many he used, with revisions and adaptations, as lyrics to Scottish folk tunes for which he was known to collect. Such is Robert Burns's stature that memorials, including fellowships, statues, art museums, cities, monuments and memorials, are placed in Scotland, Canada, United States, New Zealand, Australia, and England. Robert Burns died, after a long struggle with heart disease, at the early age of thirty-seven in 1796. More information on Robert Burns can be obtained by visiting www.robertburns.org.

Michael Sweeney arranged this melody for concert band. He studied music education and composition at Indiana University and subsequently spent five years in Ohio and Indiana teaching music in the public schools. He worked for the Hal Leonard Music Publishing Company since 1982. In addition to his current position as director of band publications, he also contributes as composer and arranger. With more than 500 works to his credit, Mr. Sweeney is well known as composer/arranger for young musicians. Born in 1952, he is the winner of multiple ASCAP awards.

Unit 2: Composition

Adjustments and alterations of the tune have promoted its acceptance as a Scottish folk melody. The use of a Scottish drone by the arranger is indicative. The two-minute, thirty-five-second arrangement is comprised of seventy-three measures and was published in 2006 by "*MUSICWORKS*," a division of Hal Leonard Corporation. The title reflects an attractive image (bonnie) of the banks and braes (Scottish: slopes or hillside) of the river Doon. Robert Burns immortalized the river, which runs in southwest Scotland, in his poetry. Burns's lyrics, listed below, describe a love-lost girl as she wanders by the banks of the river Doon in Ayrshire.

First verse only of three versions:

Ye banks and braes o' bonnie Doon, How can ye bloom sae fresh and fair?
How can ye chant, ye little birds, And I'm sae weary, fu' o' care!
Ye'll break my heart, ye warbling bird, That wontons through the
    flow'ring thorn
Ye mind me o'departed joys, Departed never to return.

Unit 3: Historical Perspective

The melody for *Ye Banks and Braes O' Bonnie Doon* has a long tradition of recognition. A resemblance of the tune is documented in John Playford's *Apollo Banquet* (1690) titled *A Scotch Tune*. Antiquarian William Chappell purports the tune is English based on a citing in Dale's *Collection of English Songs* (ca. 1780) with the title *Lost is my Quiet*.

Example 1. Ye Banks and Braes O' Bonnie Doon

LOST IS MY QUIET FOR EVER

The English original of the air, "Ye Banks and braes," ca. 1780

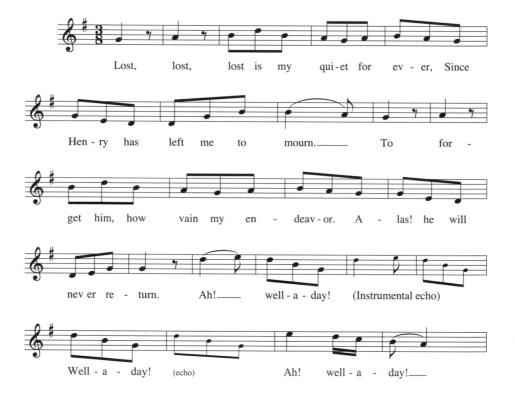

An 1896 article in *The Musical Times and Singing Class Circular* disputes this claim, referring to Mr. Miller's composition as the first. Composer Neil Gow published, in his *Second Collection of Strathspey Reels* (1788), Mr. James Miller's version, called *The Caledonian Hunt's Delight*. It is this version on which poet Robert Burns wrote lyrics to his song *Ye Banks and Braes O' Bonnie Doon.*

Example 2. Ye Banks and Braes O' Bonnie Doon

THE CALEDONIAN HUNT'S DELIGHT

From "Gow's Second Collection of Strathspey Reels," 1788

Burns's song first appeared in Volume 4 of James Johnson's *Scots Musical Museum* in 1792. Many arrangements, adaptations, and versions of this tune have been discovered throughout the centuries. Band educators often recognize Percy Grainger's 1932 scoring for concert band, among other Grainger settings, as their introduction to this beautiful air.

Unit 4: Technical Considerations

The following considerations apply:

1. The tune is written on a pentatonic scale in E-flat.
2. Rhythmic durations include dotted half notes, quarter notes, half notes and eighth notes.
3. Dynamic areas include *piano, mezzo piano, mezzo forte* and *forte*.
4. A vocal legato is the basic articulation requirement.
5. Musical terminologies to be studied are drone, ritard., molto ritardando, *crescendo, diminuendo,* and *a tempo*.
6. The bells and suspended cymbal are the only percussion parts, and both are used sparingly.

7. The metronome markings indicated are quarter note = 92, 104, and 110 beats per minute.
8. Comfortable ranges are used. The melody is an octave range.
9. Clarinet I crosses the break six times, all during the B section of the tune.
10. The meter is 3/4.

Unit 5: Stylistic Considerations

The basic style throughout this arrangement, as it relates to accomplished performance technique, is legato. Developing a true legato on a wind instrument, one that reflects the song style and tone of the singing voice, is primary for effective performance. Style is also a consideration when realizing the musical genre. *Ye Banks and Braes O' Bonnie Doon* is an example of "song," defined as a short, solo composition for voice often based on a poetic text. Robert Burns's text is also a good example of a folk music topic.

The song enjoys a long history throughout most of recorded musical time and is found in all periods of music history across the world. Several major composers have used the song as a significant form of musical communication in their music compositions. For example, Franz Schubert's songs were the pinnacle of the German style and inspired the French tradition of song called *melodie*.

Folk music also exists throughout the world and is mostly heard in the form of vocal songs. The subject matter of folk music often explores the various aspects of life, including work songs, love songs, drinking songs, cradle songs, and a variety of other topics. This repertoire usually communicates community traditions. Major composers have discovered their native folk songs and included them in all genres of composition. Béla Bartók, Antonin Dvorak, Ralph Vaughan Williams, Gustav Mahler, and Aaron Copland are composers of different nationalities who used folk songs in their compositions.

Unit 6: Musical Elements

MELODY:

The tune is based on a pentatonic scale in E-flat.

Example 3. Ye Banks and Braes O' Bonnie Doon

Its form is AABA. Young performers are challenged to create a vocal-sounding line across the octave range.

HARMONY:

The harmony that accompanies the first A section of the melody is presented with a drone on E-flat and B-flat (See Example 3). The moving bass line combined with counter melody creates an interesting diatonic chord structure in the second statement of A. The B section follows a I–IV–V–I harmonic structure. The final statement of A includes a secondary dominant and some passing tones.

RHYTHM:

The original settings of this folk tune were placed in 3/8 and 6/8 meters (see Examples 1 and 2). Sweeney chose to set *Ye Banks and Braes O' Bonnie Doon* in 3/4 meter to allow young performers to focus more on the musical aspects of the tune rather than the 3/8 and 6/8 meters. Challenge students to keep the lines long by not emphasizing the downbeats.

TIMBRE:

The arranger has been attentive to comfortable ranges, allowing students greater opportunity to create a musical tone. The pentatonic scale does present some intervallic challenges for young players. One of the most interesting characteristics of this arrangement is the variety of instrumentation that presents the tune. Examples include: 1) The flute section is accompanied by a drone. 2) The trumpet section carries the melody during the second statement of A. 3) Unaccompanied woodwind choir presents the B portion of the melody. 4) The repeat of the full tune is first seen in the low brass, only to be taken away by the trumpets halfway through the statement. This type of variety may help young performers remain attentive while rehearsing slow music.

TEACHING:

Each piece of music presents instrumental technical challenges that, if not mastered, lessens the overall musical effect of a performance. Some research indicates students are able to raise their level of musical performance by a varied approach in rehearsal. Using the song style of *Ye Banks and Braes O' Bonnie Doon* as an example, students often find it difficult to create a singing style through an unnatural sound source such as a wind instrument. Varied exploration during rehearsal might include:

1. Class voice lessons – Many choral teachers are willing to attend other classes to teach singing. Sensing a singing style more naturally aids in transfer to the instrument.

2. Viewing a variety of images of curved lines – Draw thick or thin lines on paper, the wall, or the board. These visual cues reflect continuous air-flow, shape, character, and style and, when transferred to the instrument often produce more clarity.

3. "Touching" the music – Allow students to move their hands in the air or across their bodies reflective of the manner in which the song flows. A physical connection to the music aids in performance and understanding.

4. Air control–Learning to inhale and exhale air effectively through or across a wind instrument is perhaps the single most important skill a student can develop. The level of musical tone and singing style is determined by the student's ability to use air properly. A variety of exercises is essential. Many teaching examples can be seen in a video and workbook combination called *The Breathing Gym*. Sam Pilafian and Patrick Sheridan are two noted tubists who have created this teaching video. For more information, visit www.breathinggym.com.

Unit 7: Form and Structure

SECTION	MEASURE	EVENT AND SCORING
Intro	1–2	Drone and bells
A	3–10	Drone continues; melody in flutes bass line moves; countermelody enters
A	11–18	Melody in trumpets
B	19–26	Flute melody accompanied by woodwind choir
A	27–34	Melody in trumpets; countermelody in low brass and woodwinds
A	35–42	Melody begins in low brass and is taken by trumpets
A	43–50	Melody begins in low brass and is taken by trumpets
B	51–58	Melody in flutes accompanied by woodwind choir
A	59–66	Full ensemble; melody in flutes
Extension	67–73	Echo of last two measures of melody in woodwind choir Final quiet chords in brass and low reeds

Unit 8: Suggested Listening

Robert Burns, *Robert Burns, The Complete Songs*. Vol. 9. Linn Records, 2001.
Percy Grainger, *Grainger Edition, Vol. 4, Works for Unaccompanied Chorus*. Richard Hickoy, Conductor. Chandos, 2002.
Jack Stamp, *Wind Music Celebrations*. The Keystone and IUP Wind Ensembles. Conductor, Jack Stamp. Citadel Records, 1995.

Unit 9: Additional References and Resources

Aldrich, Mark. *A Catalogue of Folk Song Settings for Wind Band.* Galesville, MD: Meredith Music Publications, 2006.

Apel, Willi. "Folk Music." *Harvard Dictionary of Music.* Cambridge, MA: The Belknap Press of Harvard University Press, 1972.

Burns, Robert. *The Poetical Works of Robert Burns.* Whitefish, MT: Kessington Publishing, 2003.

Cole, William, ed. *Folk Songs of England, Ireland, Scotland and Wales.* Garden City: Doubleday & Co. Inc., 1961.

Fennell, Frederick. "Ye Banks and Braes O' Bonnie Doon" *The Instrumentalist,* September 1981, 29–32.

Graham, George Farquahr. *The Popular Songs of Scotland with their Appropriate Melodies.* Edinburgh, Scotland: Wood and Co. 1887, 300–301 and Appendix.

Miles, Richard, ed. *Teaching Music through Performance in Band,* Vol. II. Chicago: GIA Publications, 1998.

Stade, G., L. Urgen, and W. Litz, eds. *Poets, American and British.* "Burns, Robert" by (David Daihes). New York: Charles Scribner's & Sons, 1998.

Stevens, Dennis William. *History of Song.* Wesport, CT: Greenwood Press, 1982.

Uncited Author. "New Lights upon Old Tunes. No. VII. Ye Banks and Braes." *The Musical Times and Singing Class Circular,* Vol. 37, No. 643. September 1, 1896, 593–595.

Contributed by:

Richard A. Greenwood
Professor of Music
University of Central Florida
Orlando, Florida

Index by Composer, Arranger, and Transcriber for Teaching Music through Performance in Beginning Band, Volumes 1 and 2

Note: The grading nomenclature used in Volume 1 differs from that of Volume 2 due to a change in the prevailing terminology since the release of Volume 1. Here the two systems are presented for comparison:

VOLUME 1	VOLUME 2
E – Entry-level	1–
I = Intermediate	1
A = Advanced	1+
	2–
	2

Index by Title for Teaching Music through Performance in Beginning Band, Volumes 1 and 2

Note: The grading nomenclature used in Volume 1 differs from that of Volume 2 due to a change in the prevailing terminology since the release of Volume 1. Here the two systems are presented for comparison:

VOLUME 1	VOLUME 2
E = Entry-level	1–
I = Intermediate	1
A = Advanced	1+
	2–
	2

Index by Difficulty Level for Teaching Music through Performance in Beginning Band, Volume 2

Index by Composer, Arranger, and Transcriber for Teaching Music through Performance in Beginning Band, Volume 2

Index by Title for Teaching Music through Performance in Beginning Band, Volume 2